RESEARCH HANDBOOK ON DISABILITY AND ENTREPRENEURSHIP

To all the people with visible and invisible disabilities,
We see you,
We feel you,
We hear you.
– Shumaila Yousafzai

To the many millions of remarkable people worldwide with impairments who draw on their condition to improve and enrich all our lives, including those of us who do not (yet) suffer impairments.
– Wilson Ng

The magic lies within the ability to do things differently.
–Shandana Sheikh

For the problem-solvers
– Thomas Coogan

Research Handbook on Disability and Entrepreneurship

Edited by

Shumaila Yousafzai

Graduate School of Business, Nazarbayev University, Kazakhstan and Cardiff University, UK

Wilson Ng

Professor of Entrepreneurship, IDRAC Business School, Campus de Lyon, France and Adjunct Professor of Entrepreneurship and Family Business, Regent's University London, UK

Shandana Sheikh

Avicenna Medical and Dental College, Pakistan

Thomas Coogan

Assistant Professor of Entrepreneurship and Innovation, Hadyn Green Institute, Nottingham University Business School, UK

 Edward Elgar
PUBLISHING

Cheltenham, UK • Northampton, MA, USA

Published by
Edward Elgar Publishing Limited
The Lypiatts
15 Lansdown Road
Cheltenham
Glos GL50 2JA
UK

Edward Elgar Publishing, Inc.
William Pratt House
9 Dewey Court
Northampton
Massachusetts 01060
USA

Paperback edition 2024

A catalogue record for this book
is available from the British Library

Library of Congress Control Number: 2022943292

This book is available electronically in the **Elgar**online
Business subject collection
http://dx.doi.org/10.4337/9781789905649

ISBN 978 1 78990 563 2 (cased)
ISBN 978 1 78990 564 9 (eBook)
ISBN 978 1 0353 3897 9 (paperback)

Printed and bound by CPI Group (UK) Ltd, Croydon, CR0 4YY

Contents

List of figures   viii
List of boxes   ix
About the editors   x
List of contributors   xii
Introduction to the Research Handbook on Disability and Entrepreneurship   xix
Shumaila Yousafzai, Wilson Ng, Shandana Sheikh and Thomas Coogan

PART I   THE PUSH AND THE PULL FACTORS FOR
DISABLED ENTREPRENEURS

1   Follow your dreams? Push and pull motivations of
entrepreneurs with disabilities in Hungary   2
Sara Csillag, Zsuzsanna Gyori, Anna Laura Hidegh and Carmen Svastics

2   "Underdog" entrepreneurs? Identifying processes of
opportunity creation among visually impaired founders of new
ventures   20
Wilson Ng

3   Creating my own job: Australian experiences of people
with disability with microenterprises, self-employment and
entrepreneurship   35
Simon Darcy, Jock Collins and Megan Stronach

4   The push and pull of entrepreneurship for individuals with
autism spectrum disorder   59
Eric Patton

5   Entrepreneurial activity among disabled entrepreneurs with
visible and invisible impairments: a literature review   77
Wilson Ng

6   Entrepreneurship and disability: research in a Spanish university   85
Rosa M. Muñoz, Yolanda Salinero and M. Valle Fernández

7   Awareness and attitudes towards social entrepreneurship
among university students and disabled people: the case of the
Czech Republic   99
Ondřej Kročil, Richard Pospíšil and David Kosina

PART II   ENTREPRENEURIAL ECOSYSTEM: BARRIERS
            AND FACILITATORS

8   Enterprising? Disabled? The status and potential for disabled
        people's microenterprise in South Korea   114
        Se Kwang Hwang and Alan Roulstone

9   Designing public policy to support entrepreneurial activity
        within the disabled community in Ireland   131
        Thomas M. Cooney

10   How entrepreneurs with physical and mental health challenges
        can benefit from an entrepreneurial ecosystems approach   143
        Mirza Tihic, Gary Shaheen and Felix Arndt

11   The role of government policies in establishing a conducive
        entrepreneurial environment for disabled entrepreneurs in China 160
        *Tiansheng Yang, Shandana Sheikh, Shumaila Yousafzai and
        Xiangxin Yang*

12   The need for an inclusive entrepreneurial ecosystem for
        women with disability in Pakistan   182
        Shandana Sheikh

13   Disabled women entrepreneurs and microfinance: a road less
        travelled (for a reason)?   196
        Nadeera Ranabahu and Farzana Aman Tanima

14   A preliminary analysis of the impact of COVID-19 on the
        mental wellbeing of entrepreneurship students   208
        Sylvie Studente, Filia Garivaldis and Wilson Ng

15   The hidden entrepreneurs: disability and entrepreneurship in
        Kazakhstan   221
        Shumaila Yousafzai and Yerken Turganbayev

16   Inclusive entrepreneurship in Palestine: context and prospects
        of people with disabilities   238
        Wojdan Omran and Leila Farraj

PART III   THE IDENTITY AND CONTRIBUTION OF
            DISABLED ENTREPRENEURS

17   The making of a (dis)abled entrepreneur: an entrepreneurial
        identity perspective   247
        Mukta Kulkarni and Yangerjungla Pongener

18   The opportunity to contribute: disability and the digital entrepreneur   262
      Tom Boellstorff

19   Disabled entrepreneurs creating value in Iran's entrepreneurial
      ecosystem   279
      *Vahid Makizadeh, Shumaila Yousafzai, Siavash Aein Jamshid and
      Adel Mohebbi*

20   The contribution of disabled entrepreneurs in the Sultanate of Oman   297
      Eric V. Bindah

Index   309

Figures

2.1   A theoretical conception of visually impaired entrepreneurship   28

3.1   Industry sector of business, % response   43

8.1   Economic activity status of disabled people in 2010   118

8.2   Categories of disability entrepreneurs compared to working
        age disabled profile   123

8.3   Motivation for venturing into business   124

9.1   The Funnel Approach   139

11.1   Isenberg's model of an entrepreneurship ecosystem   167

11.2   Suggestions for overcoming existing barriers   175

13.1   Pathways for entrepreneurship and support initiatives   203

14.1   Data collection survey themes   211

14.2   Reported impact of closure of university premises on social wellbeing   212

14.3   Reported impact of closure of university premises on
        psychological wellbeing   213

19.1   Value creation perspective in disabled entrepreneurs   293

Boxes

3.1   A personal story: from work experience to self-employed winemaker   48

3.2   A personal story: from a childhood spinal cord injury to
       a global business in assistive technology   53

15.1   Birzhan Kuzhakov from Uralsk, Kazakhstan   227

15.2   Ablaikhan Asylbay from Semey, Kazakhstan   229

19.1   Farah (female, 34, mother of two daughters, seven and two-years old)   283

19.2   Alborz (male, 29, single)   286

19.3   Amir (male, 39, married, one-year-old daughter)   288

About the editors

Shumaila Yousafzai is an Associate Professor of Entrepreneurship at Nazarbayev University, Kazakhstan where she teaches entrepreneurship, marketing and consumer behavior. She is on leave as a Reader in Entrepreneurship at the Cardiff Business School, Cardiff University, UK. After her undergraduate studies in Physics and Mathematics (University of Balochistan), and an MSc in Electronic Commerce (Coventry University, UK), she finished her PG Diploma in Research Methods from Cardiff University. Shumaila received her Doctoral degree in 2005 from Cardiff University. In her research, Shumaila focuses mainly on topics linked to contextual embeddedness of entrepreneurship, firm performance, institutional theory, and entrepreneurial orientation. She has published articles in various international journals, such as *Entrepreneurship Theory and Practice, Journal of Small Business Management, Industrial Marketing Management, Technovation, Journal of Business Ethics, Psychology and Marketing, Journal of Applied Social Psychology*, and *Computers in Human Behavior*. She has co-edited a special issue on women's entrepreneurship for *Entrepreneurship and Regional Development*, and nine edited volumes on entrepreneurship published with Edward Elgar Publishing and Routledge.

Wilson Ng (PhD Management Studies, University of Cambridge, UK) is a Professor of Entrepreneurship at IDRAC Business School, Campus de Lyon, France and an Adjunct Professor of Entrepreneurship and Family Business at Regent's University London, UK. Wilson's research focuses on processes of opportunity creation among severely challenged entrepreneurs and their ventures. He is interested in the ways in which creative actors in challenge-based enterprises leverage their capabilities to achieve goals that they have established because of their extreme challenges. Wilson's current research advances this interest by exploring processes of opportunity creation among sight-impaired entrepreneurs. He has published and guest-edited special issues in management and small business journals, including the *Journal of Management Studies, Human Relations, International Small Business Journal, Technological Forecasting and Social Change, Technology Analysis and Strategic Management,* and *Journal of Small Business Strategy*. Wilson has co-authored a research methods primer for novice postgraduate researchers, and he has contributed chapters on challenge-based entrepreneurship in several edited books, including the *World Encyclopaedia of Entrepreneurship* (2nd edition, 2021).

Shandana Sheikh received her Doctorate in Entrepreneurship from Cardiff Business School, Cardiff University, UK. Her research particularly focuses on women's entrepreneurship and value creation that accrues within it. In addition, Shandana is interested in disabled entrepreneurship and transgender entrepreneurship, particularly in the context of developing economies. Prior to her Doctoral studies, Shandana received her MBA in Marketing from Lahore School of Economics, Pakistan and an MSc in Marketing and Strategy from Warwick Business School, University of Warwick, UK.

Thomas Coogan (PhD, University of Leicester, UK) is an Assistant Professor of Entrepreneurship and Innovation in the Hadyn Green Institute at Nottingham University Business School, UK. Tom's practice focuses on teaching entrepreneurship theory and practice to students from undergraduate to MBA level. He has a long-standing interest in the intersection of disability and entrepreneurship, most recently as co-author of the Innovation Caucus report *Supporting Diversity and Inclusion in Innovation* (July 2021). His current research is focused on pedagogies of entrepreneurship and innovation in higher education.

Contributors

Felix Arndt is the John F. Wood Chair in Entrepreneurship in the Department of Management, a Research Fellow at the Center for Business and Sports of the Stockholm School of Economics, Sweden, and a Visiting Professor at the University of Agder, Norway. His research intersects strategy, entrepreneurship, and innovation. He looks at how firms use organizational renewal and technological innovation to stay ahead of the competition (dynamic capabilities, ecosystems, business models). His second field of interest is best captured by the question of how entrepreneurs overcome extreme challenges (for example, of a socio-economic or medical nature). Before academia, he was a consultant, entrepreneur, and lobbyist.

Eric V. Bindah obtained his PhD in Business Administration (Marketing) and MBA (International Business) from University of Malaya. His research interests include marketing (consumer science), entrepreneurship, management, qualitative and quantitative research methodologies. He is an academic at the University of Mauritius, at the Faculty of Law and Management.

Tom Boellstorff is Professor in the Department of Anthropology at the University of California, Irvine, USA. A former Editor-in-Chief of *American Anthropologist*, the flagship journal of the American Anthropological Association, he co-edits the Princeton University Press book series Princeton Studies in Culture and Technology.

Jock Collins is Professor of Social Economics in the Management Department at the UTS Business School, Sydney, Australia, where he has been teaching and conducting research since 1977. His research interests centre on an interdisciplinary study of immigration and cultural diversity in the economy and society and minority entrepreneurship. He is the author or co-author of 12 books, and the author of over 150 articles in international and national academic journals and book chapters. His latest co-authored book, *Minority Entrepreneurship: Australian Insights and Global Implications*, will be published by Routledge in 2022.

Thomas M. Cooney is Professor of Entrepreneurship at Technological University Dublin, Director of the Institute for Minority Entrepreneurship and Adjunct Professor at the University of Turku (Finland). He is a former President of the International Council for Small Business (2012–2013) and of the European Council for Small Business (2009–2011), and he was Chair of the ICSB 2014 World Entrepreneurship Conference. He is a policy advisor to Governments, European Commission, OECD, and other international organisations. He is a Director of four enterprises and works in various capacities with a range of businesses. He has published 11 books and specializes on the topic of minority entrepreneurship. Further details of his work can be found at www.thomascooney.ie.

Sara Csillag (PhD) is Dean of the Faculty of Finance and Accountancy at Budapest Business School, Hungary. Her main research interests are ethical and responsible human resource management (HRM), participatory methods, and disability issues in the workplace. She is member of the editorial board of *Journal of Business Ethics*, *Action Learning: Research and Practice*, and *Human Resource Development International*.

Simon Darcy is a Professor of Social Inclusion in the Management Department of the UTS Business School, University of Technology Sydney, Australia. He specializes in developing accessible and inclusive processes, policies, and procedures for people with disability across all areas of social participation and citizenship. Simon has over 35 years involvement the disability community and is a person with a high-level spinal cord injury. His current research examines the lived experiences of people with disabilities in employment, self-employment, microenterprises, social enterprises, and entrepreneurship

Leila Farraj has an MSc in Gender and Development Studies and currently works with the international, for-impact organization MENA Catalyst on the design and implementation of gender-inclusive empowerment programs, primarily within the field of innovation and entrepreneurship. Leila's work also extends to developing and managing content that strategically reflects on the overall developmental and entrepreneurial ecosystem in Palestine and the Middle East and North Africa (MENA) region.

M. Valle Fernández, PhD, is Vice Dean and Professor of Management at the Faculty of Law and Social Sciences, University of Castilla-La Mancha (UCLM), Spain. She has published in leading journals such as *Proceedings of Rijeka Faculty of Economics* and *Frontiers in Psychology*. She is a member of the research team Group for Research in Organizational Knowledge, Innovation and Strategy (GROKIS) and participates in the European project ENDURUNS of the INGENIUM research group of the UCLM. She has extensive teaching experience on all academic levels (MBAs such as the Máster Universitario en Estrategia y Marketing de la Empresa of the UCLM). Her current research focuses on strategic management, human resources management, sustainability, and disability and corporate social responsibility.

Filia Garivaldis is a Senior Lecturer and behavioural scientist at the Monash Sustainable Development Institute (MSDI), Australia, specializing in designing, developing, and evaluating impactful online learning experiences, including a micro-credential and a massive open online course (MOOC) on behaviour change. An expert in the field, she has published widely in peer-review journals, and has co-edited the book *Tertiary Online Teaching and Learning*, published by Springer.

Zsuzsanna Gyori (PhD), teaches courses on Business Ethics, Responsible and Sustainable Company and Entrepreneurship at Budapest Business School, Hungary as Associate Professor. Her research fields include corporate social responsibility, sustainability in higher education, entrepreneurs with disabilities, as well as values-driven business.

Anna Laura Hidegh (PhD) is an Associate Professor at Budapest Business School, Hungary. She wrote her dissertation on critical human resource management, analysing corporate Christmas from a Habermasian perspective. Her main research interest is critical management studies, disability studies, gender, and diversity. She has published articles in *Human Resource Development International* and *Action Learning: Research and Practice*.

Se Kwang Hwang is a Senior Lecturer at Northumbria University, UK. He was a program lead of the Disability Studies joint honours undergraduate degree program. He has been involved in various funded research projects on disability issues, especially autism. He has published many articles in international journals. He has a professional background in social work with disabled people and their families for 15 years in South Korea. He has been on the editorial board of several reputed journals, including *Disability and Society*.

Siavash Aein Jamshid is a research assistant (RA) in the Faculty of Management and Accounting at the University of Hormozgan, Iran. He holds a Master's degree in Business Management with Strategic Orientation from the University of Hormozgan, Iran. His research interests focus on entrepreneurship, innovation management, and business and sustainability. Also, working as a research assistant provides him with hands-on opportunities to learn more about research methods. Besides working as an RA, he also advises an early-stage environmental technology company, Aria Plasma Gostar Co., on business development and strategy.

David Kosina is an Assistant Professor at the Department of Economic and Managerial Studies, Faculty of Arts, Palacký University Olomouc, Czech Republic. In his research he focuses on new challenges in management, namely management of virtual teams, global leadership, and new approaches to entrepreneurship. Beside his academic career, David has more than 15 years of practical experience in managing educational projects.

Ondřej Kročil is Head of Department and Assistant Professor at Department of Economic and Managerial Studies, Faculty of Arts, Palacký University Olomouc, Czech Republic. In his PhD thesis, he dealt with social entrepreneurship as a possible tool of active employment policy. He is the author of several professional articles focused on social entrepreneurship.

Mukta Kulkarni is a Professor at the Indian Institute of Management Bangalore. She has published in leading journals such as the *Academy of Management Journal*, *Human Relations*, the *Leadership Quarterly*, and the *Journal of Organizational Behavior*. She serves on the editorial boards of *Human Relations*, *Journal of Organizational Behavior*, and as an Associate Editor for the *Journal of Management Inquiry*.

Vahid Makizadeh is an Assistant Professor in the Faculty of Management and Accounting at the University of Hormozgan, Iran. He has a Masters degree in Business Management and a PhD in Strategic Management from Shahid Beheshti University (formerly known as the National University of Iran), Tehran, Iran. His main area of interest is strategic management and entrepreneurship, particularly entrepreneurship among disadvantaged people. Also, he has spent several years working for businesses within a consultative role.

Adel Mohebbi is an active researcher in the fields of entrepreneurship, small business management, and branding at Islamic Azad University of Bandar Abbas, Iran. Adel's primary interest focuses on the entrepreneurship of disabled people. He is also active in social activities related to disabled people.

Rosa M. Muñoz PhD, is Associate Professor of Management at the Faculty of Law and Social Sciences, University of Castilla-La Mancha (UCLM), Spain. She has published in leading journals such as *International Journal of Human Resource Management*, *European Journal of International Management*, and *Universia Business Review*. She has been a reviewer of journals such as *Organization* and *Accounting and Finance*. She is a member of the research team Group for Research in Organizational Knowledge, Innovation and Strategy (GROKIS) of the UCLM. She has extensive teaching experience at all academic levels (MBAs such as the Máster Universitario en Estrategia y Marketing de la Empresa of the UCLM) and at several international institutions (Bialystok University, Poland; Universidad Cuenca del Plata, Argentina; Universidad de Santa Cruz de la Sierra, Bolivia). Her current research focuses on human resource management, strategic management, entrepreneurship and corporate social responsibility.

Wojdan Omran is a PhD research student at Cardiff Business School, Cardiff University, UK. Her Doctoral thesis topic features internally displaced Palestinian women entrepreneurs and how they perceive success in the context of their particular environments. Based on her research thus far, she has presented at several conferences, co-hosted an online seminar, and contributed to a documentary film which premiered at Global Entrepreneurship Week (GEW) UK in 2020. Prior to starting her PhD studies, Wojdan's professional experience was heavily based in academia as a lecturer of management at Birzeit University in Palestine, where she also served the administration, most notably as director of the Alumni and Career Services Office. Her published work to date includes topics on organizational processes, gender, and entrepreneurship, with particular emphasis on marginalized groups.

Eric Patton is Associate Professor of Management at Saint Joseph's University (SJU), USA. A native of Montreal, Canada, Dr Patton's research focuses on absence from work, gender issues in management, and disabilities in the workplace. His research has been published in several journals including the *Journal of Occupational and Organizational Psychology*, *Human Relations*, *Personnel Review*, the *Journal of Management History*, and the *Journal of Workplace Behavioral Health*. He has appeared on KYW News Radio in Philadelphia, CBS 3/CW Eyewitness News in

Philadelphia, National Public Radio, and his research has been featured on MSNBC. com, in the *Huffington Post*, and in the *Philadelphia Inquirer*. He is a member of the Academy of Management and the Society for Human Resource Management, and was the founding director of SJU's Managing Human Capital undergraduate program.

Yangerjungla Pongener is a Doctoral student at the Indian Institute of Management Bangalore. Her research interests include identity in organizations, religion in organizations, plural careers and work environments, socio-materiality in organizations, and organizational sustainability.

Richard Pospíšil (PhD), graduated from the Faculty of Business and Economics, Mendel University in Brno, the Czech Republic, where he was appointed Associate Professor in 2009. He works in the Department of Economics and Managerial Studies, Palacký University Olomouc, Czech Republic. His area of research interest includes theoretical and practical concepts of monetary and fiscal policy and budgets, as well as the central banking and applied and general economic policy of the state.

Nadeera Ranabahu is a Senior Lecturer in entrepreneurship and innovation in the Department of Management, Marketing and Entrepreneurship at the University of Canterbury, New Zealand. She obtained her PhD in Business from the University of Wollongong (Australia) in 2018. Her research focuses on disadvantaged or underrepresented people in entrepreneurship, employment and innovation. She also studies the use of innovative initiatives, such as microfinance and financial technology (fintech), for entrepreneurship and employment among the disadvantaged. She has ongoing research projects focused on women, refugees, youth/students, migrants, and low-income people.

Alan Roulstone was most recently Professor of Disability Studies, University of Leeds, UK. He has held senior academic posts at Glasgow, Sunderland, De Montfort and Northumbria University, UK. Alan has co-produced 12 books, over 100 journal articles and official reports. He specializes in disability, policy, work, technology, welfare, and hate crime. Alan is a disabled person and has strong links with disabled people's organizations globally. He has been a long-standing editor of the journal *Disability and Society*.

Yolanda Salinero (PhD) is Professor of Management at the Faculty of Law and Social Sciences, University of Castilla-La Mancha (UCLM), Spain. She has published in leading journals such as *International Journal of Human Resource Management*, *Revista Brasileira de Gestao de Negocios*, *Frontiers in Psychology*, and *Universia Business Review*. She has been a reviewer of several journals. She is a member of the research team Group for Research in Organizational Knowledge, Innovation and Strategy (GROKIS) of the UCLM. She has extensive teaching experience at all academic levels (MBAs such as the Máster Universitario en Estrategia y Marketing de la Empresa of the UCLM) and at several international institutions (Universidad de Santa Cruz de la Sierra, Bolivia; Universidad ORT, Uruguay, Universidade do

Minho, Portugal). She is a member of the social business incubator Social Business Factory. Her current research focuses on human resource management, entrepreneurship and disability and corporate social responsibility.

Gary Shaheen (PhD). For over 40 years in the public, private, and academic sectors, Gary Shaheen has been instrumental in improving policies and programs that help people with mental illnesses, co-occurring substance abuse disorders, and those who are homeless, including veterans, to achieve employment and/or entrepreneurial success. He has worked with several organizations on projects focused on increasing employment for these populations throughout the United States and its territories, and internationally. He developed curricula and was a lead trainer for the Syracuse University (SU) Entrepreneurship Bootcamp for Veterans with Disabilities (EBV), USA. While serving as Senior Vice President of the SU Burton Blatt Institute, Gary developed the StartUp NY and SBA PRIME projects with colleagues at the SU Whitman School to create entrepreneurship education and training in Onondaga County, New York, for people with disability and others with low incomes, including veterans.

Megan Stronach (PhD), is a Lecturer in Dementia at the University of Tasmania. She is also a Research Fellow at the University of Technology Sydney, Australia. Megan has published widely in areas of sport management, cultural and women's issues in sport, and has a keen interest in sport history. Most recently her attraction to history has culminated in publications focusing on issues of topical relevance in Tasmania, including cultural challenges resulting from the interface between tourism and extractive industry development in Southern Tasmania. Her current research interests centre on exploring the histories of Indigenous people in Van Diemen's Land, knowledge that has been largely lost, but which deserves to be both investigated and celebrated.

Sylvie Studente (PhD) is an Assistant Professor and Course Leader at Regent's University London, UK. With over 20 years research experience, Sylvie has led and contributed to a number of international projects. Sylvie obtained her PhD in 2008. Her research interests span the areas of education, assessment, and e-learning and technology. She has industry experience in project management, artificial intelligence and interaction design in both business and education systems. Sylvie is also an External Examiner at the University of Westminster, UK, and a Doctoral Supervisor for the University of Northampton, UK.

Carmen Svastics has degrees in humanities and sociology. She has worked in areas of equal opportunities in Hungarian central administration, and in partnership with the European Commission and international and civil society organizations. She is a full-time lecturer at the Bárczi Gusztáv Faculty of Special Needs Education at Eötvös Loránd University of Budapest, Hungary, and is conducting her PhD research on the relationship between language, power, and disability.

Farzana Aman Tanima (PhD) is a critical qualitative researcher in accounting with an interest in the role that accounting plays in women's empowerment issues, particularly in developing-country contexts. With personal interest in the growth and socio-political issues in her home country, her PhD research focused on Bangladesh, where poverty continues to be an overarching factor affecting poorer echelons of society. She joined the University of Wollongong (UOW), Australia in January 2017 as a Lecturer, and is currently working as a co-network leader for the Alternative Accounting Research Network (AARN).

Mirza Tihic is Postdoctoral Researcher with the Department of Entrepreneurship and Emerging Enterprises (EEE) at Whitman School of Management at Syracuse University, USA. Tihic serves in a dual role, based within EEE and as a member of the Institute for Veterans and Military Families (IVMF) Research and Analytics team. At Whitman, he contributes to the department's scholarly output and teaches entrepreneurship courses. Within IVMF, he plays a leading scientific role in the launch and day-to-day management of the National Survey on Military-Connected Entrepreneurs initiative, a multi-year study of military-connected (veteran and military spouse) entrepreneurs.

Yerken Turganbayev is an Administrative Director at the Nazarbayev University Graduate School of Business, Kazakhstan. He received a PhD in Economics from the Robert Gordon University (Aberdeen, UK) and a PhD in Mathematics from the Novosibirsk State University (Novosibirsk, Russia). His research interests lie in regional economics, regional policy, and economic growth. Prior to joining Nazarbayev University in August 2016, Yerken Turganbayev was a Fulbright Visiting Scholar at Harvard University, USA.

Tiansheng Yang is a PhD Student at Cardiff Business School, Cardiff University, UK. He completed his Masters at Swansea University, UK. His research interest lies in exploring the potential of entrepreneurship in improving the status of people with disabilities.

Xiangxin Yang is the Senior Manager of Suzhou Science and Technological University, China, a consultant of the Law Society, and a fellow of the China Photographers Association. His research intersects modern history and law.

Introduction to the *Research Handbook on Disability and Entrepreneurship*

Shumaila Yousafzai, Wilson Ng, Shandana Sheikh and Thomas Coogan

Datasets in entrepreneurship studies continue typically to reflect characteristics of able, white, male entrepreneurs. Entrepreneurship scholars such as Léo-Paul Dana (2002) observed that a principal reason for this bias (possibly prejudice, in a few societies worldwide) was that the identification of opportunities for entrepreneurship was primarily a function of cultural context. Relatedly, there has been little research on how social and economic contexts, specifically in terms of barriers that hinder venture activities, may initiate or attenuate the development of successful ventures. Man-made barriers include socio-cultural and economic barriers arising from life-changing physical and mental disabilities (Miller and Le Breton-Miller, 2017). We refer to disability and disabled entrepreneurs in this book purely as a shorthand. The accurate term for disability is 'impairment', either physical or mental. This is because most disabled people are not incapable of work, as the term 'disability' suggests. Disabled-impaired entrepreneurs may possess important advantages in new venture creation based on personality traits and/or adaptive capabilities that are particularly suited for successful enterprise activities. Apart from a few studies on entrepreneurs with paraplegia, sight loss and attention deficit hyperactive disorder (ADHD), there has been little research on (any type of) severely disabled entrepreneurs who appear to have overcome their challenges in creating successfully ventures and what may be learnt from these entrepreneurs and their ventures.

Researchers in and beyond entrepreneurship have voiced the need to explore the social and organizational impact of visible, physical disabilities and invisible, (largely) mental conditions (see, for example, Santuzzi et al., 2014). This is because of the rising costs of workplace inefficiencies from employees who become impaired, commonly with mental conditions such as depression. The negative effects of mental conditions are magnified in a typically high-pressure work culture that compels employees to keep their disabilities purposely hidden from employers in order to avoid demotion, or worse (Jack, 2019). For the study of entrepreneurship, this social tendency to disregard people with disabilities has contributed to the paucity of knowledge about the millions of disabled people worldwide who create ventures, often out of necessity (Jones and Latreille, 2011; Block et al., 2015). Unsurprisingly, we also know little about the possible economic and social value of people with positive, entrepreneurial traits (Wiklund et al., 2017) and adaptive skills (Ng and Arndt, 2019) who are labelled, pejoratively, as 'disabled'.[1] In too many societies, disabled entrepreneurs are still bracketed with women entrepreneurs, disabled and otherwise. Arguably, all entrepreneurs outside the normative focus on male, white entrepreneurs are bracketed as inconsequential, 'disabled', with the related sense of being econom-ically and/or socially burdensome, often both.

Worldwide, over 1 billion males and females are registered with a severe impair-ment, either physical and or mental, and as a hereditary condition or as a consequence of disease and/or injury. Most of this registered population are of working age (World Bank, 2021). Many more people with severe impairments are unregistered, often because of negative social and/or workplace consequences. United Kingdom (UK) residents with physical impairments now represent circa 15 per cent of the UK's population (RNIB, 2021). This proportion of 15 per cent of disabled people in the UK largely holds across economies worldwide, regardless of any country's economic and social development. The vast majority of disabled people live in poverty, often in extreme poverty (https://humanity-inclusion.org.uk). By 2022, the number of registered disability residents in the UK is expected to rise to over 10 million (RNIB, 2021). Unemployment among this population remains high, with only one in four UK residents who are registered as blind engaged in paid employment (Jones and Latreille, 2011). While organizations in Western economies now recruit disabled staff, the number of these employees remains pitifully small; virtually non-existent in industries such as finance and banking where the need for innovation, paradoxi-cally, is persistently high (see, for example, Tufano, 2003). In this scenario, disabled people are rarely employed for their skills and competencies. And yet we know that disabled people often face extreme challenges of many kinds, and entrepreneurship scholars have suggested how disabled entrepreneurs have responded to persistent challenges by developing adaptive skills, for example in oral communication, net-working and creative problem-solving (Block et al., 2015). In turn, astute application of these skills has contributed to work outcomes that can be advantageous for any organization; for example, in terms of work discipline, a collaborative and yet indi-vidually creative work culture, and in risk evaluation and tolerance (Miller and Le Breton-Miller, 2017).

This edited book aims to present a collection of international studies that would further explore, rethink, and recognize the value created by disabled entrepreneurs beyond economic, cultural and geographical contexts. The chapters in this book co-create useful knowledge and expertise of a range of disabled entrepreneurs and their ventures, that can feed joint learning, innovative practices and evidence-based policy-making for all types of entrepreneurs to build and grow successful ventures and gender-inclusive growth in any context, worldwide. In particular, this book highlights the importance of disabled women entrepreneurs as agents of change for society and the economy. Several chapters in this book suggest how, in certain devel-oping economies, negative social views of venture creation by women and disabled people dominate. These social views can be value-destructive. Accordingly, a prin-cipal goal of the focus in this book on disability and women entrepreneurs is to gen-erate better understanding of the significant contributions of disabled entrepreneurs to the economy, regardless of the nature of their ventures and of their social, political and economic status. It follows that by publicly recognizing the contributions of disa-bled entrepreneurs, the contributions in entrepreneurship of other marginalized social segments would also be better understood. One of the largest social segments world-wide, which remains underresearched, is women entrepreneurs. Much less is known about disabled women entrepreneurs. Yet the economic, social and political contributions of women entrepreneurs in many economies have now been established, thanks largely to the pioneering scholarship of women scholars from the United States of America (USA) and Europe. Moreover, the growing literature on women entrepreneurs has established the importance of their value-creating activities, including the activities of female micro-entrepreneurs in developing economies. This literature, however, has been located largely in Western economies. The literature on disabled entrepreneurs is similarly based largely in the USA and Western European contexts, and on data from the majority of white disabled people in those economies.

This 'Western' focus on disability and entrepreneurship is unsurprising, given the need for social and political openness as a fundamental basis for public conversations about the interests particularly of segments of society that have had, and which in many economies continue to have, little or no voice. The interests of disabled entrepreneurs and women entrepreneurs are timely topics of public interest, thanks to Western-inspired movements, such as those that campaign for equality, diversity and inclusion in every part of society. This book draws inspiration from contemporary mass social movements and locks into the current zeitgeist principally for social change of the poorly informed, and typically persistently negative, public views of disabled entrepreneurs in and beyond Western economies. Too often, even among empathetic audiences, disability and entrepreneurship is viewed as a niche topic. This view is reflected, for example, in the paucity of any discussion, including scholarly discussion, of disabled entrepreneurs. Yet there is broad public appreciation of the value of entrepreneurs who create value because of their disabilities. Indeed, publicly visible entrepreneurs such as Stevie Wonder, Ray Charles, Andrea Bocelli, and many others, continue to create pleasure for everyone, including many music-lovers who attend their performances and yet remain blind to the work of these entrepreneurs in creating public value because of their blindness.

This book offers support in dissembling mainly socially institutionalized barriers to important sources of value creation by disabled entrepreneurs by extending knowledge of this phenomenon. A notable contribution of this book is in building knowledge of disabled entrepreneurs in non-Western economies, such as China, India, Iran, Kazakhstan, Pakistan, Palestine, South Korea and Oman, and of multiple ways in which disabled entrepreneurs in those environments must negotiate the significant social and other barriers, often invisible but institutionalized (such as in the requirement in several Islamic societies for women to open any bank account with the written consent of any male), that continue to be placed before them, often on a daily basis. Aside from the social injustice of these barriers, which is a topic that is beyond the focus of this book, the studies herein are concerned with the loss of value-creative activities by marginalizing disabled entrepreneurs. Moreover, the silencing of the work of disabled women entrepreneurs in certain large economies such as Pakistan is likely to decrease the economic contributions of entire families, including males, in those economies. This is because of the multiple, negative effects on all family members, notably in finding good employment, that can arise from the social stigma of having a single, disabled female member of the family.

The principal outcome of generating public understanding of disability and entrepreneurship would therefore be to build public interest in, and support for, disabled entrepreneurs and their ventures. As disabled women entrepreneurs feature significantly in the book, a further, core outcome would be in building knowledge of this phenomenon. The editors of this book believe that this outcome would follow from public understanding and recognition of the value-creation activities of all disabled entrepreneurs in every type of enterprise, worldwide. For example, following studies in this book of disabled enterprise in many contexts, we expect researchers to have additional, up-to-date knowledge to be able to continue challenging the underperformance hypothesis associated with disabled entrepreneurs, including women entrepreneurs. We seek to support this challenge by presenting evidence that disabled entrepreneurs, as a whole, do not underperform in their businesses. Instead, disabled entrepreneurs add value, even in socially constrained environments. It is hoped that the chapters which we have included in this edited book will direct researchers to shift the focus of research from questions such as 'What do entrepreneurs do?' to 'how' questions, such as 'How do entrepreneurs create successful, value-creating ventures?'. This realignment of research focuses attention on the processes in which disabled entrepreneurs create value, and the multiple value outcomes that both able and disabled entrepreneurs create, as well as on the benefits and beneficiaries of the value that is created (cf. Zahra et al., 2009).

Accordingly, we argue that not all entrepreneurs are cut out for, or aspire to, high growth and performance. Because disabled entrepreneurs are often labelled 'underperformers' in business for their perceived low growth rate and low success rates, their activities are underrecognized, for example, in value creation. In a sense, low growth and success rates are what society expects disabled people who work to achieve. Failure, of course, is not what disabled people expect or want to achieve. Accordingly, a follow-on outcome of the studies in this book is in suggesting the ambitions and myriad related activities that disabled entrepreneurs as a whole expect and seek to achieve from venture creation. We present this anthology, as far as possible, in the perspectives and words of our disabled entrepreneurs, and on their own terms.

THE CHAPTERS IN THIS BOOK

In response to the limitation in the current entrepreneurial literature regarding the full impact of and value creation through disabled people's entrepreneurial activity, we seek to fill part of the resulting gap by co-creating expertise that can feed joint learning, innovative practices and evidence-based policy-making for an inclusive promotion and growth of disabled entrepreneurship around the globe. In doing so, we highlight what influences and restrains the growth of disabled entrepreneurship, and offer useful insights into disabled entrepreneurship as they apply to specific contexts.

This line of research has the potential to initiate a break from dominant methods of positivistic research to more exploratory ones that involve qualitative techniques that help to capture the real impact of entrepreneurship at multiple levels.

In particular, contributions were sought from researchers in geographic regions that are not sufficiently represented in the women's entrepreneurship literature. We received chapters based on data from Australia, Canada, China, the Czech Republic, Hungary, India, Iran, Ireland, Kazakhstan, Oman, Pakistan, Palestine, South Korea, Spain, the UK and USA. Collectively, these studies make a substantial contribution to the literature on disabled people's entrepreneurial activity, provide numerous insights and provoke fruitful directions for future research on the important role of the context in which disabled people's entrepreneurial activity takes place.

PART I: THE PUSH AND THE PULL FACTORS FOR DISABLED ENTREPRENEURS

In Chapter 1, Sara Csillag, Zsuzsanna Gyori, Anna Laura Hidegh and Carmen Svastics contribute to the growing body of empirical research on entrepreneurs with disability by exploring the goals and motivational background of people with disabilities who have established and managed their own businesses. While the authors contribute to the theory of entrepreneurship and disability, the regional scope of the empirical research – the Central European region – is also of importance. Both the current Hungarian entrepreneurial ecosystem and its historical development show specific characteristics due to the 45 years of socialist economy, which has impacted on the situation of entrepreneurs with disabilities. The authors suggest that both push and pull types of motivation are present in the decisions of disabled entrepreneurs to start and run a business venture. While various sources of personal and social-economic pull motivation are evident, economic pressure and the lack of any further alternatives are at least equally strong push motivating factors. They further suggest that while categorization is possible, it is often difficult to identify a leading motivation as they intertwine into each other in the course of a person's life, and may also change over time or shift because of actual economic trends or changes in social policy. From the complexity of the motivational background, however, two distinct patterns emerge: of those who were born with impairments, and those who acquired impairments later in life. Respondents who were born with an impairment tended to prepare consciously for their chosen professional field (choosing vocations or training programmes) and also for a career in entrepreneurship. This high level of consciousness, long-term orientation and planning, as well as family support, helped them to start their businesses and become successful. In their case, pull motivations seem to be more relevant in becoming entrepreneurs. The second pattern they identified seems typical in the case of acquired impairments, that happened mainly due to accidents. Those who became disabled later in life made use of their competencies, skills and previous experiences, based on which they were able to create and build a new venture, or continue the previous business activities despite the disability.

Another important finding is that it seems that sometimes social and personal motivations complement each other, but are exchanging push and pull sides. Social push motivations tend to complement personal pull factors. The authors conclude that while disabled entrepreneurs believe that having personal and business goals and a solid positive identity are important – as opposed to the general image of people with disabilities – they wish to facilitate social and cultural change. They would like to give something back to the disability community, either by becoming role models and agents of change, or by providing services for them free of charge or at low cost.

Despite substantial scholarship on opportunity creation, the field still does not understand how impactful ideas are identified. Specifically, there is little clarity on how processes of generating ideas that produce new-to-the-world products and services are created. The principal reason for this focus is because of the potential, game-changing nature of opportunity creation in satisfying unmet market needs and wants. Miller and Le Breton-Miller (2017) and Winschiers-Theophilus et al. (2015) sought to address the question of opportunity creation by proposing a preliminary, 'challenge-based' model of entrepreneurs who create ventures to overcome a variety of life-changing challenges, including severe physical disability (Miller and Le Breton-Miller, 2017), and chronic social and economic barriers (Winschiers-Theophilus et al., 2015). Moreover, 'necessity and opportunity' scholars (Block and Wagner, 2010; Block et al., 2015) have developed understanding of 'necessity entrepreneurship', where entrepreneurs are locked out of employment and discover or create ventures because they are immigrants (Hart and Acs, 2011). For opportunity creation, Miller and Le Breton-Miller's (2017) model of challenged entrepreneurs offers a platform and rationale for addressing the question of opportunity creation. The model does so by enabling research of cognitively and physically impaired entrepreneurs with its guiding framework of how extreme challenges may compel adaptive behavior that, in turn, drives entrepreneurial initiatives. By drawing from the challenge-based model of Miller and Le Breton-Miller (2017), in Chapter 2, Wilson Ng begins to explore how their model may be operationalized in opening up the little-known phenomenon of opportunity creation. The research that draws on the model has begun with a pilot study of serial, visually impaired entrepreneurs. What may be learned about processes of opportunity creation from these entrepreneurs? The chapter reports findings from the pilot study and puts forward two propositions that relate certain effects on entrepreneurs of sudden, severe disability with key elements of opportunity creation.

The employment of people with disability in Australia is low in comparison to other Organisation for Economic Co-operation and Development (OECD) nations. Government has sought to bring about change through a combination of open employment initiatives, specific disability employment services and Australian Disability Enterprises. The barriers that they face in mainstream employment have been well documented over the last 30 years, yet identifying the barriers and implementing policy has not changed the effective employment rate. One response by some people with disability is to establish microenterprises, become self-employed or enter into entrepreneurship. Labour force statistics show that, paradoxically, people with disability in Australia have higher rates of self-employment than the non-disabled, even though they are faced with higher barriers to entry. In Chapter 3, Simon Darcy, Jock Collins and Megan Stronach outline research undertaken to investigate the self-employment, microenterprise and entrepreneurship of people with disability in Australia. The research involved a partnership with service providers in the disability services sector – National Disability Services, Settlement Services International (SSI) and Break-Thru People Solutions – and was funded by the Australian Research Council. The authors explore the lived experiences of entrepreneurs with disability through their underlying motivations, the barriers they face, the enablers that assist them along their journey, the outcomes they experience, and the benefits beyond the financial rewards that they report on. Their experiences have a complexity depending upon their disability, level of support needs, and those who join them on their journeys.

According to the Centers for Disease Control and Prevention (2015), one in every 50 to 68 children in the United States is diagnosed with autism, with an estimated 500 000 young adults on the autism spectrum disorder (ASD) expected to join the workforce in the next decade (Chu, 2015; Johnson and Joshi, 2016). While being on the autism spectrum makes success in the workplace a challenge, individuals with ASD have a great deal to offer employers, as they are generally very hardworking, detail-oriented, have an extraordinary memory, are visual learners and thinkers, are very loyal, honest, perseverant and reliable, are non-judgemental, and are highly skilled in particular areas (Parr et al., 2013). In Chapter 4, Eric Patton focuses on the push and pull of entrepreneurship for individuals with ASD by exploring the factors that make entrepreneurship a viable option for these individuals. Specifically, drawing on strategic models of entrepreneurship (Hitt et al., 2011), challenge models of entrepreneurship (Miller and Le Breton-Miller, 2017) and social entrepreneurship (Harris et al., 2013), both pull factors which lead ASD individuals to seek entrepreneurial opportunities, and push factors which make entrepreneurship and small business among the few options for ASD workers to find employment, are underlined. In doing so, Eric highlights challenge or necessity-based entrepreneurship (Miller and Le Breton-Miller, 2017) as a form of entrepreneurship that is particularly relevant to ASD individuals. He further suggests that individuals on the spectrum may opt for self-employment due to biases, stigmas and fears around neurocognitive disabilities that exclude them from consideration by many employers, or pigeonhole them into low-level positions.

Continuing with the theme of push and pull factors, in Chapter 5, through an extensive literature review, Wilson Ng answers the questions of how extreme disabilities, visible and invisible, relate with entrepreneurial activity and how severely disabled entrepreneurs create ventures. His literature review presents research on these questions that have principally concerned entrepreneurs with ADHD and with severe visual impairments. For example, a recent study of entrepreneurs with ADHD has suggested a strong positive correlation between ADHD and entrepreneurial intention and action. Wilson concludes that entrepreneurs with ADHD are more likely to choose business venturing, without having to do so out of necessity, and to self-select entrepreneurial activities. He based his conclusions on the evidence from literature; for example, in a study of severely visually impaired entrepreneurs, insights were generated on processes of opportunity formation based on the entrepreneurs' skills in adapting routinely to their sighted environment (Ng and Arndt, 2019). These insights are thought to be located in the following five principal areas of entrepreneurial activity, and may illuminate processes of opportunity formation based on: (1) skills development; (2) origins and sources of entrepreneurial motivation; (3) empowerment of disabled people; (4) creation of unique strategies; and (5) entrepreneurial education.

There is a considerable amount of research concerning the issue of entrepreneurial intentions, which has generated mixed findings. Integrating sustainability, in the sense of considering disabled people, into the current entrepreneurial intention research makes it possible to fill an important research gap. The main objective of this chapter is to clarify the contribution that education, students' traits, and contextual factors make to an individual's entrepreneurial intent when disabled students are incorporated into the analysis as an innovative field of study. In Chapter 6, Rosa M. Muñoz, Yolanda Salinero and M. Valle Fernández analyse the entrepreneurial intentions of disabled people who are studying in higher education, and compare them with non-disabled students, while considering the main factors described in previous studies. In order to achieve this objective, the authors have carried out a logistic regression with a sample of Spanish students. Their findings suggest that education does not influence students' entrepreneurial intentions, which are affected by only some of the students' traits and background conditions. Regarding the disabled students' entrepreneurial intentions, they found no significant differences compared with those of students who are not disabled. Initiatives such as those of the University of Castilla-La Mancha (UCLM) described in the chapter should therefore be encouraged, keeping in mind that disabled students do not always show a lack of confidence in themselves, as some studies have claimed.

In the Czech Republic, the concept of social entrepreneurship is still being developed and lacks, for example, systematic public support and regulation. In addition, the total number of social enterprises operating in the Czech Republic is low, and thus social entrepreneurship cannot reach its potential. To accelerate this development, raising awareness of social entrepreneurship among the Czech population may be important. Based on the survey carried out among 200 possible stakeholders of Czech social enterprises, in Chapter 7, Ondřej Kročil, Richard Pospíšil and David Kosina explored the awareness and attitudes of selected groups of people towards social entrepreneurship. These groups are disabled people, as typical employees of Czech social enterprises, and university students as possible future founders of these enterprises. Their research project focuses on three issues: (1) the level of awareness of the concept of social entrepreneurship among university students and disabled people; (2) the position of disabled people in the current labour market; and (3) the willingness of students to become entrepreneurs and to start business with social purpose. Their research shows that the awareness of the concept of social entrepreneurship is generally low. Nevertheless, students consider becoming entrepreneurs and starting a business with a social purpose. The research also shows that, according to the opinion of the respondents, it is difficult to find employment as a disabled person, and that the current labour market does not offer enough vacant positions which could be interesting for these persons. From this perspective, further development of Czech social enterprises (especially of work integration social enterprises) is very important.

PART II: ENTREPRENEURIAL ECOSYSTEM: BARRIERS AND FACILITATORS

The current harsh economic climate is demanding more innovative pathways to increasing disabled people's employment. Disability enterprise has many benefits, such as increasing independence, greater choices and self-determination, and the development of management and wider transferable skills. Although it is not yet at a satisfactory level where disabled people can fully participate in their business activities, disability enterprise is absorbing many disabled people who cannot prosper in paid employment. In Chapter 8, Se Kwang Hwang and Alan Roulstone explore the position, potential and scope for self-employment and microenterprise for disabled South Koreans. The chronic barriers experienced by disabled people to gaining paid work suggest that self-employment and enterprise might offer a good alternative. The self-determined nature of running a microenterprise has been shown to connect with disabled people who may not conform to the standardized notions of body and brain that underpin many mainstream work contexts. Despite this promise, several barriers continue to beset disabled people's access to microenterprise activity; barriers ranging from Confucian precepts, to employment protections that are geared largely towards paid employment, and to the lack of training, finance and business support for disabled people starting up and sustaining microenterprises in Korea. The extension of legal protections, meaningful start-up subsidies, better business support, and bridges between paid work and microenterprise are all seen as important policy correctives that would better support disabled people. For example, the Korean government introduced the Promotion of Disabled Persons' Enterprise Activities Act in 2005, and the government's attention has been directed toward disability enterprise as a more innovative solution to ameliorate the economic and social challenges relating to employment of disabled people.

People with disabilities are disproportionately inactive in the labour market, and their rates of incomes are much lower than for people without disabilities (OECD, 2014). An OECD (2014) report highlighted that there is a large variation in self-employment rates for people with disabilities across European Union (EU) Member States. The self-employment rates of people with disabilities are relatively low in many north-eastern EU countries, and higher in southern EU countries. There is limited academic research relating to public policy initiatives that target people with disabilities who are potential, nascent or existing entrepreneurs. In designing and implementing support initiatives, policy-makers face a trade-off between extensive, generic advice to large numbers of disabled recipients, and intensive, tailored support to highly targeted subgroups. In Chapter 9, Thomas M. Cooney addresses this knowledge gap by examining the challenges policy-makers face in supporting disabled entrepreneurs. He investigates a middle-ground approach, while considering resource constraints and the specific support needs of potential entrepreneurs with diverse impairments and health conditions. He further proposes a novel policy model that considers the distinctive challenges encountered by aspiring disabled entrepreneurs. The chapter draws upon entrepreneurship literature and primary data to address these objectives. The principal barriers identified include accessibility of information and support, the low expectations of support providers, and the inflexibility of the benefits system. A 'Funnel Approach' is designed to provide support that is open to all people with disabilities initially, but through a series of stages the support becomes ever more focused towards an increasingly smaller group of potential users. The Funnel Approach provides a useful framework for the design and delivery of supports sensitive to the specific and diverse needs of people with disabilities, and it is considerate of likely resource constraints.

While all entrepreneurs can face struggles in creating business ventures, nevertheless entrepreneurs with disabilities can face challenges that are not usually encountered by business owners without disabilities. Assisting them to start their own businesses can present unique challenges for social entrepreneurs. In Chapter 10, Mirza Tihic, Gary Shaheen and Felix Arndt describe how social entrepreneurs can assist prospective entrepreneurs with disabilities by addressing three dimensions that affect venture creation: (1) how life circumstances of prospective entrepreneurs with disabilities affect their ventures (micro level); (2) addressing infrastructure and operations of the venture being created (meso level); and (3) negotiating the various external environments that affect successful venture creation. Inherent in these (macro-level) considerations is addressing stigma and negative public perceptions about persons with disabilities. The authors further argue that social entrepreneurs must consider these micro, meso and macro challenges that entrepreneurs with disabilities can face. When these barriers are surmounted, social entrepreneurs can assist more persons with disabilities to become successful business owners and achieve income stability and social equality.

Entrepreneurship plays an important role in reducing social exclusion and economic discrimination, which are often found in marginalized groups. In Chapter 11, Tiansheng Yang, Shandana Sheikh, Shumaila Yousafzai and Xiangxin Yang suggest that self-employment is likely to help disabled people out of underemployment, unemployment and low income, which may improve their perceived social value and self-sufficiency. High rates of self-employment among disabled people and such enterprises not only provide an economic contribution, but also make a significant contribution in the provision of jobs for other disabled people. Nevertheless, despite disabled people having a broadly positive attitude towards entrepreneurship, the entrepreneurial environment can still cause extreme challenges for them. Highlighting the importance of the relationship between an individual with disability and their environment, the authors of this study explore the role of government policies in China in supporting disabled entrepreneurs. Drawing upon institutional theory and entrepreneurial ecosystem literature, their results reflect on how disabled entrepreneurs in China face discrimination in employment and other career pathways. Through in-depth interviews with Chinese disabled entrepreneurs, the study also explores the role of government in creating a conducive environment for disabled entrepreneurs in China.

Despite the fact women with disability constitute more than 50 per cent of the total disabled population in Pakistan, there has been little research on this marginalized population, and thus underappreciation of their contribution towards economic output. Recognizing that entrepreneurship is a pathway for empowerment and independence for women with disability, Chapter 12 aims to discuss the entrepreneurial environment for women with disability in the context of Pakistan. Undertaking the entrepreneurial ecosystem framework, Shandana Sheikh calls attention to the factors that impact upon entrepreneurial women with disability in pursuing their entrepreneurial efforts. Drawing excerpts from the narrative of disability rights activist and entrepreneur Tanzila Khan, she discusses how disabled women navigate in their entrepreneurial journey.

Development practitioners use microfinance as a tool to promote women's entrepreneurship in low- and middle-income economies. Institutions that provide microfinance services (microfinance institutions, MFIs) often target women who own and operate businesses, or who have the willingness to engage in entrepreneurial activities. A key reason for targeting women is to integrate them into mainstream economic activities, move them out of poverty and/or economically empower them. However, certain groups of women, such as those with disabilities, are more vulnerable than others and often get excluded even from microfinance initiatives. The mainstream pro-poor financial discourse, however, has largely ignored discussing issues faced by people/women with disabilities, or opportunities available for them to access microfinance for entrepreneurship. In Chapter 13, Nadeera Ranabahu and Farzana Aman Tanima address this gap and aim to outline challenges faced by people/women with disabilities in accessing microfinance, and opportunities associated with MFI services, and to explain how MFIs shape disabled women's entrepreneurial activities. Their study reviews the way disability shapes women's access to microfinance and, subsequently, their entrepreneurial behaviours. Using peer-reviewed journal articles collected systematically, they found that microfinance has a direct role in promoting entrepreneurship among both disabled people and among caregivers. However, only some women with disabilities use loans for businesses; others are reluctant to engage in businesses due to the risks. Further, the study points out that microfinance also promotes entrepreneurial activities indirectly by addressing rehabilitation needs. Almost all face discrimination and exclusion at multiple levels of the lending process. Their findings are presented as a conceptual framework which scholars could use in future to further study disabled women entrepreneurs. Microfinance practitioners could employ the framework to identify areas requiring inclusive policies.

In response to the COVID-19 pandemic, universities were required to close their physical premises and promptly shift to online delivery to enable students to continue their studies (Bisht et al., 2020; Crawford et al., 2020). However, the rapid transition to remote learning led to negative impacts on student motivation, engagement, anxiety and psychological wellbeing (Petillon and McNeil, 2020; Wester et al., 2021; Prowse et al., 2020). Specifically, research widely reports that university students have struggled to maintain motivation and engagement following the transition to remote learning (Perets et al., 2020). Academic performance has also reportedly declined as a consequence of the mitigation strategy toward remote learning (Mudenda et al., 2020). Worldwide trends report increased stress levels, anxiety and depression amongst university students (Liu et al., 2020; Rajab and Alkattan, 2020), and the correlation between increased anxiety and declining academic performance is also noted (Bledsoe and Baskin, 2014). In Chapter 14, Sylvie Studente, Filia Garivaldis and Wilson Ng extend current research on students' mental health, offering a preliminary investigation on the impact of the COVID-19 pandemic on the learning and activities of entrepreneurship students. Specifically, this chapter reports upon a study conducted at a London University with a largely international student base. Study participants were undergraduate students enrolled on an entrepreneurship pathway. The study sought to investigate social and psychological impacts experienced by entrepreneurship participants due to the lack of physical access to the university campus during lockdown. The chapter concludes with implications and recommendations for the study and nurture of students in higher education in and beyond the research context.

In Chapter 15, Shumaila Yousafzai and Yerken Turganbayev discuss disability and entrepreneurship in the post-Soviet context of Kazakhstan. In Kazakhstan's public spaces and workspaces, one rarely encounters a person in a wheelchair, with a white cane, with a guide dog, or with Down's syndrome or cerebral palsy. While research and information on policy support for entrepreneurs with disabilities in Kazakhstan is limited, in terms of the information available on the initiatives and the economic and social impact of such support programmes, the information provided in this chapter and the narratives of Kazakh entrepreneurs with disabilities show a clear recognition in Kazakhstan of the potential for entrepreneurship among people with disabilities. Kazakhstan's government has initiated and implemented several policies to support entrepreneurial activity among people with disabilities, but gaps in the scope of the support provided to entrepreneurs with disabilities remain. Being a person, or indeed an entrepreneur, with disabilities in Kazakhstan still means significant hardship in terms of physical infrastructure, access to education, training, finance, and other social and psychological barriers. The authors recommend that attention should be paid to ensuring that potential entrepreneurs get access to mainstream entrepreneurship support by, for example, ensuring that the frontline staff in entrepreneurship support centres are sensitive to the needs of entrepreneurs, and offer them adapted support and services. Institutions of higher education, vocational training colleges and schools can offer training and education to improve entrepreneurial knowledge among people with disabilities. For example, these institutions offer no disabilities-focused entrepreneurship training courses, and the support for entrepreneurs does not include financing. In general, the initiatives reported in the chapter do not provide integrated packages of support that combine skill development, advice and mentoring, access to finances, and networking, all of which could increase their effectiveness. In addition, a range of dedicated mentoring and training services could be developed for entrepreneurs with disabilities, and sensitivity training could be provided to staff on how to adapt mainstream business advisory and other services to serve the specific needs of entrepreneurs with disabilities. Finally, there is a need to improve institutions' capabilities with respect to entrepreneurship, disability and inclusion, to motivate and inspire people with disabilities to choose an entrepreneurial career.

In Chapter 16, Wojdan Omran and Leila Farraj explore the potential of inclusive entrepreneurship in Palestine. They illustrate the realities of Palestinian people with disabilities, in light of their context as a marginalized group at the hands of both their own society and that of the colonial occupation, and how this impacts upon their potential as part of the Palestinian entrepreneurial ecosystem. They suggest that promoting entrepreneurship amongst people with disabilities would not only provide a gateway for their own enhanced economic activity, but also foster the development of people with disabilities as contributors to society. Enabling people with disabilities to create impactful social enterprises that may address some of the most pressing challenges faced by their own and other marginalized communities would not only create jobs in a rather adverse labour market, but would also serve on a broader, long-term scale by fostering meaningful progress towards socio-economic inclusion and institutional reform.

PART III: THE IDENTITY AND CONTRIBUTION OF DISABLED ENTREPRENEURS

Entrepreneurial identity is described as the set of claims about who the entrepreneur is (Navis and Glynn, 2011). It is not a static property of the founder, but is a discursively negotiated outcome where the individual is in a state of becoming (Essers and Benschop, 2007), based on evolving self and social feedback (Demetry, 2017). In Chapter 17, Mukta Kulkarni and Yangerjungla Pongener examine the identity-making of entrepreneurs with a disability, and extend prior conversations about entrepreneurial identity. Entrepreneurial identity can be a confluence of internal and external influences (Demetry, 2017; Gill and Larson, 2014). The authors outline how these influences interact to inform identity-making of the entrepreneur with a disability. They further examine the intersectionality of the two identities – of being an entrepreneur and an individual with a disability – as it informs ongoing identity-making during the entrepreneurial process. This is important because there is a contradiction between the neoliberal view of the able-bodied successful entrepreneur, and the view of disability based on dependence and inability or weakness (Jammaers and Zanoni, 2020). The interview-based study presents three broad findings. First, participants seem to question whether they are really an entrepreneur. This is because they see themselves as accidental or forced migrants to entrepreneurship (for example, given no other employment options) who sometimes curtail venture growth (for example, given bodily limitations, or to pursue disability-related goals). Second, participants wonder whether others think of them as an entrepreneur. This is driven by a perception of uneven support from parents who dissuade participants from entrepreneurship, and by a perceived lack of client faith in participants' entrepreneurial ability. Finally, participants seem to question whether being an entrepreneur makes for an inferior self. This is driven by the perception that employees and clients behave as if the entrepreneur's disability matters more than their ability. Taken together, the findings indicate that the entrepreneurial journey does not always imply a salient, constant, or a positive entrepreneurial identity for all entrepreneurs. This chapter serves as a nudge to render visible the experiences of entrepreneurial identity-making for those precariously positioned in society with regard to their social status.

A range of scholarly work has identified entrepreneurs as central to an emerging paradigm of digital labour. Drawing on data from a multi-year research project in the virtual world Second Life, in Chapter 18, Tom Boellstorff explores disability experiences of entrepreneurism, focusing on intersections of creativity, risk and inclusion. Disability is typically assumed to be incompatible with work; an assumption often reinforced by policies that withdraw benefits from disabled persons whose income exceeds a meagre threshold. Responses to such exclusion appear when disabled persons in Second Life frame 'entrepreneur' as a selfhood characterized by creativity and contribution, not just initiative and risk. In navigating structural barriers with regard to income and access, including affordances of the virtual world itself, they implicitly contest reconfigurations of personhood under neoliberalism, where the labouring self becomes framed not as a worker earning an hourly wage, but as a business with the 'ability' to sell services. This reveals how digital technology reworks the interplay of selfhood, work and value; but in ways that remain culturally specific and embedded in forms of inequality.

Disabled entrepreneurship traditionally has been seen as a challenge-based phenomenon. Nevertheless, beyond common measures of performance and success of disabled entrepreneur, they offer a value to themselves and their multiple stakeholders such as business, family and society. In Chapter 19, Vahid Makizadeh, Shumaila Yousafzai, Siavash Aein Jamshid and Adel Mohebbi explore how disabled entrepreneurs create value at multiple levels in the context of Iran's entrepreneurial ecosystem. The authors adopted a narrative approach to understand lived experiences of disabled entrepreneurs in Iran, and their contributions towards value creation. They draw upon the narrative reports of three disabled entrepreneurs in Bushehr province in Iran, and explore their value contributions at multiple levels. Thematic analysis of the interviews and narratives show that disabled entrepreneurship forms four value dimensions: of values related to individual, business, household and society levels. The multi-level value that disabled people in Iran find through engaging in entrepreneurial activity provides a robust and substantial motive to keep putting effort into their businesses. Such substantial, multidimensional values are revealed in the behaviour of disabled entrepreneurs, who by their behaviour could act as role models to their families and their local communities. The new position that disabled experience through engaging in entrepreneurship may indicate that entrepreneurship is a fruitful route for the disabled in society, and a way to raise disabled people's potential to contribute to the economic growth of a country (Falch and Hernæs, 2012).

In our final chapter, Chapter 20, Eric V. Bindah talks about his research on exploring the motivational intention and challenges faced by disabled entrepreneurs. During his interaction with disabled entrepreneurs in the Sultanate of Oman, Eric noticed that the one area which was highly neglected was the potential contribution of disabled entrepreneurs. He wanted to explore this neglected area of research, and the untapped potential of entrepreneurship by people with disability in this part of the world. Hence, based on this observation, further research was undertaken which is reported in this chapter, to understand disabled entrepreneurs' contribution, their motivation and challenges in the Sultanate of Oman. As an exploratory study, this research initiation is aimed at identifying the potential factors which affect the business ventures of disabled entrepreneurs and their growth. It was first observed that disabled entrepreneurship is relatively unfamiliar both to people with disability themselves, and to disability organizations in Oman. Furthermore, within most entrepreneurship research there seems to be little room for disability: most theories assume that entrepreneurs are able people. This study is exploratory in nature and identifies the important factors which could undermine the success of disabled entrepreneurship. For the purpose of this study, a snowball sampling method was utilized, and several semi-structured interviews were conducted with identified disabled entrepreneurs in specific geographical regions of Oman. The researcher had to identify a key informant to help identify hard-to-reach participants.

CLOSING REMARKS

We extend special thanks to Edward Elgar Publishing and its staff, who have been most helpful throughout this entire process. We also warmly thank all of the authors who submitted their manuscripts for consideration for this book. They showed their desire to share their knowledge and experience with the book's readers, and a willingness to present their research and their views for possible challenge by their peers. We also thank the reviewers, who provided excellent independent and incisive consideration of the anonymous submissions.

We hope that this compendium of chapters and themes stimulates and contributes to the ongoing debate surrounding disabled entrepreneurship. The chapters in this book can help to fill some gaps in what we know, while stimulating further thought and action.

NOTE

1. 'Disability' is an English word that is unique among most, if not all, languages in being
    pejorative. It follows that disabled people are often called, synonymously, 'spastics'.
    Hence disability carries a wholly negative meaning.

REFERENCES

Bisht, R. K., Jasola, S., and Bisht, I. P. (2020). Acceptability and challenges of online higher
    education in the era of COVID-19: A study of students' perspective. *Asian Education and
    Development Studies*. Doi: 10.1108/AEDS-05-2020-0119.
Bledsoe, T. Scott, Baskin, Janice J. (2014). Recognizing student fear: The elephant in the
    classroom. *College Teaching*, 62(1), 32–41.
Block, J. and Wagner, M. (2010). Necessity and opportunity entrepreneurs in Germany.
    Schmalenbach Business Review, 62(2), 154–174.
Block, J., Kohn, K., Miller, D. and Ullrich, K. (2015). Necessity entrepreneurship and compet-
    itive strategy. *Small Business Economics*, 44(1), 37–54.
Centers for Disease Control and Prevention. (2015, February 26). Autism spectrum disorder:
    Data & statistics. Available at: http://www.cdc.gov/ncbddd/autism/data.html.
Chu, F. (2015, June). "Making it work", *Inc. Magazine*, 34.
Crawford, J., Butler-Henderson, K., Rudolph, J., Malkawi, B., Glowatz, M., Burton, R.,
    Magni, P. and Lam, S. (2020). COVID-19: 20 countries' higher education intra-period
    digital pedagogy responses. *Journal of Applied Teaching and Learning (JALT)*, 3(1), 9–28.
Dana, Léo-Paul. (2002). *When Economies Change Paths: Models of Transition in China,
    the Central Asian Republics, Myanmar and the Nations of Former Indochine Française*.
    Singapore: World Scientific Publishing.
Demetry, D. (2017). Pop-up to professional: Emerging entrepreneurial identity and evolving
    vocabularies of motive. *Academy of Management Discoveries*, 3(2), 187–207.
Essers, C. and Benschop, Y. (2007). Enterprising identities: Female entrepreneurs of Moroccan
    or Turkish origin in the Netherlands. *Organization Studies*, 28(1), 49–69.
Falch, R. and Hernæs, U. J. V. (2012). *Disability, Social Identity, and Entrepreneurship:
    Evidence from a laboratory experiement in rural Uganda* (Master's thesis). Available at:
    https://openaccess.nhh.no/nhh-xmlui/bitstream/handle/11250/169963/falch_hernaes2012
    .pdf?sequence=1.
Gill, R. and Larson, G. S. (2014). Making the ideal (local) entrepreneur: Place and the regional
    development of high-tech entrepreneurial identity. *Human Relations*, 67(5), 519–542.
Harris, S. P., Renko, M. and Caldwell, K. (2013). Accessing social entrepreneurship:
    Perspectives of people with disabilities and key stakeholders. *Journal of Vocational
    Rehabilitation*, 38, 35–48.
Hart, D. and Acs, Z. (2011). High-tech immigrant entrepreneurship in the United States.
    Economic Development Quarterly, 25(2), 116–129.
Hitt, M.A., Ireland, R.D., Sirmon, D.G. and Trahms, C.A. (2011). Strategic entrepreneur-
    ship: creating value for individuals, organizations, and society. *Academy of Management
    Perspectives*, 25, 57–74.
Jack, A. (2019). Survey data highlight need for health interventions. *Financial Times*,
    21 November. Available at: https://www.ft.com/content/5eea0cdc-d940-11e9-9c26
    -419d783e10e8. Accessed 27-10-2021.
Jammaers, E. and Zanoni, P. (2020). Unexpected entrepreneurs: The identity work of entre-
    preneurs with disabilities. *Entrepreneurship & Regional Development*, 32(9–10), 879–898.

Johnson, T. D. and Joshi, A. (2016). Dark clouds or silver linings? A stigma threat perspective on the implications of an autism diagnosis for workplace well-being. *Journal of Applied Psychology*, 101, 430–449.

Jones, M. and Latreille, P. (2011). Disability and self-employment: Evidence for the UK. *Applied Economics*, 43(27), 4161–4178.

Liu, Y. C., Kuo, R. L. and Shih, S. R. (2020). COVID-19: The first documented coronavirus pandemic in history. *Biomedical journal*, 43(4), 328–333.

Miller, D. and Le Breton-Miller, I. (2017). Underdog entrepreneurs: A model of challenge-based entrepreneurship. *Entrepreneurship Theory and Practice*, 41(1), 7–17.

Mudenda, S., Zulu, A., Phiri, M., Ngazimbi, M., Mufwambi, W., Kasanga, M. and Banda, M. (2020). Impact of coronavirus disease 2019 (Covid-19) on university students: A global health and education problem. *Aquademia*, 4, 2. Article No: ep20026.

Navis, C. and Glynn, M. A. (2011). Legitimate distinctiveness and the entrepreneurial identity: Influence on investor judgments of new venture plausibility. *Academy of Management Review*, 36(3), 479–499.

Ng, W. and Arndt, F. (2019). "I never needed eyes to see": Leveraging extreme challenges for successful venture creation. *Journal of Business Venturing Insights*, 11 (June), 1–10.

OECD (2014). Policy Brief on Entrepreneurship for People with Disabilities. OECD, Paris.

Parr, J. R., Jolleff, N., Gray, L., Gibbs, J., Williams, J. and McConachie, H. (2013). Twenty years of research shows UK child development team provision still varies widely for children with disability. *Child: Care, Health and Development*, 39(6), 903–907.

Perets, E., Chabeda, D., Gong, A., Huang, X., Fung, T., Ng, K., Bathgate, M. and Yan, E. (2020). Impact of the emergency transition to remote teaching on student engagement in a non-STEM undergraduate chemistry course in the time of COVID-19. *Journal of Chemical Education*, 97, 2439–2447.

Petillon, R. and McNeil, S. (2020). Student experiences of emergency remote teaching: Impacts of instructor practice on student learning, engagement, and well-being. *Journal of Chemical Education*, 97(9), 2486–2493.

Prowse, R., Sherratt, F., Abizaid, A., Gabrys, R., Hellemans, K., Patterson, Z. and McQaid, R. (2020). Coping with the COVID-19 pandemic: Examining gender differences in stress and mental health among university students. *Frontiers in Psychology*. Doi: https://doi.org/10.3389/fpsyt.2021.650759.

Rajab, M. and Alkattan, K. (2020). Challenges to online medication education during the COVID-19 pandemic. *Cureus*, 12, 7.

RNIB (2021). UK Disability survey research report. Available at: https://www.gov.uk/government/publications/uk-disability-survey-research-report-june-2021/uk-disability-survey-research-report-june-2021.

Santuzzi, A., Waltz, P., Finkelstein, L. and Rupp, D. (2014). Invisible disabilities. Unique challenges for employees and organizations. *Industrial and Organizational Psychology*, 7(2), 204–219.

Tufano, P. (2003). *Financial innovation*. (Chapter 6). In: Constantinides, G., Harris, M. and Stulz, R. (eds). *Handbook of the Economics of Finance*, Vol 1, Part A, *Corporate Finance*, 307–335. Elsevier: Amsterdam.

Wester, E., Walsh, L., Arango-Caro, S. and Callis-Duehl, K. (2021). Student engagement declines in STEM undergraduates during COVID-19 driven remote learning. *Journal of Microbiology and Biology Education*, 22, 1.

Wiklund, J., Yu, W., Tucker, R. and Marino, L. D. (2017). ADHD, impulsivity and entrepreneurship. *Journal of Business Venturing*, 32(65), 627–656.

Winschiers-Theophilus, H., Cabrero, D., Angula, S., Chivuno- Kuria, S., Mendonca, H. and Ngolo, R. (2015). A challenge-based approach to promote entrepreneurship among youth in an informal settlement of Windhoek. AOM Conference Proceedings, 7–11 August, Vancouver, Canada. https://www.researchgate.net/profile/Daniel-G-Cabrero/publication/

283346056_A_Challenge-based_Approach_to_promote_Entrepreneurship_among
_Youth_in_an_Informal_Settlement_of_Windhoek/links/56351cb508aebc003fff70cc/A
-Challenge-based-Approach-to-promote-Entrepreneurship-among-Youth-in-an-Informal
-Settlement-of-Windhoek.pdf. Accessed 2-11-2021.

World Bank (2021). Disability inclusion. Available at: https://www.worldbank.org/en/topic/
disability#1. Accessed 2-11-2021.

Zahra, S. A., Gedajlovic, E., Neubaum, D. O. and Shulman, J. M. (2009). A typology of
social entrepreneurs: Motives, search processes and ethical challenges. *Journal of Business
Venturing*, 24, 519–532.

PART I

THE PUSH AND THE PULL FACTORS FOR DISABLED ENTREPRENEURS

1. Follow your dreams? Push and pull motivations of entrepreneurs with disabilities in Hungary

Sara Csillag, Zsuzsanna Gyori, Anna Laura Hidegh and Carmen Svastics

INTRODUCTION

Disability has a wide-ranging effect on social and economic circumstances, including not only participation in the labour market but also on factors such as education and transport, which also affect employment opportunities. One possible solution to the problems of low labour market participation rates lies in the potential for people with disabilities to become self-employed or to start and run their own businesses. The advantages of entrepreneurship for people with disability (PWD) may outweigh any risk involved (Doyel, 2002). Some argue that self-employment and business ownership can be used as a potential means of vocational rehabilitation to achieve faster and better integration into the labour market, and eventually social inclusion and a higher quality of life in general (Kitching, 2014). This loosely connects to one of the priorities of the European Union (EU): promoting entrepreneurship as part of the Europe 2020 strategy, leading to a smart, sustainable and inclusive growth of the European economy (Pagán, 2009).

Despite an increased scientific interest in recent years regarding entrepreneurship and social minorities, there remains a significant lack of theoretical and empirical research on the topic of entrepreneurs with disabilities (EWD), who Cooney (2008) calls the 'forgotten minority'. Parker Harris et al. (2014) note that the theoretical work exploring entrepreneurship for PWD started in the late 1980s in the United States (US) and the United Kingdom, but there is a scarcity of existing theory and empirical evidence, for several reasons. First, as Pagán (2009) emphasises, there is very little reliable global or nationwide data on the exact number or characteristics of EWD: official statistics do not cover, or only partially cover, the field, so preparing reliable quantitative analyses is difficult. Second, disability is a heterogeneous social construct and refers to an extremely diverse set of individuals (Renko et al., 2015). It can vary in type, severity, stability, time of onset, duration, and so on: no two people's experiences or impairments are the same (Dhar and Farzana, 2017). Entrepreneurial motivation, personal characteristics and socio-economic conditions may also vary individually; besides which, certain entrepreneurial challenges may also be limited to only particular groups. This makes theorising or researching different aspects of EWD very challenging. Third, as Yamamoto et al. (2012) indicate, there is an uncertainty in the extant literature: the terms 'self-employment', 'business ownership', 'microenterprise' and 'entrepreneurship' are at times used interchangeably, which creates theoretical confusion. Scholars in the field urge focused, theoretically sound and high-quality empirical research in refining the present picture and supporting future policy development (Parker Harris et al., 2014).

In this chapter we would like to contribute to the growing body of empirical research on EWD, highlighting the results of our exploratory research project in the field. Our objective is to explore and analyse the goals and motivational background of PWD establishing their own enterprises. While we aim to contribute to theory, the regional scope of the empirical research may also be of importance, insofar as very little empirical research has been conducted in the Central European region about EWD.

The structure of our chapter is as follows: first, we introduce the labour of PWD within the socio-economic context and environment of Hungary. Then the chapter presents an overview of the theoretical background of the research project, focusing on goals and motivation. Next, we describe the methodology used, after which the main results of the research are presented. The chapter closes with a discussion providing arguments for our answers and contributions.

BACKGROUND

The lack of employment opportunities and secure employment for PWD pose personal, societal and economic difficulties and challenges worldwide (Yamamoto et al., 2012). Where reliable statistics are available, they show that the unemployment rates of PWD are considerably higher than, and their labour market participation rates and economic activity are well below, those of non-disabled people. Evidence shows that the right of PWD to meaningful work is frequently denied, mostly based on a medical picture of disability which frames disability as an individual's medical or health problem requiring cure and care (Barnes and Mercer, 2005).

Being present in the labour market offers several advantages and may also mean a variety of work options: moreover, salaried employment, self-employment, business ownership or entrepreneurship may provide viable and realistic options toward overcoming at least some of the traditional obstacles to employment (such as negative attitudes and ignorance; environmental barriers, especially mobility barriers; inadequate vocational rehabilitation services; and lack of opportunities for career development). At the same time, some obstacles may remain (such as lower levels of, or lack of, educational or social networks) and new challenges may also appear (such as competence-deficit). Although self-employment as a career option is nothing new, as a strategy it has been neglected by policy-makers and rehabilitation agencies, considering it a last option, or a safety valve for PWD (Ashley and Graf, 2018). This attitude might arise from traditional Western culture, which sees the entrepreneur as a proud and independent (white male) hero achieving something outstanding, which is in distinct contrast to the widespread and distorted image of PWD as dependent and vulnerable people who expect others to make decisions on their behalf, or wait for job offers rather than take the initiative to actively seek employment (Cooney, 2008; Harper and Momm, 1989). All in all, Pagán's (2009) analyses of the European Community Household Panel (ECHP) and other data from the US suggest that self-employment rates are indeed higher among PWD than non-disabled people, along with interesting national differences (Kitching, 2014; Renko et al., 2015).

People with Disability in Hungary

The Hungarian picture of employment for PWD is not favourable. According to the latest state census of the Hungarian Central Statistical Office in 2011, 490 000 people (4.9 per cent of the population) were officially classified as being disabled, and 82 per cent claimed that they perceived serious obstacles in their everyday lives: transport, education and employment were the most frequently mentioned fields. Data shows that PWD in Hungary on average tended to have lower levels of education and lower income than others. As for the duration of impairment, 40 per cent acquired their impairments before the age of 18. Nearly 300 000 of them were between 18 and 59 years of age (that is, were of 'active age'), but only 18.1 per cent were actually active in the labour market (Hidegh and Csillag, 2013). Based on recent estimations, due to certain financial incentives introduced in 2012 the employment rate has increased significantly to about 30 per cent. Unfortunately, official data about the ratio of self-employment or business ownership for PWD does not exist, and there is no available Hungarian data in the European Community Household Panel (Pagán, 2009; Csillag et al., 2019). As the rate of self-employment is lower in Hungary than the European average, this would imply a lower rate of self-employment among PWD as well.

Concerning disability affairs, Hungary is following the European Disability Strategy 2010–2020 (EU), while also being a state party of the United Nations Convention on the Rights of Persons with Disabilities (UNCRPD). According to the latest 'Concluding observations on the initial periodic report of Hungary' adopted by the CRPD Committee (17–28 September 2012), although the legal background has been secured in several aspects, Hungary is still lagging behind in a number of areas. Among others, PWD and disability organisations are generally not involved in the planning, execution and monitoring of public decision-making processes at all levels; efforts to meet the deadlines for removal of accessibility barriers and monitoring are not adequate; and programmes are needed for the integration of PWD into the open labour market and the education and professional training systems, besides ensuring that all workplaces and educational and professional training institutions are made accessible. All in all, it can be stated that general conditions for becoming and being an entrepreneur as a person with disabilities are not very favourable.

With regard to national policy, the development of vocational rehabilitation and the system of social benefits are handled by the Ministry of Human Capacities, while entrepreneurship development networks, programmes and services are the responsibility of the Ministry of Innovations and Technology. Unfortunately, these two fields of activity do not seem to have had any strong connections so far: despite various government initiatives supporting the employability and employment of PWD in the last ten years (that is, modification of the complex rehabilitation system and offers of financial incentives in 2012) there are no official strategies or any incentives specifically targeting their entrepreneurship.

LITERATURE REVIEW

Entrepreneurs are 'individuals who exploit market opportunity through technical and/or organizational innovation' (Schumpeter, 1965: 45). Entrepreneurs represent a driving force for economic development and job creation, at the same time playing a significant role in local and broader social connections and personal fulfilment. This is because the process of becoming an entrepreneur requires certain (internal) competences and suitable (external) conditions, which can both shape the strengths and weaknesses of the business venture. 'Entrepreneurial competence has been defined as the capability to apply the required knowledge, personal characteristics, skills and attitudes to effectively fulfil the demands of the highly complex and challenging tasks and roles in different stages of new venture creation and growth' (Bagheri and Abbariki, 2017: 71). Entrepreneurial competences have cognitive, attitudinal, behavioural, social and functional sides, and can be both inborn and acquired through education, training and experience (Bagheri and Abbariki, 2017). As they form a rather complex set of expectations, naturally nobody can perfectly fit all characteristics. Nevertheless, with sufficient awareness, abilities can be detected and improved; moreover, strengths or weaknesses can be complemented by partners and business associates. This makes entrepreneurship a viable opportunity for PWD to use and develop their own competencies, be flexible in terms of management, time and place (Jones and Latreille, 2011) and, finally, to improve their economic standing (Dhar and Farzana, 2017).

Besides internal competencies, entrepreneurs also need external support, an assistive environment ('entrepreneurial ecosystem') for their activities, in which they can innovate and develop their business (Maroufkhani, 2018). 'The concept of an entrepreneurial ecosystem refers to the interaction that takes place between a range of institutional and individual stakeholders so as to foster entrepreneurship, innovation and SME growth' (Mazzarol, 2014: 5). Such an ecosystem enables the optimal use of new ideas, concepts and business models as its players interact and impact upon each other. The complexity of the entrepreneurial ecosystem is high, due to the variety of players and different conditions, and the complexity of the national culture and legal and institutional environments in which they are embedded (Maroufkhani, 2018). The ecosystem of entrepreneurship development is composed of several multifaceted actors: entrepreneurs, resource providers, competitors, complementary organisations and allies, beneficiaries and customers, opponents and problem-makers; while the ecosystem is also affected by influential bystanders (Muldoon et al., 2018). In the case of EWD, the number of actors involved in the ecosystem is multiplied, including those such as organisations of disabled groups, and rehabilitation experts.

Prior research suggests that over the past decade PWDs tend to prefer self-employment and entrepreneurship to being employed more than others do (Parker Harris et al., 2013; Bagheri et al., 2015). The reason and motivation behind their decision may be diverse and complex, just as the enabling and disabling environment and the aspects of the entrepreneurial ecosystem (Isenberg, 2011) around them may also differ. The next section of the chapter gives an overview of the goals and motivations EWD have, as we provide some insights into the general entrepreneurial factors, then list some of the special characteristics of EWD from our findings.

Motivations

A significant body of the existing literature on EWD examines the potential motivations and barriers of entrepreneurial activities of PWD, analysing individual perceptions or macro-level national policies (or both) (Cooney, 2008; Kitching, 2014). The main motivations for becoming an entrepreneur are as follows: need for income; independence/freedom; job satisfaction; willingness to pursue an idea/opportunity; educational or occupational skills/experience; need for new challenges; and self-realisation or encouragement from others, such as from family or the broader society (Stephan et al., 2015; Vecsenyi, 2017). One of the main goals of our research was to investigate whether these were the same as in the case of EWD. Based on our literature review we identify four motivation groups for PWD becoming and being entrepreneurs. The two dimensions of our matrix are pull and push factors (incentives and disincentives, based on Amit and Muller, 1995) and personal as well as social and economic factors (internal and external). Table 1.1 shows the four groups of factors concerning potential motivations of EWD below.

The reason for becoming an entrepreneur or self-employed is of the utmost importance. Motivation arising from a constraint or a fear of something (for example, unemployment or employer discrimination) creates a different situation than if entrepreneurship were based on an independent and positive decision. Rizzo (2002) distinguishes 'self-employment' and 'self-directed employment', while Howard (2017) uses the terms 'need-driven entrepreneurs' and 'opportunity-driven entrepreneurs'. In the case of self-directed employment:

> people with disabilities, to a significant degree, have a prime, decision-making role in the kind of work that is done, how time is allocated, what kinds of investment in time and money should be made, and how to allocate revenue generated. The essential feature is that the people taking responsibility for doing the work also have a significant say in how the work is organized and managed. (Rizzo, 2002: 98)

Cooney (2008) distinguishes between the situation of taking the initiative to start one's own business, and when the person has no real alternatives. Based on these, we distinguish between pull factors and push factors.

Table 1.1   *Potential motivations of EWD*

	Personal (internal)	Social and economic environment (external)
Pull factors (incentives)	• wealth creation and financial security (Cooney, 2008) • flexibility (Bagheri et al., 2015) • self-determination (Howard, 2017) • higher level of job satisfaction (Pagán, 2009) • 'making an impact' (Atkins, 2013)	• network connections (Atkins, 2013) • role models (Parker Harris et al., 2013) • supportive family (Renko et al., 2015) • ecosystem: policy, finance, supports, human capital (Bagheri et al., 2015); market (Miller and Le Breton-Miller, 2017) • rehabilitation agencies (Seekins and Arnold, 1999) • business services and context (Rizzo, 2002) • small business development programmes (Heath and Reed, 2013)
Push factors (disincentives)	• overcoming personal challenges of everyday life (Dhar and Farzana, 2017) • coping with personal disadvantages and previous unpleasant experiences (Miller and Le Breton-Miller, 2017) • dissatisfaction with previous job (Yamamoto et al., 2012)	• fighting for social acceptance and existential independence (Dhar and Farzana, 2017) • recovery from poverty and a disadvantaged situation (De Clercq and Honig, 2011) • fighting against prejudice (Miller and Le Breton-Miller, 2017) • ecosystem: changing of culture (Miller and Le Breton-Miller, 2017)

Personal features and previous experience also determine the starting and successful operation of an enterprise. Yamamoto et al. (2012) list gender (for example, the discrimination experiences of women), the type of disability (for example, entrepreneurs with blindness or other physical disability are overrepresented among EWD), and qualification (for example, the self-employment of PWD is more usual in the information technology sector). De Clercq and Honig (2011) underline the importance of knowledge and competencies, while Renko et al. (2015) claim the impact of family patterns to be crucial. We call these personal, internal factors. The broader social and economic environment (its support or obstruction) is another source of motivation (Howard, 2017), which we call social and economic, or external motivation factors.

Among personal pull factors (in the top left quadrant of the table) we grouped personal incentives for being an EWD. Wealth creation and financial security (Cooney, 2008) are important for EWD, just as they are for anyone else. Some scholars also suggest that the relative independence and flexibility of entrepreneurial life could be important motivations compared to being an employee, as being disabled forces the person to overcome obstacles on a daily basis. Being an entrepreneur enables a PWD to achieve professional and personal goals and could result in a higher level of job satisfaction (Pagán, 2009), as well as involving greater flexibility in time and tasks (Bagheri et al., 2015; Dhar and Farzana, 2017). The willingness for self-determination is also identified (Howard, 2017). In some cases, this means strategic, long-term thinking, and at the same time the willingness to do good to others (the public or other PWD) as well. Atkins (2013) writes about the desire to 'make an impact' and about pursuing a passion for displaying one's experience and skills. Miller and Le Breton-Miller (2017) mention the desire to prove one's knowledge and talent.

Among the social and economic environment as pull factors (in the top right quadrant) we identified the motivating role of network connections and role models listed by Atkins (2013), Miller and Le Breton-Miller (2017), Renko et al. (2015), Bagheri et al. (2015) and Parker Harris et al. (2013). The motivating role of a supportive family is also mentioned here (Renko et al., 2015). Many US articles list the importance of a supporting ecosystem, emphasising the role that the vocational rehabilitation agency network can play (Bagheri et al., 2015; Seekins and Arnold, 1999; Ipsen et al., 2003; Walls et al., 2002; Rizzo, 2002; Miller and Le Breton-Miller, 2017). This also links to Isenberg's (2011) aspects of policy (institutional framework and removing of barriers) and finance (available funding). Potential business services such as mentoring and social services (Rizzo, 2002) and small business development programmes (Heath and Reed, 2013; Parker Harris et al., 2014) are also mentioned in the literature, which draws attention to the human capital (labour market and education), support (non-governmental organisations and venture-oriented professionals) and financial aspects of entrepreneurship (Isenberg, 2011). The appropriate business context (Miller and Le Breton-Miller, 2017) can also be connected to support (infrastructure: transport and communication, which should be accessible). All in all, Isenberg's (2011) domains of policy, market, finance, human capital and supports are mentioned as being related to EWD.

Few factors were found for the personal push factors (in the bottom left quadrant). Dhar and Farzana (2017) claim that the wish to overcome the personal challenges of everyday life can be a great motivator (for example, earning enough money to afford to pay an assistant). Howard (2017) conducted a qualitative research study with EWD and highlighted the importance of family values (such as entrepreneurial spirit, courage and education for independence), which may offset the fear of failure. Miller and Le Breton-Miller (2017) elaborate on the ability to cope with personal disadvantages and previous unpleasant experiences. Yamamoto et al. (2012) emphasise the effect of previously experienced discrimination and dissatisfaction in previous jobs.

For social and economic environment as push factors (in the bottom right quadrant) we identified the drivers for social acceptance and existential independence (Dhar and Farzana, 2017). This involves, among others, the fight against prejudice and recovery from poverty and disadvantaged situations (De Clercq and Honig, 2011; Balcazar et al., 2014). Miller and Le Breton-Miller (2017) claim that negative personal circumstances of an economic, socio-cultural, cognitive or physical nature – poor people, immigrants, PWD or those with learning disorders such as dyslexia and attention deficit hyperactivity disorder (ADHD) – show the same career path with regard to their becoming entrepreneurs while coping with their own, specific type of challenges. Moreover, 'to compound the difficulties of these populations, there is often a bias against them that makes traditional career paths, and even entrepreneurship, a most challenging endeavour' (Miller and Le Breton-Miller, 2017: 8). Dominant ideas about disability and about the roles PWD should play can be linked to Isenberg's (2011) culture domain as the only domain which shows up as a discouraging, or push factor, while others are rather encouraging incentives or pull factors for becoming an entrepreneur.

METHODOLOGY

The current study employs a qualitative research method to explore the entrepreneurial motivations of EWD experience, for two reasons. First, qualitative methodology has proved to be effective for investigating complex and multifaceted social phenomena, such as issues connected to disability (Cooper and Emory, 1995). Second, research on EWD is still in an exploratory stage and there is little information on this field of inquiry (Bagheri et al., 2015). Previous studies have also used qualitative methods to investigate EWD (Heath and Reed, 2013; Atkins, 2013; Reddington and Fitzsimons, 2013; Bagheri et al., 2015; Dhar and Farzana, 2017; Bagheri and Abbariki, 2017; Ashley and Graf, 2018). Data was collected over periods of 1–2.5 hours of semi-structured interviews in various locations, depending on the demand of the interviewee (Kvale, 2007). Interviews were recorded and transcribed word-for-word.

A snowball sample selection strategy (Silverman, 2008) was followed. First, we sent the summary of the research plan to various stakeholders (both individuals and organisations): among others, vocational and rehabilitation agencies, disability advocacy organisations and service providers, state government representatives from disability, employment, education and small business departments, private or state-funded entrepreneurship development centres, academic faculties, and network of researchers, entrepreneurs and social entrepreneurs. We asked them to suggest possible respondents, together with their availability. Interviewees were also asked for suggestions on further potential respondents.

At this stage of the research we did not restrict the sample according to the type or severity of disability or field of entrepreneurship, taking into consideration the explorative purpose of the study. We invited participants who claimed to be entrepreneurs with a disability and having experience of entrepreneurship for at least three years and having employees. The participants were located nationwide in Hungary and they had either physical impairment or sight loss. This is in line with Ashley and Graf (2018), who found that (based on US statistics) among PWD, persons with visual impairment have the highest self-employment rates. Heath and Reed (2013) and Bagheri et al. (2015), on the other hand, conclude that people with physical and mobility issues may face fewer difficulties and challenges in performing entrepreneurial tasks. Table 1.2 presents the background information of the participants.

Four members of the research team, all having experience of working with or studying PWD, took part in the coding process. In the first phase of the analysis, each interview was coded by at least two persons from the research group. Interview texts were coded around themes based on the research questions. In the second phase, the interview texts of all codes were re-read and a condensed text (Kvale, 2007) was produced about each code, with the aim of detecting significant statements, typical

Table 1.2   Background information of the participants

Code	Gender	Type of disability	Field of business	Age	Onset of the disability
BB	male	sight loss	IT services, software development	42	born with the impairment, but gradually deteriorated
TT	male	Physical	medical industry (development of wheelchairs)	41	consequence of accident
ZZ	male	Blind	construction industry, project management	56	born with the impairment, gradually deteriorated, in the last 15 years blind
GG	male	Physical	IT, cross fit room and sport event organisation	42	consequence of accident
DD	male	Physical	catering, sales	33	consequence of accident
AA	male	Physical	car sales, agriculture	40	consequence of accident
RR	male	Blind	information technology services, software development	26	born with the impairment
SS	female	Blind	sales	36	born with the impairment
OO	male	Physical	architecture, construction, advertising	70	consequence of accident
JJ	male	Physical	accounting services, clothing	60	consequence of accident

patterns and relationships, using word-for-word quotations. The researchers met several times to discuss results and formulate interpretations. Ethical standards were maintained throughout the research process, with consideration paid to participant contact, communication and behaviour.

RESULTS

According to our respondents, becoming an entrepreneur can be both a constraint and an autonomous, positive decision. Some participants failed to become employed, while for others the salary they earned was simply not enough to live on. Even now, half the respondents stressed that they still have to work on several projects or jobs at the same time in order to avoid becoming financially vulnerable. Thus, necessity-driven entrepreneurship (Howard, 2017) is strongly present in our sample.

With regard to motivations, several respondents mentioned the importance of a positive personality and self-knowledge. This applies to general entrepreneurial features, but also to the acknowledgement and acceptance of their disabilities. They emphasised that a very important step is to recognise that the disability does not define them as human beings or as entrepreneurs: 'You need to accept the state you are in, you do not need anything else. I don't need others to accept me, first I need to accept myself, and when I have accepted myself, others will also accept me for what I am' (JJ).

Some had the opinion that being a successful entrepreneur is fundamentally based on personal properties:

> I think it's just about personal qualities. So, for someone to be successful you need to be persistent, you need willpower, to run head into a brick wall, and break down any door in your way, so it depends on you. A person can only become a good entrepreneur if he has the attitude it takes. (TT)

Personal Pull Factors

Some motivations mentioned were related to the fulfilment of individual and professional goals. First of all, half the respondents mentioned that the first and main motivation was to earn a living, and they claimed that pursuing self-interest and focusing on personal gain was one of their main motivators. Independence, autonomy and flexibility were of great importance to EWD as opposed to being an employee: 'I can't imagine sitting in an office for eight hours where they are checking whether I'm on Facebook or filling out an excel chart and it is not because of my condition, but because of my attitude' (GG).

Half the entrepreneurs mentioned long-term plans for company growth, service or product development, and stressed that it was important to think in a strategic way:

> I realised that it was not my goal in life. I did not want to remain on such a financial level. So I quit my job for various reasons and started my own business. Well, of course I'm still waiting for my big dreams to come true, though I'm not doing badly at all. (RR)

At the same time it is also possible for someone to be satisfied with their achievements, and consciously not want to grow the business further, but have free time for private life, family and leisure activities. This is also a way of living a full life by thinking in more dimensions, not just in terms of fulfilling dreams of financial success:

> And thank God I can say that my life is whole, irrespective of the fact that I am in this. But is it worthwhile developing further, to let's say having fifty thousand more a month plus a five times higher stress level? I'm not sure it's worth it, on the contrary, I would say, it is not worth it. I'd rather spend my time with my family, my kid, my dog, my hobby, or whatever. (AA)

The passion for work and for related social causes also appeared as a motivation factor. The majority of the entrepreneurs spoke about determination, pursuing the passion for demonstrating one's experience, skill and pride for the achieved results. Recognition in the form of entrepreneurial or innovation prizes (for example, the Hungarian Quality Product Award) can also be part of the motivation. This does not represent a goal in itself as much as an important positive indicator that emphasises effort, making achievements visible for everyone, and making one feel part of mainstream business irrespective of any personal difference: 'It's good to know that what you do leaves a mark, and that you are motivated by high quality, pride and timelessness' (OO).

Appreciation and acknowledgement also serve as a proof of one's own value and worth, emphasising general pride over business success: 'I am basically proud of myself that with all my disadvantages, starting from below zero I am way in the positive already' (RR).

Social and Economic Environment as Pull Factors

The importance of a favourable business context and supporting business network connections was also mentioned in the interviews. Support and motivation, besides inspiration, could come from the closer circle of family or friends, or from official incubator schemes or mentor programmes (Erste Bank, NESsT). Even the idea of starting a business might come from outside, from a role model or from a family that believes in the person's talents and skills: 'Starting a business basically came from him. I saw things at his place and I also had an idea of a kind' (RR).

The need for a better supporting ecosystem was also mentioned by some respondents, which goes beyond the narrower personal business connections, but entails a whole system of support. The EWD have generally not received any help from an entrepreneurial ecosystem supporting them or targeting their (sometimes special) needs, either on the part of vocational rehabilitation agencies or from general business development programmes: 'Theoretical support, [I received] from everywhere, any practical assistance, let's say material support or something like that, not at all' (RR).

Education and the labour market situation are perceived as unfavourable: PWD are traditionally not treated equally: 'Let's switch our brains a little bit: people with disabilities are not a poor, unhappy, useless population, sitting at home, but a potential workforce, even an excellent, loyal workforce' (DD).

Support is needed in infrastructure and from other angles, but these are not present in Hungary: 'These programmes in every country, wherever they operate, are supported by the local government, or the ministry of education, there is no private funding anywhere' (DD).

EWD should also have connections to and operate on the market, but those services are not sufficient: 'They should connect us with potential customers or investors. Credit is not enough, in fact: if you are not good enough, the credit can ruin the whole enterprise: it can put you in a worse position than you were originally' (ZZ). They also feel the lack of financial resources to grow and flourish, and refer to bureaucracy as an obstacle: 'This is bureaucracy ... this is a very old regulation that is still in use today, so we had to deal with a lot, it was almost half a year, I think, or three quarters of a year before it all went through the system' (TT).

By and large, according to their answers, they cannot see the whole system as a real, formal net of supporting factors that may govern, catalyse or mediate the activities of the various actors.

Personal Push Factors

Some of the respondents drew a negative picture of PWD in general. They claimed that PWD do not usually want to change their disadvantaged positions, and it is very difficult to motivate them. Some of the causes mentioned were psychological barriers created by previous experiences (in the family, or in other communities, for example during education), failures, or not believing in oneself. As many as three respondents of the ten revealed that they themselves had been in a depressive phase, and starting an enterprise was what pushed them out of their depression. Resilience is thus crucial in overcoming everyday challenges:

'I'm not self-sufficient physically ... but if you get to the level where you are financially self- sufficient, then if we are being really pragmatic, you can also pay for your independence' (GG).

Social and Economic Environment as Push Factors

Among socially and economically driven push motivations, we have identified the need for existential independence and recovery from a disadvantaged situation, the drivers for social acceptance, and the fight against prejudice, related to Isenberg's culture domain, for example: 'The main problem is that people do not know how to help well. I always teach people how to help, but I also teach the blind to accept help' (ZZ).

Three respondents mentioned that professional excellence could make disability insignificant, or that even disability could signify an advantage in some situations (for example, during business negotiations). More than half the respondents mentioned a mission to use their own results for the sake of fellow PWD to counterbalance their deprived position. Service to the community seems motivating for EWD: 'Every obstacle that you overcome makes you stronger. Our mission is to help people with visual impairment freely access information, integrate into the "intact" society more easily, and improve their quality of life through our IT services and activities' (BB).

The topic of becoming role models for fellow PWD, to motivate and empower, was also mentioned (which can also be linked to Isenberg's culture domain): 'I would like to show my peers that there is a way other than the one followed by many. This one is a lot more difficult, but possibly a lot better in the long run' (RR).

At the same time, some EWD say that hey could not bear taking on more responsibility. The image of a successful, confident, self-sufficient (male) entrepreneur may seem too far away to achieve for someone with issues of self-esteem, physical and communicational disadvantages, or financial difficulties.

Table 1.3 summarises the motivational factors from the literature while contrasting it with the findings of the current enquiry.

Table 1.3   *Motivations of EWD in the literature and based on the interviews*

Potential motivations for becoming EWD	Theory	Pattern identified
Personal pull factors	• wealth creation and financial security; flexibility; • self-determination; • higher level of job satisfaction; 'making an impact'	• earning a living, *but also finding work/life balance (finance free time and leisure)*; • flexibility, autonomy, independency; • self-determination; 'making an impact'; • *pride in achieving professional success from a disadvantaged position*
Personal push factors	• overcoming the personal challenges of everyday life; • coping with personal disadvantages and previous unpleasant experiences; dissatisfaction with previous job	• overcoming the personal challenges of everyday life; coping with personal disadvantages and previous unpleasant experiences; dissatisfaction with previous job – *avoiding low-paid work in supported employment*
Social and economic environment as pull factors	• network connections; role models; supportive family; • ecosystem: policy, finance, supports, human capital; market; • business services and context	• supportive family; • ecosystem: policy, finance, supports, human capital; • market – *not sufficient, not tailor-made*
Social and economic environment as push factors	• fighting for existential independence and affiliation; • recovery from poverty and a disadvantaged situation; • fighting against prejudice	• fighting for existential independence and affiliation; • changing of culture; • *becoming role models and facilitate social change*; • *providing service for the 'disabled community'*

Note: Motivations of EWD in the literature (Table 1.1); and based on the interviews (additional findings in italics).

DISCUSSION AND PRELIMINARY CONCLUSIONS

The narratives of EWD show that both push and pull types of motivation are present in their decision to start and run a business venture in Hungary. While various sources of personal and social-economic pull motivation are evident, economic pressure and the lack of any further alternatives are at least as strong push motivating factors. We also found that while categorisation is possible, it is often difficult to identify a leading motivation, as they intertwine with each other in the course of a person's life, and may also change over time due to changes in the person's personal life or shifts in the economic situation or social policies.

From the complexity of the motivational background of EWD, however, two distinct patterns emerge: of those who were born with impairments, and those who acquired impairments later in life. Respondents who were born with an impairment very consciously prepared themselves for their chosen professional field (choosing vocations or training) and also for becoming entrepreneurs. This high level of consciousness, long-term orientation and planning, as well as family support, helped them to start their businesses and become successful. In their case, pull motivations seem to be more relevant in becoming entrepreneurs. The second pattern we identified seems typical in the case of acquired impairments that happened mainly due to accidents. Those who became disabled later in life made use of competencies, skills and previous experiences, based on which they were able to create and build a new venture or continue their previous business activities despite the disability. The motivations in the second pattern were at first mainly push ones, however: as they had positive entrepreneurial experiences based on pull motivations from before, returning to business activities was not an insurmountable obstacle. With accommodations in both lifestyle and business, as well as help from family and friends, it was possible to build a new career as an entrepreneur with a disability.

We realised that sometimes social and personal motivations complement each other, but swapping push and pull sides. Social push motivations complement personal pull factors. While having goals and a solid positive identity is important, as opposed to other PWD here EWD wish to facilitate social and cultural change. They would like to 'give something back' to the disability community either by becoming role models and agents of change, or by providing services for them free of charge or at low cost.

Among personal and push factors we found that EWD have a desire for clearly meaningful work and affiliation. Within the complementary domain of social and pull factors, EWD hold critical opinions about the employment system and the role of the state. The lack of quality employment for PWD and the lack of an appropriate entrepreneurial ecosystem are recurring issues in the interviews. There is a need for a better supporting ecosystem (this is also true for disability organisations and general entrepreneurial ecosystem), and PWD think that they can be a significant part of it. Accordingly, in challenging and changing mainstream culture, as well as the attitudes towards entrepreneurship of people with disabilities, PWD could play a decisive role.

Another general issue in the narratives, which seems decisive in almost all cases, is the crucial role that parents and the immediate family play both in general terms and in developing the entrepreneurial background of the PWD. The role of parents ranges from providing the necessary capital and supporting young entrepreneurs in all areas, to retraining and changing their own career paths to be of more support in business issues. The family respondents also play a crucial role in the psychological and emotional well-being of the entrepreneurs, and were generally seen as inseparable from business success. Another area that seemed decisive in relation to the family was that of an entrepreneurial tradition being passed on by the parents. This was a determining factor on the one hand, regarding the upbringing of the child with a disability. Here, parents seem to play a crucial role in providing them with the necessary education and skills to enter the labour market, and at the same time not overprotecting them, through genuine fear, from any hardships. On the other hand, parents as entrepreneurs themselves seem to have a long-term impact on the future career of their children. They become role models, at the same time giving them the opportunity to develop useful personal competences (for example, attitude, problem-solving, commitment, proactivity, resilience, networking) and business management competences (for example, planning, HR, leadership, performance) that are invaluable in starting and running a business.

As for the findings in relation to pull and push motivations, some of the issues we found were not mentioned in the literature before, and thus may be considered as contributions to the existing literature.

Regarding personal pull factors, pride in achieving professional success from a disadvantaged position appeared in almost all interviews. As overcoming physical and psychological barriers in a hardly favourable entrepreneurial ecosystem can be seen as a considerable achievement, it is little wonder that EWD are proud of their success. This might also add to the literature on disability identity, asserting that besides normalisation and compliance with mainstream expectations and norms, there exists a more radical approach to difference in identity politics known as 'disability pride'. This involves 'challenging the narrow conceptions of normality' and 'finding merit in the atypical, beauty in the uncommon and value in the unusual' (Sherry, 2001: 907). Another motivational factor that might be called atypical was also highlighted in the interviews: besides earning a living, some EWD also wish to find a work–life balance in their jobs; that is, they consider profit as a means to finance free time and leisure activities, such as travel or hobbies. In this narrative, entrepreneurship can help them to move away from existential problems and fulfil higher motivations.

Flexibility in time and tasks as an essential aspect of becoming an entrepreneur has already been mentioned in the literature, and in a sense becoming an entrepreneur might also be seen as a form of resistance to the mainstream norms of the labour market. As a personal push motivator, avoiding low-paid work and supported employment also illustrates this aspect of resistance. For a young person especially, entering the labour market with a good education and a stable family background, the perspective of a precarious, low-paid job as a lifelong career would appear unattractive. However, while there are certain risks involved in becoming an entrepreneur, the perspective of financial autonomy, a meaningful job and possible success far outweighs the hardships, the missing skills and lacking ecosystem they might encounter.

FURTHER RESEARCH

One of the issues to be discussed in further research is the difference between male and female entrepreneurs with disabilities. Studies on female entrepreneurship suggest that women's motivations, barriers, and the way they combine general entrepreneurial ideals with traditional gender roles might provide a different understanding of disability and entrepreneurship (Essers and Benschop, 2007). In our sample, the dominance of men was evident, while the issues of an overprotective family or the positive role of institutions such as universities that emerged in the narrative of the only female entrepreneur might indicate some differences that future research could elaborate.

Another direction could involve looking at entrepreneurs with various types of disabilities. As the literature suggests, there might be differences in the experience and motivations based on the actual impairment. Deaf entrepreneurs, for example, need to develop special communication strategies to be effective, while special technology is important in order to be constantly accessible, available and up to date (Atkins, 2013). Another, maybe even more disadvantaged group is that of deafblind entrepreneurs where the reliance on outside help to communicate is even more significant (Hierholzer and Bybee, 2017).

The entrepreneurial identity formation of EWD is an issue that has also been underresearched. In the case of EWD the intersections of disability, gender and entrepreneurship identities are all at work (beside many others such as age, family status, regional facilities, and so on), giving an opportunity to form the most socially valued identity possible in line with an inner, personal identity. The narratives of our respondents showed that a positive and stable disability identity is crucial in entering into business and striving for success; while, at the same time, further investigation is needed into the ways in which disability may have an effect on career choice, career transitions, sustainability and success at work (Baldridge and Kulkarni, 2017).

ACKNOWLEDGEMENTS

This research was supported by a grant from the Higher Education Institutional Excellence Programme of the Hungarian Ministry of Innovation and Technology to the Budapest Business School – University of Applied Sciences (NKFIH-1259- 8/2019).

REFERENCES

Amit, R. and Muller, E. 1995. 'Push' and 'pull' entrepreneurship. *Journal of Small Business and Entrepreneurship*, 12(4): 64–80.

Ashley, D. and Graf, N.M. 2018. The process and experiences of self-employment among people with disabilities: a qualitative study. *Rehabilitation Counseling Bulletin*, 61(2): 90–100. doi:10.1177/0034355216687712.

Atkins, S. 2013. A study into the lived experiences of deaf entrepreneurs: considerations for the professional. *Journal of the American Deafness and Rehabilitation Association (JADARA)*, 47(2): 222–236.

Bagheri, A. and Abbariki, M. 2017. Competencies of disabled entrepreneurs in Iran: implications for learning and development. *Disability and Society*, 32(1): 69–92. doi: 10.1080/09687599.2016.1268524.

Bagheri, A., Azizi, M. and Fard, M.F. 2015. Managerial skills required by entrepreneurs with physical and mobility disabilities. *International Journal of Management Sciences*, 5(8): 571–581.

Balcazar, F.E., Kuchak, J., Dimpfl, S., Sariepella, V. and Alvarado, F. 2014. An empowerment model of entrepreneurship for people with disabilities in the US. *Psychosocial Intervention*, 23: 145–150.

Baldridge, D.C. and Kulkarni, M. 2017. The shaping of sustainable careers post hearing loss: toward greater understanding of adult onset disability, disability identity, and career transitions. *Human Relations*, 70(10): 1217–1236.

Barnes, C. and Mercer, G. 2005. Disability, work and welfare: challenging the social exclusion of disabled people. *Work, Employment and Society*, 19(3): 527–545.

Cooney, T. 2008. Entrepreneurs with disabilities: profile of a forgotten minority. *Irish Business Journal*, 4(1): 119–129.

Cooper, D. and Emory C. 1995. *Business Research Method*, 5th edn. Homewood, IL: Irwin.

Csillag, S., Győri, Z. and Svastics, C. 2019. Long and winding road? Barriers and supporting factors as perceived by entrepreneurs with disabilities. *Journal of Enterprising Communities: People and Places in the Global Economy*, 13(1–2): 42–63.

De Clercq, D. and Honig, B. 2011. Entrepreneurship as an integrating mechanism for disadvantaged persons. *Entrepreneurship and Regional Development*, 23(5–6): 353–372.

Dhar, S. and Farzana, T. 2017. Entrepreneurs with disabilities in Bangladesh: an exploratory study on their entrepreneurial motivation and challenges. *European Journal of Business and Management*, 9(36): 103–114.

Doyel, A.W. 2002. A realistic perspective of risk in self-employment for people with disabilities. *Journal of Vocational Rehabilitation*, 17(2): 115–124.

Essers, C. and Benschop, Y. 2007. Enterprising identities: female entrepreneurs of Moroccan or Turkish origin in the Netherlands. *Organization Studies*, 28(1): 49–69.

Harper, M. and Momm, W. 1989. Self-employment for disabled people: experiences from Africa and Asia. International Labour Office.

Heath, K.L. and Reed, D.L. 2013. Industry-driven support (IDS) model to build social capital and business skills of low-income entrepreneurs with disabilities. *Journal of Vocational Rehabilitation*, 38: 139–148.

Hidegh, A.L. and Csillag, S. 2013. Toward the mental accessibility. Changing the mental obstacles that future HRM practicioners have about the employment of people with disabilities. *Human Resource Development International*, 16: 22–39.

Hierholzer, A.C. and Bybee, J. 2017. Working with Randolph-Sheppard entrepreneurs who are deafblind: a qualitative analysis. *Journal of Visual Impairment and Blindness*, January–February: 61–71.

Howard, T.L. 2017. Strategies for entrepreneurs with disabilities to sustain a successful small business. PhD thesis, Walden University, Minneapolis.

Ipsen, C., Arnold, N. and Cooling, K. 2003. Small Business Development Center experiences and perceptions: providing service to people with disabilities. *Journal of Developmental Entrepreneurship*, 8(2): 113–132.

Isenberg, D. 2011. The entrepreneurship ecosystem strategy as a new paradigm for economic policy: principles for cultivating entrepreneurship. Institute of International and European Affairs, Dublin, Ireland, 12 May.

Jones, M.K. and Latreille, P.L. 2011. Disability and self-employment: evidence from the UK. *Applied Economics*, 43(27): 4161–4178.

Kitching, J. 2014. Entrepreneurship and self-employment by people with disabilities. Background Paper for the OECD Project on Inclusive Entrepreneurship. Working Paper: OECD.

Kvale, S. 2007. *Doing Interviews*. London: SAGE.

Maroufkhani, P., Wagner, R. and Wan Ismail, W.K. 2018. Entrepreneurial ecosystems: a systematic review. *Journal of Enterprising Communities: People and Places in the Global Economy*, 12(4): 545–564.

Mazzarol, T. 2014. Growing and sustaining entrepreneurial ecosystems: what they are and the role of government policy. White Paper WP01-2014, Small Enterprise Association of Australia and New Zealand (SEAANZ). www.seaanz.org.

Miller, D. and Le Breton-Miller, I. 2017. Underdog entrepreneurs: a model of challenge-based entrepreneurship. *Entrepreneurship Theory and Practice*, 41(1): 7–17.

Muldoon, J., Bauman, A. and Lucy, C. 2018. Entrepreneurial ecosystem: do you trust or distrust? *Journal of Enterprising Communities: People and Places in the Global Economy*, 12(2): 158–177. https://doi.org/10.1108/JEC-07-2017-0050.

Pagán, R. 2009. Self-employment among people with disabilities: evidence for Europe. *Disability and Society*, 24(2): 217–229.

Parker Harris, S., Caldwell, K. and Renko, M. 2014. Entrepreneurship by any other name: self-sufficiency versus innovation. *Journal of Social Work in Disability and Rehabilitation*, 13(4): 317–349.

Parker Harris, S., Renko, M. and Caldwell, K. 2013. Accessing social entrepreneurship: perspectives of people with disabilities and key stakeholders. *Journal of Vocational Rehabilitation*, 38: 35–48. doi:10.3233/JVR-120619.

Reddington, T. and Fitzsimons, J. 2013. People with learning disabilities and microenterprise. *Tizard Learning Disability Review*, 18(3): 124–131.

Renko, M., Parker Harris, S. and Caldwell, K. 2015. Entrepreneurial entry by people with disabilities. *International Small Business Journal*, 1–24. doi: 10.1177/0266242615579112.

Rizzo, D.C. 2002. With a little help from my friends: supported self-employment for people with severe disabilities. *Journal of Vocational Rehabilitation*, 17: 97–105.

Schumpeter, J.A. 1965. Economic theory and entrepreneurial history. In: Aitken, H.G. (ed.), *Explorations in Enterprise*. Cambridge, MA: Harvard University Press, pp. 45–64.

Seekins, T. and Arnold, N. 1999. Self-employment and economic leadership as two promising perspectives on rural disability and work. *Work*, 12(3): 213–222.

Sherry, M. 2001. Identity. In: Albrecht, G., Seelman, D.K. and Bury, M. (eds), *Handbook of Disability Studies*. Thousand Oaks, CA: SAGE, pp. 906–914.

Silverman, D. 2008. *Doing Qualitative Research: A Practical Handbook*. London: SAGE.

Stephan, U., Hart, M., Mickiewicz, T. and Drews, C.C. 2015. *Understanding Motivations for Entrepreneurship*. BIS Research Paper No. 212. Department for Business, Innovation and Skills, London.

Vecsenyi, J. 2017. *Kisvállalkozások indítása és működtetése* (Starting and managing new ventures), Akadémiai Kiadó: Budapest.

Walls, R.T., Dowler, D.L., Cordingly, K., Orslene, L.E. and Gleer, J.D. 2002. Microenterprising and people with disabilities: strategies for success and failure. *Journal of Rehabilitation*, 6(2): 29–35.

Yamamoto, S., Unruh, D. and Bullis, M. 2012. The viability of self-employment for individuals with disabilities in the United States: a synthesis of the empirical-research literature. *Journal of Vocational Rehabilitation*, 36: 121–134.

2. "Underdog" entrepreneurs? Identifying processes of opportunity creation among visually impaired founders of new ventures

Wilson Ng

INTRODUCTION

How do good ideas come about? This question has occupied entrepreneurship scholars and practitioners throughout the 40-odd years of entrepreneurship as a field of study. Yet remarkably little progress has been made in addressing the question. Entrepreneurship scholars agree that in order to make significant progress, the processes in which impactful ideas are created need to be clarified. Accordingly, scholars, notably since a number of economic crises at the turn of the 21st century and the subsequent proliferation of start-ups, have sought to craft general theories of entrepreneurs and entrepreneurship. Emanating principally from economics, finance, cognitive psychology, and human resource management, scholars have drawn on tools and knowledge in their field and prioritized various criteria of their choice about entrepreneurs and their operating contexts to learn about the origins of good ideas.

Interestingly, however, few of those scholars, despite their diverse backgrounds, disagree with Baumol's (1990: 894) prognosis that entrepreneurial endeavor has calculable and finite limits which "depend heavily ... on the reward structure in the economy that happen[s] to prevail." Entrepreneurship therefore has finite limits, for example in creative endeavor, that are calculable. Moreover, what is calculable concerns the nature and volume of rewards that entrepreneurs anticipate from their ideas. It then follows that the stimulation of good, entrepreneurial ideas should prioritize the generation of knowledge about the nature of rewards that motivate entrepreneurs and the volume of rewards that would keep them motivated in generating a continuing stream of ideas. Controlling for the misallocation of entrepreneurial endeavor in unproductive activities, the largely unchallenged view since Baumol (1990) has been that the process of generating good ideas should focus on outcomes of entrepreneurial endeavor that could then be traceable, somewhat instrumentally, back to the motivational sources for each activity.

Indeed, entrepreneurship scholars have subsequently drawn on this approach in crafting theories of entrepreneurship that begin with a consideration of good, high-potential and bad, low-potential ideas. Here, our opening insight about this rewards-centered literature in entrepreneurship is to question what the motivation is, in the first place, to generate good ideas. What drives entrepreneurs to create new ventures? To what extent are entrepreneurs motivated by personal experience or observation of opportunities (cf. Kirzner), by an interest in new wealth (Fiet and Patel, 2008), or by their effectual need (Sarasvathy, 2001) to focus only on creating their venture? The sole focus of entrepreneurs on new venture creation is important for entrepreneurship, following Baumol's (1990) prognosis of its finite stock. Yet none of these answers to the question of how entrepreneurs are (or should be) motivated to embark on their finite stock of entrepreneurial endeavor have been convincing because theories of entrepreneurship do not really tackle the question of motivation.

We argue that motivation, namely, a sustained, and perhaps primordial, "blind" drive to target only the search for good ideas should constitute a principal concern for entrepreneurship researchers prior to addressing any other questions. Accordingly, the question in entrepreneurship research of how good ideas come about should be preceded by an overarching question of the nature of the (bald) motivation behind certain entrepreneurs who seek to produce good ideas with a sense of their "mission" (Dacin et al., 2011). This mission would be in the nature of entrepreneurs' commitment to new venture creation above and beyond all other concerns. Once this commitment is understood, then we believe that the processes in which high- and low-potential ideas are identified will also be clarified. Attempting to theorize the latter processes before understanding the former phenomenon of commitment has led, unsurprisingly, to an unconvincing body of theories that remains largely unused and undeveloped.

The latter question of motivation (input stimuli) and commitment (behaviors arising from motivation) inspired me to explore why severely visually impaired (VI) entrepreneurs set about creating ideas. In choosing this endeavor, our initial intuition was that VI entrepreneurs would tend to create opportunities, as opposed to be satisfied with merely discovering them, because of the extreme nature of their disability, for which there is typically no cure. Indeed, blindness remains a permanent, incurable condition; and blindness contrasts with a number of other disabilities, such as a loss of a limb, which can be compensated for with prosthetics. Moreover, when much of the human world is experienced by sight, loss of sight has been considered across cultures to be the gravest possible condition in life; recall, for example, the penalty of blindness as the most extreme sentence for the sin of Œdipus Rex.

How, then, when they cannot see, would VI entrepreneurs be able to create entrepreneurial ideas? This question seems to be central in understanding, initially, how good ideas arise in the minds and activities of VI entrepreneurs. Follow-up research, which we consider at the end of this chapter, may then address a potentially more impactful question of the learning that can be drawn from the motivation of VI entrepreneurs in opportunity creation for sighted entrepreneurs.

FRAMING VISUALLY IMPAIRED RESEARCH

We focus on exploring processes in generating impactful ideas for new ventures, which is known in the entrepreneurship literature as opportunity creation (see, e.g.,

Mainela and Puhakka, 2009). Our subsequent discussion of this process draws principally on an ongoing pilot study of how VI entrepreneurs based in the European Union have created new opportunities. All of the entrepreneurs under study set up ventures to address social and/or physical problems that they and other disabled adults faced following their incurable disabilities. Additionally, as a control group, we also followed the work of a physically disabled entrepreneur, still of working age, who had been self-employed throughout their working life, and who continues to make a living from their own venture in making and selling walking aids for VI people. The self-funded pilot has been closely following the activities of two United Kingdom (UK)-based VI entrepreneurs (who we consider to be serial entrepreneurs because of their continuing record of new venture creation) in their ongoing process of creating and developing their ventures. The aim of this research is to generate knowledge of the ways in which the two entrepreneurs identified opportunities. Breaking down our question on the motivation of these entrepreneurs, we sought to learn the origins and processes in which their ideas had been, and perhaps continue to be, identified. Opportunity creation contrasts with the discovery or recognition of existing opportunities, which scholars have considered to be inadequate to meet the extreme challenges of certain disabled entrepreneurs (Miller and Le Breton-Miller, 2017). The process of creating opportunities would involve a transformation of entrepreneurs' knowledge of social, economic, and physical challenges, into new, valuable goods and/or services for their targeted end-users, mostly if not wholly comprising extremely disabled people such as them (Alvarez et al., 2010; Mitchell et al., 2008).

This process (or processes) of imagining and forming new opportunities we define as opportunity creation,[1] and this chapter reflects on the pilot study to begin to understand how challenged VI entrepreneurs generate ideas. Here, our further intuition is that these entrepreneurs seek to create new opportunities consequent upon the extreme challenges that they and other disabled people face. We believe that a perspective of studying opportunities that are formed as an outcome of challenges faced by entrepreneurs has much to yield in contrast, for example, to a view of "stubborn" entrepreneurs (Ramamurti, 1986) who persist with planned activities despite unplanned intervening factors.[2] While there is also learning from "stubborn" entrepreneurship, including necessity entrepreneurs who form ventures as a necessary source of income in order to survive (Block et al., 2015), this learning would appear to be incremental. For example, a focus of necessity entrepreneurs has been on the environment and conditions of their activities, as opposed to our interest in the creative aspects and processes of our VI entrepreneurs. Here, we do not presume that the purpose of the subsequent activities of VI entrepreneurs is to try to relieve their disabilities. Instead, we view venture creation by our entrepreneurs as a possible outcome of a relentless drive to create opportunities that continues to be inspired by their sight loss.

As part of this view, we also consider venture creation, generally among disabled entrepreneurs, to be motivated by an interest to engage with, and possibly to exploit, social perceptions of the limitations of their "disabled" condition (Ng and Arndt,

2019). In this view, the audiences for these entrepreneurs would have a limited, or poor, understanding of disability, but those audiences would nonetheless participate in activities created by disabled entrepreneurs. Such audiences could be large, as with the worldwide following of Stevie Wonder, Andrea Bocelli, and other sight-impaired performers. An assumption among these entrepreneur-performers would appear to be that their sight impairment was part of their attraction for audiences, an attraction that Bocelli has played up (Express, 2021).

Learning about creating opportunities from the pilot will then feed into a wider project on VI entrepreneurship between serial VI entrepreneurs, on the one hand, and novice (first-time) and nascent (aspiring) entrepreneurs on the other, beyond the UK, with different institutional perspectives of disability and its support. To build a basis for this wider research, the pilot's objective sets out to trace and articulate possible processes, motivated by their disability, that VI entrepreneurs may draw upon in forming their opportunities.

We contend that this aim and objective of opportunity creation among VI entrepreneurs begins to address the question that has persisted in the entrepreneurship literature, despite a number of theories that have sought to address its processes, of how entrepreneurs can generate impactful, influential ideas (see, e.g., Sarasvathy et al., 2010). The pilot intends to throw some light on this question by beginning to explore the physical, economic, and social challenges faced by two VI entrepreneurs who have formed opportunities apparently despite their disabilities. To date, the little that is known about these processes is based on limited knowledge of the capabilities of sighted entrepreneurs. Here, the common feature of this knowledge is that entrepreneurs experience only what they see, while the question among VI entrepreneurs, with potentially, highly impactful implications for the exclusively "sighted" view of opportunity creation, is how VI entrepreneurs may form valuable entrepreneurial opportunities when they cannot see, and when they would thereby appear to create opportunities by observing and experiencing differently from sighted entrepreneurs.

These experiences comprise the routine challenges faced by VI entrepreneurs, and in this perspective, they may be "underdog" entrepreneurs (Miller and Le Breton-Miller, 2017), unheralded and somewhat unsupported as entrepreneurs in a sighted world that is naturally set up with support mechanisms, including funding and on the terms of a sighted audience, that distinguishes between able and disabled entrepreneurs. An ordinary example of the challenges that disabled people face is in the activities that they are presumed to be restricted from performing, and the associated premium that investors would need to add in funding disabled ventures. An investment belief therefore is that funding the activities of disabled entrepreneurs (in both social and commercial enterprises) should normally be a public undertaking for social welfare, as opposed to being the subject of private projects, which would have to be expensively costed (Casey, 2017; Ng and Arndt, 2019).

We proceed by explaining our focus on VI entrepreneurs. Based on this interest, we critique principal theories of opportunity creation and relate their core themes with one another. We then present exploratory research in our pilot and propose theoretical and practical implications from our preliminary findings for further research, principally in developing potential contributions of VI entrepreneurship in and beyond disability research.

LITERATURE ON OPPORTUNITY CREATION

We have suggested that the question of opportunity creation remains central to entrepreneurs and scholars, as clarifying the processes in creating new and impactful opportunities potentially opens up answers to the persistent puzzle of how valuable ideas arise. At various periods over the past four decades, entrepreneurship scholars have championed the prior importance chiefly of suitable personality traits, intentions, behaviors and beliefs, wealth, networks, and environmental conditions in explaining the "unique" nature of entrepreneurs and their ideas. These "subjective criteria" (Floyd and Wooldridge, 1999: 10) are thought to lie behind diverse ideas, and are produced when information on possible opportunities is produced "from outside the dominant social structure" (ibid.). A number of subjective criteria have been developed into general and specific theories of entrepreneurial behavior. The perspective of opportunity creation with the oldest provenance is a behavioral economics view of "entrepreneurial alertness," which argues that major influences on opportunity creation are typically based on the entrepreneur's sighted observations, social networks, and personal experiences (see, e.g., Kirzner, 1997). Clarifying and enacting entrepreneurial alertness can then become a necessary condition for the success of the opportunity identification "triad" of recognition, development, and evaluation (Ardichvili et al., 2003).

By contrast, subsequent perspectives of opportunity creation have developed along two principal paths. Fiet and Patel (2008) suggested that opportunities may be discovered by a learnable causal procedure of "constrained, systematic search" (Fiet and Patel, 2008) involving five clearly identified activities in discovering opportunities (Patel and Fiet, 2009). Taking an exploratory, process-driven approach, Sarasvathy (2001) suggested how opportunities may be discovered or created by effectual reasoning, which is also learnable and demands exploratory skills, principally of imagination and spontaneous thinking. Additionally, effectual reasoning would involve domain-specific skills and training, which the causal reasoning approach of systematic search and entrepreneurial alertness also demands. Each of these three perspectives of opportunity creation continues to attract scholarly debate, often within, as opposed to across, the founding disciplines of entrepreneurship scholars (Mary George et al., 2016). This limited development of a general theory of opportunity creation has meant that knowledge of the creative and potentially highly impactful processes of opportunity creation remains "fragmented and empirically underdeveloped" (ibid.: 309). The literature review of Mary George et al. (2016) on opportunity creation found that only a few scholars have really contributed to understanding this phenomenon, which is considered by many management journals to be an ancillary issue in entrepreneurship despite its obvious importance.

Accordingly, despite substantial scholarship on opportunity creation since the 1970s, the field still does not really know how impactful ideas are identified (Floyd and Wooldridge, 1999; cf. Nonaka, 1994). Specifically, there is little clarity on how processes of generating ideas that produce new-to-the-world products and services are created, which remains a focus of debate because of the importance of high-impact, new-to-the-world products (Alvarez et al., 2010; Sarasvathy et al., 2010). The principal reason for this focus is because of the potential game-changing nature of opportunity creation in satisfying unmet market needs and wants (see, e.g., Mary George et al., 2016; Ng and Arndt, 2019). Miller and Le Breton-Miller (2017) and Winschiers-Theophilus et al. (2015) have sought to address the question of opportunity creation by proposing a preliminary "challenge-based" model of entrepreneurs who face a variety of life-changing challenges, including severe physical disability (Miller and Le Breton-Miller, 2017), and chronic social and economic barriers (Winschiers-Theophilus et al., 2015). Moreover, "necessity and opportunity" scholars (Block and Wagner, 2010; Block et al., 2015) have developed understanding of "necessity entrepreneurship," where entrepreneurs are locked out of employment and discover or create ventures because they are immigrants (Hart and Acs, 2011). Necessity entrepreneurs may also be unable to overcome perceived handicaps to employment, such as dyslexia and attention deficit hyperactivity disorder (Dimic and Orlov, 2014).

For opportunity creation, however, Miller and Le Breton-Miller's (2017) model of challenged entrepreneurs offers a platform and rationale for researching impaired entrepreneurs, with its guiding framework of how extreme challenges may compel adaptive behavior that, in turn, drives entrepreneurial initiatives. Although these initiatives may appear unremarkable, in aggregate they have in fact contributed significantly to economic wealth (Jones and Latreille, 2011). Furthermore, individual ventures have helped to ease the extreme challenges of disabled people (Shaheen and Myhill, 2009; Tihic et al., Chapter 10 in this book), while augmenting public understanding of the potential contributions of a large segment of the population of many economies worldwide that continue to undervalue people with any kind of disability.

Accordingly, drawing from the challenge-based model of Miller and Le Breton-Miller (2017), this chapter begins to explore how their model may be operationalized in addressing the pilot's research question: What may be learned about processes of opportunity creation from serial, visually impaired entrepreneurs? The pilot project enquired how two VI entrepreneurs have created and targeted suitable opportunities, and how they have formed ideas that can capture their perceived opportunities. The rest of this chapter reports on the pilot study, which began in November 2019 principally to explore the feasibility of an international project on opportunity creation among VI entrepreneurs. A principal follow-on question, which we begin to address, enquires how high-potential ideas are identified, and when they fail to be identified, among VI entrepreneurs by distinguishing between the cognitive, socio-cultural, and other processes of VI and sighted entrepreneurs (cf. Miller and le Breton-Miller, 2017).

RESEARCH ON VISUALLY IMPAIRED ENTREPRENEURS

Research Context

The statistics of visual impairment in most, if not all, economies worldwide support a picture of negative public perception of VI people. In the UK, over two million residents live with visual impairment, either as a hereditary condition or as a consequence of disease and/or injury. UK residents with visual impairment now represent circa one in 30 of UK's population (RNIB, n.d.). By 2020, the number of UK-based VI residents is expected to rise to over 2 250 000 (ibid.). Unemployment among this population has remained high, with one in four UK residents who are registered as blind working in paid employment (ibid.). While many organizations in Western economies now recruit VI staff, the number of these employees remain pitifully small; and virtually non-existent in industries such as finance and banking where the need for innovation, paradoxically, is extremely high. In this scenario, VI people are rarely employed for their skills and competencies. And yet we know that disabled people often face extreme challenges of many kinds, and entrepreneurship scholars have suggested how blind entrepreneurs have responded to their challenges by developing adaptive skills, for example in oral communication, networking, and creative problem-solving (Block et al., 2015). In turn, astute application of these skills has contributed to work outcomes that can be advantageous for any organization; for example, work discipline, a collaborative and yet individually creative work environment, and risk tolerance (Miller and Le Breton-Miller, 2017; Ng and Arndt, 2019; Yu et al., 2021).

Among UK VI entrepreneurs, running their own ventures has been a significant activity at least over the past 20 years, with a number of VI entrepreneurs whose activities have been publicly reported (Jones and Latreille, 2011). These activities have included extraordinary projects that VI entrepreneurs have undertaken because they are blind, by applying skills they have developed to create substantial, impactful ventures (Casey, 2017). A number of these ventures have centered on developing and publicizing the potential contributions of disabled people to business organizations, initially in developed economies, with further, challenging follow-on opportunities in developing economies such as China, where many disabled people continue to be stigmatized, marginalized from mainstream opportunities and activities, and physically abused (Palmer, 2014). In this scenario, while there appears to be clear potential in the social impact of disabled and VI entrepreneurship, our purpose, similarly, is to be able to draw potential impact on knowledge of opportunity creation from the persistent, high level of motivation that certain VI entrepreneurs have publicly shown in new venture creation (Casey, 2017). Hence our pilot study.

Pilot Study

The research began with a pilot study that observed the activities of two serial VI entrepreneurs over six months. We contacted the entrepreneurs directly following an internet search of VI entrepreneurs with a record of venture creation that could be studied. Entrepreneurs with this record were also naturally discoverable on the internet. The pilot drew on an exploratory research design to address the research question of how opportunities were created. This design involved a grounded approach (Glaser and Strauss, 1967) where we followed and interacted with two prominent VI entrepreneurs in England and Ireland as case studies of potentially contrasting approaches to opportunity creation among serial VI entrepreneurs. The design drew elements of qualitative research techniques from Glaser and Strauss (1967), principally theoretical sampling, where the pilot's small dataset has driven inductive understanding of a process, which appears to be still evolving, of opportunity creation in a number of ventures set up by the two VI entrepreneurs. Additionally, from data collected from sit-in observations of management meetings and project-related discussions with each of the two entrepreneurs, we began to compare the pilot data by moving back and forth from features of Miller and Le Breton-Miller's (2017) challenge-based model to the data in articulating the nature and processes of a VI-motivated form of opportunity creation within the respective operating contexts of the two entrepreneurs.

The first entrepreneur (VI-1) is a white European male who has been legally blind (defined as at least 80 percent visual impairment) from a congenital condition since his late teens. Since 2010, VI-1 has also become paraplegic and confined to a wheelchair following an accident that resulted from his blindness. VI-1 launched a number of ventures between 2015 and 2017 to raise funds for, and awareness of, disabled people, including VI citizens, and to improve mobility for the disabled, permanently through spinal research, and on demand by developing a portable body-suit constructed from a combination of technologies that enable strong and enduring movement from paralyzed legs.

By contrast, the pilot's second participant (VI-2) is a white European female who was born with severe sight loss. However, she was diagnosed as legally blind only in her twenties. Because of her entrepreneurial activities that she conducts publicly, VI-2 is now known internationally as a paid speaker and fundraiser for all disabled people of working age. A number of these ventures promote employment opportunities and the development of professional skills among disabled employees and entrepreneurs. VI-2 was chosen initially because she appears to have drawn on her considerable personal networks as a former finance executive, to fund her ventures and, equally, in providing a source of professional organizational assistance to develop her ventures (cf. Miller and Le Breton-Miller's, 2017 model of "underdog" entrepreneurs).

The pilot project has now begun to learn the approaches to venture development of these VI entrepreneurs. Agreed areas of interaction between the two entrepreneurs and the research team are in collaborative work on new projects: namely, in crowd-funding a proposed venture (VI-1), and a public awareness and fundraising event in China (VI-2) where institutional support for the health and well-being of disabled citizens remains absent. As both entrepreneurs work in the UK but were born and raised outside the UK, there is a further relationship with Miller and Le Breton-Miller's

(2017) disability-based model, where their social differences as a national minority may potentially compound the routine challenges faced by these entrepreneurs.

Preliminary Findings

Preliminary findings of the pilot suggest that the two VI entrepreneurs developed a process of opportunity creation with a number of principal features. These features are based on the venture's (as opposed to merely the entrepreneur's) market-sensitive anticipation of a range of market signals; for example, in the market's interest in stem cell research for paraplegic and other disabilities (VI-1), and in the timing for and social receptivity to fundraising for disability projects (VI-2).[3] Within each feature, our sampled entrepreneurs have developed specific skills that they believe can produce effective outcomes to address their personal condition and/or life experiences (Figure 2.1).

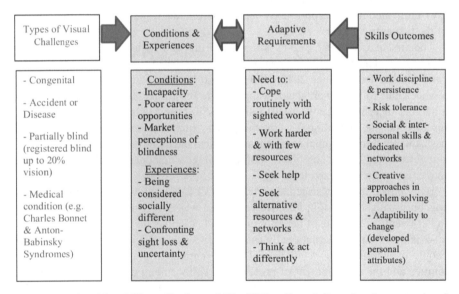

Source: Developed from Miller and Le Breton-Miller (2017, p. 9) on challenge-based competencies of disabled entrepreneurs.

Figure 2.1   *A theoretical conception of visually impaired entrepreneurship*

Here, the two VI entrepreneurs appear to have applied their respective personal skills to alter their ventures' strategic and marketing approaches to adapt to, and capture, changes typically in perception and preferences of the wider market to support their ventures' disabled projects. This ambitious appeal to the wider market beyond disability contrasts with the personal networks-focused nature of the principal perspectives of opportunity creation where entrepreneurs (are expected to) have limited, specific knowledge of their product market based on their eclectic "information channels" (Fiet and Patel, 2008) and affordable means (Sarasvathy, 2001).

Accordingly, the market-oriented focus of the two VI entrepreneurs' skills appears to have altered their adaptive, "coping" responses to challenging personal conditions and experiences by reacting to changing/changed preferences of their sighted audiences in different ways from coping mechanisms that originated from their routine personal experiences as blind individuals. The skills that the two experienced VI entrepreneurs developed of (sighted) market behavior therefore appear to have prompted them to adapt differently to their experiences; and this skills-based capability as experienced entrepreneurs has, in turn, produced different routine experiences of their challenges as VI entrepreneurs.

In sum, both VI entrepreneurs seem to possess an unusual skillset, consequent upon an apparently identical process of opportunity creation, that they applied astutely, for example, in envisaging adaptive requirements of their particular disabilities. In both cases, this process involved the entrepreneurs applying their adaptive skill to turn their disabilities to the advantage of their ventures, for example in seeking non-traditional funding and popular support, in one case by setting up a series of open night-time runs in parkland. These runs have become popular and provide operational funding and seed funding for their spinal research venture (VI-1). Figure 2.1 presents the pilot's key findings to date.

POTENTIAL CONTRIBUTIONS

The pilot has produced a number of potentially important findings. These findings are set out in the section above and in Figure 2.1. Each finding requires further research for substantiation, but promises significant implications principally for our understanding of the little-understood, and yet obviously core, front end of identifying new and, in particular, creative opportunities. Based on the findings of opportunity creation, a key potential contribution is in the adaptive way, based on crafting new skills, in which our two VI entrepreneurs continue to cope with established practices of new venture creation (such as in observing or experiencing the need for new opportunities). The adaptive process exposed a deep determination to produce novel, impactful ideas, not in terms of any outcome-related interests, but because of the sudden condition of their visual impairment. The inspiration and imagination to generate novel and impactful ideas therefore seemed to emanate from this sudden, extreme disability.

For the sampled entrepreneurs, this condition, being permanent, was viewed as something to be embraced as a positive, motivating factor. The fact of their visual impairment was therefore an opportunity in itself, while the desire—a nagging need that both entrepreneurs demonstrated in drawing on their "disabilities" to create ideas (Ng and Arndt, 2019)—for new venture creation drove the identification of impactful, and hence "good," ideas. Accordingly, VI-2's view that she did not need eyes to see became an inspirational epithet that drove her to create new opportunities when she discovered, somewhat late in her life, that she did not, in fact, need eyes to see (ibid.). By contrast, VI-1 was driven by his sight loss to create ventures to alleviate the physical burden of paralyzed limbs. While VI-1's sight loss could not be treated, his paralysis and that of other paralyzed sufferers could be treated. Both VI-1 and VI-2 therefore found motivation for new venture creation only when, from their late teens, they suffered sight loss. From their moment of sight loss, their incurable condition became a persistent source of motivation for new venture creation.

These preliminary data have potentially significant implications for Baumol (1990), as well as for subsequent theories of systematic search and effectuation that have accepted the notion of a fixed proportion of entrepreneurship in any social setting. A principal, potential implication of VI entrepreneurship is that as the source of enterprise is the VI entrepreneur, and specifically in their "disability," entrepreneurship is "fixed" only to the extent of the entrepreneur's continuing desire to move forward and create new opportunities because of their incurable condition. A notable feature of VI entrepreneurship is the way that both VI entrepreneurs in our pilot project saw their sudden visual impairment as positive motivation for opportunity creation. Accordingly, because they were visually impaired, they would now, henceforth, not need eyes to see. It cannot yet be known whether this feature is shared, and the conditions under which it may be shared, among other entrepreneurs, sighted and otherwise. However, we would offer the following propositions, extemporizing forward from our preliminary data, and in the positive spirit of our VI entrepreneurs: The more sudden and more extreme the physical impairment, such as permanent sight loss, the greater the potential ability of entrepreneurs with the disability to create impactful opportunities, following the "release" of creative endeavor triggered by the shocking nature of the disability. Hence, we propose that severe disability may loosen the creative constraints of entrepreneurs, such as from their personal risk preference and experience of socio-cultural norms, and may release their ability to imagine opportunities that they had previously felt constrained from imagining.

For these courageous, inspired entrepreneurs, the permanence of their disability then becomes a watershed for expansive entrepreneurial endeavor that seems to pay little attention to social, institutional, and other structural factors that, in Baumol's (1990) view, have typically constrained the volume of enterprise through history. Perhaps in the manner of a prisoner on death row who has enjoyed an unexpected reprieve, our VI entrepreneurs seem to have turned around the physical and social constraints of their disability and grabbed their own reprieve, which they clearly seek to enjoy to the full.

REFLECTIONS ON FURTHER RESEARCH

Relatedly, our conversations and observations have also yielded emerging data on processes of opportunity creation based on the adaptive skills of the two sampled VI entrepreneurs in exploiting, as opposed to passively responding to, their challenges. These preliminary data on skills such as a well-developed, market-oriented adaptability to external change (Figure 2.1) suggest that VI entrepreneurship can throw light on processes of opportunity creation that may produce substantial economic and social impact. If so, VI and more generally disabled entrepreneurship may provide an important dimension of entrepreneurial activity by helping to reduce failure in new ventures (Lorenzo et al., 2009), without serving merely as an example of social diversity in advanced economies.

Equally, the data thus far suggest that VI entrepreneurship may involve an identifiable and homogenous process of skills adaptation and development that can inform the basis of a general theory of opportunity creation. Following entrepreneurship scholars, we have argued that this theory is imperative for advancing knowledge of how game-changing ideas can be created as a traceable, systematic process (Figure 2.1), without reprising the substantial knowledge that has already been generated about personality traits and preferences of individual entrepreneurs. To convincingly attain this goal, further study of individual elements of VI entrepreneurship is required (see, for example, elements identified in Figure 2.1), and we have suggested how studies should take place across legal, cultural, and other divides worldwide that are in fact unified by their severe undervaluation of the potential contributions of disabled people as a whole.

For VI entrepreneurs, who we have argued are exemplars of such contributions, further study will benefit from exploring the range of features in VI opportunity creation as well as from assessing the extent of creative processes among types of VI entrepreneurs. The purpose of this focus would be to assess the approaches to opportunity creation of serial VI entrepreneurs against those of novice VI entrepreneurs with few skills or little training, and with extremely low affordable means because of their handicap. This question needs to be asked of how novice-nascent and not merely serial VI entrepreneurs may develop entrepreneurial skills and knowledge (Fiet and Patel, 2008) before beginning to compare contributions to opportunity creation between VI and sighted entrepreneurs. Overall, the questions we have posed are researchable because, ironically, VI and many other physically disabled entrepreneurs are in plain view. Yet this research of visibly impaired entrepreneurs has yet to be conducted, while the field of entrepreneurship has already begun to learn about the possible contributions, in and beyond entrepreneurship, of invisibly impaired entrepreneurs with mental conditions (see, e.g., Wiklund et al., 2018; Yu et al., 2021; Hsieh et al., 2019; Lerner et al., 2019). This chapter has sought to bridge this gap in knowledge of visibly impaired entrepreneurs by suggesting the potential rich learning from a number of these entrepreneurs who appear to create opportunities because of, and not despite, their sudden, severe impairment.

NOTES

1. We distinguish opportunity creation from opportunity recognition which merely involves the discovery or identification of existing opportunities (Mary George et al., 2016).

Opportunity recognition or discovery is assumed to be an inadequate process for meeting or satisfying extreme challenges faced by VI entrepreneurs.

2.   We therefore assume that VI entrepreneurs who have created ventures because of their blindness would potentially yield more learning about opportunity creation (and other areas of entrepreneurship research, such as intrinsic motivation) than anyone else, including VI entrepreneurs who go about their activities despite their disabilities and challenges.

3.   A number of senior associates of each venture share this ability to anticipate market signals, as opposed to the entrepreneur possessing the sole capability to do so. This suggests that this feature is an organizational capability.

REFERENCES

Alvarez, S., Barney, J. and Young, S. (2010). Debates in Entrepreneurship: Opportunity Formation and Implications for the Field of Entrepreneurship. In: Acs, Z. and Audretsch, D. (eds), *Handbook of Entrepreneurship Research*, International Handbook Series on Entrepreneurship, Volume 5, pp. 23–45. New York, NY: Springer.

Ardichvili, A., Cardozo, R. and Ray, S. (2003). A Theory of Entrepreneurial Opportunity Identification and Development. *Journal of Business Venturing*, 18(1), pp. 105–123.

Baumol, W. (1990). Entrepreneurship: Productive, Unproductive, and Destructive. *Journal of Political Economy*, 98(5), Part 1, pp. 893–921.

Block, J., Kohn, K., Miller, D. and Ullrich, K. (2015). Necessity Entrepreneurship and Competitive Strategy. *Small Business Economics*, 44(1), pp. 37–54.

Block, J. and Wagner, M. (2010). Necessity and Opportunity Entrepreneurs in Germany. *Schmalenbach Business Review*, 62(2), pp. 154–174.

Casey, C. (2017). Disability is Uncomfortable. https://www.theguardian.com/small-business -network/2017/aug/21/disability-is-uncomfortable-caroline-casey-valuable-binc-one -young-world (accessed February 11, 2021).

Dacin, M.T., Dacin, P.A. and Tracey, P. (2011). Social Entrepreneurship: A Critique and Future Directions. *Organization Science*, 22(5), pp. 1203–1213.

Dimic, N. and Orlov, V. (2014). Entrepreneurial Tendencies among People with ADHD. *International Review of Entrepreneurship*, 13(3), pp. 187–204.

Express (27-2-2021). Andrea Bocelli Blind: What Happened to Andrea Bocelli? https:// www.express.co.uk/entertainment/music/1398725/Andrea-Bocelli-blind-what-happened -to-Andrea-Bocelli-eyesight-accident-evg (accessed February 11, 2021).

Fiet, J. and Patel, P. (2008). Entrepreneurial Discovery as Constrained, Systematic Search. *Small Business Economics*, 30(3), pp. 215–229.

Floyd, S. and Wooldridge, B. (1999). Knowledge Creation and Social Networks in Corporate Entrepreneurship: The Renewal of Organizational Capability. *Entrepreneurship: Theory and Practice*, 23(3), pp. 123–144.

Glaser, B. and Strauss, A. (1967). *The Discovery of Grounded Theory: Strategies of Qualitative Research*. London: Weidenfeld & Nicholson.

Hart, D. and Acs, Z. (2011). High-Tech Immigrant Entrepreneurship in the United States. *Economic Development Quarterly*, 25(2), pp. 116–129.

Hsieh, Y-C., Molina, V. and Weng, J. (2019). The Road to Entrepreneurship with Impairments: A Challenges–Adaptive Mechanisms–Results Model for Disabled Entrepreneurs. *International Small Business Journal*, 37(8), pp. 761–779.

Jones, M. and Latreille, P. (2011). Disability and Self-employment: Evidence from the UK. *Applied Economics*, 43(27), pp. 4161–4178.

Kirzner, I. (1997). Entrepreneurial Discovery and the Competitive Market Process: An Austrian Approach. *Journal of Economic Literature*, 35(1), pp. 60–85.

Lerner, D., Verheul, I. and Thurik, R. (2019). Entrepreneurship and Attention Deficit/ Hyperactivity Disorder: A Large-Scale Study Involving the Clinical Condition of ADHD. *Small Business Economics*, 53(2), pp. 381–392.

Lorenzo, T., van Niekerk, L. and Mdlokolo, P. (2009). Economic Empowerment and Black Disabled Entrepreneurs: Negotiating Partnerships in Cape Town, South Africa. *Disability and Rehabilitation*, 29(5), pp. 429–436.

Mainela, T. and Puhakka, V. (2009). Organising New Business in a Turbulent Context: Opportunity Discovery and Effectuation for IJV Development in Transition Markets. *Journal of International Entrepreneurship*, 7(2), pp. 111–134.

Mary George, N., Parida, V., Lahti, T. and Wincent, J. (2016). A Systematic Literature Review of Entrepreneurial Opportunity Recognition: Insights on Influencing Factors. *International Entrepreneurship and Management Journal*, 12(2), pp. 309–350.

Miller, D. and Le Breton-Miller, I. (2017). Underdog Entrepreneurs: A Model of Challenge-Based Entrepreneurship. *Entrepreneurship: Theory and Practice*, 41(1), pp. 7–17.

Mitchell, R., Mitchell, J. and Smith, J. (2008). Inside Opportunity Formation: Enterprise Failure, Cognition, and the Creation of Opportunities. *Strategic Entrepreneurship Journal*, 2(3), pp. 225–242.

Ng, W. and Arndt, F. (2019). "I Never Needed Eyes to See": Leveraging Extreme Challenges for Successful Venture Creation. *Journal of Business Venturing Insights*, 11(June), e00125, pp. 1–10. DOI: https://doi.org/10.1016/j.jbvi.2019.e00125.

Nonaka, I. (1994). A Dynamic Theory of Organizational Knowledge Creation. *Organization Science*, 5(1), pp. 14–37.

Palmer, K. (2014). Crippling Injustice. Disabled People in China are Still Stigmatized, Marginalized, and Abused. What Hope is There for Reform? https://aeon.co/essays/what-is -life-like-for-disabled-people-in-china (accessed February 11, 2021).

Patel, P. and Fiet, J. (2009). Systematic Search and Its Relationship to Firm Founding. *Entrepreneurship Theory and Practice*, 33(2), pp. 501–526.

Ramamurti, R. (1986). Public Entrepreneurs: Who They are and How They Operate. *California Management Review*, 28(3), pp. 142–158.

RNIB (Royal National Institute for the Blind) (n.d.). http://www.rnib.org.uk/professionals/ knowledge-and-research-hub/research-reports/employment-research (accessed February 11, 2021).

Sarasvathy, S. (2001). Causation and Effectuation: Toward a Theoretical Shift from Economic Inevitability to Entrepreneurial Contingency. *Academy of Management Review*, 26(2), pp. 243–263.

Sarasvathy, S., Dew, N., Velamuri, S. and Venkataraman, S. (2010). *Three Views of Entrepreneurial Opportunity*. In: Acs, Z. and Audretsch, D. (eds), *Handbook of Entrepreneurship Research*, International Handbook Series on Entrepreneurship, Volume 5, pp. 77–96. New York, NY: Springer.

Shaheen, G. and Myhill, W. (2009). Entrepreneurship for Veterans with Disabilities: Lessons Learned from the Field. *In Brief Newsletter*. New Brunswick, NJ: Intar Leadership Center.

Wiklund, J., Hatak, I., Patzelt, H. and Shepherd, D. (2018). Mental Disorders in the Entrepreneurship Context: When Being Different Can Be an Advantage. *Academy of Management Perspectives*, 32(2), pp. 182–206.

Winschiers-Theophilus, H., Cabrero, D., Angula, S., Chivuno- Kuria, S., Mendonca, H. and Ngolo, R. (2015). A Challenge-Based Approach to Promote Entrepreneurship among Youth in an Informal Settlement of Windhoek. *AOM Conference Proceedings*, August 7–11, Vancouver, Canada. https://www.researchgate.net/profile/Daniel-G-Cabrero/publication/ 283346056_A_Challenge-based_Approach_to_promote_Entrepreneurship_among _Youth_in_an_Informal_Settlement_of_Windhoek/links/56351cb508aebc003fff70cc/A

-Challenge-based-Approach-to-promote-Entrepreneurship-among-Youth-in-an-Informal
-Settlement-of-Windhoek.pdf (accessed February 11, 2021).
Yu, W., Wiklund, J. and Pérez-Luño, A. (2021). ADHD Symptoms, Entrepreneurial Orientation
(EO), and Firm Performance. *Entrepreneurship Theory and Practice*, 45(1), pp. 92–117.

3. Creating my own job: Australian experiences of people with disability with microenterprises, self-employment and entrepreneurship

Simon Darcy, Jock Collins and Megan Stronach

INTRODUCTION

Over 4.4 million or 17.7 per cent of people in Australia have some form of disability, and the number of people with disability (PwD) who are of working age is increasing. In fact, the disability rate for Australians of 'prime working age' is currently around 15 per cent (2.2 million people). Yet, nearly half (46.6 per cent) of these people were not in the labour force, and more than half (59 per cent) were permanently unable to work (Australian Bureau of Statistics, 2012, 2019). Labour force participation for PwD of working age has stubbornly remained constant at approximately the same rate for some two decades (53.4 per cent), whereas those without disability had significantly higher rates of workforce participation which increased further with the most recent data collection (84.1 per cent) (Australian Bureau of Statistics, 2019).

Governments often focus their efforts on encouraging inclusion and facilitating PwD to find traditional employment within organisations (Boylan and Burchardt, 2002). While the general population have significant issues in having a work–life balance, research has shown that this is far more problematic for PwD (Jammaers and Williams, 2021). It may not be surprising, then, that given both the barriers they face and the complexity of the work environment for PwD in some Western countries, PwD are 'more likely to be self-employed than the general population' (Renko et al., 2016). For example, in the United States 'PwD are almost twice as likely to be self-employed' (ODEP, 2014), while in Europe PwD also have high rates of self-employment (Pagán, 2009).

In starting to research this area in Australia, the secondary data revealed that, like the United States and European countries, PwD have a higher rate of self-employment (13.1 per cent) than people without disability (9.2 per cent) (Australian Bureau of Statistics, 2012). Despite these statistics, PwD continue to face considerable economic and social exclusion, both in Australia and elsewhere. Indeed, it could be argued that learning from other Australian research on minority entrepreneurship of migrants, refugees and first nations people (Collins and Low, 2010; Collins et al., 2017; Collins and Norman, 2018; Collins and Shin, 2014) identifies that the relatively higher rate of PwD entrepreneurship is itself a function of – and a response to – the very economic and social exclusion from employment or 'blocked mobility' that other minorities in Australia face (Alaslani and Collins, 2017). Yet, the experiences of PwD with self-employment, microenterprise, social enterprise and entrepreneurship is largely an underresearched area of scholarship in Australia (Darcy et al., 2019; Maritz and Laferriere, 2016).

International research has traditionally focused on entrepreneurship in a generic sense, but in recent years an increasing interest in entrepreneurs with disability (EwD) has emerged. However, research in Australia on PwD seeking to pursue self-employment is scant. Nevertheless, there is rising awareness that PwD are likely to have their own set of aspirations, needs and adjustment patterns in employment (NDIS, 2020a). These factors, along with the roll-out of the National Disability Insurance Scheme (NDIS) and the Australian Disability Strategy 2021–2031 (AND) should be of vital interest to vocational rehabilitation organisations, disability support groups, business groups and government policy-makers. Yet, for those receiving the NDIS who have higher and more complex levels of support needs than most other PwD, their employment rates are only 25 per cent, and at the time of the research beginning the NDIS had not included self-employment or entrepreneurship as employment options (NDIS, 2020b).

This chapter outlines research undertaken to investigate the self-employment, microenterprise and entrepreneurship of PwD in Australia. The research involved a partnership with service providers in the disability services sector – National Disability Services, Settlement Services International (SSI) and Break-Thru People Solutions – and was funded by the Australian Research Council.[1] The project had two components. The first examined the experiences of EwD in Australia; while the second focused on the support programs (accelerators, incubators and the like) for EwD, other business development, together with the macro policy environment. The research aimed to better understand the pathways of PwD into entrepreneurship to support Australia's capacity for developing evidence-based policy initiatives that increase the number and success of EwD. The research hypothesis was that entrepreneurship increases social inclusion and improves employment opportunities for PwD. The specific project aims were:

1. Identify and understand the experiences of men and women with disability who own and operate private enterprises.
2. Investigate the extent to which EwD are embedded in family and personal social networks, and the role of gender in disability entrepreneurship.
3. Identify the role of networks of disability service organisations in the establishment of, and nature and success of, Australian disability entrepreneurship.
4. Follow the entrepreneurial journeys of ten PwD participating in the IgniteAbility® Small Business Startups.

This chapter addresses objectives 1 and 2, focusing on their lived experiences, with objectives 3 and 4 addressed in other papers and the publicly available reports (Darcy et al., 2020, 2021, 2022).

BACKGROUND AND APPROACH

The research draws on a social approach to disability by focusing on the lived experience of the group. In doing so, the theoretical framework takes direction from the United Kingdom (UK) social model of disability that places disability and the lived experiences of those with disability at the centre of the research paradigm. The UK social model of disability developed from the 1960s and 1970s disability social movement by disabled (deliberate use of the term) activists and disability advocacy groups, who sought to influence social policy and bring about change for a group within society who, on every social metric, were described as 'disadvantaged', stigmatised through institutionalisation and living in poverty (Oliver, 1996, 2004). The disability social movement drew on both civil rights and human rights movements before them, including those movements focusing on race and gender. In understanding the marginalisation, oppression and discrimination affecting the group, it is important not just to hear the experiences of PwD but also to actively engage with those with disability and work in partnership. This is encapsulated by the slogan 'Nothing about Us without Us' (Charlton, 1998), which expresses that as individuals and as a collective they wish to use their agency to effect social change to be co-designed so they have control and choice over their lives. Hence, rather than just hearing their lived experiences it is important for other allies or stakeholders to truly listen to what PwD are saying, to understand what the barriers to social participation and citizenship are and seek to develop transformative solutions for social change. Social approaches to disability also underpinned the United Nations Convention on the Rights of Persons with Disabilities (United Nations, 2006).

Disability in Australia

The two primary sources of data on PwD in Australia are: (1) the Australian Census, conducted every five years, the most recently available in 2016 (Australian Bureau of Statistics, 2017); and (2) the Survey of Disability, Ageing and Carers (SDAC), conducted every three years, and most recently in 2018 by the Australian Bureau of Statistics (ABS), through a survey of around 75 000 people (ABS, 2019). These two sources of population data measure disability in different ways which, when combined, give us a picture of the extent of disability in the Australian population. In 2018 in Australia, all PwD totalled 4.4 million people, or 17.7 per cent of the Australian population. People with profound or severe disability of all ages were 1.42 million, or 5.7 per cent of the Australian population (ABS, 2019). People with higher levels of disability have significantly lower levels of employment. In 2018, 2.1 million PwD living in households were of working age (15–64 years). Of these:

- over half (53.4 per cent) were in the labour force, compared with 84.1 per cent of those without disability;
- almost half (47.8 per cent) were employed, compared with 80.3 per cent of people without disability;

- 46.6 per cent were not in the labour force, compared with 15.9 per cent of those without disability. (ABS, 2019).

Table 3.1 gives Australian PwD data for 2018.

Table 3.1   PwD in Australia, 2018

Disability definition	Number	% of population
All PwD	4.4 million	17.7
Profound or severe disability – all ages	1.42 million	5.7

Source: Data from the Australian Bureau of Statistics (2019).

Australian Government Disability Employment Programs

The Australian Government, through the Department of Social Services, funds two types of specialist programs to help PwD find and maintain work: Australian Disability Enterprises (ADEs) and Disability Employment Services (DES). ADEs are not-for-profit and commercial businesses that employ and support PwD who need a higher level of ongoing support, often in specialist working environments, work crews or contract labour arrangements. However, PwD in ADEs are not paid award wages, with their terms and conditions set by the Supported Employment Services Award 2010, which has a base rate of 12.5 per cent of the minimum pay rate for their classification (Fair Work Ombudsman, 2020). Not surprisingly ADEs are highly controversial amongst many people with disability, their supporters and other social support not-for-profits.

DES by contrast deliver employment assistance for job seekers with disability. This assistance is delivered by a network of organisations around Australia which play a specialist role in helping PwD, with injury or health conditions, to prepare and search for a job, find a job and keep a job (Department of Social Services, 2020b; Women with Disabilities Australia, 2020). Employers are supported through wage subsidy for a specified period, and workers with disability are paid at standard award rates for the industry with the subsidy being withdrawn after a period of time. Critics point to the relatively low levels of permanent employment positions that are sustained beyond the subsidy (Devine et al., 2020). Self-employment is not part of the DES model (Department of Social Services, 2020a).

National Disability Insurance Scheme (NDIS)

In 2019 the focus on employment for PwD changed with the release of the NDIS Participant Employment Strategy 2019–2022. This strategy aims to 'improve employment outcomes for NDIS participants by connecting them to supports to seek and maintain employment in a setting of their choice, including through open employment and/or supported employment' (NDIS, 2020b: 5). Initially employment support through the NDIS focused primarily on paid employment in the mainstream workforce or through the DES system. However, with the development of this strategy the focus of employment participation has expanded to include any and all types of employment, including private and public employment, family business, microenterprises (including self-employment and entrepreneurship), as well as ADEs. More significantly it suggests that the NDIS will provide supports for all employment opportunities for PwD including commercially successful businesses as well as social enterprises (NDIS, 2020a, 2020b).

RESEARCH DESIGN

The research study involved multiple populations including entrepreneur/ self-employed people with disability (EwD), and key stakeholders involved in the entrepreneurial ecosystem with an in-depth understanding of the entrepreneurial journeys of those involved in one disability-specific accelerator program. A mixed methodology research design was adopted for the study involving a quantitative survey, qualitative in-depth interviews and action research methods.

The survey employed snowballing or networking approaches to attract 100 respondents drawn from disability organisations from across Australia (Veal and Darcy, 2014). This was deemed an appropriate approach given that there was no census or list of EwD from which to draw a random sample (Darcy and Burke, 2018; Darcy et al., 2017). The survey was conducted online, or by telephone or on a face-to-face basis if required. This data was supplemented by 60 PwD to the 2018 Startup Muster® Surveys who identified as having a disability.

Semi-structured interview schedules guided in-depth interviews involving key stakeholders in the field of disability entrepreneurship (state and local government, disability employment organisations and the broader disability sector), and EwD who identified as being self-employed, involved in microenterprises, or commercial or social enterprises either currently or in the past. Table 3A.1 in the Appendix outlines the key characteristics of the entrepreneurs interviewed in the study. This chapter draws on this fieldwork to focus on the lived experience of people who are self-employed, involved in microenterprises or commercial or social enterprises.

Data Analysis

The survey data was collected by the Qualtrics online survey design and analysis package. Initial descriptive analysis was undertaken on Qualtrics including frequencies, percentages, cross-tabulations and graphics. For more complex inferential analysis, the data was exported from Qualtrics to the Statistical Package for the Social Sciences (SPSS) v23. The data was interrogated for any between-group differences based on disability, support needs and other appropriate socio-demographic data. The analysis included chi square, t-tests, ANOVA, correlation and regression. Further, inclusion of the Startup Muster® data provided an opportunity to be able to compare EwD to non-disabled entrepreneurs through the use of descriptive statistics.

NVivo is a comprehensive qualitative data analysis software and was used to organise, analyse and find connections across all the interview transcripts, open-ended survey questions and any other textual data collected (for example, documents). Coding themes (or nodes) were identified based upon theoretical background research to the project and the previously explained research design. Manual coding was undertaken, and then common themes identified across the data. Comparisons were made between the different interview subjects to determine whether there were significant differences in concepts identified, based on the experience and priorities of the interview subject groups.

FINDINGS: THE ENTREPRENEURIAL JOURNEYS

The findings firstly present an analysis of the secondary data from the Australian Bureau of Statistics (2012, 2015) on the comparative rate of self-employment of PwD and the non-disabled. This data is then further analysed through the comparative rate of self-employment by disability type and the non-disabled that has not been analysed previously in Australia. Secondly, the entrepreneurial journey is examined through an analysis of quantitative data from two separate surveys outlined in the research design to complementary qualitative research. The qualitative research examines in-depth interviewees of some 52 PwD who are self-employed or entrepreneurs. The quantitative and qualitative data is then presented somatically through examining the motivations, barriers, facilitators, outcomes and benefits of the entrepreneurial journey. To provide further depth of understanding to the qualitative interview participants, they were given pseudonyms and were allocated a code to indicate their disability as follows: hearing (H); speech (S); intellectual disability (I); physical/mobility (PM); psychosocial (P); head injury, stroke or brain damage (ABI); and other (O).

SECONDARY ANALYSIS DISABILITY EMPLOYMENT STATISTICS

Self-employment and entrepreneurship have not regularly featured in Australian secondary data collection (ABS, 2012). Table 3.2 identifies the number and proportion of PwD by status in employment, self-employment and by disability type. Our research reports for the first time that the rate of self-employment (entrepreneurship) varies significantly by disability type with the range compared to the general population, going from 2.5 per cent less for those with intellectual/cognitive disability, through to those with psychosocial disability having 76 per cent higher levels of self-employment than non-disabled Australians.

The reason for self-employment by PwD are complex, including the economic, social and cultural milieu that is affected by disability type, level of support needs, and the relative levels of social, human, digital and bodily capital that they have

Table 3.2   *Employee vs self-employment by disability group*

	Employee %	Self-employed %	% +/- No disability
Disability group	Estimate '000		
Sensory and speech	89.4	10.9	19.0
Intellectual	89.3	9.0	-2.5
Physical/Mobility	84.4	15.3	66.8
Psychological	84.3	16.2	76.2
Head injury, stroke or brain damage	85.9	15.0	63.6
Other	85.8	15.0	62.7
All with reported disability	86.8	13.1	43.0
No reported disability	90.8	9.2	0.0

Source: Reproduced from Darcy et al. (2020) with permission.

access to (Jammaers and Williams, 2020). Further, the intersectionality of disability with gender, ageing, indigeneity, sexuality and cultural background are all considerations that affect the choice of people to become self-employed or to explore entrepreneurial opportunities, including social enterprises (McCall, 2005; Meyer et al., 2021; Settlement Services International, 2018; Williams and Patterson, 2018). As shown in Table 3.2, on average, PwD are 43 per cent more likely to be self-employed than non-disabled Australians, supporting similar overseas findings (ODEP, 2014; Pagán, 2009; Renko et al., 2016). Unfortunately, we do not have any further Australian secondary data insights into self-employment or entrepreneurship for PwD.

Online Survey

Survey respondents' most predominant disability types were mobility/physical (47 per cent), deaf or hearing impairment (20 per cent), and intellectual/cognitive disability (10 per cent); followed by mental health, blind or vision disability and speech/API. Most (65 per cent) identified as having no or low levels of support needs, with only 20 per cent having high or very high support needs. There was a relatively even representation of females (50 per cent) to males (47 per cent), with the majority born with their disability (51 per cent) as opposed to having a traumatic injury (38 per cent). The respondents were well educated, with 43 per cent having an undergraduate or postgraduate qualification, and the majority completing year 12 high school or above. Most were married (60 per cent), with either no dependents (42 per cent), or 1–2 children (47 per cent). The majority were born in Australia (79 per cent) – 21 per cent were born overseas – with only 3 per cent speaking a language other than English at home. Aboriginal and Torres Strait Islander people were underrepresented as respondents (1.2 per cent), even though there has been some targeted research examining the experiences of this group (Collins et al., 2017; Collins and Norman, 2018). Most identified as being self-employed (48 per cent), entrepreneurs (29 per cent), or would like to be self-employed or an entrepreneur in the future (23 per cent).

Startup Muster® Survey

While there were similarities between the online survey conducted for the study and a sample drawn from Startup Muster® who were identified as having a disability (n = 60 of 600 or 10 per cent), there are also decided contrasts. The major disability type in Startup Muster® was again mobility/physical (39 per cent), but with substantially more entrepreneurs with mental health issues (29 per cent), intellectual/cognitive/ learning (22 per cent), deaf or hearing impaired (14 per cent), and blind or vision impaired (12 per cent). Two in three (66 per cent), identified as being independent and not requiring any assistance, while a further 20 per cent had low support needs. No one identified as having a high or very high level of support needs. Slightly more EwD were male (58 per cent), and while most (95 per cent) spoke English at home, some 38 per cent also spoke another language. Again, the respondents had very high levels of formal education, with the majority (70 per cent) having a bachelor or higher degree, and the remainder attending technical and further education or completing high school. With respect to their entrepreneurial journey, a smaller proportion identified as founders (35 per cent), with a higher proportion identifying as future founders (43 per cent), and the remainder identifying as supporters of start-ups.

Identity as Self-Employed or Entrepreneurs

In the online survey, 48 per cent identified as being self-employed, while 29 per cent identified as entrepreneurs, and 23 per cent were intending to be self-employed or entrepreneurs. The fieldwork revealed that that PwD who identified as self-employed or entrepreneurs had very different in mindsets, formative experiences and business experience, and even used a different language or discourse in describing their enterprise. Many had not formally been involved with what many entrepreneurs would recognise as the 'entrepreneurial ecosystem' (Acs et al., 2017; Stam and van de Ven, 2021) – including accelerators, incubators, co-sharing environments, pitching competitions, angel investors or crowdfunding – or been exposed to other entrepreneurial educational experiences. The word 'entrepreneur' just did not resonate with them. Much of the entrepreneurial ecosystem in Australia was not accessible or inclusive to PwD, as for other marginalized identities including gender, migrants, refugees, seniors or first nation people (Darcy et al., 2020, 2021). Other EwD did identify with the start-up or entrepreneurial development process or stages from ideation to concept, committing, validating, scaling and establishing (Jack and Anderson, 2002; Startup Commons, 2021).

Types of Businesses Established

Living with disability gives people a world of experience that other people do not have. In many instances this involves discrimination and other negative experiences that have affected them throughout their life or since acquiring the disability, as evidenced through complaint cases and federal court actions instigated through the

Australian Human Rights Commission (Darcy et al., 2016). However, many – a third of those surveyed – use their experiences to be a basis for their business enterprise, giving them insider disability knowledge that they regard as an advantage to start a business designed to assist others in similar situations in the disability niche market. In the language of economic theory, EwD have a comparative advantage in businesses that relate to their experiences as PwD. They know the market well and can spot market niches that have not been addressed or have been addressed inadequately. These wide-ranging business activities as described by survey respondents are illustrated in Figure 3.1. The clear lesson is that while EwD are concentrated in the healthcare and social assistance, education and training, professional, scientific and technical services, and arts and recreation services industries in Australia, they are not confined to these industries. If the question is 'What is the typical PwD business?', the answer is that there is not one.

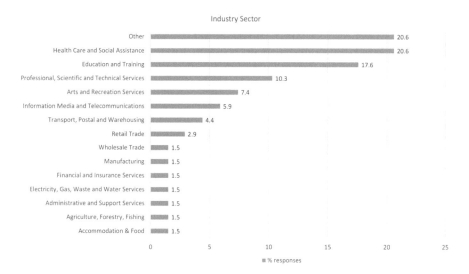

Figure 3.1   Industry sector of business, % response

There is a diversity of disability business start-ups, encompassing service, merchandising and manufacturing enterprises: manufacturing car hand controls, personal care service delivery and oversight, providing travel, parking space advice, and legal services. Others described transforming a hobby such as craftwork into a microenterprise. Technological advances have opened new avenues for EwD, who described a variety of assistive technologies such as messaging apps, screen readers, wheelchair stair-climbers, electronic conveyancing and speech recognition software. About half of the respondents had developed enterprises for non-disabled purposes, including winemakers, transport operators, landscaping, and information technology support.

The businesses identified by Startup Muster® respondents were similarly across a variety of industries, including education, transport, agriculture and manufacturing.

However, there was a greater EwD involvement in technology-related industries – including social media, software development, MedTech/Healthtech/biotech, internet of things, artificial intelligence, virtual/augmented reality and fintech – and much lower levels of disability-specific enterprises and professional consulting services. About 85 per cent of the respondents' enterprises were not for disability purposes.

Motivations

The shift to entrepreneurship and self-employment for PwD may be perceived as a combination of pull/anti-pull and push/anti-push factors (Chevalier et al., 2013). The attraction of self-employment stems from a desire by PwD for economic and personal independence in a way that can accommodate an individual's intrapersonal lifestyle needs. Pull factors related to the possibility of higher income, flexibility in the workplace in terms of hours and location, and reasonable recognition of support needs, as well as the ability to bring about social change, and the likelihood of increased work satisfaction. Anti-pull factors were aversion to the risks involved in starting up a business, and the resultant uneven cash flow, particularly if that meant they needed to relinquish their Disability Support Pension. Hence, the interrelationship between risk and social security played heavily on the minds of some EwD.

From a push perspective, lack of opportunities, or what the literature calls 'blocked mobility' (Alaslani and Collins, 2017), was identified by many participants. Largely associated with employer discrimination, EwD faced individual and institutional barriers and constraints to being embraced as an 'ideal' or viable employee (Foster and Wass, 2013; Scholz and Ingold, 2021). They often experienced a lack of recognition of their qualifications, resulting in a mismatch between their skills and the labour market opportunities made available to them. As a result, participants felt that they had no choice but to start their own business. This course of action was seen as a necessity after long-standing discrimination had resulted in blocked mobility or occupational skidding in the workplace (Block et al., 2015; Brewer and Gibson, 2014). Counterintuitively, it appeared that experiences of discrimination indirectly prepared participants with the resilience required for the challenges, persistence, determination, and even a higher appetite for risk on the entrepreneurial journey. Disability entrepreneurship in Australia, it seems, is a highly contradictory phenomenon.

Anti-push factors related to the security of having permanent employment and/ or the risk of losing their disability support pension. Sometimes motivations were a combination of push and pull factors. Whether pushed or pulled towards entrepreneurship, the EwD had a desire for autonomy: the potential for acquiring independence, enhancing work–life balance, resulting in improved agency with control over their lives through the instrumental improvement of being their own boss, flexibility around their own lifestyle, and the challenge of skill development where they are testing their ability for their new business enterprise. These motivations must be situated within the social ecology of the individual EwD themselves: the nature and timing of their disability, their education, personal circumstances, social support

Table 3.3   *Current entrepreneurs with disability: top ten motivations*

Motivator	Mean*
To help others	4.26
To be my own boss	4.24
To have a flexible work schedule and lifestyle	4.19
To develop new skills	4.01
To take advantage of my own creative talents	4.01
The opportunity for financial success	4.00
To test and prove myself	3.89
To realise my dream	3.75
To solve a problem I was experiencing	3.70
To meet people	3.63

Note: * Mean calculated using Likert scale 1–5 values, where 1 = strongly disagree, 2 = disagree, 3 = neutral, 4 = agree, 5 = strongly agree.
Source: Based on data from Darcy et al. (2021), with permission.

networks, gender, age, linguistic, cultural and religious background, where they live, and their individual circumstances. Table 3.3 lists the top ten motivating factors as identified by survey respondents, with push factors common.

Interestingly, however, interviewees had a slightly different focus. While they noted the need for financial success, they also described their passion to develop their own enterprise, particularly when they had identified a service or product that may be of use to other PwD. For example:

Having a spinal injury costs a fortune, and so I realised my situation, of living with this, if I was going to live, being poor was not something I could think about. So that was a bit of a motivator, to be honest. (Judy, PM)

I don't want anybody else to have to go through what I did. I don't think it's fair that when you're choosing university it's based on parking, rather than their program, or quality of university. That's not okay. It's not okay to not be able to go into the city to work because you don't think you can park there, it's too expensive, and you don't know any other way to get there. There's a whole bunch of fear that comes with taking public transport when you have limited mobility, and the whole point of what I built is to take away some of that fear. (Liz, O)

In addition, this cohort described significant push factors which they had encountered in the workplace. Discrimination is described as treating an individual or an entity differently before the law, due to their age, ability, sexuality, ethnicity, indigeneity or gender. Apart from being unlawful, such stereotypical attitudes were very hurtful:

I was told I was unemployable by the CES in [location]. They told me when I went there, not long after my accident, looking for their help to get a job, 'No, I don't think you're employable Gus'. (Gus, PM)

I was waiting in the waiting room and overheard the people who were about to interview me, there were two people. The man said, 'Oh, don't worry about the next interview, we're only doing it to be seen to be doing the right thing'. Great! (Caroline, PM)

Table 3.4   *Top ten barriers that hinder entrepreneurial aspirations*

Barriers	Mean*
Financial constraints	2.95
Uncertainty of the future	2.84
Lack of capital	2.78
Financial dependents	2.61
Lack of time	2.57
Physical access to spaces and places	2.42
Lack of confidence in my own ability	2.39
Transport-related barriers	2.26
Compliance with government regulations/redtape	2.25
Access or cost of providing my own assistive technologies (equal 10th)	2.21
No one to turn to get some help (equal 10th)	2.21

Note: *Mean calculated using Likert scale 1–5 values, where 1 = not a barrier, 2 = minor barrier, 3 = moderate barrier, 4 = high barrier, 5 = very high barrier.
Source: Based on data from Darcy et al. (2021), with permission.

> Hah! Choice had nothing to do with it. I tried to fit into traditional structured workplaces for several years, but it never worked. Across 8+ workplaces I've been bullied, undervalued, underpaid and even told to 'work on fixing' my disability because it's inconvenient for someone! Self-employment was the only option I had left for workforce participation. Workplaces say they're all about disability inclusion but in reality, only a very short list of disabilities are welcome. If you've got a visible disability that doesn't get in other people's way – you're OK – but if you have an invisible disability that annoys people, you're screwed. (Survey Respondent, PM)

Barriers and Challenges

Table 3.4 lists the top ten barriers identified by survey respondents.

Many of these factors were at the individual level, including lack of confidence in their own ability:

> But working with a disability and having a disability can be really overwhelming. And the fear that I always had, the sort of anxiety that I had, was that people would think that I was in that job because I had a disability, NOT because I was competent and providing a unique result. (Kenan, S)

Simply being a PwD presented huge barriers to self-employment or entrepreneurship, and participants described only being able to work to a certain level because of having to accommodate the disability. They described frequent and ongoing episodes of ill-health:

> And while I was in between being sick ... I was in the hospital when I started my NEIS [New Enterprise Incentive Scheme] program. I was working from a hospital bed during three of those months. I'm calling people, doing websites, I had the computer with me ... yeah. (Pamela, PM)

So, we got to the end of the accelerator, and we presented to investors and we did really well. We absolutely did excellent on the pitch night, but a week later I was in intensive care. (Liz, O)

However, most barriers for those with mobility, vision and cognitive disability were structural, involving facilities, access and transport: 'I mean I'm only a 15 minute drive to the city, but it would take me two hours by public transport just to get there in the morning because some buses weren't accessible, and I'd have to wait, and it would rain and I can't hold umbrellas' (Joan, PM).

In addition, many EwD experienced challenges in obtaining start-up funding or loans. The following experiences encapsulate many of the financial constraints and barriers experienced by the group:

Yeah, well, they wouldn't really give me a bank loan. I've got a mortgage, but because I'm not actually working at the moment because I've been sick, I can't get a loan. So, I'm on Centrelink for Newstart, but I'm not eligible for a pension even though I'm full-time in a wheelchair. So, credit card was our only option. (Pamela, PM)

I've done it all myself, so, I had to fund it. I had to use my own private capital, and I have an overdraft. I pay the staff. It's been very lean. I'm only three years in, and it's definitely showing signs of promise, but the cash flow is difficult. (Gail, PM)

Financially it was absolute hell, because I got no compensation from my motorbike accident. It was not a compensable claim, because I swerved to miss a dog on the road. There was no third-party insurance for me, nothing. So, bankruptcy was right there. That was another reason why I had to get out of hospital, because we just would have gone broke. (Hudson, PM)

But you know, we are running out of money, and now that's why these crowdfunding campaigns are so important in the short term. I think what we want to do is basically stay afloat and carry on developing the site. What we want to do is stay afloat until we find a big corporate supporter who will enable us to roll out comfortably and employ and meet people, and pay ourselves, and become more than a one-man band. (Dave, PM)

Negative societal attitudes towards disability were commonplace, and while some EwD mentioned small-scale personality conflicts, in a small number of instances the conflict involved appeared to border on bullying. Participants found that compliance with social service agencies such as Centrelink (Australian Government, 2018) and the NDIS was challenging, cumbersome, confrontational and laborious:

It's quite frustrating that I am not taken seriously, because I don't have an assistive device, and that has always been the way, and the assumption that if you have a disability you don't work, you can't work, you are constantly dependent on somebody else, just getting through that whole stigma and stereotype program. (Liz, O)

Other people who had been quite close friends, who also work in this space, just immediately saw me as threatening their work, and the things they do. When I was individual, I became a bit of a target. As a person with disability, which is what we're all meant to be supporting, it's been particularly disappointing to see that. (Neal, V)

Another dominant theme that occurred in the interview group was the intersectionality of multiple issues that heighten vulnerabilities and compound the barriers and challenges to employment that they face. When people have multiple identities such as ability, gender, sexuality, seniority and indigeneity, they can become further marginalized through the intersectionality of those identities (McCall, 2005; Meyer et al., 2021; Williams and Patterson, 2018). This is exemplified by the lived experience of one participant:

> The issues I have with my mental health make it difficult for me to have self-confidence. Also knowing a lot of the statistics around investment in tech and all the bias and glass ceilings that women face, let alone, you know, people with disabilities, and people from like LGBTIQ [lesbian, gay, bisexual, trans, intersex, queer] backgrounds like me. I mean, the best thing I've got going for me is that I'm white. (Janet, P)

For all PwD, there are enablers that assist them to overcome the barriers that they face. Indeed, focusing solely on barriers – on what PwD lack – creates a deficit model that draws attention away from what they have: their determination, their abilities to shape their lives despite their disability constraints, and the institutional and personal discrimination that they face because of it. In other words, a deficit approach to PwD entrepreneurship detracts attention from the agency of EwD and the strategies that they employ to overcome barriers. In highlighting the change in mindset from focusing on barriers to understanding enablers, we present a short case (Box 3.1) of one entrepreneur with disability who encapsulates the need to focus on ability and the importance of enablers.

BOX 3.1   A PERSONAL STORY: FROM WORK EXPERIENCE TO SELF-EMPLOYED WINEMAKER

I have mild cerebral palsy, affecting my coordination, my speech and the pace of my walking. I'm a self–employed winemaker. I've always found it hard to gain employment. I get to the interviews, but find people very much judge me on my disability. I have a strong need to prove myself, both at work and socially. Twenty years ago, in my first job I had to do three month's work experience to prove myself. All my employment, and now my business, have all been based on that three month's work experience. Now, if I had sat back and waited for a job to come along, who knows how my career may have ended up? But because I went out there and said, 'Guys, this is who I am, and these are my abilities', they were able to see for themselves that I had the abilities to go further. I think my strong work ethic has come from my brothers, who were both very much sports minded. I was always down there watching them play sport, achieving, and I needed to achieve. I needed to show people I had abilities and I needed to work out where that was. For me it was in the workplace.

From a workplace perspective there are a couple of people in the wine industry who have been my mentors. They've shown me how to make wine, and more importantly, they have shown me I've got the ability in the wine industry. I regard those couple of people highly, and when I have my down days, I think of them and the way they've told me I can do things. I am very proud of my own wine business. When I was sixteen years old I dreamt that one day I would like my own wine business to be able to make my own wine, and have my own wine label, and at the age of thirty-five, I was able to release my first wine. So, it was a nineteen-year dream, but I'm a big believer in setting goals, and if I went through each individual goal to get where I was, I reckon there'd be hundreds of goals. I think it's also important to look at the 'glass half-full' instead of the 'glass half-empty'. To me it is all about looking at all the positives, looking at everything we can do, and never worrying about the things you can't do. There's no point worrying about things because you can't do them. So, achieve what you can and strive hard for it. (Kenan, S)

Enablers and Ways Forward

Table 3.5 lists the top ten enablers identified by survey respondents.

Table 3.5   *Top ten enablers assisting in entrepreneurial aspirations*

Enabler	Mean*
I can see opportunities for new businesses	3.52
Being in contact with people with positive attitudes towards disability	3.32
I have social and/or family support	3.05
I have access to mentors	3.00
I can see opportunities for entrepreneurship education	2.83
I am financially independent	2.74
Attending a start-up, innovation, entrepreneurship program or course	1.96
There is commercial or legal infrastructure that supports me	1.94
Previous experience starting an enterprise	1.92
I am single	1.87

Note: * Mean calculated using Likert scale 1–5 values, where 1 = not enabling, 2 = somewhat enabling, 3 = moderately enabling, 4 = highly enabling, 5 = very highly enabling.
Source: Based on data from Darcy et al. (2021), with permission.

The characteristics inherent in PwD – their agency – also positioned them to succeed in entrepreneurship. These characteristics included innovative problem-solving skills, flexibility, tenacity, sense of humour, preparedness to seek assistance, grace under pressure, and creativity. Many had juggled salaried jobs while developing their start-ups, and pivoted their original business plans while refining their future ideas:

You don't need to have a disability to be entrepreneurial. Entrepreneurial isn't a reason to – it's not something that you've got to say, well, I have this disability, therefore I can't be entrepreneurial. The roots of entrepreneurialism stems from your psychology. It's a psychological construct, this idea of self-efficacy, and the more you do, the more you conquer, the more you believe you can conquer. (Stan, PM)

I just see myself as a successful businessperson who's making the best of everything … I think persistence and having a positive attitude are very important. I'm a massive believer of make the most of every day and don't let your disabilities hold you down. So, you have your down days but then you need to bounce back. (Ivana, PM)

Importantly, a range of schemes including incubator and accelerator programs provided support to nascent entrepreneurs, and some participants had successfully identified organisations and institutions that they had enlisted for support or to add value to the enterprise. Some of these included funding opportunities such as grants or loans. While a third of respondents mentioned the importance of mentors, virtually all respondents benefited from high levels of backing from family and friends, in shaping and supporting their ventures:

> I was able to get about four mentoring sessions, and that time was the most effective prob- ably because she [mentor] has a disability herself and she's been involved in the training sphere for a very, very long time. So, with my time with her I basically structured and wrote three training programs. (Taylor, ABI)

> Yeah, so through these, whether it be Facebook groups or Slack channels, that's how I keep in touch with lots of people and Twitter as well, LinkedIn, always asking people that I am talking to, meeting people at entrepreneurial events, 'Can you introduce me to someone?' and building my network that way, has really helped me. Then those people that connect with my business idea or that connect with me personally have offered their time and they help me regularly. (Janet, P)

> I rely on my ex-husband a whole lot, we're best mates, best, best friends. So, we completely do 50/50 custody, raise our children together. He's still my best friend that I tell everything to, he's the only person who knows everything about me. So he's a massive, massive key support to me. And then my mum is a really, really key support and I've got some really close friends who live very nearby who are ... Yeah, so I've got a lot of supports around me and they're all aware of everything to do with me. (Brooke, P)

Outcomes and Benefits

Benefits to EwD involve personal and community benefits. Many report having enhanced meaning in their life, greater purpose, opportunities to contribute, increased self-esteem, and a wider range of relationships with people in community spaces. A need shared by these individuals is to be positively regarded for their inherent skills and expertise, and their human potential, rather than being regarded through the lens of their deficits and negative stereotypes. Over half of our respondents identified a desire to benefit the community around them, whether that be providing opportunities for employment, showing that those with disability can contribute eco- nomically and socially in a positive way, and providing role models for other PwD to forge their own journey through life. EwD – like other entrepreneurs in the small and medium-sized business sector – are embedded in family and social relations and net- works, and make business decisions for altruistic as well as personal wealth reasons. Table 3.6 lists the top ten outcomes identified by survey respondents.

Interviewees identified some additional outcomes, such as their autonomy in decision-making, the flexibility afforded by self-employment, and enjoying their new lifestyle: 'I'm very happy with the lifestyle. You know, how are we going to measure lifestyle? If I'd stayed in the banking industry, and just plodded along, and

Table 3.6   *Outcomes of having your own business*

Outcomes	Mean*
I have a sense of purpose	4.53
I have a sense of future	4.29
I now contribute to the community	4.27
I have increased my self esteem	4.11
I now have a better quality of life / I am happy	3.98
I have a larger social network	3.91
I have a job that keeps me employed	3.84
I create employment for others	3.44
I have secured an income stream	3.42
I have turned a profit	3.40

Note: * Mean calculated using Likert scale 1–5 values, where 1 = strongly disagree, 2 = disagree, 3 = neutral, 4 = agree, 5 = strongly agree.
Source: Based on data from Darcy et al. (2021), with permission.

was still there now, I'd be way, way, way better off financially, but that's not the best measure' (Stan, PM).

SUMMARY OF KEY FINDINGS

First, our research has identified the great diversity in EwD business types spread across a wide range of industries in Australia. PwD have a comparative advantage in businesses that relate to their experiences as a PwD. They know the market well and can spot market niches that have not been addressed or have been addressed inadequately. Despite that, half of our informants were directed to business opportunities in the non-disability market. While EwD are concentrated in the healthcare and social assistance, education and training, professional, scientific and technical services, and arts and recreation services industries in Australia, they are not confined to these industries. If the question is 'What is the typical PwD business?', the answer is that there is not one.

Second, this research also shows that men and women with a range of disabilities in Australia have set up their own businesses to move into entrepreneurship. Those with an intellectual disability have the lowest rate of entrepreneurship amongst PwD (9.0 per cent), but this is only slightly below the average rate of entrepreneurship in Australia (9.2 per cent). People from all other disability types have a higher rate of entrepreneurship than average: sensory and speech (10.9 per cent), head injury, stroke or brain damage (15 per cent), physical/mobility (15.3 per cent) psychological (16.2 per cent) and other (15 per cent).

Third, gender is an important aspect of PwD entrepreneurship. Across Australia the rate of female entrepreneurship is significantly lower than male entrepreneurship: in 2016, 33 per cent of all business owner managers in Australia were female (ABS, 2018), with the rate increasing much faster than for male entrepreneurship. Many women with disability also enter entrepreneurship, though there is a gap in research into their experiences. In the qualitative research conducted for this research grant, female informants (54 per cent) outnumbered male informants (46 per cent). In future work we will examine female EwD in more detail.

Fourth, the research identified the major barriers that our EwD informants experienced in setting up and running their businesses. In declining order of importance, the barriers identified were financial constraints, lack of capital, uncertainty about the future, financial dependents, physical access to spaces and places, and lack of confidence. While the first two barriers are common to all those who start up a business, the final four are influenced strongly by the social ecology of disability in Australia today. Policies designed to support existing EwD and encourage other PwD to set up a business should include innovative responses to addressing these barriers.

Fifth, the research identified the major reasons that motivated our PwD informants to set up their own business. Like most small business start-ups, the desire to 'be my own boss' was most important. The next most important factor reported by our informants was 'to help others'. This is a striking finding, since economic theory focuses almost exclusively on individual wealth maximisation as the sole motivator for businesses in the capitalist market economy. Our EwD informants were equally driven to assist others as they were to help themselves. The other motivating factors were to have a flexible work schedule and lifestyle, to develop new skills and achieve financial success.

Sixth, the outcomes for PwD that emerge from acting on the risky task of creating jobs for themselves by starting up a business have been revealed by this research project. EwD report that they have a sense of purpose, a sense of the future, and now contribute to the community. Increased self-esteem and a better quality of life accompany their move into entrepreneurship. They report a larger social network by creating jobs for themselves and others, and a more secure income stream.

Seventh, given these strong outcomes of PwD moving into entrepreneurship, policies designed to assist more PwD generate significant economic and social dividends. Few PwD have drawn on existing, mainstream, entrepreneurship start-up or business accelerator programs to assist them setting up their own business. We have identified an important gap in the space of disability entrepreneurship start-up programs.[2]

Finally, while the research identified the barriers that PwD face when deciding to set up their own business in Australia an overemphasis on the barriers that PwD face can lead to a deficit model approach to PwD entrepreneurship, one that focuses more on what they cannot do and less on what they can do: their agency, determination and ability to overcome the barriers. This helps to explain what we can call the apparent paradox of disability entrepreneurship in Australia today: PwD face very high barriers, yet they have much greater rates of entrepreneurship than other Australians. This is an apparent paradox, because once attention moves to the agency of PwD and their abilities to overcome constraints in their lives, their higher rate of entrepreneurship becomes explained.

It is fitting that we conclude the chapter with the words of the lived experience of one of our entrepreneurs (Box 3.2).

BOX 3.2 A PERSONAL STORY: FROM A CHILDHOOD SPINAL CORD INJURY TO A GLOBAL BUSINESS IN ASSISTIVE TECHNOLOGY

I was injured in 1963 in a motor vehicle accident which left me a paraplegic. There was very little rehab and there was probably a little less expectation on people with disabilities back then in terms of life outcome, social participation and even longevity. I'm very lucky because I was a pretty mobile kid. I was the fastest kid in the wheelchair, and I was able to get around. When I left school, I did business studies there and then a short course in computing. I now work for myself as a private business consultant specialising in helping businesses and associations involved in the supply of assistive technology (aids and equipment). Throughout my working life, the only modification I have needed was the installation of hand controls in my motor vehicle to allow me to get to and from my workplace. I also own a pair of portable hand controls so I can drive hire cars when required. To this day when I meet new people, they're astounded to know I'm married to an able-bodied woman and then they're stunned that I've worked all my life. This is truly surprising whereas to me the assumption should be well, why shouldn't you work? Having a job is a major enabler of all facets of my life. The income I earn enables me to enjoy a much higher standard of living, it allows me to connect and interact with a broad range of people. Through my work I travel and build relationships and self-esteem. I also feel proud that I am earning a wage and paying tax in Australia rather than having to survive on government payments. (Don, PM)

ACKNOWLEDGEMENTS

First, we would like to thank all those entrepreneurs with disability who contributed their time to answer the survey and be interviewed. Second, we thank Barbara Almond, who assisted with the research data collection and report preparation. Third, we would like to dedicate this chapter to John Moxon who was a noted disability advocate, public servant and self-employed consultant, who was also featured in the video vignettes on the website as he passed away 5 September 2022 after a battle with COVID-19. Lastly, we thank the funding body of the Australian Research Council Linkage Grant Program (LP160100697) with the support of industry partners National Disability Services, Settlement Services International and BreakThru People Solutions. The original research reports on which this chapter is based, Darcy et al. (2020, 2021), were published on the project website together with other resources: https://www.uts.edu.au/about/uts-business-school/management/projects/disability-entrepreneurship.

NOTES

1. ARC Linkage Grant (2016-18) LP 160100697 'Disability Entrepreneurship in Australia'.
2. An exception is the SSI IgniteAbility program https://www.ssi.org.au/services/disability -services/ignite-ability-small-business-start-ups.

REFERENCES

Acs, Z.J., Stam, E., Audretsch, D.B., and O'Connor, A. (2017). The lineages of the entrepreneurial ecosystem approach. *Small Business Economics*, *49*(1), 1–10.

Alaslani, M., and Collins, J. (2017). The blocked mobility hypothesis and muslim immigrant entrepreneurship in Sydney, Australia. *Review of Integrative Business and Economics Research*, *6*(3), 333–357.

Australian Bureau of Statistics (ABS) (2012). *4433.0.55.006 Disability and Labour Force Participation, 2012*. Retrieved 1 November 2018 from http://www.abs.gov.au/ausstats/abs@.nsf/mf/4433.0.55.006.

Australian Bureau of Statistics (ABS) (2015). *4430.0 – Disability, Ageing and Carers, Australia: Summary of Findings, 2015*. Retrieved 1 November from http://www.abs.gov.au/ausstats/abs@.nsf/Latestproducts/4430.0Main%20Features202015.

Australian Bureau of Statistics (ABS) (2017). *2071.0 Census of Population and Housing: Reflecting Australia – Stories from the Census, 2016*. Canberra: Australian Bureau of Statistics.

Australian Bureau of Statistics (ABS) (2018). *Business Owner Managers across Australia*. Canberra: Australian Bureau of Statistics.

Australian Bureau of Statistics (ABS) (2019). *4430.0 – Disability, Ageing and Carers, Australia: Summary of Findings, 2018, 2020*. https://www.abs.gov.au/Ausstats/abs@.nsf/0/0CD3AF801A5AF108CA25804F000F61FB?OpenDocument.

Australian Government (2018). Centrelink. Retrieved 1 November 2018 from https://www.humanservices.gov.au/individuals/centrelink.

Block, J., Kohn, K., Miller, D., and Ullrich, K. (2015). Necessity entrepreneurship and competitive strategy. *Small Business Economics*, *44*(1), 37–54.

Boylan, A., and Burchardt, T. (2002). *Barriers to Self-Employment for Disabled People. Report for the Small Business Services*. London: Department of Trade and Industry.

Brewer, J., and Gibson, S. (eds) (2014). *Necessity Entrepreneurs: Microenterprise Education and Economic Development*. Cheltenham, UK and Northampton, MA, USA: Edward Elgar Publishing.

Charlton, J.I. (1998). *Nothing About Us Without Us: Disability Oppression and Empowerment*. Berkeley, CA: University of California Press.

Chevalier, S., Fouquereau, E., Gillet, N., and Demulier, V. (2013). Development of the Reasons for Entrepreneurs' Retirement Decision Inventory (RERDI) and preliminary evidence of its psychometric properties in a French sample. *Journal of Career Assessment*.

Collins, J., and Low, A. (2010). Asian female immigrant entrepreneurs in small and medium-sized businesses in Australia. *Entrepreneurship and Regional Development*, *22*(1), 97–111.

Collins, J., Morrison, M., Basu, P.K., and Krivokapic-Skoko, B. (2017). Indigenous culture and entrepreneurship in small businesses in Australia. *Small Enterprise Research*, *24*(1), 36–48.

Collins, J., and Norman, H. (2018). Indigenous entrepreneurship and indigenous employment in Australia. *Journal of Australian Political Economy*, 82, 149–170.

Collins, J., and Shin, J. (2014). Korean immigrant entrepreneurs in the Sydney restaurant industry. *Labour and Management in Development Journal*, 15, 1025.

Darcy, S., and Burke, P.F. (2018). On the road again: the barriers and benefits of automobility for people with disability. *Transportation Research Part A: Policy and Practice*, *107*(Supplement C), 229–245.

Darcy, S., Collins, J., and Stronach, M. (2020). *Australia's Disability Entrepreneurial Ecosystem: Experiences of People with Disability with Microenterprises, Self-Employment and Entrepreneurship*. University of Technology Sydney UTS Business School, National Disability Services, Settlement Services International and BreakThru People Solutions.

Darcy, S., Collins, J., and Stronach, M. (2021). *Australia's Disability Entrepreneurial Ecosystem: Experiences of People with Disability with Microenterprises, Self-Employment and Entrepreneurship – Report 2 Policy and Organisational Level Initiatives*. University of Technology Sydney UTS Business School, National Disability Services, Settlement Services International and BreakThru People Solutions.

Darcy, S., Collins, J., and Stronach, M. (2022). Entrepreneurs with disability: Australian insights through a social ecology lens. *Small Enterprise Research*, published online 13 July 2022 in Latest Articles, pp. 1–25, https://doi.org/10.1080/13215906.2022.2092888.

Darcy, S., Lock, D., and Taylor, T. (2017). Enabling inclusive sport participation: effects of disability and support needs on constraints to sport participation. *Leisure Sciences*, *39*(1), 20–41.

Darcy, S., Taylor, T., and Green, J. (2016). 'But I can do the job': examining disability employment practice through human rights complaint cases. *Disability and Society*, *31*(9), 1242–1274.

Darcy, S., Yerbury, H., and Maxwell, H. (2019). Disability citizenship and digital capital: engagement with a social enterprise telco. *Information, Communication and Society*, *22*(4), 538–553.

Department of Social Services (2020a). Disability and carers. https://www.dss.gov.au/our-responsibilities/disability-and-carers/programmes-services/disability-employment-services.

Department of Social Services (2020b). Disability and carers: employment for people with disability. Retrieved 10 March 2020 from https://www.dss.gov.au/disability-and-carers-programs-services-for-people-with-disability/employment-for-people-with-disability.

Devine, A., Vaughan, C., Kavanagh, A., Dickinson, H., Byars, S., et al. (2020). 'I'm proud of how far I've come. I'm just ready to work': mental health recovery narratives within the context of Australia's Disability Employment Services. *BMC Public Health*, *20*(1), 325.

Fair Work Ombudsman (2020). Employees with disability pay rates. Retrieved 1 November 2020 from https://www.fairwork.gov.au/pay-and-wages/minimum-wages/employees-with-disability-pay-rates.

Foster, D., and Wass, V. (2013). Disability in the labour market: an exploration of concepts of the ideal worker and organisational fit that disadvantage employees with impairments. *Sociology*, *47*(4), 705–721.

Jack, S.L., and Anderson, A.R. (2002). The effects of embeddedness on the entrepreneurial process. *Journal of Business Venturing*, *17*(5), 467–487.

Jammaers, E., and Williams, J. (2020). Turning disability into a business: entrepreneurs with disabilities' anomalous bodily capital. *Academy of Management Proceedings*, *2020*(1), 19091.

Jammaers, E., and Williams, J. (2021). Care for the self, overcompensation and bodily crafting: the work–life balance of disabled people. *Gender, Work and Organization*, *28*(1), 119–137.

Maritz, A., and Laferriere, R. (2016). Entrepreneurship and self-employment for people with disabilities. *Australian Journal of Career Development*, *25*(2), 45–54.

McCall, L. (2005). The complexity of intersectionality. *Signs: Journal of Women in Culture and Society*, *30*(3), 1771–1800.

Meyer, V., Pakura, S., and Seidel, V. (2021). Engaging with entrepreneurial diversity: an intersectional framework. *International Journal of Entrepreneurial Venturing*, *13*(3), 288–318.

NDIS (2020a). Let's talk about work. Retrieved 1 November 2020 from https://www.ndis.gov.au/participants/finding-keeping-and-changing-jobs/lets-talk-about-work.

NDIS (2020b). Participant Employment Strategy. https://www.ndis.gov.au/about-us/strategies/participant-employment-strategy.

ODEP (2014). Self-employment for people with disabilities. Washington, DC: United States Department of Labor.

Oliver, M. (1996). *Understanding Disability: From Theory to Practice*. Basingstoke: Macmillan.

Oliver, M. (2004). The social model in action: if I had a hammer? In C. Barnes and G. Mercer (eds), *Implementing the Social Model of Disability: Theory and Research*. Leeds: Disability Press.

Pagán, R. (2009). Self-employment among people with disabilities: evidence for Europe. *Disability and Society*, 24(2), 217–229.

Renko, M., Parker Harris, S., and Caldwell, K. (2016). Entrepreneurial entry by people with disabilities. *International Small Business Journal*, 34(5), 555–578.

Scholz, F., and Ingold, J. (2021). Activating the 'ideal jobseeker': experiences of individuals with mental health conditions on the UK Work Programme. *Human Relations*, 74(10), 1604–1627.

Settlement Services International. (2018). Still outside the tent. https://www.ssi.org.au/images/stories/documents/publications/Still_Outside_the_Tent_Final.pdf.

Stam, E., and van de Ven, A. (2021). Entrepreneurial ecosystem elements. *Small Business Economics*, 56(2), 809–832.

Startup Commons (2021). Startup or entrepreneurial development process. Retrieved 19 October 2021 from https://www.startupcommons.org/startup-development-phases.html.

United Nations (2006). *Convention on the Rights of Persons with Disabilities (CRPD)*. https://www.un.org/development/desa/disabilities/convention-on-the-rights-of-persons-with-disabilities.html.

Veal, A.J., and Darcy, S. (2014). *Research Methods for Sport Studies and Sport Management: A Practical Guide*, 1st edn. Abingdon: Routledge.

Williams, J., and Patterson, N. (2018). New directions for entrepreneurship through a gender and disability lens. *International Journal of Entrepreneurial Behaviour and Research*, 25(8), 1706–1727.

Women with Disabilities Australia (2020). Employment programs for people with disabilities. Retrieved 15 July 2020 from http://wwda.org.au/govtdis/govtdisprogram/employprog1/#:~:text=People%20With%20Disabilities-,Employment%20Programs%20for%20People%20With%20Disabilities,Disability%20Employment%20Services%20(DES).

APPENDIX

Table 3A.1   Typology of in-depth interviewees

	Pseudonym	Gender	Age	State	Disability type	Self-described impairment	Lives with	Supp. needs	M/ status	Children	Type of business
1	Janine	F	31–64	NSW	Mental health	Anxiety	separated	None	partner	1	Entrepreneur/Manager
2	Brooke	F	31–64	ACT	Mental health	Anxiety	family	None	separated	2	Entrepreneur/Managing Director
3	Dave	M	31–64	NSW	Mental health	ASD/SCI	alone	Low	single	0	Sole trader
4	Jenny	F	31–64	NSW	Mental health	ASD/vision	partner	Low	single	0	Sole trader
5	Julianne	F	31–64	NSW	Mental health	Anxiety	family	None	married	2	Nascent Entrepreneur
6	Vern	M	18–30	NSW	Mental health	ASD/ADHD	family	Low	single	0	Nascent Entrepreneur
7	Josie	F	31–64	NSW	Mental health	Anxiety	alone	None	single	0	Nascent Entrepreneur
8	Valerie	F	31–64	NSW	Mental health	Anxiety	alone	None	single	1	Nascent Entrepreneur
9	Adrienne	F	31–64	NSW	Mental health	Anxiety	family	Low	married	6	Sole trader
10	Beatrice	F	31–64	NSW	Mental health	Anxiety	alone	Low	single	0	Nascent Entrepreneur
11	Maurice	M	18–30	NSW	Mental health	ASD/ADHD	family	Low	single	0	Nascent Entrepreneur
12	Janet	F	31–64	NSW	Mental health	Bi-polar	family	Low	single	0	Sole trader
13	Glenys	F	31–64	NSW	Other	Diabetes	family	Low	separated	2	Sole trader
14	Martin	M	31–64	VIC	Other	Fibromyalgia	partner	Low	partner	0	Sole trader
15	Adam	M	65+	NSW	Other	Stroke	alone	Low	single	0	Nascent Entrepreneur
16	Fran	F	31–64	VIC	Other	CBI	alone	Low	single	0	Sole trader
17	Hamish	M	18–30	NSW	Other	MS	alone	Low	single	0	Sole trader
18	Liz	F	31–64	NSW	Other	CHD	spouse	Low	married	0	Entrepreneur/partnership
19	Wendy	F	31–64	NSW	Daughter has ID	IL	family	None	married	2	Sole trader on behalf of daughter
20	Liam	M	31–64	NSW	Sensory/Hearing	Hearing impaired	family	None	married	1	Sole trader
21	Sarah	F	31–64	NSW	Sensory/Hearing	Hearing impaired	alone	Low	single	0	Sole trader
22	Jack	M	31–64	NSW	Sensory/Vision	Vision impaired	partner	Low	partner	0	Sole trader
23	Neal	M	31–64	WA	Sensory/Vision	Vison impaired	spouse	Low	married	2	Sole trader
24	Kenan	M	31–64	SA	Sensory/Speech	CP	partner	Low	partner	0	Sole trader
25	Gregor	M	31–64	NSW	Physical injury	Leg injury	family	None	single	0	Sole trader
26	Pauline	F	31–64	QLD	Physical injury	Leg injury	family	None	married	1	Sole trader
27	Heath	M	18–30	TAS	ID	Congenital condition	family	Low	single	0	Sole trader

	Pseudonym	Gender	Age	State	Disability type	Self-described impairment	Lives with	Supp. needs	M/ status	Children	Type of business
28	Isabel	F	18–30	TAS	ID	Congenital condition	family	Low	single	0	Sole trader
29	Alex	F	18–30	QLD	ID	Congenital condition	family	Low	single	0	Sole trader
30	Dave	M	31–64	NSW	Physical/Mobility	SCI/ABI	family	Medium	married	0	Entrepreneur/Manager
31	Hudson	M	31–64	SA	Physical/Mobility	SCI	spouse	Medium	married	1	Sole trader
32	Bill	M	31–64	NSW	Physical/Mobility	SCI	spouse	Medium	married	3	Entrepreneur/Managing Director
33	Nate	M	31–64	NZ	Physical/Mobility	SCI	spouse	Medium	married	1	Entrepreneur/Managing Director
34	Lillian	F	65+	NSW	Physical/Mobility	Post-polio	alone	Low	single	2	Sole trader
35	Gus	M	65+	NSW	Physical/Mobility	SCI	spouse	Medium	married	3	Entrepreneur/Manager
36	Stan	M	31–64	NSW	Physical/Mobility	SCI	family	Medium	single	0	Sole trader
37	Don	M	31–64	NSW	Physical/Mobility	SCI	spouse	Low	married	0	Entrepreneur/Manager
38	Leigh	M	31–64	NSW	Physical/Mobility	SCI	spouse	Medium	married	2	Sole trader
39	Judy	F	31–64	NSW	Physical/Mobility	SCI	alone	High	single	0	Sole trader
40	Gail	F	31–64	QLD	Physical/Mobility	SCI	spouse	Medium	married	1	Entrepreneur/Manager
41	Lucas	M	31–64	NSW	Physical/Mobility	SCI	spouse	Low	married	0	Entrepreneur/partnership
42	Tom	M	31–64	NSW	Physical/Mobility	SCI	spouse	Medium	married	2	Sole trader
43	Pamela	F	31–64	NSW	Physical/Mobility	Congenital condition	family	Low	single	0	Entrepreneur/Manager
44	Joan	F	31–64	NSW	Physical/Mobility	Congenital condition	alone	Low	divorced	1	Sole trader
45	Taylor	F	31–64	VIC	Physical/Mobility	ABI	alone	None	single	0	Sole trader
46	Deanne	F	31–64	NSW	Physical/Mobility	Amputee	partner	Medium	single	0	Sole trader
47	Ivana	F	31–64	TAS	Physical/Mobility	Degenerative cond	alone	Medium	single	1	Entrepreneur/partnership
48	Kate	F	31–64	NSW	Physical/Mobility	Degenerative cond	partner	Medium	partner	0	Sole trader
49	Michelle	F	18–30	NSW	Physical/Mobility	Degenerative cond	family	High	single	0	Entrepreneur/partnership
50	Caroline	F	18–30	QLD	Physical Mobility and speech	CP	mother	Low	single	0	Sole Trader
51	Mack	M	31–64	NSW	Physical Mobility	CP	alone	Low	single	0	Entrepreneur/partnership
52	Joe	M	18–30	VIC	Physical Mobility and speech	CP	alone	Medium	single	0	Sole trader

Notes: Abbreviations in full as follows: ASD (autistic spectrum disorder); SCI (spinal cord injury); ADHD (attention deficit hyperactivity disorder); CBI (congenital brain injury); MS (multiple sclerosis); CHD (congenital heart disease); ID (intellectual disability); CP (cerebral palsy); ABI (acquired brain injury).

4. The push and pull of entrepreneurship for individuals with autism spectrum disorder

Eric Patton

His wife now handed him the stack of books that she had accumulated on autism and related disorders … After a few pages, Michael Burry realized that he was no longer reading about his son but about himself … it explained an awful lot about what he did for a living, and how he did it: his obsessive acquisition of hard facts, his insistence on logic, his ability to plow quickly through reams of tedious financial statements. People with Asperger's couldn't control what they were interested in. It was a stroke of luck that his special interest was financial markets and not, say, collecting lawn mower catalogues. (Lewis, 2010: 183)

In the *Big Short*, the bestselling book by Michael Lewis and subsequent Academy Award winning film about the subprime mortgage implosion which caused the 2008 financial crisis, we are introduced to Dr Michael Burry, who was one of the very few people to have seen the crisis coming. His laser-like focus on financial data, especially around the fine print, allowed his company Scion Capital, which he had started with a small inheritance and loans from his family, to reap returns of 489 percent (over $800 million in profit), with $100 million for him personally. This, when most investors were losing a large portion of their savings. Dr Burry's autism spectrum disorder (ASD), a condition typically characterized by hard work, a strong focus on detail, extraordinary memory, and visual learning and thinking (Parr et al., 2013), was a contributing factor in his success.[1] The book also chronicles Dr Burry's difficulties with navigating relationships, his problems connecting with people, and his obsessive nature. Michael Burry's story can be viewed as a shining example of how one can harness a neuro-cognitive disorder into amazing entrepreneurial success. Still, as noted in the opening passage, he was fortunate that his area of interest was very lucrative, as opposed to the mundane. Michael Burry is also clearly on the very high-functioning part of the ASD spectrum. As such, while his story is fantastic, it is one story. As Dr Stephen Shore famously said, "If you've met one person with autism, you've met one person with autism" (Palmer and Shore, 2012). ASD comprises a wide range of people often with different talents, different interests, different ability levels, and who live in very different financial and social circumstances from one another.

One could also say that when anyone has learned about one entrepreneur, then they have only learned about one entrepreneur. Each entrepreneurial endeavor is different, and each entrepreneur has their own story. While research has sought to uncover the positive characteristics that entrepreneurs share, an emerging area of research has focused on the more atypical characteristics that certain entrepreneurs have, which may hinder them in typical employment pursuits but may encourage entrepreneurship.

A specific focus has centered on neuro-cognitive disorders, whereby disorders such as attention deficit and hyperactivity disorder, dyslexia, and obsessive-compulsive disorder (Logan, 2009; Wiklund et al., 2017; Wolfe and Patel, 2017) can represent strengths in entrepreneurship through the ability to hyperfocus or to process visual patterns. The link between disability/different-ability and self-employment has been demonstrated in both the United States and the United Kingdom (Jones and Latreille, 2011). While the current focus on neuro-diversity and entrepreneurship has highlighted the positive nature of this connection (Wiklund et al., 2018), an important question is whether the neuro-diversity–disability–entrepreneurship link is the result of employer discrimination and other barriers that block people from traditional employment, or instead represents a positive voluntary choice of employment that is better suited to the particular needs of a disabled person (Jones and Latreille, 2011).

This chapter explores the factors that make entrepreneurship a viable option for individuals with autism spectrum disorder (ASD). Specifically, drawing on strategic models of entrepreneurship (Hitt et al., 2011), challenge models of entrepreneurship (Miller and Le Breton-Miller, 2017) and social entrepreneurship (Harris et al., 2013), both pull factors which lead ASD individuals to seek entrepreneurial opportunities, and push factors, which make entrepreneurship and small business among the few options for ASD workers to find employment will be underlined.

Throughout, an underlying social belief is that beyond financial success, participation in economic activity and the dignity of work are fundamental expressions of humanity. As highlighted by Roux et al. (2013), employment represents a socially normative activity that often occupies the majority of adult lives, is a key component of passage into adulthood, and an important factor in quality of life. Regardless of where any individual falls on the autism spectrum or how/why they become employed through a small business, entrepreneurship can serve as a vital pathway to meaningful work for individuals with autism.

In the following pages, an overview of entrepreneurship is provided with an emphasis on issues important to neuro-diversity. Specifically, in addition to the strategic conceptualization of entrepreneurship, the chapter highlights social entrepreneurship and the concept of challenge/necessity entrepreneurship. Next, employment challenges facing individuals on the autism spectrum are discussed, followed by an exploration of the links between entrepreneurship and ASD. Both push factors (that is, factors that can force ASD individuals into entrepreneurship) and pull factors (that is, factors that make entrepreneurship attractive for ASD individuals) are highlighted. Throughout, stories of entrepreneurship and individuals on the autism spectrum collected through the media and through interviews are presented.

THE DIFFERENT FACES OF ENTREPRENEURSHIP

Teaching and scholarship on any form of diversity always struggles with the need to describe issues subject to stereotypes while being careful not to perpetuate stereotypes. Highlighting the variety within groups is always as important as highlighting similarities within groups and variety between groups. In the same way, it is essential not to oversimplify the idea of entrepreneurship to a single model. An entrepreneurial enterprise can be a multimillion-dollar venture or a small lawn-mowing business; it can be a self-employed independent contractor, or a firm with dozens of employees; it can be service- or product-oriented; it can be for-profit or have more of a social mission; it can be a family business or have no family component.

Strategic Entrepreneurship

In what might be considered the traditional or strategic form, Hitt et al. (2011) point to Davidsson (2005) as offering a strong definition of entrepreneurial activity in three parts: "(1) entrepreneurship is starting and running one's own firm; (2) entrepreneurship is the creation of new organizations; and (3) entrepreneurship is … the creation of new-to-the-market economic activity" (Davidsson, 2005: 80). Hitt et al. (2011) also define the traditional entrepreneurial mindset as composed of alertness, real-option reasoning, and opportunity recognition, which facilitates quickly identifying and exploiting opportunities, regardless of uncertainty. In terms of individuals with neuro-cognitive conditions such as ASD, as described in the next section, such traditional entrepreneurial activities are not out of bounds if the conditions are right. The opening story of this chapter about Dr Michael Burry is one example.

Social Entrepreneurship

As noted above, one of the important variations within entrepreneurship is in the desired outcomes and goals of its entrepreneurs. While profit, innovation, and wealth are what most people think of when they consider entrepreneurship, not all entrepreneurial organizations share these goals. Whereas entrepreneurship as a discipline focuses on the emergence of new organizations and innovations, social entrepreneurship, as a subfield of entrepreneurship, is defined as an innovative social value-creating activity with a goal of addressing unmet societal need, and an objective of financial sustainability (Austin et al., 2012; Mair and Martí, 2006). Social entrepreneurs establish enterprises primarily to meet social objectives rather than solely to generate personal financial profit (Dacin et al., 2010).

The literature suggests that some of the most successful social entrepreneurs solve problems that they have personally experienced by using their familiarity with economic and social problems to inspire relevant and effective strategies (Shaw and Carter, 2007; Zahra et al., 2009). Subsequently, people with disabilities may be uniquely positioned to become social entrepreneurs. Furthermore, social entrepreneurs can have as a goal to employ and/or serve less powerful social groups, such as those with physical or neuro-cognitive disabilities.

Challenge/Necessity Entrepreneurship

A third form of entrepreneurship that exists, and may be particularly relevant to ASD individuals, has been called challenge or necessity entrepreneurship (Miller and Le Breton-Miller, 2017). An underlying assumption of most entrepreneurship, including both the strategic model and the social entrepreneurship model, is that engaging in entrepreneurial activity is voluntary. Another reality is that many people who would like to have a traditional employer–employee relationship are blocked out of employment opportunities. In such cases, self-employment becomes one of the few options available.

Miller and Le Breton-Miller (2017) highlight research showing that those who start and run their own businesses are overrepresented among people who have difficulty finding jobs such as immigrants (Hart and Acs, 2011), those with neuro-cognitive disorders (Dimic and Orlov, 2014; Logan, 2009), and the physically disabled (Pagán, 2009).

The forces highlighted by Miller and Le Breton-Miller (2017) that push individuals into entrepreneurship are entirely, or very largely, beyond the control of the individual concerned. Bias and discrimination make traditional career paths difficult to achieve. Unfortunately, those with cognitive problems confront failure, fear and ridicule, and immigrants may find themselves ostracized or out of place in their new surroundings, while those with physical disabilities may be objects of curiosity or unwelcome pity as they grapple with everyday life (Miller and Le Breton-Miller, 2017). Pagán (2009) notes that self-employment has commonly served as a safety valve where victims of discrimination (for example, women, racial minorities or people with disabilities) can find jobs. In fact, Jones and Latreille (2011) found that the work-limited disabled, in particular, are more likely than other disability groups to class themselves as working for themselves, with nearly 80 percent having no employees. Jones and Latreille (2011) suggest that overrepresentation of the disabled in self-employment may be a rational response to the presence of employer discrimination in the salaried sector.

Beyond bias and discrimination, Miller and Le Breton-Miller (2017) suggest that disadvantaged groups face other barriers to regular employment, such as poor language skills for recent immigrants, lack of required cognitive abilities in certain jobs for individuals with neuro-cognitive disorders, and physical requirements of certain workplaces or jobs that limit the positions that are possible or available for those with physical impairments. As noted by Miller and Le Breton-Miller (2017: 9): "In adulthood, given the need to seek economic support or gainful employment, a challenged population may have to resort to unusual types of work, with self-employment in one's own business establishment becoming an important option." In this vein, Pagán (2009) and Jones and Latreille (2011) suggested that self-employment is a means toward better work–life balance for individuals with disabilities, as they themselves can create their own accommodations, set their own schedules, and design their own work environment.

Entrepreneurship as a Spectrum Phenomenon

Overall, entrepreneurship is also something of a spectrum phenomenon. Entrepreneurial activities can be encouraged by positive, proactive forces that pull individuals to deliberately choose self-employment to fulfill their desires; or by negative forces or constraints that push individuals into self-employment out of necessity. Furthermore, there are few limits to the types of activities that entrepreneurs can engage in, and these activities can be aimed at wealth or profit maximization, or bettering society. The rest of this chapter will examine how two complex spectrum phenomena, entrepreneurship and autism spectrum disorder, may interact.

THE CHALLENGES AND OPPORTUNITIES OF ENTREPRENEURSHIP AND ASD

According to the Centers for Disease Control and Prevention (2015), one in every 50 to 68 children in the United States is diagnosed with autism, with an estimated 500 000 young adults on the autism spectrum expected to join the workforce in the next decade (Chu, 2015; Johnson and Joshi, 2016). How can entrepreneurship represent a way forward for millions of ASD individuals who are willing and able to work?

The 2013 fifth edition of the *Diagnostic and Statistical Manual of Mental Disorders* (American Psychiatric Association, 2013: 31) defines ASD as follows: "A neuro-developmental disorder that is characterized by persistent deficits in social communication and social interaction across multiple contexts, including deficits in social reciprocity, non-verbal communicative behaviors used for social interactions, and skills in developing, maintaining and understanding relationships." Consistent with the concept of a spectrum, there is a wide range of severity levels within the ASD umbrella. While every individual case is different, the three primary characteristics of the disorder for highly functioning individuals on the autism spectrum concern: (1) difficulties with social interactions; (2) difficulty in verbal and non-verbal communication; and (3) a pattern of ritualized and repetitive behaviors (American Psychiatric Association, 2013; Hendrickx, 2008; World Health Organization, 2013). In terms of social interactions, individuals on the spectrum often have difficulty initiating conversations, may not respond when called by name or spoken to directly, may not respond or take an interest in the feelings or preferences of others, may not respond to praise, have difficulty comforting others, and may have an aversion to physical contact with others. From a communications perspective, individuals on the autism spectrum often have difficulty with a range of issues, including pragmatic language, difficulty in expressing wants and needs, and clarification when misunderstood. ASD people may also speak with unusual volume, pitch, and rhythm; they may have great difficulty in understanding the nuances of sarcasm, idioms, and humor; and often fail when it comes to making eye contact and understanding facial expressions and body language. Individuals on the autism spectrum may exhibit ritualized behavior, follow routines very tightly, resist change or unplanned events to an excessive degree, adopt rule-bound and inflexible thinking, and repetitively question and speak on the same topic.

Although these factors make success in the workplace a challenge, individuals on the autism spectrum also have a great deal to offer employers. Workers with ASD are generally very hardworking, detail-oriented, and have an extraordinary memory; are visual learners and thinkers; are very loyal, honest, perseverant, and reliable; are non-judgmental; and are highly skilled in particular areas (Parr et al., 2013). In line with the general characteristics of ASD, they are also willing to do repetitive work and are able to develop a high level of expertise in narrow and specialized areas (Austin and Pisano, 2017; Wright, 2016). Many ASD individuals have above-average intelligence (Austin and Pisano, 2017; Parr et al., 2013).

Despite the fact that the United States, Canada, the United Kingdom, the European Union, and Australia have enacted legislation to protect workers with neuro-cognitive disorders such as ASD, and although several high-profile companies such as SAP, Hewlett Packard, Microsoft, Willis Towers Watson, Ford, and Ernst & Young are actively implementing programs to hire ASD individuals (Austin and Pisano, 2017), the employment statistics for individuals on the spectrum are deeply troubling. The National Autistic Society (2016) estimates that 85 percent of individuals with autism are unemployed, including 80 percent of individuals with the highest-functioning level of autism (Austin and Pisano, 2017; Barnard et al., 2001; Parr et al., 2013). Of those who are employed, underemployment in low-level, unskilled jobs not corresponding to their intelligence and abilities is another common phenomenon (Bjelland et al., 2010). According to Roux et al. (2013), young adults with an ASD fare worse on the job market compared to other types of disabilities. In another empirical study of young adults with ASD, Wei et al. (2018) found that, compared to other young adults with different disabilities, ASD youth were less likely to seek paid employment, more likely to spend a long time searching for a job, less likely to attempt to or to be successful at finding a job on their own, and less likely to have been employed since leaving high school. Given these difficulties and the skill level versus employment rate discrepancy for individuals with ASD, entrepreneurship may be a viable pathway to employment for those on the spectrum. Indeed, Harris et al. (2013) report that, over the course of the last decade, people with disabilities have chosen self-employment over traditional employment options at a higher rate than the general population. With that in mind, what are the push and pull factors that may influence a foray into entrepreneurship? Both theoretical work on organizational behavior and human resource management, as well as the stories of entrepreneurs as reported in the popular press and in interviews, can shed light on this question. In terms of the stories, they are from seven sources: three articles on ASD entrepreneurs (Ansberry, 2017; Morel, 2012; Rosenberg, 2014), two articles about family members who have created small businesses to employ their ASD family members (Stolman, 2018; French-Dunbar, 2016), and interviews with two entrepreneurs (C.S. and D.M. for confidentiality) who have started ASD-focused businesses.

PUSH FACTORS FOR ASD INDIVIDUALS AND ENTREPRENEURSHIP

As noted by Ng and Arndt (2019), strictly medically based lenses of disability frame an individual's impairment as "tragic" or as a defect. Alternatively, the social model emphasizes environmental, structural, and attitudinal barriers that impaired people must overcome. While this conceptualization is more positive, as it contains the underlying assumption that disabilities can indeed be overcome and are more perceived differences than defects, the reality that people with physical or neuro-cognitive conditions face is a society founded on "ableist" (able-bodied) perceptions of impaired people's "disabilities" (Williams and Patterson, 2019). For neuro-diverse populations, the dominant norms are centered on neuro-typical people, which can pose difficulties for individuals with ASD by pushing them into self-employment out of necessity.

Discrimination and Low Expectations

As a neuro-cognitive condition, ASD and those who live with it are subject to discrimination and fears based on social stigmas. A stigma represents a social phenomenon in which a person's social identity does not fit an expected social identity in a particular context (Goffman, 1963). As highlighted by many researchers (Newheiser and Barreto, 2014; Russinova et al., 2011; Stone and Colella, 1996), individuals with neurological and psychological disorders are often perceived to be incompetent, unintelligent, awkward, cold, unsociable, and hypersensitive, and are subject to fears about aggressiveness and being potentially dangerous. The result of these perceptions is a generalized fear on the part of managers about the behavior of employees with neurological and psychological disorders (Freeman et al., 2004), and expectations of poor performance (Erickson et al., 2014; Santuzzi et al., 2014). Russinova et al. (2011) found that individuals with neurological and psychological disorders were subject to insensitive language, patronizing and condescending remarks, and social exclusion. Schur (2003) found discrimination to be an important explanation of higher self-employment rates among the disabled, while Pagán (2009) notes that self-employment may be the only option to be integrated into the labor market, and to increase their well-being and income levels. This view follows Baldwin and Johnson's (1995) finding that discrimination against disabled people was more intense for those impairments or limitations that are subject to greater prejudice by employers (for example, persons with mental health problems).

While individuals at the lower-functioning end of the ASD spectrum will be particularly subject to these negative perceptions, individuals on the higher-functioning end of the spectrum are also disadvantaged. For example, Richards (2012) found that individuals with Asperger's faced exclusion in the workplace; while Johnson and Joshi (2016) suggest that milder versions of neuro-cognitive disorders, such as high-functioning ASD, may be more publicly stigmatized than severe forms of mental disorders, as these individuals will not have an obvious neuro-cognitive condition and may be perceived as simply being difficult, antisocial, or rude. From the social perspective, severe and obvious impairments may generate sympathy, while less-severe and less-obvious conditions may be contested in terms of how "real" each condition is (Conrad and Barker, 2010).

Accounts of entrepreneurs and autism demonstrate challenges regardless of where the individual lies on the autism spectrum. A feature for the Associated Press (Rosenberg, 2014), on an autistic entrepreneur named Matt Cottle who had opened a successful bakery and catering business, noted that when he worked at a grocery store and asked his boss to let him work in the supermarket's bakery, he was told he would never do anything more than collect grocery carts. When he did gain employment at a bakery, he encountered people who did not understand him, and who ended up yelling at and insulting him. Upon disclosure of his condition to other potential employers, and explanations that he would need more time to understand instructions, companies would either refuse to make accommodations or would assume that he might do or say inappropriate things. Another feature of disabled entrepreneurship (on entreprenurship.com, Stolman, 2018) explained that many parents created entrepreneurial ventures for their children who otherwise would be limited to jobs as baggers in grocery stores, or unsanitary manual labor jobs, but had more to offer. A story in the *Wall Street Journal* (Ansberry, 2017) on an autistic entrepreneur named Chris Tidmarsh, who has university degrees in chemistry, environmental studies, and French, reported that he lost a promising job as an environmental researcher due to social and communication problems. For these individuals on the spectrum, entrepreneurship represented a pathway to get beyond typically problematic social judgments.

Interviewing and Selection

The social interaction characteristics of individuals on the ASD spectrum make the interview process a true barrier to employment. Before they can even demonstrate their skills and excellent work habits, they are often derailed at the moment of first encounter with employers. Interviewing practices that place an emphasis on eye contact and small talk represent a dead end for both ASD workers and employers. Grooming can also be an issue with neuro-diverse individuals (Dipeolu et al., 2015), and this issue can further complicate first contact in interviews. Drawing on a meta-analysis by Ren et al. (2008) and other research, Erickson et al. (2014) suggest that the concept of employee–organization "fit" in hiring practices severely hinders applicants with disabilities in the selection process, as fit criteria are not conducive to the differently abled. While avant-garde companies interested in engaging with ASD workers are using alternatives to interviews to tap ASD talent such as work samples, trial runs, individual and team games and projects using building and construction materials, and also offer training and support for neuro-diverse applicants and employees (Chu, 2015; Hurley-Hanson and Giannantonio, 2017), most neuro-typical workplace individuals are not adequately informed about neuro-minorities. Unfortunately, the unstructured and social-style interview is an established ritual in the corporate world that has a truly adverse impact on neuro-diverse populations. This, despite the fact that strong evidence exists that a more structured interview and selection process yields better outcomes for neuro-typical candidates (Rynes et al., 2002; Schmidt and Hunter, 1998). For neuro-diverse workers, traditional interview practices contribute to the high unemployment rate and represent a push factor towards self-employment.

Actual Skill Deficiencies and Lack of Preparation

Not all challenges result from discrimination or social interaction issues. Depending on the nature and severity of an individual's ASD, certain jobs may not be feasible or desirable for people on the spectrum. The feature stories on autistic entrepreneurs noted in the opening quote portray this reality. In the case of Eileen Parker (Morel, 2012), her issues with sitting in chairs, working at a computer, and decoding and prioritizing sounds in crowded environments, made it difficult to hold down a job. For Chris Tidmarsh (Ansberry, 2017) and Matt Cottle (Rosenberg, 2014), difficulties with verbal communication are true limitations, which in the case of Chris led to serious problems in a traditional employment setting. Furthermore, the education system, which in many ways is more advanced in accommodating neuro-diversity than workplaces, nevertheless appears often to set low expectations for students with ASD. In Stolman's (2018) feature on parents creating companies for their ASD children, one parent commented that the education system was letting ASD children down, stating: "They don't believe in the kids, they don't believe in their capabilities. In most countries, they're not being educated, they're being trained" (ibid.: para. 24). Another mother from a different part of the United States noted that ASD students, at some point as they age, receive fewer programs tied to special education: "The jobs these kids were sampling and training at included packing toiletries for prisoners and wiping down tables with harsh chemicals. It smelled terrible. The adults supervising and supposedly training the students were not interacting with them. The kids wanted to connect though. It broke my heart. I said 'not my kid'" (ibid.: para. 14). Interviews conducted for this chapter also confirmed that parents worry about their child's lack of preparation around employment. C.S. (initials used for confidentiality), noted that she and her husband were extremely worried about their ASD son's prospects after high school. While their son's high school was supportive from an educational standpoint, they were not equipped or oriented to prepare special needs teens for employment. The result was C.S. creating a pet-sitting business for her son. Both C.S. and another interviewee, D.M., noted that the limitations of ASD individuals make entrepreneurship necessary, as jobs and firms can be tailored to abilities, rather than attempting to change the ASD person to fit an organizational position.

Systemic Issues

Overall, there are systemic issues around bias and discrimination, common work-place practices around interviewing and selection, deficiencies in the education system, and actual skill issues that push individuals with ASD into entrepreneurship out of necessity. At the same time, there are other factors which make entrepreneurship an attractive option rather than an only or last resort.

PULL FACTORS FOR ASD INDIVIDUALS AND ENTREPRENEURSHIP

Many manifestations of ASD are, in fact, well aligned with the characteristics of successful entrepreneurs. Certain common characteristics of individuals on the spectrum—such as being very hardworking and detail-oriented; very loyal, honest, perseverant, reliable, and non-judgmental; and having extraordinary memory and above average intelligence (Austin and Pisano, 2017; Parr et al., 2013)—are valuable in any employment circumstance. Austin and Pisano (2017) underline that such neuro-diverse employees should be viewed as differently abled rather than disabled. In her profile of companies such as SAP, HP, and Freddie Mac that hire ASD workers in high-skilled and high-paying technical jobs, such as management specialists and proofreaders, Wright (2016) quotes managers who underline that integrating these workers is not a form of charity, but a strategic business decision. One business owner with ASD workers representing over 70 percent of his workers commented: "Very quickly, you realize that our employees tend to bring to the table the qualities of a good worker without the negatives of a bad worker. No drinking, coming in late, smoking etc., very timely and follow directions to the T" (Stolman, 2018: para. 9). While these characteristics would be valued in any organization, certain other manifestations of ASD and social factors relating to these individuals represent true pull factors towards entrepreneurship.

Hyperfocus and Specialized Skills

Thinking and acting differently, and going against the grain, are common characteristics of entrepreneurs (Mullins, 2017). Furthermore, the ability to think very narrowly and serve markets deemed too insignificant for large corporations has been a proven path to success for many entrepreneurial firms (Cooper, 2008; Mullins, 2017). The think differently–narrow focus combination represents a strong pull factor for ASD entrepreneurs.

For example, in addition to her ASD, Eileen Parker has a form of sensory disorder, which led her to create the firm Cozy Calm specializing in heavy blankets (Morel, 2012). Working with professional sewers and hiring a small staff, Ms Parker's products found a market through medical supply stores and hospitals. Her sales tripled in a single year after the founding of her company. Her product was a result of her own medical conditions. ASD entrepreneur Chris Tidmarsh of Green Bridge Growers spends hours researching natural and effective pesticides to deal with small insects, while his degree in chemistry matches his ability to perfectly space rows of kale and spinach, and to monitor water chemistry and soil acidity (Ansberry, 2017). Returning to the opening passage of the chapter, Michael Burry's interest and ability to read even the fine print of voluminous financial prospectuses allowed him to recognize patterns that made him a multi-millionaire.

Similarly, there is a growing literature in the entrepreneurship–disability field demonstrating that conditions such as attention deficit and hyperactivity disorder (ADHD), dyslexia, and obsessive compulsive disorder (OCD) can be beneficial for entrepreneurial activity. As highlighted by Antshel (2018), one manifestation of neuro-cognitive disorders that is positively associated with successful entrepreneurship is hyperfocusing:

> The Wiklund et al. proposed model has hyperfocusing attention as a moderator of the relationship between these entrepreneurial actions and outcomes. Hyperfocusing attention is specifically linked to passion, persistence, and time commitment. Over time, hyperfocus leads to expertise that, in turn, further moderates the relationship between entrepreneurial actions and outcomes (Wiklund et al., 2016). (Antshel, 2018: 249)

While Wiklund and his colleagues' work focuses primarily on ADHD, and hyperfocusing is also associated with OCD, the laser-like focus and attention that defines hyperfocusing is a core characteristic of ASD. Hyperfocus combined with specialized skills can thus represent an important pull factor for ASD entrepreneurs. As noted by Dipeolu et al. (2015), students with ASD may have obsessions about particular subjects which, if harnessed properly, can propel them into well-paying careers. In our interview, D.M. also emphasized that ASD workers in his entrepreneurial firms were excellent learners and had increased efficiency in several areas of his firm.

Ability to Shape One's Own Accommodations

As highlighted previously, individuals with ASD are usually covered under the Americans With Disabilities Act and several other pieces of legislation from around the world. Again, underlining the socially constructed aspect of mental health, von Schrader et al. (2014) found that many individuals with disabilities choose non-disclosure of their condition due to a myriad of factors. Clearly, legal protections are not sufficient to ensure accommodations in the workplace. In this vein, Jones and Latreille (2011) suggest that work-limited, disabled people may be better able to 'accommodate' their disability by being able to choose their own duties, hours, and location, which acts as a pull factor that might encourage a disabled individual to be self-employed. In an empirical study on this question, Pagán (2009) investigated whether disabled people use self-employment to achieve a better balance between disability status and working life by selecting specific types of work, determining their own work conditions and environment, and their schedule. Results supported their hypothesis that self-employment may be a valid option for many disabled individuals since it facilitates achieving a better balance between disability status and working life. Principally, Pagán (2009) found that disabled people in the European Union were using self-employment as an option to accommodate their impairment.

As C.S. noted in our interview, ASD individuals can excel in suitable work where their limitations can be turned into collective strengths.

Newspaper and magazine features on ASD entrepreneurs also provide support for these findings. In the case of Eileen Parker, by owning her own business she was able to hire and train her own staff to understand and accommodate her communication problems:

> On a recent trip with a staff member to check out office space, Parker started waving her arms and walking on her toes … 'Sandy, my staff member, picked up on my movements; she knew my autism was getting agitated and that I didn't know how to deal with the situation, Parker says. She knew from my actions that I didn't like the space but just couldn't say it, so she got us out of there'. (Morel, 2012: 11–12)

The ability of other ASD entrepreneurs to delegate certain tasks to accommodate their condition also occurred for baker Matt Cottle and chemist/horticulturalist Chris Tidmarsh. In Mr Cottle's case, given his difficulty with verbal communication and talking over the phone, his mother takes orders and does the marketing (Rosenberg, 2014). For Mr Tidmarsh, his family members handle most of the administrative functions, and Ansberry (2017) notes that for Mr Tidmarsh and others like him:

> By launching their own companies, people on the spectrum can create a work environment that fits their comfort level and doesn't force them to navigate the traditional, heavily social office setting. Very often, though, their key to success is not to try for independence, but to build up a network of supporters who will help them with the business. (ibid.: para. 11)

Overall, the ability to shape one's own workplace is a very proactive and positive pull towards entrepreneurship for individuals on the spectrum. At the same time, the quotations above also point to another important factor that represents a strong pull to entrepreneurship: the commitment and support of family members.

Motivated Family and Supportive Networks

One of the factors that has emerged as important in the ASD employment relationship is family involvement and support. Given that a high proportion of adults with autism live with their parents, companies such as SAP get parents involved in the recruitment and selection phase of employment. In fact, factors related to employment and other outcomes in adults with ASD include intelligence, communication abilities, adaptive functioning level, co-occurring mental health and medical issues, and family socio-economic status (Roux et al., 2013).

While crucial for navigating employment opportunities, parents and family are also indispensable in entrepreneurial activities. In their study on disabled entrepreneurs, Harris et al. (2013) reported that family and friends not only provide a source of information and opportunity, but are also an important source of support and motivation; and all the entrepreneurs with disabilities who they studied agreed that they could not do what they were doing without their support network. The authors also found that families help to provide support in self-employment that typically has not been provided by vocational rehabilitation services.

Specific to ASD, published examples highlight the essential role that parents and family members play. As previously highlighted in the cases of Matt Cottle and Chris Tidmarsh, their family members work side-by-side with them to provide workplace accommodations. Also, a previous passage on the limits of education in preparing ASD individuals for the workplace positioned parents as the key driver for self-employment. In fact, many parents and family members actually create companies with the specific goal of creating employment for their ASD relatives. While the ASD individuals may not be the owners of these companies, family business is a hallmark of entrepreneurship and small entrepreneurial businesses created because of ASD individuals are certainly an important part of the ASD-entrepreneurship reality. For example, mothers Pamela Kattouf and Patricia Miller created Beloved Bath, a soap and candle company, for their teenage boys and others with ASD, some of whom do not have the ability to speak (Stolman, 2018). Stolman also reports the story of Drs Steven and Barbie Bier, owners of Popcorn for the People, who created the company for their son Samuel, who has autism. Samuel's passion for popcorn, combined with the Biers' resolve that their son should have the opportunity to earn a living doing what he loves, motivated them to open the business that now employs 41 employees, 28 of whom are on the ASD spectrum. While the company has a lucrative business making popcorn in noiseless packaging for local theatres and for Rutgers University, the Biers decided that Popcorn for the People would be a non-profit social entrepreneurship organization. The Biers also maintained their medical practices.

Parents are not the only ones creating companies to employ family members. John and Tom D'Eri created the award-winning Rising Tide Car Wash to employ their autistic son/brother, who they knew had much to offer but seemed stuck in a friendless world of video games (French-Dunbar, 2016). According to Yam (2017), 80 percent of the car wash's employees have autism, and while the purpose of the company is ASD employment, the business is highly profitable.

Parents and family of individuals on the spectrum are creating businesses and social entrepreneurship ventures not only to employ their children/family members, but also to serve the ASD community. Jonah Zimiles and his wife decided to open a bookstore, Words, for the sake of their teenage son with ASD. Beyond the retail aspect of selling books, the store also serves as a training program for workers with ASD. Since opening in 2009, the Zimiles family has trained more than 100 people with autism (Stolman, 2018). Similarly, Stolman (2018) reports that ASD parent Moish Tov created Joy Dew, an umbrella organization which includes a foundation and a for-profit arm that provides continuing education, job training, and employment for young adults with ASD. With two sons with ASD, Mr Tov felt compelled to put his entrepreneurial experience into this venture for his boys and the larger ASD community. Explaining the need for Joy Dew, Tov noted that few countries have supportive educational systems that educate ASD individuals, rather they merely train them for menial jobs: "Schools don't believe in them. I was naïve enough to believe someone figured out what to do. There is no program. I have to build it" (Stolman, 2018: para. 24).

Interviewee D.M. explained that his ice cream business that employs ASD individuals is primarily concerned with providing funds for an ASD foundation, and that the company is partnering with the local high school to prepare its students for the future. Similarly, interviewee C.S. started her pet-sitting business for her son with ASD, but has also partnered with local organizations and schools to recruit other individuals with ASD.

Consistent with Harris et al. (2013), it is important to note the families featured above have sufficient income and wealth to create these businesses. This, of course, is not the case for every ASD family. As such, beyond family, several organizations—such as https://the-art-of-autism.com/sponsors/directory-of-programsstudios/—have programs to help ASD individuals to start their own businesses. These organizations are also an important pull for ASD individuals to engage in entrepreneurial activities.

CONCLUSION

In the end, there are both push and pull reasons why individuals with ASD take an entrepreneurship route. However, through the stories of actual entrepreneurs and the growing awareness of the strengths associated with ASD, and the human goal of finding meaningfulness through employment, the positive aspects seem to emerge as most important. Barriers and discrimination do exist for neuro-minorities, but the ability to shape one's own work environment, benefit from a supportive network, and pursue activities one is passionate about, are reasons enough to engage in entrepreneurial activities. In fact, while the challenge model/push notion of entrepreneurship often positions entrepreneurship as a first step in securing a desired job with a firm, there is evidence that individuals with neuro-cognitive disorders, once they find their preferred area of interest, will stick with their entrepreneurial firm as their desired destination (Lerner et al., 2019). If "fit" blocks individuals with ASD and other neuro-cognitive conditions out of regular employment (Erickson et al., 2014), "fit" may be what makes entrepreneurship the employment solution for this population. The grassroots solutions and stories presented in this chapter represent a growing wave of ASD entrepreneurship in our economy. It is a great developing story. As noted by Hitt et al. (2011), successful entrepreneurs always benefit from a good story.

NOTE

1.   Michael Burry has Asperger's, which is an ASD condition.

REFERENCES

American Psychiatric Association (2013). *Diagnostic and Statistical Manual of Mental Disorders* (5th edn). Washington, DC.

Ansberry, C. (2017, November 27). An entrepreneur with autism finds his own path: for Chris Tidmarsh, the key is building a support network to help execute his vision. *Wall Street Journal*. https://ezproxy.sju.edu/login?url=https://www-proquest-com.ezproxy.sju.edu/doc view/1968298910?accountid=14071.

Antshel, K.M. (2018). Attention Deficit/Hyperactivity Disorder (ADHD) and entrepreneurship. *Academy of Management Perspectives*, *32*, 243–265.

Austin, J., Stevenson, H., and Wei-Skillern, J. (2012). Social and commercial entrepreneurship: same, different, or both? *Revista de Administração*, *47*, 370–384.

Austin, R.D., and Pisano G.P. (2017). Neurodiversity as a competitive advantage. *Harvard Business Review*, *95*, 96–103.

Baldwin, M.L., and Johnson, W.G. (1995). Labor market discrimination against women with disabilities. *Industrial Relations*, *34*, 555–577.

Barnard, J., Harvey, V., Potter, D., and Prior, A. (2001). *The Reality for Adults with Autism Spectrum Disorders*. London: National Autistic Society.

Bjelland, M.J., Bruyère, S.M., von Schrader, S., Houtenville, A.J., Ruiz-Quintanilla, A., and Webber, D.A. (2010). Age and disability employment discrimination: occupational rehabilitation implications. *Journal of Occupational Rehabilitation*, *20*, 456–471.

Centers for Disease Control and Prevention (2015, February 26). Autism spectrum disorder: data and statistics. Retrieved from http://www.cdc .gov/ncbddd/autism/data.html.

Chu, F. (2015). Making it work. *Inc. Magazine*, June, p. 34.

Conrad, P., and Barker, K.K. (2010). The social construction of illness: key insights and policy implications. *Journal of Health and Social Behavior*, *51*, S67–S79.

Cooper, R.G. (2008). Perspective: the stage-gate idea-to-launch process—update, what's new, and nexgen systems. *Journal of Product Innovation Management*, *25*, 213–232.

Dacin, P.A., Dacin, M.T., and Matear, M. (2010). Social entrepreneurship: why we don't need a new theory and how we move forward from here. *Academy of Management Perspectives*, *24*, 37–57.

Davidsson, P. (2005). *Researching Entrepreneurship*. New York: Springer.

Dimic, N., and Orlov, V. (2014). Entrepreneurial tendencies among people with ADHD. *International Review of Entrepreneurship*, *13*, 187–204.

Dipeolu, A.O., Storlie, C., and Johnson, C. (2015). College students with high-functioning autism spectrum disorder: best practices for successful transition to the world of work. *Journal of College Counseling*, *18*, 175–190.

Erickson, W.A., von Schrader, S., Bruyère, S.M., VanLooy, S.A., and Matteson, D.S. (2014). Disability-inclusive employer practices and hiring of individuals with disabilities. *Rehabilitation Research, Policy, and Education*, *28*, 309–328.

Freeman, D., Cromwell, C., Aarenau, D., Hazelton, M., and Lapointe, M. (2004). Factors leading to successful workplace integration of employees who have experienced mental illness. *Employee Assistance Quarterly*, *19*, 51–58.

French-Dunbar, M. (2016, March 5). Rising Tide car wash is turning autism into an advantage. *Conscious Company Media*. Retrieved September 5, 2019 from https://consciousco mpanymedia.com/workplace-culture/rising-tide-car-wash-is-turning-autism-into-an -advantage/.

Goffman, E. (1963). *Stigma*. New York: Simon & Schuster.

Harris, S.P., Renko, M., and Caldwell, K. (2013). Accessing social entrepreneurship: perspectives of people with disabilities and key stakeholders. *Journal of Vocational Rehabilitation*, *38*, 35–48.

Hart, D.M., and Acs, Z.J. (2011). High-tech immigrant entrepreneurship in the United States. *Economic Development Quarterly*, *25*, 116–129.

Hendrickx, S. (2008), *Asperger Syndrome and Employment: What People with Asperger Syndrome Really Really Want*. London: JKP.

Hitt, M.A., Ireland, R.D., Sirmon, D.G., and Trahms, C.A. (2011). Strategic entrepreneurship: creating value for individuals, organizations, and society. *Academy of Management Perspectives*, *25*, 57–74.

Hurley-Hanson, A.E., and Giannantonio, C.M. (2017). LMX and autism: effective working relationships. In Scandura, T.A., and Mouriño-Ruiz, E. (eds), *Leading Diversity in the 21st Century*. Charlotte, NC: IAP Information Age Publishing, pp. 281–302.

Johnson, T.D., and Joshi, A. (2016). Dark clouds or silver linings? A stigma threat perspective on the implications of an autism diagnosis for workplace well-being. *Journal of Applied Psychology*, *101*, 430–449.

Jones, M., and Latreille, P. (2011). Disability and self-employment: evidence for the UK. *Applied Economics*, *43*, 4161–4178.

Lerner, D.A., Verheul, I., and Thurik, R. (2019). Entrepreneurship and Attention Deficit/Hyperactivity Disorder: a large-scale study involving the clinical condition of ADHD. *Small Business Economics*, *53*, 381–392.

Lewis, M. (2010). *The Big Short: Inside the Doomsday Machine*. New York: W.W. Norton.

Logan, J. (2009). Dyslexic entrepreneurs: the incidence; their coping strategies and their business skills. *Dyslexia*, *15*, 328–346.

Mair, J., and Martí, I. (2006). Social entrepreneurship research: a source of explanation, prediction, and delight. *Journal of World Business*, *41*, 36–44.

Miller, D., and Le Breton-Miller, I. (2017). Underdog entrepreneurs: a model of challenge-based entrepreneurship. *Entrepreneurship Theory and Practice*, *41*, 7–17.

Morel, K. (2012, April 30). The success and challenges of an autistic entrepreneur. *American Express Trend and Insights*. Retrieved September 10, 2019 from https://www.americanexpress.com/en-us/business/trends-and-insights/articles/the-success-and-challenges-of-an-autistic-entrepreneur/.

Mullins, J. (2017). The counter-conventional mindsets of entrepreneurs. *Business Horizons*, *60*, 597–601.

National Autistic Society (2016). About the campaign. Retrieved from National Autistic Society website, www.autism.org.uk.

Newheiser, A., and Barreto, M. (2014). Hidden costs of hiding stigma: ironic interpersonal consequences of concealing a stigmatized identity in social interactions. *Journal of Experimental Social Psychology*, *52*, 58–70.

Ng, W., and Arndt, F. (2019). "I never needed eyes to see": leveraging extreme challenges for successful venture creation. *Journal of Business Venturing Insights*, https://doi.org/10.1016/j.jbvi.2019.e00125.

Pagán, R. (2009). Self-employment among people with disabilities: evidence for Europe. *Disability and Society*, *24*, 217–229.

Palmer, A., and Shore, S.M. (2012). *A Friend's and Relative's Guide to Supporting the Family with Autism: How Can I Help?* London: Jessica Kingsley Publishers.

Parr, A.D., Hunter, S.T., and Ligon, G.S. (2013). Questioning universal applicability of transformational leadership: examining employees with autism spectrum disorder. *Leadership Quarterly*, *24*, 608–622.

Ren, L.R., Paetzold, R.L., and Colella, A. (2008). A meta-analysis of experimental studies on the effects of disability on human resource judgments. *Human Resource Management Review*, *18*, 191–203.

Richards, J. (2012). Examining the exclusion of employees with Asperger syndrome from the workplace. *Personnel Review*, *5*, 630–646.

Rosenberg, J.M. (2014, August 13). Entrepreneurship the answer for some with autism. Associated Press State Wire, North Carolina.

Roux, A.M., Shattuck, P.T., Cooper, B.P., Anderson, K.A., Wagner, M., and Narendorf, S.C. (2013). Postsecondary employment experiences among young adults with an autism spectrum disorder. *Journal of the American Academy of Child and Adolescent Psychiatry*, *52*, 931–939.

Russinova, Z., Griffin, S., Bloch, P., Wewiorski, N.J., and Rosoklija, I. (2011). Workplace prejudice and discrimination toward individuals with mental illnesses. *Journal of Vocational Rehabilitation*, *35*, 227.

Rynes, S.L., Colbert, A.E., and Brown, K.C. (2002). HR professionals' beliefs about effective human resource practices: correspondence between research and practice. *Human Resource Management*, *41*, 149–174.

Santuzzi, A.M., Waltz, P.R., Finkelstein, L.M., and Rupp, D.E. (2014). Invisible disabilities: unique challenges for employees and organizations. *Industrial and Organizational Psychology*, *7*, 204–209.

Schmidt, F.L., and Hunter, J.E. (1998). The validity and utility of selection methods in personnel psychology: practical and theoretical implications of 85 years of research findings. *Psychological Bulletin*, *124*, 262–274.

Schur, L.A. (2003). Barriers or opportunities? The causes of contingent and part-time work among people with disabilities. *Industrial Relations*, *42*, 589–622.

Shaw E., and Carter, S. (2007). Social entrepreneurship: theoretical antecedents and empirical analysis of entrepreneurial processes and outcomes. *Journal of Small Business and Enterprise Development*, *3*, 418–434.

Stolman, L. (2018, October 16). Entrepreneurship is how families are creating meaningful jobs for their children with autism spectrum disorder. *Entrepreneur*. Retrieved September 8, 2019 from https://www.entrepreneur.com/article/321421.

Stone, D.L., and Colella, A. (1996). A model of factors affecting the treatment of disabled individuals in organizations. *Academy of Management Review*, *21*, 352–401.

von Schrader, S., Malzer, V., and Bruyère, S.M. (2014). Perspectives on disability disclosure: the importance of employer practices and workplace climate. *Employee Responsibilities and Rights Journal*, *26*, 237–255.

Wei, X., Yu, J.W., Wagner, M., Hudson, L., Roux, A.M., et al. (2018). Job searching, job duration and job loss among young adults with Autism Spectrum Disorder. *Journal of Vocational Rehabilitation*, *48*, 1–10.

Wiklund, J., Hatak, I., Patzelt, H., and Shepherd, D.A. (2018). Mental disorders in the entrepreneurship context: when being different can be an advantage. *Academy of Management Perspectives*, *32*, 182–206.

Wiklund, J., Patzelt, H., and Dimov, D. (2016). Entrepreneurship and psychological disorders: how ADHD can be productively harnessed. *Journal of Business Venturing Insights*, *6*, 14–20.

Wiklund, J., Yu, W., Tucker, R., and Marino, L.D. (2017). ADHD, impulsivity and entrepreneurship. *Journal of Business Venturing*, *32*, 627–656.

Williams, J., and Patterson, N. (2019). New directions for entrepreneurship through a gender and disability lens. *International Journal of Entrepreneurial Behavior and Research*, *8*, 1706–1726.

Wolfe, M.T., and Patel, P.C. (2017). Persistent and repetitive: Obsessive-Compulsive Personality Disorder and self-employment. *Journal of Business Venturing Insights*, *8*, 125–137.

World Health Organization (2013). *Autism Spectrum Disorders and Other Developmental Disorders: From Raising Awareness to Building Capacity*. Geneva: WHO Document Production Services.

Wright, A.D. (2016, October). Autism speaks, and employers listen. *HR Magazine, 61*(8), 60–64.

Yam, K. (2017, December 6). Company's staff is 80% employees with autism, provides model for other businesses. *Huffington Post*. Retrieved September 8, 2019 from https://www .huffpost.com/entry/rising-tide-car-wash_n_6604506.

Zahra, S.A., Gedajlovic, E., Neubaum, D.O., and Shulman, J.M. (2009). A typology of social entrepreneurs: motives, search processes and ethical challenges. *Journal of Business Venturing, 24*, 519–532.

5.   Entrepreneurial activity among disabled entrepreneurs with visible and invisible impairments: a literature review

Wilson Ng

Entrepreneurship research has often sought to distinguish success from failure on the basis of entrepreneurial characteristics. The subsequent, stereotypical presentation of entrepreneurial success has implications for narrowly defined factors in research designs, such as in the selection of datasets that typically concern non-disabled white males (Carter et al., 2013). By contrast, there has been little research on how extreme challenges may have initiated or produced successful ventures. Extreme challenges include socio-cultural and economic barriers arising from life-changing physical and mental disabilities[1] (Miller and Le Breton-Miller, 2017). Apart from a few studies on entrepreneurs with paraplegia, sight loss, and attention deficit hyperactive disorder (ADHD), there has been little research on severely disabled entrepreneurs who appear to have drawn on and/or overcome their challenges in creating successful ventures. What may be learned from these entrepreneurs and their ventures?

Moreover, researchers in and beyond entrepreneurship have voiced a need to explore the social and organizational impact of visible (physical) disabilities and invisible (mental) conditions (see, e.g., Santuzzi et al., 2014). This is because of the rising costs of workplace inefficiencies from employees who pick up impairments, commonly mental conditions such as depression. The negative effects of mental conditions are magnified in a typically high-pressure workplace culture that compels employees to keep their disabilities hidden from employers in order to avoid demotion, or worse (Jack, 2019). For the study of entrepreneurship, this social tendency to disregard people with disabilities has contributed to the paucity of knowledge about the millions of disabled people worldwide who create ventures, often out of necessity (Jones and Latreille, 2011; Block et al., 2015). Relatedly, we also know little about the possible contribution to enterprise of people with positive, entrepreneurial traits (Wiklund et al., 2017) and adaptive skills (Ng and Arndt, 2019) who are labelled, pejoratively, as "disabled."[2]

There are several guiding perspectives on the phenomenon of venture creation among disabled entrepreneurs. A major perspective that is based on employment studies of disability is the social model of disability. This model adopts a social constructivist view of the nature of disabled enterprise. In this view, disability is a socially constructed phenomenon founded on "ableist" (able-bodied) perceptions of impaired people's "disabilities" (Williams and Patterson, 2019). Deviating from normative behavior can then produce oppressive consequences, including emotional trauma from social exclusion, which the social model has made explicit in "lived" accounts of these experiences (French, 1998; French and Swain, 2006).

A principal implication of the social model is that knowledge about disabled entrepreneurs is viewed in terms of their environmental, structural, and social-attitudinal barriers (cf. French, 2001). As these barriers impede their ordinary activities, where possible they should be designed out of, or removed from, structures (cf. French and Swain, 1997). Knowledge about all disabled people is sourced primarily from their presentations of their own experiences (Oliver et al., 2012). First-hand narratives of typical barriers in the lives of impaired people have therefore underpinned the social model's influence on disability research and practice (Williams and Mavin, 2012). The model, however, has been criticized for its non-disabled ontology that reflects "normative expectation[s] of western, white, middle-class, non-disabled, hetero-sexual male[s]" (Williams and Mavin, 2012: 164).

Relatedly, the challenge-based view (Miller and Le Breton-Miller, 2017) may also be criticized for assuming that its socially constructed ontology is a workable setting for the activities of disabled entrepreneurs. The challenge-based view suggests that disabled entrepreneurs may develop a propensity for envisaging adaptive requirements of their particular challenges. These challenges can be physical, social, and/or cognitive. Challenged entrepreneurs draw on their challenges as resources in shaping adaptive requirements. These requirements—such as, for example, a "need to do things differently" (Miller and Le Breton-Miller, 2017: 9) —then motivate the development of "outcomes" that meet particular requirements, such as where creativity satisfies the need to do things differently.

To date, few studies in any field have drawn on the social model of disability. However, recent studies in entrepreneurship have begun to explore the activities of disabled entrepreneurs in liberal socio-cultural ("Western") environments with a socially constructed basis of ableism as a given social context in which the sampled entrepreneurs live and work. These entrepreneurs in the United States and the European Union are either visibly disabled—namely, visually or otherwise physically impaired (Ng, 2018, 2021; Ng and Arndt, 2019; Ng, Chapter 2 in this book)—or invisibly impaired with mental conditions, such as ADHD (Wiklund et al., 2016, 2017, 2018; Lerner et al., 2019). In these Western contexts, research has drawn on the adaptive mechanisms of the challenge-based model of entrepreneurship (Ng and Arndt, 2019; Ng, Chapter 2 in this book) and the person–environment fit literature to explore how certain personality traits (Wiklund et al., 2017) and extreme personal challenges (Ng and Arndt, 2019) of disabled entrepreneurs may relate with entrepreneurial intention and positive outcomes of entrepreneurial activities.

A number of insights have been produced by this research. For example, the most striking finding of Ng and Arndt's (2019) research on visually impaired ("blind") entrepreneurs was that their venture creation process was not driven by a self-employment motive. Instead, as indicated in Table 5.1, the persistent way in which the sampled entrepreneurs sought opportunities out of the ordinary requirements of a "sighted" world exposed a determination to produce impactful ideas that attained clearly defined goals, consequent upon their blindness.

Table 5.1   *Attributes of a possible process of opportunity formation among disabled entrepreneurs*

Personal challenges	Possible drivers of venture creation	New venture opportunities (not related exclusively to any specific challenges)		Special attributes of paraplegic and blind entrepreneurs' ventures
Economic:		Paraplegic	Blind	"I never needed eyes to see"
Paraplegic Entrepreneur: Limited career prospects	Paraplegic: Financially driven outlook	Commercial fund-raising events for research to cure paralysis from paraplegia	Business sponsorship to increase employment across industries	(Blind): Ability to assess and accept high-risk activities despite sight loss (adventure lifestyle:
Blind Entrepreneur: Enforced change of career	Blind: Social welfare-driven outlook	Development of exo-skeleton bodysuit to	of physically impaired workers with generic and	paraplegic entrepreneur), and because of sight loss (new public candor, following her sight
Sociocultural:		enable temporary	special skills	loss, to speak to an international
Paraplegic and Blind: New social perception of "disability" following UK Equality Act (2010)	Paraplegic and Blind: Desire to interact with public audiences sympathetic to "disability"	(paralyzed) limb movement Stem cell research to reverse paraplegia	Social fund-raising for skills development among physically impaired people	audience on behalf of disabled people unfettered by social expectations of her limited capabilities as a sight-impaired individual: blind entrepreneur)
Cognitive:		Cross-disciplinary	Research and	Outcomes driven: more
Paraplegic: Nagging sense of physical inadequacy following paraplegia	Paraplegic: Urge to reverse paralysis. Refusal to accept immobility	medical and psychology research of adaptive sensory	dissemination of capabilities of visually impaired	materialistic attitude (focused on financial goals because of passion to cure his paraplegia: paraplegic)
Blind: Sudden sight loss enabled entrepreneurial development	and change of lifestyle following paraplegia	capabilities of physically impaired people	employees for organizations Scientific	Process driven: less materialistic attitude (focused on social welfare goals because of poor employment
	Blind: Sense of "liberation" from constraints as employee	Paid motivational and problem-solving talks to business organizations	research on problem-solving capabilities of employees with different physical and mental	opportunities for disabled: blind) Passion for continuing venture creation. Adapted employment skills from long-term sight loss. (paraplegic)
Physical and Emotional:			impairments	High self-belief in own skills and
Paraplegic: Loss of mobility from paraplegia and consequent trauma. Personal sense of "disability"	Paraplegic: Personal sense of "disability" from paralysis. Urge to "cure paralysis", but not sight loss		Public motivation and educational talks	capabilities (blind) Empathetic relationship with non-disabled audiences to leverage social perception of disability for profit (paraplegic) and social
Blind: Sense of exhilaration and anxiety from life-changing sight loss	Blind: Self-driven pressure to achieve social goals following sight loss			welfare (blind) Commercial exploitation of non-disability views of blindness by developing blind skills for the non-disabled (paraplegic) Ability to build distinctive public identity by leveraging social trends for equality and diversity (blind)

Source: Adapted from Ng and Arndt (2019).

The debilitating nature of the entrepreneurs' condition was in fact drawn upon as a motivating resource for venture creation. Visual impairment then became a basis for generating new opportunities, and the desire of blind entrepreneurs for creating impactful ventures drove the identification of simple ideas that would connect mainly with large Western businesses. Their entrepreneurial motivation seemed to originate from, and draw on, the suddenness of the "disabilities" that spurred the entrepreneurs to create ventures; for example, the paraplegia of one of the entrepreneurs (who was also blind), and the late-onset blindness of another entrepreneur. The latter's declaration that they "never needed eyes to see" then became a powerful mantra for engaging with disabled people who also possess often overlooked attributes, for example to see in ways that sighted people cannot.

By contrast, the paraplegic entrepreneur in Ng and Arndt (2019) pursued physical adventures that defied his early sight loss, and his most ambitious ventures were motivated by the physical burden of paralyzed limbs. While his blindness was incurable, his paraplegia from an accident that resulted from his blindness was more likely to secure a treatment for recovery during his lifetime. Thus, following his paraplegia, this entrepreneur focused his energies on finding a cure for paralysis that he viewed as a temporary constraint on his adventure lifestyle. Notably, this entrepreneur found motivation for venture creation only when he experienced physical impairments that compelled a change of lifestyle. Yet there was a notable difference in the connection between their respective impairment(s) and entrepreneurial activity: whereas the paraplegic entrepreneur did not accept the permanence of his paraplegia and sought to reverse it, the sight loss of the blind entrepreneur inspired them to pursue radically new activities. It seemed, therefore, to follow that were the paraplegic entrepreneur to successfully reverse his paraplegia, then his entrepreneurial passion would decline. For the blind entrepreneur however, their blindness liberated a new, passionate social calling on behalf of the world's disabled. Here, potentially, it also seemed to follow that scholars and managers in and beyond entrepreneurship have more to learn from the "foresight" of the blind entrepreneur than the personal interests of the paraplegic entrepreneur, which focused merely on repairing his paraplegia. That foresight potentially links creative outcomes of opportunity formation, for example in the identification of little-known networks and skills of disabled people (Miller and Le Breton-Miller's, 2017: 9, column 4 model) that may be drawn on, by employing organizations, as capabilities.

Findings from Ng (2018) and Ng and Arndt (2019) have a number of theoretical implications, principally for the challenge-based view. This view represents a major stride toward classifying different challenges, while bringing together several hitherto unconnected research streams. Chiefly, the respective conditions of the sampled entrepreneurs inspired expansive entrepreneurial endeavor that paid little attention to social norms of disabled people, such as their traditional employment in low-paid, menial work. Instead, this research on disabled entrepreneurs yielded insights on processes of opportunity formation based on the adapted skills of the two entrepreneurs in exploiting, as opposed to passively reacting to, their personal challenges (Table 5.1, columns 1 and 2). The subsequent, market-oriented ventures of the sampled entrepreneurs suggest that their activities can throw light on processes in which valuable goods and services are produced for targeted end-users, specifically for physically challenged people who entrepreneurship scholars know little about, but also for non-disabled entrepreneurs who typically face challenges. The suggestion here is how different drivers for a severely challenged form of entrepreneurship may produce different types of ventures with personal goals that satisfy the sponsoring entrepreneur (Table 5.1, columns 2 and 3). Accordingly, by understanding and ena- bling drivers of venture creation, it may prove possible for disabled and non-disabled entrepreneurs to develop suitable attributes for producing successful outcomes of for-profit and social ventures.

In respect of opportunity formation, the challenges faced by the entrepreneurs in Ng and Arndt (2019) proved to be a vital resource that they returned to for venture funding and networks, initially in launching their ventures, and then in sustaining their public impact. This insight offers a fresh perspective of the social model that locates the source of disability in public perceptions. The suggestion here is that the popular, punitive weakness of disability in a non-disabled world in fact became a lucrative source for the access to funding and networks that were critical for the disabled entrepreneurs' venture success.

The nascent studies of physically and mentally disabled entrepreneurs also have practical implications in the ways that the entrepreneurs leveraged their physical and mental conditions to discover and/or to exploit novel opportunities. For example, the necessity-based literature has contributed to understanding the empowerment of disabled people. This empowerment may be experienced where disabled people in impoverished settlements develop entrepreneurial skills as a means of addressing their multiple challenges. Community leaders then empower the entrepreneurs by por- traying their skills as a special endeavor (Lorenzo et al., 2007). By contrast, a recent, large-scale study of entrepreneurs with ADHD has demonstrated a strong positive correlation between the clinical condition of ADHD and entrepreneurial intention and action. This finding suggests that entrepreneurs with ADHD are more likely to choose business venturing, rather than doing so out of necessity, and to self-select entrepreneurial activities (Lerner et al., 2019). Consequently, it may be possible to identify and develop suitable skills to capture high-potential opportunities for venture creation, regardless of the severity of any challenges (Miller and Le Breton-Miller, 2017). This is because physically impaired people, through daily experience, have acquired close understanding of the non-disabled world in which they must live. The opposite is not the case, unless able-bodied people develop late-onset impairments. Hence the persistence of a socially constructed, "bourgeois" view of disability. In this view, because the socially constructed view reflects psychological and emotional beliefs (Williams and Mavin, 2012), it may be possible for most, if not all, disabled people to develop special attributes in venture creation and development.

FURTHER RESEARCH

The pioneering studies on physically and mentally disabled entrepreneurs suggest opportunities for further research on venture creation and development in a number of areas in new venture creation and development. For example, following Ng and Arndt (2019), further research may: (1) shed light on generic processes of skills adaptation and development; (2) illuminate possible origins and sources of entrepreneurial motivation; (3) help to empower disadvantaged people; (4) offer new areas of study in entrepreneurial education; and (5) provide examples of how effective strategies are created, without disabled entrepreneurship serving merely as an example of social diversity and tolerance. Disabled entrepreneurship may involve an identifiable, homogenous process of skills adaptation and development. Ng and Arndt (2019) and Wiklund et al.'s (2017, 2018) research have suggested how this process can shed light on possible ways in which game-changing ideas among disabled entrepreneurs may be systematically created (Ng and Arndt, 2019), and relate with entrepreneurial success (Wiklund et al., 2017). To achieve this goal, process studies of disabled entrepreneurship may be conducted by exploring possible drivers and adapted skills of opportunity-driven behavior among disabled entrepreneurs (Ng, 2021). Those drivers and skills can then be drawn on in developing "special attributes," perhaps most influentially in the empathetic relationship between disabled entrepreneurs and their non-disabled audiences that enabled the entrepreneurs to leverage their challenges for personal goals. Here, further research may be conducted to compare the behavior of entrepreneurs with congenital impairments and those with late-onset impairments. This work could expose the important issue of the relationship between impairments and entrepreneurial endeavor, and ultimately of success.

Learning of the ways that sudden sight loss may motivate a change in priorities resonates with a number of fields, including entrepreneurship education. Here, knowledge of potentially different approaches to new venture creation among disabled entrepreneurs may run deep among entrepreneurship students who are trained to develop and launch innovative ventures (Kuratko, 2005). Entrepreneurship scholars now know that entrepreneurship education can have a significant, measurable impact in creating more and better entrepreneurs (Martin et al., 2013). Accordingly, the innovativeness and motivation of disabled entrepreneurs in Ng and Arndt (2019) may form an important part, for example, of a psychology-driven framework of attributes that can predict future success in new venture creation (Kickul and Gundry, 2002). Processes in which blind entrepreneurs build entrepreneurial skills, such as in creative thinking and use of technology (Kuratko, 2005), as tools in a sighted world could therefore become core components of entrepreneurship education.

A further important field of research in disabled enterprise is in the relationship between behavioral traits of invisible disabilities and entrepreneurial activities. In the current climate of growing business concern over the costs of invisible disabilities, research is needed in exploring how employees with normally invisible disabilities such as ADHD and Asperger's syndrome may in fact draw positively from their impairments for their own as well as for their employers' benefit. For example,

Wiklund et al. (2017) suggest that future research might examine how individuals with ADHD gather resources and organize teams when starting ventures. As venture founders with ADHD symptoms tend to move quickly to gather financial and human resources, this may prove to be advantageous in "striking while the iron is hot" in securing funding for venture creation and in capturing the attention of venture capitalists in a crowded field of new venture proposals.

NOTES

1. We refer to disability and disabled entrepreneurs in this book entry purely as a shorthand. The accurate term for disability is "impairment," either physical or mental. This is because most disabled people are not incapable of work, as the term "disability" suggests. In fact, disabled-impaired entrepreneurs may possess important advantages in new venture creation based on personality traits and/or adaptive capabilities that are particularly suited for successful enterprise activities, as outlined in this chapter.
2. "Disability" is an English word that is unique among most, if not all, languages in being pejorative. To call someone "disabled" is also used in an insulting way. Unsurprisingly, "disability" carries a wholly negative meaning.

REFERENCES

Block, J., Kohn, K., Miller, D., Ullrich, K., 2015. Necessity entrepreneurship and competitive strategy. Small Bus. Econ. 44 (1), 37–54.

Carter, S., Ram, M., Trehan, K., Jones, T., 2013. Diversity and SMEs: Existing evidence and policy tensions. Enterprise Research Centre White Paper No. 3. Available at: https://www.enterpriseresearch.ac.uk/wp-content/uploads/2013/12/ERC-White-Paper-No_3-Diversity-final.pdf.

French, S., 1998. Surviving the institution: Working as a visually disabled lecturer in higher education. In: Malina, D., Maslin-Prothero, S. (eds), Surviving the academy: Feminist perspectives. Falmer, London, 31–41.

French, S., 2001. Disabled people and employment. A study of the working lives of visually impaired physiotherapists. Ashgate, Aldershot.

French, S., Swain, J., 1997. From a different viewpoint: The lives and experiences of visually impaired people. Royal National Institute for the Blind, London.

French, S., Swain, J., 2006. Telling stories for a politics of hope. Disability Soc. 21 (5), 383–396.

Jack, A., 2019 (November 21). Survey data highlight need for health interventions. Financial Times. Available at: https://www.ft.com/content/5eea0cdc-d940-11e9-9c26-419d783e10e8.

Jones, M., Latreille, P., 2011. Disability and self-employment: Evidence from the UK. App. Econs. 43 (27), 4161–4178.

Kickul, J., Gundry, L., 2002. Prospecting for strategic advantage: The proactive entrepreneurial personality and small firm innovation. J. Small Bus. Manag. 40 (2), 85–97.

Kuratko, D., 2005. The emergence of entrepreneurship education: Development, trends, and challenges. Entrep. Theory Pract. 29 (5), 577–597.

Lerner, D., Verheul, I., Thurik, R., 2019. Entrepreneurship and attention deficit/hyperactivity disorder: A large-scale study involving the clinical condition of ADHD. Small Bus. Econ. 53 (2), 381–392.

Lorenzo, T., Van Niekerk, L., Mdlokolo, P., 2007. Economic empowerment and black disabled entrepreneurs: Negotiating partnerships in Cape Town, South Africa. Disability Rehab. 29 (5), 429–436.

Martin, B., McNally, J., Kay, M., 2013. Examining the formation of human capital in entrepreneurship: A meta-analysis of entrepreneurship education outcomes. J. Bus. Ventur. 28 (2), 221–224.

Miller, D., Le Breton-Miller, I., 2017. Underdog entrepreneurs: A model of challenge-based entrepreneurship. Entrep. Theory Pract. 41 (1), 7–17.

Ng, W., 2018. "Underdog" entrepreneurs? Processes of opportunity creation among visually-impaired founders of new ventures. British Academy of Management Annual Conference, Entrepreneurship Track, Bristol Business School, University of the West of England, September 6.

Ng, W., 2021. Disabled entrepreneurs. In: Dana, L-P. (ed.), World encyclopedia of entrepreneurship. Second Edition, Chapter 11. Edward Elgar Publishing, Cheltenham, UK and Northampton, MA, USA, 105–111.

Ng, W., Arndt., F., 2019. I never needed eyes to see: Leveraging extreme challenges for successful venture creation. Journal of Business Venturing Insights 11 (June), 1–10. DOI: https://doi.org/10.1016/j.jbvi.2019.e00125.

Oliver, M., Sapey, B., Thomas, P., 2012. Social work with disabled people. Practical social work series. 4th edition. Palgrave Macmillan, London.

Santuzzi, A., Waltz, A., Finkelstein, L., Rupp, D., 2014. Invisible disabilities. Unique challenges for employees and organizations. Ind. and Org. Psych. 7 (2), 204–219.

Wiklund, J., Hatak., I., Patzelt, H., Shepherd, D., 2018. Mental disorders in the entrepreneurship context: When being different can be an advantage. Academy of Management Perspectives 23 (2), 182–206.

Wiklund, J., Patzelt, H., Dimov, D., 2016. Entrepreneurship and psychological disorders: How ADHD can be productively harnessed. J. Bus. Ventur. Insights 6, 14–20.

Wiklund, J., Yu, W., Tucker, R., Marino, L., 2017. ADHD, impulsivity and entrepreneurship. J. Bus. Ventur. 32 (6), 627–656.

Williams, J., Mavin, S., 2012. Disability as constructed difference: A literature review and research agenda for management and organization studies. Int. J. Manag. Revs. 14 (2), 159–179.

Williams, J., Patterson, N., 2019. New directions for entrepreneurship through a gender and disability lens. Int. J. Entrepreneurial Beh. Res. 25 (8), 1706–1726.

6. Entrepreneurship and disability: research in a Spanish university

Rosa M. Muñoz, Yolanda Salinero and M. Valle Fernández

INTRODUCTION

After the recent global financial crisis, European institutions developed various measures in an attempt to improve employment and achieve economic growth. One of those measures was the Entrepreneurship 2020 Action Plan, the main objective of which is to extend a culture of entrepreneurship throughout the European Union. The European Commission is focused particularly on the weaker groups from the point of view of their economic circumstances: seniors, family businesses, migrants, women, and liberal professions (European Commission, 2020). However, one group does not appear on this list: that of disabled people. We consider that there is a gap as regards the potential role these individuals could play in entrepreneurial activities, and in this chapter we therefore showcase an innovative course dealing with entrepreneurship for disabled students developed by a Spanish University.

The concept of entrepreneurship includes various phenomena, such as the opening of a new company, the expansion of a business, innovation, the personal traits of a leader, or a social process. This last phenomenon is a movement regarding social concerns that allows entrepreneurs to change existing production and consumption trends (Mair and Martí, 2006). This aspect of entrepreneurship, in many respects, is related to sustainability. Sustainability and entrepreneurship should not be considered as mutually exclusive. The sustainability-related entrepreneurship approach is increasingly important as it is considered to be a process by which to not only produce profits, but also solve environmental and social problems (Criado-Gomis et al., 2017). In this respect, entrepreneurship should contribute to the realization of sustainable innovations that will provide benefits for the majority of society. This process can therefore satisfy the demands of a larger group of stakeholders. As we know, stakeholders are individuals, institutions, or groups that influence or are influenced by a company's actions in different ways. Stakeholders such as non-governmental organizations (NGOs) or consumer associations usually demand environmental or social improvements (Schaltegger and Wagner, 2011). In our research, disabled people have become one of these groups of stakeholders, and their needs are the ultimate sources of entrepreneurial opportunities.

A considerable amount of research has been carried out as regards entrepreneurial intentions, although the findings have been mixed. The integration of sustainability, in respect of including disabled people in the current entrepreneurial intentions field of study, will allow us to fill an important research gap.

The principal objective of the present chapter is, consequently, to clarify the contribution made by education, students' traits, and contextual factors to an individual's entrepreneurial intent, but by incorporating disabled students into the analysis in order to provide a new field of study. The aim of this research is to analyze the entrepreneurial intentions of disabled people who are studying in higher education, and to compare them with non-disabled students, while considering the main factors described in previous studies. We carried out a logistic regression with a sample of Spanish students. The main conclusions reached are: education does not influence students' entrepreneurial intentions, and these intentions are influenced by only some of the students' traits and background conditions. No significant differences were found when comparing disabled students' entrepreneurial intentions with those of non-disabled students.

The rest of the chapter is structured as follows. We first present a literature review in which we collect the main ideas and previous research concerning disability, entrepreneurship, education, and sustainability. We then go on to explain the methodology employed to carry out the research, and show the main results. In the last section, we show our conclusions and discuss the limitations and our future research.

LITERATURE REVIEW

Determinants of Entrepreneurial Intentions

An entrepreneur is an economic agent who starts, organizes, manages, and controls the activities required to develop new projects. This person may discover a gap within the market and try to fill it (Eugine Tafadzwa et al., 2017; Dijkhuizen et al., 2016). Several authors claim that personal inputs such as individual predispositions and differences, and background conditions such as geographic and environmental variables, determine people's expectations and beliefs as regards self-efficacy, which in turn lead to the formation of entrepreneurial intentions (Schaub and Tokar, 2005; Brown and Lent, 2019).

With regard to entrepreneurs' dimensions, those most cited by researchers include the perception of obstacles, risk tolerance, locus of control, educational level, business experience, gender, place of residence, and an existing family business (Brown and Lent, 2019; Vanevenhoven, 2013; Bae et al., 2014). Risk tolerance is the "tendency of a decision maker either to take or to avoid risks" (Sitkin and Pablo, 1992), and is considered a variable that is positively related to entrepreneurial intentions (Liguori et al., 2019). Locus of control is the extent to which people attribute the control over situations to themselves (internal locus of control) or to external factors (external locus of control). When entrepreneurs wish to control circumstances themselves, internal locus of control is present in entrepreneurship (Hansemark, 2003).

The individual's experience is one of the factors that authors have most frequently found to be significant as regards distinguishing between successful and unsuccessful entrepreneurs. Moreover, if the first venture has something to do with starting a business activity during the individual's youth, this makes the person more likely to begin another entrepreneurial activity later (Miettinen and Littunen, 2013).

Entrepreneurial family background refers to the influence that self-employed parents may have on their children's career choices. They are role models, or share similar preferences for venture business (Bae et al., 2014). The family evolution plays an important role in students' career preferences and, subsequently, in their entrepreneurial intention (Fietze and Boyd, 2017). Previous studies have shown that an important proportion of students from families with self-employed parents also choose to become self-employed (Laspita et al., 2012).

Sustainability and Entrepreneurship

Since the emergence of the concept of sustainable development, social, economic, and environmental dimensions of sustainability have been considered (Aldieri et al., 2009; Khan et al., 2020; Aldieri et al., 2020), all of them with the main objective of fulfilling the necessities of people living today, but within the carrying capacity of the Earth so that future generations are not damaged. The so-called social and solidarity economy addresses current challenges such as social exclusion, inequality, climate change, and unemployment. Its priorities are to create a sustainable society where socially weaker groups also have opportunities (Lee, 2020; Kulkarni, 2016).

Entrepreneurship and sustainability are currently viewed as binary concepts because many researchers consider that entrepreneurial action is desirable in order to discover opportunities, innovate, and produce profits, while social and environmental challenges are included in the process (Cohen and Winn, 2007; Shepherd and Patzelt, 2011).

The relationship between sustainability and entrepreneurship has been addressed from several points of view, such as those of ecopreneurship, institutional entrepreneurship, sustainable entrepreneurship, and social entrepreneurship (Cohen, 2006; Schaltegger, 2002). In this chapter, we have adopted the last approach, incorporating disabled people into the analysis. This type of entrepreneurship is focused on "improving social wealth through the creation of social capital, social change, or focus on social needs" (Zhiwei et al., 2018). We consider that this is an appropriate point of view because social entrepreneurship is the desire to attain societal objectives by means of business and entrepreneurship approaches (Schaltegger and Wagner, 2011). The factor that distinguishes social entrepreneurship from commercial entrepreneurship is that it attempts to solve social problems rather than covering market needs (Parker Harris et al., 2014). Inclusive entrepreneurship leads to social inclusion, giving target groups such as women, seniors, youth, immigrants, minorities, and disabled people an equal opportunity to launch a business (Maritz and Laferriere, 2016).

The establishment of new ventures by disabled people is an important aspect of sustainable employment strategies. We should not, however, confuse entrepreneurship with self-employment. The former concerns providing something innovative to the market, while the latter concerns performing work for personal profit. Simply encouraging self-employment will not, therefore, have a significant effect on employment. Policies should focus on disabled people who carry out entrepreneurial activities that may lead to the hiring of others.

Entrepreneurship, Education, and Disability

Disability is growing in all countries. There are more than 1000 million people with disabilities throughout the world; that is, about 15 percent of the world's population, or one in seven people. The World Health Organization defines disability as a general term that covers activity limitations, impairments, and participation restrictions (WHO, n.d.). It is an individual limitation that can be different in type, duration, and severity. This signifies that, as disabilities vary, so do entrepreneurial motivations (Dhar and Farzana, 2017).

Several studies have highlighted the important role that entrepreneurship education, business incubators, and university initiatives play in students' intentions to start a new venture (Zahari et al., 2018). In addition to entrepreneurs' traits, university activities that lead students to launch a new business have also been considered in earlier research (Nowiński et al., 2019). However, little has been written about the factors that influence the entrepreneurial intentions of disabled starters entering the labor market. Some of these factors are not changeable, such as gender or age, but other factors can be improved. Education, an important promoting activity for employment, is a clear example of this (Achterberg et al., 2019).

Disabled people's entrepreneurial challenges can be financial, personal, or societal. They often have difficulties in financing their new ventures, as they do not manage their own funds and banks are reticent to provide them with loans (Eugine Tafadzwa et al., 2017). At a personal level, these potential entrepreneurs often lack training and business, legal, and financial knowledge. They also show a lack of confidence in themselves (Maritz and Laferriere, 2016). From the societal point of view, discrimination by stakeholders is a reality that is related to the way in which people with disabilities are viewed by society (Jones and Latreille, 2011). Disabled people are underrepresented in the workforce, since employers underestimate their capabilities and are particularly wary of hiring employees with intellectual or psychiatric disabilities (Balcazar et al., 2014). However, several studies conclude that individuals with disabilities succeed to roughly the same extent as non-disabled entrepreneurs (Roni and Baines, 2012), and are even significantly more likely to confront greater challenges when compared to other potential entrepreneurs (Uddin and Jamil, 2015).

The main ideas presented above in relation to entrepreneurs' characteristics, education, and disability have led to the following hypotheses:

Hypothesis (H1). Students' traits and background conditions influence their entrepreneurial intentions.

We analyze those variables included in previous studies that were considered as most influential in entrepreneurial behavior: the perception of obstacles, risk tolerance, locus of control, educational level, business experience, gender, place of residence, and an existing family business.

Hypothesis (H2). Education influences students' entrepreneurial intentions.

The knowledge acquired about how to plan, finance, manage, and start a business works as an incentive for entrepreneurship.

Hypothesis (H3). Disabled students and non-disabled students do not have different entrepreneurial intentions.

Regardless of the final result, in a first step, disabled students show entrepreneurial intentions at a similar level to students without disabilities.

METHODOLOGY

The Department of Business Administration at the University of Castilla-La Mancha (UCLM) offers an entrepreneurship education course, entitled "Entrepreneurship and Disability," for disabled students. This course is equivalent to nine credits in the European Credit Transfer and Accumulation System. The objectives of this course are to provide students with the opportunity to acquire abilities regarding entrepreneurship and to teach them the basic capabilities required to carry out and develop a whole business plan.

The 2018/19 course was the third edition, with 15 students in each class. This has resulted in the setting up of one company, while another is starting the necessary procedures to be created. The former is a co-operative that produces ecologic plant substratum from coffee dregs, while the latter is also a co-operative whose activity consists of assembling guitars. This is the first time that a course with these characteristics has been offered at a Spanish university, signifying that there are no similar publications of this nature. This chapter, therefore, is a contribution to the field owing to its originality (Muñoz et al., 2019).

The students were surveyed using a written standardized questionnaire. The participants were the disabled students on the entrepreneurship course and students on different degrees at the UCLM during their classes. The second hypothesis was tested by collecting data from the first year and last year of each degree during the period from September 2018 to November 2018. We received 234 responses (92 percent of the students).

A lot of works have researched the variables that drive potential entrepreneurs through the process of starting a business. However, a gap exists in relation to the understanding of the motives that lead disabled people to start a business. We have adapted a model proposed in previous research (Van der Zwan et al., 2010), in an attempt to develop it in the context of a sample that includes disabled students. We used a logistic regression in which the dichotomous dependent variable was created by means of the following question: "Have you started a business recently or are you taking steps to start one?" (1 = yes, 0 = no). We included the following as independent variables (Van der Zwan et al., 2010):

- Four perceptions of obstacles. We asked the students whether they consider it difficult to start a business owing to a possible lack of *financial support*, the complexity of *administrative procedures*, difficulty in *obtaining information*, and an unfavorable *economic climate*. The individuals had to respond: strongly agree, agree, disagree, or strongly disagree. We constructed a dummy variable with a value of 1 in the case of strongly agree or agree.
- A measure of *risk tolerance*. The students had to evaluate the sentence "It is not advisable to start a business if there is risk of failure." A variable was constructed with the value of 1 in the case of disagree or strongly disagree.
- *Locus of control*. Internal locus of control is related to the feeling that everything in life depends on one's own efforts and actions, while external locus of control is related to the feeling that external conditions determine the results. In this case, the students had to respond to the question "What most influences a company's success?" by choosing from among the following five options: director's personality, general management of the firm (if they chose these, the dummy internal locus of control variable = 1), overall economy, political context, or external entities (if they chose these, the dummy internal locus of control variable = 0 because these answers are linked to the external locus of control).

We also included other external variables, such as educational level, business experience, gender, location or place of residence, and whether the students' parents are/were self-employed, because these are present in the literature concerning entrepreneurship.

Some previous studies confirm that entrepreneurship education has a positive influence on the perceived attractiveness of new business initiation. However, they have rarely involved control groups or employed pre-testing and post-testing controls. Most studies focus on individuals with an existing predisposition toward entrepreneurship, which biases the conclusions in favor of educational activities (Von Graevenitz et al., 2010). We consequently included "before–after" education by using a dummy variable that we denominated as *educational level* (0 = before education, 1 = after education).

We additionally employed a dummy variable for *business experience* (0 = no, 1 = yes) and for *gender* (1 = male, 0 = female).

Location has two possibilities: 1 = urban area, and 0 = rural area.

The question regarding whether the students' father, their mother, or both are/were self-employed was used to include the family context (and was denominated as *entrepreneurial parents*). This variable was recoded to a dummy variable (0 = no entrepreneurial parents, 1 = entrepreneurial parents).

The characteristic *disability* is also another dummy variable (0 = not disabled, 1 = disabled). The aforementioned factors were the independent variables, while the response to the question concerning the possible attempt to start a business was the dependent variable.

Logistic regression is an extension of regression, but with an outcome variable that is a categorical variable and predictor variables that are continuous or categorical. This means that, given certain other information, it is possible to predict to which of two categories a company is likely to belong.

Logistic regression analysis is well suited when the dependent variable is non-metric and consists of just two groups. Compared to discriminant analysis, choosing logistic regression is justified by the fact that the multivariate normality assumptions do not need to be met. Logistic regression is much more robust when these assumptions are not met. But even if they are met, many researchers prefer this methodology to discriminant analysis because the interpretation of the results is similar to that of regression analysis results (Hernan-Gómez et al., 2006).

We therefore used a binomial logit model in order to find out which variables influence somebody when deciding whether to start a business. In simple linear regression, the outcome variable, Y, is obtained from the equation of a straight line. In logistic regression, rather than predicting the value of a variable, Y, from several explanatory variables, we predict the probability of Y occurring by using given values of several explicative variables.

As with linear regression, it is necessary to decide how we enter explicative variables in the model. Stepwise methods are not generally recommended because they take important decisions away from the researcher and base them on mathematical criteria rather than sound theoretical logic. They are only really appropriate when one is proposing a hypothesis from scratch and has no empirical evidence or sensible theories about which explanatory factors are most important. We usually have some idea about which are determinant and their relative importance. We therefore chose the entry method for the logistic regression analysis.

RESULTS

The categorical variable coding is presented in Table 6.1. The results of the model parameter estimation are shown in Table 6.2 (the corresponding hypothesis appears next to each variable).

The fourth column in Table 6.2 shows which parameters are significant according to the test. Thus, for example, the parameter linked to the *entrepreneurial parents* variable is significant, with a confidence margin of 99 percent. The variables *unfavorable*

Table 6.1   *Categorical variable coding*

Variables	Coding	Frequency	Parameter coding
Educational level	Before education	97	1.000
	After education	137	0.000
Gender	Male	136	1.000
	Female	98	0.000
Location	Urban area	102	1.000
	Rural area	132	0.000
Business experience	No	146	0.000
	Yes	88	1.000
Entrepreneurial parents	No	146	0.000
	Yes	88	1.000
Locus of control	Internal locus of control	166	1.000
	External locus of control	68	0.000
Lack of financial support	Strongly agree	149	1.000
	Strongly disagree	85	0.000
Risk tolerance	Strongly agree	111	0.000
	Strongly disagree	123	1.000
Unfavorable economic climate	Strongly agree	147	0.000
	Strongly disagree	87	1.000
Difficulty in obtaining information	Strongly agree	53	1.000
	Strongly disagree	181	0.000
Complexity of administrative procedures	Strongly agree	111	1.000
	Strongly disagree	123	0.000
Disability	Not disabled	202	0.000
	Disabled	32	1.000

Table 6.2   *Binomial logit model*

Variables	B	S.E.	Wald	Sig.	Exp(B)
Disability (H3)	0.549	0.468	1.374	0.241	1.732
Gender (H1)	0.420	0.292	2.073	0.150	1.523
Location (H1)	0.519	0.290	3.190	0.074	1.680
Business experience (H1)	0.497	0.303	2.693	0.098	1.644
Entrepreneurial parents (H1)	0.925	0.304	9.248	0.002	2.521
Locus of control (H1)	0.127	0.347	0.134	0.714	1.136
Lack of financial support (H1)	−0.137	0.317	0.188	0.665	0.872
Complexity of administrative procedures (H1)	0.003	0.314	0.000	0.992	1.003
Difficulty in obtaining information (H1)	−0.219	0.399	0.300	0.584	0.804
Unfavorable economic climate (H1)	0.518	0.315	2.703	0.096	1.678
Risk tolerance (H1)	0.265	0.295	.806	0.369	1.303
Educational level (H2)	−1.07	0.309	0.120	0.729	0.898
Constant	−1.531	0.504	9.225	0.002	0.216

Table 6.3   *Goodness of the adjustment*

Hosmer–Lemeshow statistic			2LogLikelihood	Cox and Snell R^2	R^2-Nag
Chi-square	df	Sig.			
9.570	8	0.297	294.556[a]	0.112	0.150

Note: Author's calculation. a. The estimate ended in iteration number 4 because the parameter estimates had changed by less than 0.001.

economic climate, location, and business experience have an associated coefficient that is significant for a confidence level of 90 percent.

The present findings partially support the first hypothesis regarding the influence of students' traits and background conditions on their entrepreneurial intentions, because only four dimensions are significant. The second hypothesis is not corroborated; that is, in this case, education does not influence entrepreneurial intentions. However, a clear difference is not found in the entrepreneurial intentions of those with and without disabilities, which is consistent with the third hypothesis.

With regard to the goodness of the adjustment, we have chosen three measures: the Cox and Snell R^2, the R^2-Nag (the percentage of variation explained by the model's independent variables is between 11.2 percent and 15 percent), and the Hosmer–Lemeshow statistic (in our case, this value is 0.297 for a Chi-square of 9.570 with 8 degrees of freedom, signifying that an acceptable adjustment exists because a non-significant parameter is desirable when using this test) (see Table 6.3).

DISCUSSION AND CONCLUSIONS

This research helps to better understand the factors that influence entrepreneurial intentions, in addition to focusing on the gap in existing theory, policy, and practice in relation to the pressing sustainable-related issue of disability employment.

The perception of lack of *financial support* does not influence the probability of starting a business. The same conclusion is obtained for the lack of sufficient *information*. Moreover, the complex *administrative procedures* do not play a role in beginning an entrepreneurial activity. Only the fact of perceiving an unfavorable *economic climate* has a positive impact on the probability of developing a new enterprise. The difficulties involved in getting a job may lead the students to consider the possibility of starting a new venture. The *risk tolerance* does not have any influence on the students' entrepreneurial intentions. The variable *locus of control* does not appear to be relevant. Whether or not an individual believes that they can change events through their abilities does not have a significant influence on their entrepreneurial activity, and the same can be said for the acknowledgment that external factors affect events. The variable *educational level* does not appear to be relevant; that is, we were unable to find any influence of education on the perceived attractiveness of starting a new business. This is also true of the variable *gender*, because the result does not support the general perception that men have a greater entrepreneurial intention than women (Zhao et al., 2005). *Business experience* significantly increases the probability of engaging in entrepreneurial activities, a conclusion obtained in many other studies. *Location* has a positive impact; that is, an urban environment favors entrepreneurial attitudes. An urban location provides more opportunities in every aspect related to new ventures: technical, financial, commercial, and so on. Having *entrepreneurial parents* significantly increases the probability of considering starting a business. The students have seen that a successful venture is a way of life that provides a lot of satisfactions, such as achievement, control, power of decision, growth potential, and so on.

This study has shown that only some dimensions have an influence on the students' entrepreneurial intentions (H1): perception of unfavorable *economic climate*, *entrepreneurial parents*, *location*, and *business experience*. With regard to *locus of control*, the students in this case show a lack of belief in their own abilities to successfully engage in the creation of a new business. This conclusion is similar to those obtained in other studies developed in Bangladesh, Portugal, and Malaysia (Zahari et al., 2018; Uddin and Bose, 2012; Ferreira et al., 2012).

The variable *educational level* was unable to demonstrate a significant relationship with entrepreneurial intentions (H2), which is a similar result to that obtained by some other authors (Von Graevenitz et al., 2010; Zahari et al., 2018). Our recommendation, therefore, is that universities should increase their efforts regarding entrepreneurship education in order to make it more effective. They should strengthen different options, such as business incubators, technology transfer offices, or reward systems, in order to influence students' intentions.

With regard to the variable *disability*, the fact that a respondent is disabled does not affect the probability of having entrepreneurship intentions. This is an important conclusion in the sense that disabled people can be considered on the same level as "capable" people in relation to this issue (H3). Innovations such as the "Entrepreneurship and Disability" course at the UCLM should be replicated in most universities.

Table 6.4, which is a summary of Table 6.2, shows the main results of the research.

The results of this research will allow us to develop an intervention approach focused on supporting and promoting entrepreneurship among people who are interested in beginning a new venture. Moreover, the addition of individuals with disabilities to the model may allow us to attain a sustainability-related initiative in order to link demand from small companies with the underutilized labor supply of these types of employees.

In terms of policy implications, disabled people's low employment rates have negative consequences, such as economic implications by having underutilized productive resources and high costs through more impact on social security systems. Therefore, public policies should seek solutions for the unemployment and low activity rates among disabled people (Zhao et al., 2005). We consider that changes should continue with these types of initiatives, that is, the creation of educational programs that will provide entrepreneurship candidates with training that will lead to a business plan. Initiatives such as educational programs at different educational levels,

Table 6.4   *Model's variables*

Sign of parameter B	Significance (Wald)	Conclusions
+	0.096	The unfavorable economic climate has a positive impact on the probability of developing a new enterprise
+	0.002	Having entrepreneurial parents has a positive influence on the students' entrepreneurial intentions
+	0.074	Urban location has a positive effect on the students' entrepreneurial intentions
+	0.098	Business experience has a positive influence on the students' entrepreneurial intentions
−	0.729	Educational level does not appear to have a significant relationship with entrepreneurial intentions
+	0.241	Being disabled does not affect the probability of showing entrepreneurial intentions

business mentoring, technical assistance, business incubators, or start-up company grants, could increase the presence of disabled people in the workforce. Furthermore, the findings of many studies evidence the influence of university collaborations for academic performance (Aldieri et al., 2018). Knowledge exchange among universities is crucial to develop and share these types of initiatives. While policies are in place to amend some of the inequalities, it is clear that the implementation of new actions is a challenge. In this sense, this research contributes to the planning of policies on education for people with disabilities, as it shows factors that can boost their entrepreneurial inclinations.

This research provides useful conclusions in the field of entrepreneurship and its link to sustainability, but has some limitations. The survey tool may incorporate a common method bias, although self-report measures are frequently used in entrepreneurial intention research. The conclusion in relation to disabled students should be viewed carefully, because it has been obtained from a small sample. Moreover, the data was obtained from only one region in Spain. In future research, it would be useful to extend the sample to include more regions and countries, which would allow comparative studies. We also consider it advisable to carry out a longitudinal study in order to check whether entrepreneurial intentions eventually lead to actual entrepreneurial behavior.

REFERENCES

Achterberg, T.J., Wind, H., de Boer, A.G.E.M. and Frings-Dresen, M.H.W. 2019. Factors that promote or hinder young disabled people in work participation: A systematic review. *J. Occup. Rehabil.*, 19(2), 129–141. DOI: 10.1007/s10926-009-9169-0.

Aldieri, L., Grafström, J., Sundström, K. and Vinci, C.P. 2020. Wind power and job creation. *Sustainability*, 12(1), 45. DOI: 10.3390/su12010045.

Aldieri, L., Kotsemir, M. and Vinci, C.P. 2009. The role of environmental innovation through the technological proximity in the implementation of the sustainable development. *Bus. Strategy Environ.*, 29(2), 493–502. DOI: 10.1002/bse.2382.

Aldieri, L., Kotsemir, M. and Vinci, C.P. 2018. The impact of research collaboration on academic performance: An empirical analysis for some European countries. *Socio-Econ. Plan. Sci.*, 62, 13–30. DOI: 10.1016/j.seps.2017.05.003.

Bae, T.J., Qian, S., Miao, C. and Fiet, J.O. 2014. The relationship between entrepreneurship education and entrepreneurial intentions: A meta-analytic review. *Entrep. Theory Pract.*, 38(2), 217–254. DOI: 10.1111/etap.12095.

Balcazar, F.E., Kuchak, J., Dimpfl, S., Sariepella, V. and Alvarado, F. 2014. An empowerment model of entrepreneurship for people with disabilities in the United States. *Psychosoc. Interv.*, 23, 145–150. DOI: 10.1016/j.psi.2014.07.002.

Brown, S.D. and Lent, R.W. 2019. Social cognitive career theory at 25: Progress in studying the domain satisfaction and career self-management models. *J. Career Assess.*, 27(4), 563–578. DOI:10.1177/1069072719852736.

Calderón-Milán, M.-J., Calderón-Milán, B. and Barba-Sánchez, V. 2020. Labour inclusion of people with disabilities: What role do the social and solidarity economy entities play? *Sustainability*, 12(3), 1079. DOI: 10.3390/su12031079.

Cohen, B. 2006. Sustainable valley entrepreneurial ecosystems. *Bus. Strategy Environ.*, 15(1), 1–14. DOI: 10.1002/bse.428.

Cohen, B. and Winn, M.I. 2007. Market imperfections, opportunity and sustainable entrepreneurship. *J. Bus. Ventur.*, 22(1), 29–49. DOI: org/10.1016/j.jbusvent.2004.12.001.

Criado-Gomis, A., Cervera-Taulet, A. and Iniesta-Bonillo, M.-A. 2017. Sustainable entrepreneurial orientation: A business strategic approach for sustainable development. *Sustainability*, 9, 1667. DOI:10.3390/su9091667.

Dhar, S. and Farzana, T. 2017. Entrepreneurs with disabilities in Bangladesh: An exploratory study on their entrepreneurial motivation and challenges. *Eur. J. Bus. Manag.*, 9(36), 103–114.

Dijkhuizen, J., Gorgievski, M., Van Veldhoven, M. and Schalk, R. 2016. Feeling successful as an entrepreneur: A job demands–resources approach. *Int. Entrep. Manag. J.*, 12(2), 555–573. DOI:10.1007/s11365-014-0354-z 7.

Eugine Tafadzwa, M., Welcome, M. and Thobekani, L. 2017. Entrepreneurial barriers that are confronted by entrepreneurs living with physical disabilities: A thematic analysis. *J. Econ. Behav. Stud.*, 9(1), 27–45. DOI:10.22610/jebs.v9i1.1555.

European Commission. 2020. The Entrepreneurship 2020 Action Plan. https://ec.europa.eu/growth/smes/promoting-entrepreneurship/action-plan_en (accessed on February 10, 2020).

Ferreira, J.J., Raposo, M.L., Gouveia Rodrigues, R., Dinis, A. and do Paco, A. 2012. A model of entrepreneurial intention: An application of the psychological and behavioral approaches. *J. Small Bus. Enterp. Dev.*, 19(3), 424–440. DOI: 10.1108/14626001211250144.

Fietze, S. and Boyd, B. 2017. Entrepreneurial intention of Danish students: A correspondence analysis. *Int. J. Entrep. Behav. Res.*, 23(4), 656–672. DOI: 10.1108/IJEBR-08-2016-0241.

Hansemark, O.C. 2003. Need for achievement, locus of control and the prediction of business start-ups: A longitudinal study. *J. Econ. Psychol.*, 24(3), 301–319. DOI:10.1016/s0167-4870(02)00188-5.

Hernan-Gómez, J., Martín, N. and Rodríguez, A.I. 2006. Education and training as non-psychological characteristics that influence university students' entrepreneurial behaviour. *J. Entrep. Educ.*, 9, 99–112.

Jones, M.K. and Latreille, P.L. 2011. Disability and self-employment: Evidence for the UK. *Appl. Econ.*, 43(27), 4161–4178. DOI: 10.1080/00036846.2010.489816.

Khan, J., Hildingsson, R. and Garting, L. 2020. Sustainable welfare in Swedish cities: Challenges of eco-social integration in urban sustainability governance. *Sustainability*, 12(1), 383. DOI: 10.3390/su12010383.

Kulkarni, M. 2016. Organizational career development initiatives for employees with a disability. *Int. J. Hum. Resour. Manag.*, 27(14), 1662–1679. DOI: 10.1080/09585192.2015.1137611.

Laspita, S., Breugst, N., Heblich, S. and Patzelt, H. 2012. Intergenerational transmission of entrepreneurial intentions. *J. Bus. Ventur.*, 27(4), 414–435. DOI: 10.1016/j.jbusvent.2011.11.006.

Lee, S. 2020. Role of social and solidarity economy in localizing the sustainable development goals. *Int. J. Sustain. Dev. World Ecol.*, 27(1), 65–71. DOI: 10.1080/13504509.2019.1670274.

Liguori, E., Winkler, C., Vanevenhoven, J., Winkel, D. and James, M. 2019. Entrepreneurship as a career choice: Intentions, attitudes, and outcome expectations. *J. Small Bus. Entrep.*, 1–21. DOI: 10.1080/08276331.2019.1600857.

Mair, J. and Martí, I. 2006. Social entrepreneurship research: A source of explanation, prediction, and delight. *J. World Bus*, 41, 36–44. DOI: 10.1016/j.jwb.2005.09.002.

Maritz, A. and Laferriere, R. 2016. Entrepreneurship and self-employment for people with disabilities. *Aust. J. Career Dev.*, 25(2), 45–54. DOI: 10.1177/1038416216658044.

Miettinen, M.R. and Littunen, H. 2013. Factors contributing to the success of start-up firms using two-point or multiple-point scale models. *Entrep. Res. J.*, 3(4), 449–481. DOI: doi.org/10.1515/erj-2012-0012.

Muñoz, R.M., Salinero, Y., Pena, I. and Sanchez de Pablo, J.D. 2019. Entrepreneurship education and disability: An experience at a Spanish university. *Adm. Sci.*, 9(2), 34. DOI: 10.3390/admsci9020034.

Nowiński, W., Haddoud, M., Lančarič, D., Egerová, D. and Czeglédi, C. 2019. The impact of entrepreneurship education, entrepreneurial self-efficacy and gender on entrepreneurial intentions of university students in the Visegrad countries. *Stud. High. Educ.*, 44(2), 361–379. DOI: 10.1080/03075079.2017.1365359.

Parker Harris, S., Renko, M. and Caldwell, K. 2014. Social entrepreneurship as an employment pathway for people with disabilities: Exploring political–economic and socio-cultural factors. *Disabil. Soc.*, 29(8), 1275–1290. DOI:10.1080/09687599.2014.924904.

Roni, N.N. and Baines, S. 2012. Why entrepreneurship process as a battle for business resources recognition for disadvantaged people? *J. Bus. Stud.*, 33, 55–90.

Schaltegger, S. 2002. A framework for ecopreneurship: Leading bioneers and environmental managers to ecopreneurship. *Greener Manag. Int.*, 38, 45–58. DOI: 0.9774/GLEAF.3062.2002.su.00006.

Schaltegger, S. and Wagner, M. 2011. Sustainable entrepreneurship and sustainability innovation: Categories and interactions. *Bus. Strategy Environ*, 20(4), 222–237. DOI: 10.1002/bse.682.

Schaub, M. and Tokar, D.M. 2005. The role of personality and learning experiences in social cognitive career theory. *J. Vocat. Behav.*, 66 (2), 304–325. DOI: 10.1016/j.jvb.2004.09.005.8.

Shepherd, D.A. and Patzelt, H. 2011. The new field of sustainable entrepreneurship: Studying entrepreneurial action linking "what is to be sustained" with "what is to be developed." *Entrep. Theory Pract.*, 35, 137–163. DOI: 10.1111/j.1540-6520.2010.00426.x.

Sitkin, S.B. and Pablo, A.L. 1992. Reconceptualizing the determinants of risk behavior. *Acad. Manag. Rev.*, 17(1), 9–38. DOI: 10.2307/258646.

Uddin, M. and Jamil, S.A. 2015. Entrepreneurial barriers faced by disabled in India. *Asian Soc. Sci.*, 11(24), 72–78. DOI:10.5539/ass.v11n24p72.

Uddin, M.R. and Bose, T.K. 2012. Determinants of entrepreneurial intention of business students in Bangladesh. *Int. J. Bus. Manag.*, 7(24), 128–137. DOI: 10.5539/ijbm.v7n24p128.

Van der Zwan, P., Thurik, R. and Grilo, I. 2010. The entrepreneurial ladder and its determinants. *Appl. Econ.*, 42(17), 2183–2191. DOI: 10.1080/00036840701765437.

Vanevenhoven, J. 2013. Advances and challenges in entrepreneurship education. *J. Small Bus. Manag.*, 51(3), 466–470. DOI: 10.1111/jsbm.12043.

Von Graevenitz, G., Harho, D. and Weber, R. 2010. The effects of entrepreneurship education. *J. Econ. Behav. Organ.*, 76(1), 90–112. DOI: 10.1016/j.jebo.2010.02.015.

WHO. n.d. Disability. https://www.who.int/disabilities/en/ (accessed on December 10, 2019).

Zahari, A.R., Tamyez, P.F.M., Azizan, N.A. and Hashim, F. 2018. Student spin-off intentions in Malaysian higher educational institutions: Founders' characteristics and university roles. *J. Entrep. Educ.*, 21, 1–15.

Zhao, H., Seibert, S.E. and Hills, G.E. 2005. The mediating role of self-efficacy in the development of entrepreneurial intentions. *J. Appl. Psychol.*, 90(6), 1265–1272. DOI: 10.1037/0021-9010.90.6.1265.

Zhiwei, Y., Xuanwei, C., Hongyi, D. and Yun, H. 2018. Is entrepreneurial orientation a good predictor of sustainable performance? *J. Asia Entrep. Sustain.*, 14, 124–165.

7. Awareness and attitudes towards social entrepreneurship among university students and disabled people: the case of the Czech Republic

Ondřej Kročil, Richard Pospíšil and David Kosina

INTRODUCTION

Social entrepreneurship represents one of the possibilities entrepreneurs can employ to contribute to the solution of pressing social problems such as social exclusion, crime and unemployment. The general definition identifies social enterprises as the enterprises selling products and providing services to achieve economic self-sufficiency and at the same time following a social purpose. The term 'social enterprise' is often conflated with that of 'work integration social enterprises' (WISE) in public understanding in European Union (EU) countries (Borzaga et al., 2020). These enterprises focus on the employment of labour market disadvantaged persons with the objective to integrate them into society or prevent their social exclusion. The labour market disadvantaged persons are disabled persons, socially excluded persons, low-qualified persons, and older or long-term unemployed people.

Although the typical feature of the pre-coronavirus pandemic labour market (EU-28: 6.3 per cent in September 2019) (Eurostat, n.d.) is the low rate of unemployment, it is necessary to pay continuous attention to disadvantaged persons because they face many specific social and health risks. According to Eurostat data, in 2018, 28.7 per cent of the EU population with a physical activity limitation was at risk of poverty or social exclusion, compared with 19.2 per cent of those with no limitations. Social entrepreneurship can be an effective tool for the integration of these people into society, and an innovative way to protect them against social exclusion.

In EU countries, social entrepreneurship is not based on uniform principles. In some EU countries, social entrepreneurship is included in national legislation (for example, Slovakia and Finland). In other countries, social entrepreneurship is not yet officially regulated (for example, the Czech Republic and Austria). Social entrepreneurship principles introduced by EMES (the research network of university research centres and individual researchers of social enterprise) are widely recognized in the EU countries (Defourny and Nyssens, 2012). These principles are provided in Table 7.1.

Social Entrepreneurship in the Czech Republic

Currently, the Czech Republic lacks formal legislative regulation of social entrepreneurship. For this reason, unofficial principles created by the non-profit organization TESSEA (n.d.-a), inspired by the principles of EMES (introduced above), are used in the Czech Republic. These principles are intended primarily for the allocation of subsidies and not for including social enterprises in the indicative database administered by the Czech Ministry of Labour and Social Affairs (listing in the database is voluntary). The principles are recorded in Table 7.2.

The research carried out in the Czech Republic in 2018 by the authors of this chapter suggests that WISEs are the most frequent type of social enterprises. Czech WISE focus predominantly on the integration of disabled people back into society by giving them job opportunities (Kročil et al., 2019). At the same time, the research showed that in 2018 there was an excess of supply over demand for the work of disabled people. That suggests the even higher importance of the existing WISEs, as without them the excess supply would be even more significant.

According to TESSEA (n.d.-b) there are currently 300 social enterprises operating in the Czech Republic, and 90 per cent of them have the character of WISE. Eighty per cent of these companies focus on the integration of people with disabilities. In 2018 they employed almost 4000 such disadvantaged people (according to the Czech Labour Office, n.d.), and in December 2019 there were 33 000 unemployed disabled people in the labour market. However, in the Czech Republic, the concept of social entrepreneurship is still being developed and lacks, for example, systematic public support and regulation. In addition, the total number of social enterprises operating in the Czech Republic is low, and thus the concept of social entrepreneurship cannot reach its potential. To accelerate this development, raising awareness of social entrepreneurship among the Czech population may be important. In this pilot study we focus on two selected groups of people within Czech population: disabled people as typical employees of Czech social enterprises, and Czech university students of humanities as potential founders of new social enterprises. This study was originally published in the journal *Economic and Social Changes: Facts, Trends, Forecast* (Kročil et al., 2020). The relationship between social entrepreneurship on the one hand, and university students and people with disabilities on the other, is supported by the following literature review.

Definition and Characteristics of European WISE

The literature approaches the field of WISE from various perspectives. A significant contribution to WISE research in Europe was made by experts from the EMES network. Social enterprises can be active in many areas, as meeting the socially beneficial objective relates to a wide range of activities (Defourny and Nyssens, 2008). However, so-called integration social enterprises, commonly called WISE, are dominant in Europe. The lasting structural unemployment in some groups, limitations to traditionally perceived active labour market policies, and the increasingly needed innovative policies in this area, bring questions concerning the role of a social entrepreneur in combating the unemployment and support of employment opportunities (Defourny and Nyssens, 2008). To help unemployed people with low qualifications who are facing permanent labour market exclusion is exactly the objective of work integration social enterprises. Social enterprises integrate these people into society, providing the possibility fot them to engage in productive activity.

Defourny et al. (2004) describe the integration social enterprises as autonomous economic subjects whose main objective is the professional integration of persons facing employment difficulties. The integration happens through a productive activity or training aimed to increase the qualifications of the disadvantaged persons. According to the cited experts, the most frequent activities that WISE focus on are manual work, waste treatment, gardening and packaging work.

Defourny et al. (2004) distinguish four main types of social enterprises according to the way they integrate persons:

1. Temporary employment. The focus is on providing the target group with work experience (temporary employment) or training at the workplace with the purpose to integrate these disadvantaged workers in the open labour market. The target persons participate in traineeships or are employed for a fixed period.
2. Creating a permanent work position financed by the social enterprise. The objective of this type of integration is to create work positions for the labour market disadvantaged persons which are stable and economically sustainable in the mid-term. In the initial phase, public subsidies are used to finance the work position, and these subsidies balance the insufficient productivity of the target group. These subsidies are temporary, and their amount decreases when the workers become competitive in the labour market. After this interim phase, the integration social enterprises pay the wages of the employees from their own resources (mainly from their revenues).
3. Professional integration supported by permanent subsidies. In the case of the most disadvantaged persons, the integration of which would be difficult in the mid-term, these people are provided with stable work positions permanently financed from public resources.
4. Socialization through productive activity. The aim of the last type of integration enterprise is not professional integration into the open labour market (however, this is not excluded), but rather social rehabilitation of the target groups through social contact, complying with roles, lifestyle improvements, and so on. The enterprises of this type work mainly with people with serious social problems (alcohol and drug addiction, former convicts), or people with a serious physical or mental handicap.

Spear and Bidet (2003) provide several views on WISE:

- The amount of financing of the social enterprise from public sources: whether the financing from the public sources is permanent, temporary, or whether the enterprise is only self-financed.

- The type of employment the social enterprise provides to the disadvantaged persons: the authors distinguish between permanent and temporary employment.
- The emphasis the social enterprise places on the training of the employees.

Defourny et al. (2004) describe the types of social enterprises from the financial perspective in a similar way. In European countries, WISE have a strong position among other types of social enterprises. As in other countries, WISE are currently the dominant and more visible model of social enterprises in Switzerland (Adam et al., 2016). The dominant position of WISE among other types of social enterprises in a number of European countries is confirmed, for example, by Greblikaite et al. (2015) in the case of Poland, and by Asmalovskij and Sadilek (2016) in the case of Slovakia and the Czech Republic. As stated by the authors, in the Czech Republic, social entrepreneurship is often perceived as the employment of disabled or otherwise disadvantaged people. WISE in Austria correspond to a high degree to the international understanding of social enterprises, as they display the social, economic and governance-related dimensions of social enterprises such as are outlined in the EMES approach, and they pursue a specific social mission of work integration (Anastasiadis, 2016).

Social Enterprises and Disabled People in the Labour Market

Disabled people are one of the groups of disadvantaged people who can be supported by WISE. In an attempt to understand the employment of disabled persons, Shier et al. (2009) carried out individual and group interviews with 56 disabled persons. The interviews revealed that they face discrimination and that it is difficult for them to find and retain a job. Thornton (2005) described the inequalities between the disabled and non-disabled persons in the context of employment; she pointed out that discrimination of disabled people during the selection process of applicants often exists and that the non-disabled candidates were 150 per cent more likely to gain a positive reply than the disabled candidates.

Social enterprises as the partners of disabled persons were the research subject of Harris et al. (2013) and Caldwell et al. (2012). According to these authors, if supported adequately, social entrepreneurship is an employment option that can lead to economic self-sufficiency, assist broader economic growth, and support businesses that address the social problems affecting people with disabilities. The connection between social entrepreneurship and social inclusion of disabled persons was made by Hall and Wilton (2011), Shaheen (2016), Buhariwala et al. (2015) and Smith et al. (2018). According to these authors, social enterprise can deliver higher wages, and extend to otherwise disadvantaged and marginalized individuals the dignity and respect of 'real work for real pay'. Based on the research of Kummitha (2016), the WISE approach helped the excluded sections to gain access to a dignified livelihood and to attain quite active participation in mainstream society. Both economic and social empowerment were identified as positive results from such initiatives. Especially through professional integration, the excluded regain dignity by participating in employment and social activities. Regaining dignity has connections to the social ties that such individuals can rebuild during the process.

The research presented supports the importance of WISE in the inclusion process of disabled people into society. For disabled people, it is necessary to be informed about the opportunities that WISE offer. For this reason, we decided to contribute to the existing literature and to reveal whether Czech disabled people are familiar with the social entrepreneurship concept, and how they perceive their situation in the labour market, which could be improved by WISE.

University Students as Future Social Entrepreneurs

As the second group of social enterprises key stakeholders, we selected university students. To support the legitimacy of our position to include university students as potential social entrepreneurs, we performed a review of relevant scientific literature on university students' intentions to become social entrepreneurs and their knowledge about the concept.

Franco et al. (2010) compared entrepreneurial intentions of university students in Eastern and Western Germany and also in central Portugal. They revealed that most of the respondents are so-called potential founders: they do not exclude the possibility of being self-employed. The largest number of students considering to become entrepreneurs (so-called founders) is in Portugal. According to Ashour (2016), a significant number of higher education students in the United Arab Emirates have positive attitudes towards entrepreneurship and social entrepreneurship as career options. The research revealed that 38 per cent of students expressed an interest in becoming entrepreneurs, and 23.3 per cent expressed an interest in becoming social entrepreneurs. Students' intentions to become social entrepreneurs were also researched by Kedmenec et al. (2015). The authors found that almost 70 per cent of the respondents (Croatian university students) intend to start a venture in the next ten years. Half of those respondents show a tendency toward commercial entrepreneurship, while the other half prefer social entrepreneurship. Ip et al. (2017) argue that university students are our society's future, and because of that they should be encouraged to treasure environmental resources and to help disadvantaged people. The study of Barton et al. (2018) shows that more than half of American business students who were interviewed reported social entrepreneurial intentions.

According to some of the latest research focused on Russian university students' knowledge of social entrepreneurship (Kireeva et al., 2019), only 34.8 per cent of respondents are familiar with the phenomenon of social entrepreneurship. Nevertheless, students' knowledge of social entrepreneurship and students' intentions to become entrepreneurs and social entrepreneurs in the Czech context are not analysed in the literature. This fact provides an opportunity for this research, which can contribute to a better understanding of this topic. The methodological approach to our research is described in the next section.

CHAPTER OBJECTIVE AND RESEARCH QUESTIONS

The aim of the chapter is to explore the awareness and attitudes of selected groups of people: possible social enterprise stakeholders towards social entrepreneurship in the Czech Republic. In our research, these groups of people are Czech disabled persons and Czech university students of the humanities.

We focus on these groups because, firstly, disabled people are the largest group of disadvantaged persons in the Czech labour market, and increasing their awareness of social entrepreneurship can support their further involvement and thus improve the overall situation of these people in the labour market. For disabled people, it is necessary to be informed about the opportunities that social entrepreneurship offers. For this reason, we decided to contribute to the existing literature and to reveal whether Czech disabled people are familiar with the social entrepreneurship concept. In addition, we tried to find out how these people perceive their situation in the labour market. A possible difficult situation can be resolved by the establishment of new social enterprises (especially by WISE), which according to previous research (e.g., Kročil et al., 2019) make a significant contribution to the integration of disadvantaged people.

Secondly, as presented in the literature review, university students often have social entrepreneurial intentions, and will become the founders of new social enterprises. Especially, students of the humanities who, based on their study direction, could be interested in social innovations, can respond to the situation of disadvantaged people in the labour market and develop new social enterprises (including WISE) that will contribute to solving societal problems in the field of unemployment.

To achieve the aim stated above, the following research questions were defined:

- Q1: To what extent do Czech university students and people with disabilities know of the existence of social entrepreneurship concept and how are they able to define it?
- Q2: Do Czech university students consider starting businesses with social purposes and helping to integrate disadvantaged people back into society?
- Q3: How do Czech disabled people perceive their position in the current labour market?

METHODOLOGICAL APPROACH

Within this research, we consider as potential entrepreneurs the students of the first year of humanities-focused programmes of the Department of Applied Economics, Palacky University Faculty of Arts. After finishing their studies, these individuals will decide whether their income will come from an employment or entrepreneurial activity. If they chose the second option, they will also need to determine their business goals. At the same time, their study focus on the humanities could contribute to increased interest in social innovations. Out of 146 students enrolled in the researched first year, 106 completed the questionnaire. The survey results do not take into account the respondents' gender, as we do not consider this factor as relevant to the objective of the survey. The structured questionnaire was provided in paper form.

The first-year students were chosen on purpose as the students of later study years meet the term 'social entrepreneurship' in their courses. This would negatively influence the research results, as the assessment of the initial awareness of students starting the university studies is one of the research outputs.

The disabled persons, who are potential employees of social enterprises, were provided with the questionnaire in electronic form, using the platform Survio. This questionnaire was shared through the social networks profiles of the Chart 77 Foundation, the main project of which is the fundraising campaign Konto Bariéry, focusing on the improvement of life of disabled persons and their integration into society; and the Brno-based association Liga vozíčkářů, z.ú. In this case as well, gender was not taken into account. Given the form of distribution of the questionnaires, it is impossible to determine the total population; 102 disabled persons completed the questionnaire.

Of course, the possibility that the social entrepreneur – that is, the social enterprise founder – can be a person from the disadvantaged group or a disabled person is not excluded. However, from the perspective of this research, disadvantaged persons are primarily considered as the employees of social enterprises. There is also a possibility that during the survey the surveyed student was at the same time a disabled person, or that the interviewed person was at the same time the student of a humanities-focused programme of the Department of Applied Economics, Faculty of Arts, Palacky University Olomouc.

The students of humanities programmes of the Department of Applied Economics – the potential social entrepreneurs/founders of social enterprises – were asked to answer the questions given in Table 7.1.

RESULTS

Responses of Czech University Students: Potential Social Entrepreneurs

More than half of the questioned students consider becoming an entrepreneur or setting up a business (Table 7.2). This result is in line with the research of Kedmenec et al. (2015). According to these authors, the majority of Croatian students expressed the intention to start an entrepreneurship career. On the other hand, according to Ashour (2016) and Franco et al. (2010), Czech university students show more interest in becoming entrepreneurs than do students in the United Arab Emirates, or in Germany and Portugal.

More than half of the questioned students can imagine following a social purpose and not only the profit in their future business activity (Table 7.2). This result is important for the development of new social enterprises in the Czech Republic, as most of the respondents are willing to follow the main social entrepreneurship principle which is to help the society, and not just to attain a profit. Our result is in line with

Table 7.1   *Questionnaire items*

Questions	Type of question
University students	
Do you consider becoming an entrepreneur or founding an enterprise in your future professional life?	Closed-ended question, answer YES – NO
Regardless of whether you want to do business or set up an enterprise, can you imagine following a social purpose as a part of your business activity?	Closed-ended question, answer YES – NO
If yes, what would be the subject matter of such a social purpose?	An open-ended question, free answer
Have you ever heard the term 'social entrepreneurship'?	Closed-ended question, answer YES – NO
If yes, please try to answer briefly: what does this term mean or what is your understanding of this term?	Open-ended question, free answer
Disabled people	
According to your opinion, is it difficult to find employment as a disabled person in the current labour market?	Closed-ended question, answer YES – NO
Do you perceive the number of work positions interesting for disabled persons as sufficient?	Closed-ended question, answer YES – NO
Have you ever heard the term 'social entrepreneurship'?	Closed-ended question, answer YES – NO
If yes, please try to answer briefly: what does this term mean or what is your understanding of this term?	Open-ended question, free answer

Table 7.2   *Summary of results (YES – NO questions)*

Question	Respondents	Positive answer (%)	Negative answer (%)
Do you consider becoming an entrepreneur or founding an enterprise in your future professional life?	Students	53	47
Regardless of whether you want to do business or set up an enterprise, can you imagine following a social purpose as a part of your business activity?	Students	66	34
Have you ever heard the term 'social entrepreneurship'?	Students	24	76
In your opinion, is it difficult to find employment as a disabled person in the current labour market?	Disabled people	89	11
Do you perceive the number of work positions interesting for disabled persons as sufficient?	Disabled people	20	80
Have you ever heard the term 'social entrepreneurship'?	Disabled people	46	54

previous research done by Barton et al. (2018). These authors concluded that more than half of the American business students they interviewed reported social entre-preneurial intentions. In comparison with Ashour's research (2016), our respondents show more interest in unconventional business. Of the 70 persons who responded positively to the previous question, 60 further specified the nature of a social purpose that they planned to follow in their business activities.

Some of them provided more purposes. Purposes such as helping disadvantaged groups of people and the creation of new work positions are typical for the nature of WISE. However, the most common purpose mentioned by Czech university students is environmental protection and improvement, which is important especially for environmental social enterprises.

Surprisingly to us, the majority of students responded that they had never heard of the term 'social entrepreneurship' (Table 7.2). In comparison with the research done by Kireeva et al. (2019), our respondents are less familiar with the concept of social entrepreneurship than the Russian university students. This result does not support the development of new WISE founded by students, and it would suggest that the Czech education system should acquaint students with the concept of social entrepreneurship.

Twenty-two students tried to define the concept of social entrepreneurship. The majority of the students connected social entrepreneurship with achieving profit and at the same time a social purpose. These respondents perceived these two principles as interconnected. We can evaluate these answers as correct: both sets of principles (economic and social) are covered in these answers. Fewer students mentioned only the aspect of following a social purpose without an effort to make a profit. One student did not generalize the features of social entrepreneurship; the student only suggested that it could be, for example, establishing a home for elderly people. Twenty-one respondents mentioned a social purpose as a feature of social entrepreneurship. More than half of those questioned did not provide any specification. These students only mentioned that it was an activity which was generally beneficial to society. However, some respondents defined social purpose in a more concrete way. Most of the students specify the main goal of social enterprises as 'general benefit to society', and 'helping disadvantaged people to find employment'. The second objective follows the idea of WISE.

The following section provides comments on the answers of the Czech disabled people, who were asked five questions.

Responses of the Czech Disabled People

The majority of the people questioned believe that it is difficult to find employment as a disabled person (Table 7.2). This result is in line with the conclusion reached by Shier et al. (2009), who reported that it is difficult for disabled people to get and retain a job. Establishing new social enterprises (WISE especially) may be particularly useful in overcoming these obstacles.

The majority of the respondents are convinced that the current labour market does not provide enough work positions suitable for disabled persons (Table 7.2). In 2018, Czech WISE provided work for almost 4000 disabled people. According to the Czech Labour Office, in December 2019 there were 33 000 unemployed disabled people in the labour market. Without existing Czech WISE, this number would have increased by 12 per cent. In terms of establishing new WISE, the current labour market situation could be further improved.

A small majority of the questioned persons responded that they had never heard of the term 'social entrepreneurship' (Table 7.2). As in the case of the students' answers, this is a surprising finding for us.

Fifty-seven per cent of all respondents tried to characterize the term 'social entrepreneurship'. Only two persons mentioned that social entrepreneurship interconnected two objectives: making a profit and pursuing a societally beneficial purpose. The majority of the respondents defined this concept as business with a societally beneficial objective, and almost one-fifth as the entrepreneurial activity of disabled people.

LIMITATIONS OF THE RESEARCH

Although the research presents original results and its conclusions can be used in practice (for example, by universities in their educational activities, or by non-profit organizations helping disabled people), it still has its limitations. First, the research sample could be extended to students of other universities, which would allow a better generalization of the conclusions. Second, the research does not focus on some other possible stakeholders of social enterprises, whose awareness and attitudes would also be appropriate to examine. These stakeholders are, for example, representatives of public administration bodies who can play an important role in the development of social entrepreneurship. Third, the research is descriptive in nature and does not answer the question of the relationship between respondents' characteristics and their awareness and attitudes towards social entrepreneurship. These limits offer room for further research.

CONCLUSION AND DISCUSSION

This research aimed to explore the awareness and attitudes of selected groups of people: possible social entrepreneurship stakeholders related to social entrepreneurship in the Czech Republic. We based our findings on the results of a questionnaire survey among possible social enterprises' stakeholders: Czech university students and disabled persons. We also tried to find out how disabled people perceive their situation in the labour market. A possibly difficult situation can be resolved by the establishment of new social enterprises (especially by WISE), which, according to previous research, make a significant contribution to the integration of disadvantaged people.

According to our findings, the level of awareness of the concept of social entrepreneurship in the Czech Republic is generally low. In the case of both groups of respondents, the majority of them has never heard of social entrepreneurship, and when compared, the level of awareness is better in the group of disabled persons. We consider these findings to be negative in terms of higher involvement of disabled people in social entrepreneurship. It is useful for people with disabilities to know about the existence and nature of social entrepreneurship, which can help to integrate them into society. As a practical contribution of our chapter, we suggest that the Czech educational system (both secondary and university) should include the topic of social entrepreneurship in its study plans: in the form of practical workshops, as part of existing subjects, or in the newly developed specialized courses. In the case of disabled people, it could be the role of the Czech social policy and non-profit organizations helping disabled people (such as the Czech National Disability Council) to increase their knowledge.

Approximately 20 per cent of the questioned students tried to define social entrepreneurship, while 50 per cent of the disabled persons responded to the same question. The cumulative results differ as well. The majority of responding students are aware of the objective to make a profit which is necessary for social entrepreneurship. The majority of disabled persons did not mention this objective, and focused their answers only on the idea of following a social purpose, which is only one of the important characteristics of social entrepreneurship. An integral part of the definition of social enterprise are the economic principles represented by the effort to make a profit, or in the case of not-for-profit social enterprises, at least by the production of products and delivery of services. According to the EMES definition, for-profit and not-for-profit social enterprises engage in economic activity. This fact was omitted by the majority of disabled respondents. In the majority of cases, the students who mentioned the profit-making did not omit the social purpose.

We can say that both students and disabled persons often relate social entrepreneurship to its integration role, although it is only one of the possible objectives of social enterprises. In the majority of cases, the students mentioned a social purpose only in a general way and did not specify it. However, a smaller number of students mentioned the objective of employment or helping disadvantaged people in the labour market. Disabled people primarily linked the social purpose of enterprises with the employment of disadvantaged persons.

As part of their responses to questioning, both students and disabled persons mentioned names of 24 enterprises which they consider to be social. However, the question is whether these enterprises are social enterprises. Ten of the 24 claim to be a social enterprise on their web pages, or by the fact that they are listed in the database of social enterprises administered by the Czech Ministry of Labour and Social Affairs. Many enterprises considered by the respondents as social do not provide this information on their web page or through the database listing. However, in these cases there can be at least identified the purpose to employ labour market disadvantaged persons.

The willingness of university students to become entrepreneurs or to start a business and consider pursuing a societally beneficial objective is very important for the further development of social entrepreneurship and integration of disabled people. From this perspective, social entrepreneurship including WISE has the potential for further development, as the majority of respondents responded positively to both questions. Our findings are in line with previous research and support the idea of university students as a group of potential social enterprise founders. University students need to increase their knowledge of social entrepreneurship during their studies. However, they must understand not only the benefits of this type of entrepreneurship, but also the threats and risks associated with it.

The majority of disabled respondents reported that it is difficult to find employment as a disabled person, and that the current labour market does not offer enough vacant positions which could be interesting for these people. Knowledge of the existing difficult position of Czech disabled people in the current labour market could be an impulse for establishing new social enterprises (especially WISE) in the Czech Republic. From this perspective, we can assess the importance of further development of social enterprises (especially WISE) as very significant. On average, one Czech WISE employs almost 15 disabled people. The establishment of new WISE would help in meeting the work needs of people with disabilities.

As a topic for the discussion and further research we suggest to focus on the causes of low awareness of social entrepreneurship among the questioned persons. One of the possible reasons can be the fact that in the Czech Republic so far there is no law in force regulating social entrepreneurship. Such a law exists in many countries of the European Union. We see an opportunity to carry out similarly oriented research in some of these states to find out whether the level of awareness differs from the results presented in this chapter. Another research topic could focus on the space given to the topic of social entrepreneurship in the study programmes of humanities-focused institutions of higher education or at lower levels of education.

ACKNOWLEDGEMENT

This research was supported by the grant IGA_FF_2020_001 Shifts in Entrepreneurial Approaches in the Contemporary Economy 2 of the internal grant agency of Palacky University Olomouc, Czech Republic.

REFERENCES

Adam, S., Aviles, G., Ferrari, D., Amstutz, J., Crivelli, L., et al. 2016. Work integration social enterprises in Switzerland. *Nonprofit Policy Forum*, 7: 509–539.
Anastasiadis, M. 2016. Work integration social enterprises in Austria – characteristics, evolution and perspectives. *Nonprofit Policy Forum*, 7: 541–564.
Ashour, S. 2016. Social and business entrepreneurship as career options for university students in the United Arab Emirates: the drive–preparedness gap. *Cogent Education*, 3. tandfonline.com.
Asmalovskij, A., Sadilek, T. 2016. The current state of social entrepreneurship in the Czech Republic and Slovakia. *Sociologia*, 48: 319–339.
Barton, M., Schaefer, R., Canavati, S. 2018. To be or not to be a social entrepreneur: motivational drivers amongst American business students. *Entrepreneurial Business and Economics Review*, 6: 9–35.

Borzaga, C., Galera, G., Franchini, B., Chiomento, S., Nogales, R., Carini, C. 2020. *Social Enterprises and Their Ecosystems in Europe, Comparative Synthesis Report.* European Commission.

Buhariwala, P., Wilton, R., Evans, J. 2015. Social enterprises as enabling workplaces for people with psychiatric disabilities. *Disability and Society*, 30: 865–879.

Caldwell, K., Harris, S.P., Renko, M. 2012. The potential of social entrepreneurship: conceptual tools for applying citizenship theory to policy and practice. *Intellectual and Developmental Disabilities*, 50: 505–518.

Czech Labour Office. n.d. Unemployment Statistics, Czech Labour Office. https://www.mpsv .cz/web/cz/statistiky#statistiky-o-trhu-prace.

Defourny, J., Gregoire, O., Davister, C. 2004. *Work Integration Social Enterprises in the European Union: An Overview of Existing Models.* https://emes.net/publications/ working-papers/work-integration-social-enterprises-in-the-european-union-an-overview -of-existing-models/.

Defourny, J., Nyssens, M. 2008. *Social Enterprise in Europe: Recent Trends and Developments.* https://emes.net/publications/working-papers/social-enterprise-in-europe-recent-trends -and-developments/.

Defourny, J., Nyssens, M. 2012. *The EMES Approach of Social Enterprise in a Comparative Perspective.* https://emes.net/content/uploads/publications/EMES-WP-12-03_Defourny -Nyssens.pdf.

Eurostat. n.d. *Unemployment Statistics, Eurostat.* https://ec.europa.eu/eurostat/statistics -explained/index.php/Unemployment_statistic.

Franco, M., Haase, H., Lautenschläger, A. 2010. Students' entrepreneurial intentions: an inter-regional comparison. *Education and Training*, 52: 260–275.

Greblikaite, J., Sroka, W., Grants, J. 2015. Development of social entrepreneurship in European Union: policy and situation of Lithuania and Poland. *Transformations in Business and Economics*, 14: 376–396.

Hall, E., Wilton, R. 2011. Alternative spaces of 'work' and inclusion for disabled people, *Disability and Society*, 26: 867–880.

Harris, S.P., Renko, M., Caldwell, K. 2013. Accessing social entrepreneurship: perspectives of people with disabilities and key stakeholders. *Journal of Vocational Rehabilitation*, 38: 35–48.

Ip, C.I., Wu, S.C., Liu, H.C., Liang, C. 2017. Revisiting the antecedents of social entrepreneurial intentions in Hong Kong. *International Journal of Educational Psychology*, 6: 301–323.

Kedmenec, I., Rebernik, M., Peric, J. 2015. The impact of individual characteristics on intentions to pursue social entrepreneurship. *Ekonomski Pregled*, 66: 119–137.

Kireeva, N.S., Zavyalov, D.V., Saginova, O.V., Zavyalova, N.B. 2019. Students' perception of social entrepreneurship. *Revista de la Universidad del Zulia*, 10: 200–210.

Kročil, O., Dopita, M., Pospíšil, R. 2019. Integration social enterprises as a tool of employment policy. *Ekonomski Pregled*, 70: 554–571.

Kročil O., Pospíšil R., Kosina, D. 2020. Awareness and attitudes toward social entrepreneurship among university students and disabled people. The case of the Czech Republic. *Economic and Social Changes: Facts, Trends, Forecast*, 13: 247–263.

Kummitha, R.K.R. 2016. Social entrepreneurship as a tool to remedy social exclusion: a win– win scenario? *South Asia Research*, 36: 61–79.

Shaheen, G.E. 2016. Inclusive entrepreneurship: a process for improving self-employment for people with disabilities. *Journal of Policy Practice*, 15: 58–81.

Shier, M., Graham, J.R., Jones, M.E. 2009. Barriers to employment as experienced by disabled people: a qualitative analysis in Calgary and Regina, Canada. *Disability and Society*, 24: 63–75.

Smith, P., McVilly, K.R., McGillivray, J., Chan, J. 2018. Developing open employment outcomes for people with an intellectual disability utilising a social enterprise framework. *Journal of Vocational Rehabilitation*, 48: 59–77.

Spear, R., Bidet, E. 2003. The role of social enterprise in European labour markets. https:// emes.net/publications/working-papers/the-role-of-social-enterprise-in-european-labour -markets/.

TESSEA. n.d.-a. *Definition and Principles of Social Enterprise, TESSEA.* http://www.tessea .cz/tessea-o-nas/definice-a-principy-socialniho-podnikani.

TESSEA. n.d.-b. *Questionnaire Survey of Social Enterprises, TESSEA.* http://www.tessea.cz/ aktuality/528-dotaznikove-setreni-socialnich-podniku-2019.

Thornton, P. 2005. Disabled people, employment and social justice. *Social Policy and Society*, 4: 65–73.

PART II

ENTREPRENEURIAL ECOSYSTEM: BARRIERS AND FACILITATORS

8. Enterprising? Disabled? The status and potential for disabled people's microenterprise in South Korea

Se Kwang Hwang and Alan Roulstone

INTRODUCTION

Over the past two decades, economic and societal trends have highlighted the centrality of paid employment as a key route to social inclusion in many 'advanced' economies. In this way, disability employment policies and vocational guidance have become far more important tools for inclusion (Burchardt, 2005; Roulstone, as quoted in Watson et al., 2012). Disabled people's economic activities can empower them financially and allow them to escape unemployment or entitlements-based programmes to employment (Cole et al., 2007; OECD, 2003). Disabled people's concerns for paid employment have inadvertently converged with neoliberal preoccupations with economic work-first models of the citizenship. For disabled people, nevertheless, moving into employment may be very difficult (Stafford, 2005; World Health Organization and World Bank, 2011), while explanations for barriers of moving to employment in each approach are very different. Disabled people have globally been significantly less likely to be in employment than non-disabled people (O'Reilly, 2007). There are currently 2 683 477 registered disabled people living in South Korea (hereinafter Korea); 96.5 per cent of them are of working age (over 18 years old), but only 35.5 per cent of disabled people were in the Korean labour market in 2011 (Ministry of Health and Welfare, 2012). Disabled people's employment in Korea has been further constrained by structural, cultural and economic barriers, while disabled people are still characterised by their lower labour market participation, lower income rates, higher unemployment levels, greater presence in low-skilled jobs and lower educational levels than the general population (KIHASA, 2011).

The disability employment legislation in Korea has been established since the 1960s and several initiatives have been promoted, most notably a quota system for employers and sheltered employment alternatives. The Korean disability employment policy has four main components: employment promotion initiatives, which are designed to ensure the employment of disabled people in the open labour market; protected employment initiatives, designed to provide sheltered or supported employment for severely disabled people in protected environments; vocational rehabilitation education and training, designed to provide specialised rehabilitation education programmes for disabled people; and disability enterprises, which are designed to support the starting and running of businesses by disabled people funded by the government (Kim and Davis, 2006). Although these varied approaches acknowledge the diverse nature of employment challenges and involve both sanctions and sweeteners (Stanley et al., 2004), the framework adopted by the Korean government for promoting the employment of disabled people in the labour market can best be characterised as passive and reactive (Cho, 2013). In this sense, the disability legislation has been unable to unravel the close and enduring relationship between impairment, disability and unemployment.

The current harsh economic climate is demanding more innovative pathways to increasing employment participation of socially disadvantaged people as concern mounts about the costs and social impact of out-of-work benefits. Enterprise has been used to help disadvantaged people enter the labour market in many global contexts, and offers a solution to the benefits–tax ratio challenges. It also offers a longer-term option for disabled people who may not fit with standardised notions of the workplace (Cooney, 2008; Pagán, 2009; Robb and Fairlie, 2009). However, disabled people have historically been considered unable to create their own businesses (Pavey, 2006) as they are assumed not to fit traditional business models. Cooney (2008: 119) notes that the general impression of disabled people intuitively implies that they are recipients of care services and protection, and that they are unsuited to running a business. This is of course an assumption; one not based on any firm evidence. Arnold and Ipsen (2005) comment that disabled people wanting to generate their income, who establish and run a business, must overcome physical barriers that face disabled employees in the wider labour market. In addition to assumptions about low productivity and risks that limit disabled people globally (Roulstone, as quoted in Watson et al., 2012), Korean cultural assumptions also add an additional layer of exclusion. The cultural precept of *ijil* ('difference') provides the broad narrative construction of disability (Grinker, 2007). *Ijil* is closely associated with the notion of 'the other'. The linked precept of *chemyon* or face-saving operates to attenuate shame by structuring separate lives for disabled people (Lim, 2002: 104–105). This mirrors Canguilheim's formulation of social orders of difference, where he notes: 'Every preference for a possible order is accompanied, most often explicitly by the aversion for the opposite order. That which diverges from the preferable in a given area ... is not the indifferent, but the repulsive' (Canguilheim, 1991: 240).

However, studies in the United States (Mathis, 2003), the United Kingdom (Anderson and Galloway, 2012), South Africa (Lorenzo et al., 2007) and Sweden (Larsson, 2006) have reported that, for disabled people, an own-account business holds many benefits, such as increasing independence, greater choices and self-determination, and the development of management and wider transferable skills (Blanck et al., 2000). As awareness of these benefits increases, the Korean government's attention is being increasingly directed towards the potential of disability enterprise as a more innovative solution to ameliorate the economic and social challenges relating to contractual employment. This realisation led the Korean government to introduce the Promotion of Disabled Persons' Enterprise Activities Act (PDEA) (Ministry of Government Legislation, 2005), a move which it was hoped might play an increasing role in providing employment opportunities, self-sufficiency and reduction of dependence.

ENTERPRISE AND DISABLED PEOPLE: COMMENSURATE BEDFELLOWS?

Within disability studies, policy studies and business studies, the concepts of self-employment and enterprise are often used interchangeably (Raheim, 1996). Since one person may have more than one job, however, the numbers of self-employed may not equal the total number of enterprises. Therefore, distinguishing enterprise from self-employment is essential for any discussion of how to improve labour force participation for disabled people. Self-employment is defined as performing work primarily for individual profit rather than for employing people (see Wickham, 2013), but enterprise refers to 'any entity engaged in an economic activity, irrespective of its legal form' (European Commission, 2005) that brings new and innovative ventures to the market. In Korea, disability enterprise is officially defined as 'a for-profit business owned and operated by the disabled entrepreneur' (PDEA Article 2; Ministry of Government Legislation, 2005). To be officially designated a disability enterprise, at least 30 per cent of a firm's employees must be disabled; paradoxically, the quota rate does not apply to micro and small disability enterprises (less than 50 employees). This entitles the business to tax advantages. The potential is then twofold as an opportunity for disabled people to front enterprises and to incentivise the employment of disabled people within these enterprises. Governments often also favour such enterprises, as they can provide innovative and novel solutions to the marketplace and respond to unmet customer needs (Shane, 2008).

Nevertheless, within both business and disability studies research, disability and enterprise at present are rarely positioned together, while there are a very small number of studies on self-employment for disabled people (Boylan and Burchardt, 2003). This contrasts with the much larger literature on enterprise, gender and ethnicity (Allen and Truman, 1993; Clark and Drinkwater, 2000; Marlow, 2002). Most commentators assume that small businesses are synonymous with non-disabled entrepreneurs. Even a cursory glance at popular images of entrepreneurs, small business owners or the self-employed shows a distinct absence of disabled people (Google image search: 'micro-enterprise', 'small business', 'self-employment'). Therefore, no comprehensive study has been completed that generates evidence relating to enterprises established and run by disabled people. Although now more heterogeneous, the archetypal image of enterprise is 'male and lean, hungry, predatory and hostile' (Greer, 1999: 299). As a result, research is needed to increase our understanding of how disability enterprises can become a realistic option for all disabled people as alternatives to paid employment.

This chapter explores the nature, activities and untapped potential of enterprise for disabled people, as a new alternative work integration and social inclusion tool for disabled people in Korea. Firstly, we look at the current nature of disability and employment in Korea, highlighting the major challenges faced. We then trace back the changes in the disability employment policies and map out the development of disability enterprise and supportive legislation in Korea. Next, we map out profiles of current disability enterprises based on the Small and Medium Business Administration's (SMBA) 2011 Biannual Nationwide Survey of Disability Enterprises (SMBA, 2011), and discuss the implications for the development of disability enterprises. We make clear which factors support or militate against greater enterprise development.

THE KOREAN LABOUR MARKET CONTEXT AND DISABLED PEOPLE

Any starting point regarding disability enterprises needs to begin with a review of the general employment situation for disabled people, as it provides contextual information of disabled people's wider employment position and re-emphasises the need for alternatives. The Korean government has supported disabled people by creating affirmative action for getting them into employment such as vocational rehabilitation centres, social enterprises and sheltered employment workshops (Oh et al., 2005). Nevertheless, it is widely recognised that having a disability has very negative effects upon employment and earnings. According to the Economic Activity Status for the Disabled Survey 2010 (Lim et al., 2011) (Figure 8.1), the employment-to-population ratio of disabled people stands at 38.5 per cent, about one-half of the national employment-to-population ratio of 61.9 per cent. A total of 915 217 disabled people aged 15 or over (36 per cent) are economically active, compared with the national economically active population (60 per cent); and 466 916 of disabled employees are waged/salaried workers, but 43 per cent of disabled employees have basic physical labouring jobs, and 63.2 per cent have part-time jobs. Earnings are similarly imbalanced, with the mean earnings in 2010 for disabled employees holding full-time jobs being 1 342 000 Korean Won (KRW) (approximately £758) per month compared to 3 112 000 KRW (approximately £1754) for non-disabled employees. It is hard for disabled people to enter employment that requires multi-skilling, higher productivity and long working hours. Similar findings emerged in Western studies (e.g., Office for National Statistics, 2012), which indicate that disabled people are more likely to work unskilled, semi-skilled or skilled manual jobs, and to earn less. Although the Korean government has employed strong strategies for disabled people's thriving and surviving (Roulstone et al., 2003), they are still less likely to sustain employment. In the study (Lim et al., 2011), 388 241 Korean disabled workers are identified as self-employed. Self-employment is an important source of paid work for disabled people, but generally they become self-employed for negative reasons. Research (Yu, 2008) established that disabled people in Korea are more likely to be self-employed because there are fewer opportunities to get paid jobs due to being considered 'less productive', with a perceived lack of interpersonal skills and relationships with colleagues; there is discrimination in the workplace (for example, less opportunity

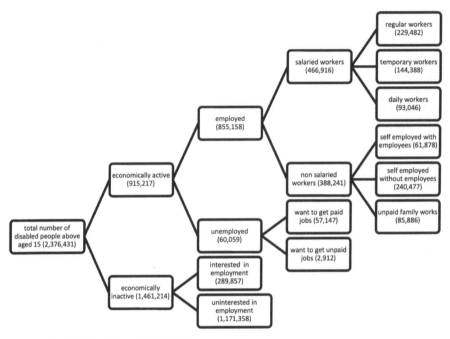

Source: Derived from Lim et al. (2011: 11).

Figure 8.1   *Economic activity status of disabled people in 2010*

for promotion, job placement, salary); accessibility in the workplace is a problem; and there is a lack of transportation from home to work. The common reasons for disabled people becoming self-employed are therefore the disadvantages and dis-criminations of mainstream paid jobs. Further evidence (e.g., Cooney, 2008; Noakes, 2006) suggests that self-employment can be seen as a survival strategy for disabled people who cannot find any other means of earning an income. However, there is no research evidence as to why and how many disabled employees transit from their current paid jobs to self-employment or enterprises in Korea.

The vast majority (61.5 per cent) of disabled people are classified as 'economically inactive'. Specifically, 80.2 per cent of disabled people who are outside the labour market are uninterested in or unable to pursue paid employment. The unemployment rate for disabled people stands at 6.6 per cent, almost twice as high as the national unemployment rate of 3.2 per cent. In particular, the highest unemployment rate (13 per cent) is for those between ages 15 and 29. These findings indicate that it is harder for young disabled females to get a paid job in Korea, due to both generic disabling barriers and cultural assumptions around a woman's role rooted in Confucian family obligations in and beyond one's blood family (Sung, 2003). The rates of employ-ment vary markedly between types of disability. For example, the Employment Development Institute (2011) survey shows that people with complex needs have the lowest probability of getting a job. This is clear evidence that the type, severity, duration and cause of the disability were found to be important determinants of paid employment (Berthoud, 2006; Hall and Wilton, 2011).

Overall, disabled people have significantly lower rates of participation in employment than the general population. Opportunities for getting a job are more restricted than other marginalised groups and are unevenly distributed because of structural, cultural and economic barriers relating to impairments (KIHASA, 2011). As a result, unemployment and poverty still remain serious problems affecting the majority of Korean disabled people and their families.

THE EMPLOYMENT POLICY CONTEXT TO KOREAN DISABILITY ENTERPRISE POLICY

Disability employment policies in Korea have developed since the 1960s. For example, the Employment Act for the Relief of Recipients 1961 required employers to offer paid jobs to people with physical disabilities, whilst the Industrial Accident Compensation Insurance Act 1963, an Act firmly rooted in a paternalist tradition (Roulstone and Prideaux, 2012: 56–81), focused on the provision of relevant medical services and rehabilitation training for employees who were wounded or had physical disabilities due to industrial accidents. In 1990, the Employment Promotion for Disabled Persons policy was introduced. The Employment Promotion for Disabled Persons focuses on promoting employment opportunities for disabled people, whilst avoiding discrimination sanctions or requiring employers to make reasonable adjustments. Thus, the Employment Promotion and Vocational Rehabilitation Act for Disabled Persons is regarded as symbolic, rather than practical in effectively enabling employment (Cho, 2013). The revision of the Employment Promotion for Disabled Persons in 2000 through the Employment Promotion and Vocational Rehabilitation Act for Disabled Persons stipulates the employment quota system, which has operated as the key system for the promotion of the employment of disabled people. Initially, employers with over 300 employees were obliged to fulfil the employment quota for disabled people. But, its remit was expanded in 2004 so that any organisation with more than 50 employees must employ disabled people at a rate of 2 per cent of the entire company's workforce. For central and local governments the figure is even higher, at 3 per cent of the workforce. If employers fail to fulfil the obligatory quota, they are supposed to pay 'burden charges'. Income from burden charges is used to support those businesses actively hiring disabled employees. The quota system was designed to increase the representativeness of disabled people through the enactment and implementation of laws governing compulsory hiring and employment quotas. Moreover, the Employment Promotion and Vocational Rehabilitation Act for Disabled Persons provided government funding for enhanced subsidies to employers who hired people with complex needs rather than 'mild or moderate' disabled people. This was in recognition of the weight of barriers facing people with the most complex impairments.

To supplement the Act, the Korean government constructed five-year plans for the employment promotion of disabled people in 1997, 2003 and 2008. Sadly, as with many other quota schemes, the Act has not actively promoted the employment and independence of disabled people, because employers have been able to buy out of their obligations, as in many other jurisdictions (see Mont, 2004: 21). It is clear that voluntarism runs through much of Korean disability employment policy. Kim (2011: 29) argues that 'the Act left much room for interpretation, owing to a compromise among major political parties, and there were a number of problems, including insufficient budget allocations, vague regulations, and poor preparedness'.

In 2007, the Disability Discrimination Act (DDA) laid down the legal foundation to prevent discrimination against the disabled in all aspects, including employment, the provision of goods and services, education and transport. The Korean DDA not only intends to prohibit discrimination against a qualified disabled person in employment, but also seeks to improve the employment opportunities and conditions for disabled people. However, there is evidence of a severe lack of public and employer awareness of discrimination against disabled people in employment (Park, 2010). Unlike, say, the United Kingdom DDA or the Americans with Disabilities Act, the Korean DDA does not identify as discrimination a failure of an employer to provide extra help for the disabled employee or applicant. Employers cite 'legitimate' reasons such as undue burden in justifying non-compliance (Chung and Cho, 2007). The Korean government stated that it does not believe quotas for disabled people reverse discrimination by themselves. It is questionable, however, whether the DDA can be compatible with the quota scheme for disabled people, or whether the quota scheme can strengthen the anti-discrimination policies in Korea. Other jurisdictions have seen the quota system and anti-discrimination policies as inimical due to the tensions between paternalist and individual constructions of legal rights (Waddington, 1996), while the Korean government continues to see these as compatible.

Despite legislation intended to root out discrimination against disabled people in the workplace and to contribute to employment promotion, high levels of exclusion of disabled people from participation in the labour market still exist. Such employment policies, programmes and practices (that is, welfare to work, employment quota system, rehabilitation, anti-discrimination) are being further constrained by structural and cultural barriers (Ablenews, 2013). Between 2008 and 2012, employment-related claims for disability discrimination made up 320 cases, but only seven cases were successful (National Human Rights Commission of Korea, 2013). Taken together, the Korean quota system and disability discrimination legislation are clearly insufficient to address the multiple structural and cultural barriers disabled people face in participating in employment.

In recognition of the limited effectiveness of the quota system, the Korean government has prompted affirmative action to promote greater participation in the labour market. In 2005, the PDEA was enacted to help disabled people start their own businesses through having easier access to financing, and encouraging public sector agencies to purchase products from disabled-owned businesses. The PDEA states that the central and local authorities should allow investments and loans to disabled entrepreneurs and their businesses (Articles 3, 8 and 10; Ministry of Government Legislation, 2005). Moreover, the PDEA clearly prohibits discriminatory practices or systems by any public agencies against disability enterprises (Article 4). As of 2011, 32 027 disability enterprises have been established, representing 1 per cent of all small and micro enterprises in Korea (Choo, 2011).

Based on the PDEA (Article 5), the SMBA has established and run the strategic annual plan for facilitation of disability enterprise activities since 2006. The Disabled Enterprise Business Centre was also established in 2008, based on article 13 of the PDEA. The major role of the Disabled Enterprise Business Centre is to establish a 'one-stop shop' to support disability enterprises. To get support from the Disabled Enterprise Business Centre, any disability enterprise must receive an authorisation from the SMBA. Furthermore, the Special Act on the Preferential Purchase of Goods Produced 2008 was passed to promote the purchase of products manufactured by people with multiple and complex needs, and to contribute to their income-earning activity. Following the proactive spirit of section 504 of the US 1974 Rehabilitation Act (Scotch, 2001), the Act recommends that public sector organisations must purchase goods produced by disabled enterprises (Article 9-2) and make such purchases tax-deductible (Article 14). The amount of disabled enterprises' products purchased by 210 public organisations, including the government, local autonomous bodies and public corporations, was expected to increase to about 315.8 billion KRW in 2009 from 86 billion KRW in 2008.

THE CURRENT STATUS OF KOREAN DISABILITY ENTERPRISES

Based on the PDEA, Article 10 (Ministry of Government Legislation, 2005), nation-wide research has been conducted biannually by the SMBA to examine the nature of disability enterprises and to support the growth of their businesses since 2005. Data drawn from the Biannual Nationwide Survey 2011 offer insights into the extent to which disabled entrepreneurs are starting up and running their own businesses. The organisations vary substantially in size, there being a polarisation between a few small (7 per cent) and medium-sized firms (1.6 per cent) and the majority of micro businesses (91.4 per cent) hiring fewer than five employees (see Table 8.1). Similar findings are reported by Cooney (2008), who examined the self-employment of disabled people in the United Kingdom and the United States. Cooney notes that disabled people's firms are more likely to be home-based and microenterprises compared with wider self-employment patterns.

With regard to the type of firm, 88.7 per cent of disability enterprises are in the service sector with sole proprietorship status, while 11.3 per cent are private limited companies. The disability employment rate in these enterprises is 40.6 per cent. These findings suggest that disability enterprises provide disabled people with a valuable opportunity to work.

Table 8.1   *Profiles of disability enterprises*

Size	No. of businesses
Micro (hiring under 5 employees)	2284
Small (hiring 5–50 employees)	176
Medium (hiring 50–300 employees)	40

Source: SMBA (2011).

With regard to the type of business, disability enterprises are predominantly home-based trading businesses that do not require a large amount of start-up funding, knowledge and skills, such as retail outlets (34 per cent), manufacturing units (18.2 per cent) and accommodation providers (15 per cent). Few small (7 per cent) and medium-sized manufacturing firms (1.6 per cent) have been set up. Due to the small size of the business, the average annual income (equivalent to £138 410) of disability enterprises is lower than that of their non-disabled counterparts (equivalent to £3 749 888). Growing revenue, improving gross and operating margins, increasing cash flow, efficiently managing both capital expenditures and working capital, and building an asset base in disability enterprises, are generally poor, so disability enterprises may be easy to set up but are hard to sustain financially without government support.

With regard to gender and age difference, males (78.6 per cent) are three times more likely to be entrepreneurially active as females (21.4 per cent). This finding is echoed in Park's (2007) study, which established that Korean disabled women found it much harder to access the labour market than disabled men, due to stereotypes relating to disabled women, more limited education and lack of employment opportunity. Research conducted by Kim et al. (2011) found a similar trend in that most Korean disabled entrepreneurs were male (95.5 per cent). Although never explicitly studied, the Confucian assumption that women will support their wider family network, including their partner's parents, may be an added barrier to the workplace and enterprise alike (Hwang and Brandon, 2012). The most entrepreneurial age group for the disabled is between 50 and 59 years old (40.9 per cent).

A high proportion (84.7 per cent) of chief executives of disability enterprises have no higher education qualification, while a small proportion (2.7 per cent) have no educational qualifications at all. There are no analyses to date of the relationship between business performance and level of education. Education qualifications are a not prerequisite for starting a disability enterprise, which might seem a positive thing (Pavey, 2006). However, low levels of educational attainment and support for chief executives in disability enterprises may have a negative influence on their business development (for example, developing effective sales, improving operational performance).

Categories of chief executives in disability enterprises are presented in Figure 8.2. People with physical disabilities are particularly likely to start and operate disability enterprises, while people with developmental disabilities and epilepsy are less likely to set up a business. The evidence suggests that finance and support are less in evidence for Koreans with epilepsy and developmental disability (this is the term closest to the Korean, elsewhere the term learning difficulty or intellectual disability is used internationally) because they are, perhaps wrongly, assumed to be seen as greater risks, having higher support needs and less scope for independent trading without support. This finding indicates that disabled people who may need more support to run a business are relatively excluded. The PDEA concentrates more on promoting the business of 'less severely' disabled people, while paying less attention to the business of 'more severely' disabled people. However, it is impossible to know what proportion of disabled people may be considered as potential entrepreneurs.

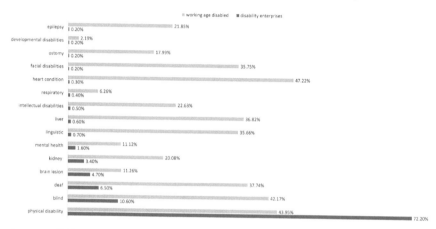

Sources: SMBA (2011) and KIHASA (2011).

Figure 8.2   *Categories of disability entrepreneurs compared to working age disabled profile*

With regard to the duration that the business has been in operation, 23.4 per cent of the respondents said that they have been operating their businesses for a period between three and 15 years, and 18.8 per cent of the respondents have been operating for less than five years. However, there is no comprehensive picture regarding the success rate of businesses owned by disabled people. Most disability enterprises are operating in or near urban areas, especially Seoul, which is the capital of Korea; this would be expected, as large urban areas present larger market potential. However, competing for the same market with other enterprises is a particular challenge.

Studies exploring motivations for starting small business enterprises are rather sobering. As Figure 8.3 shows, the reasons for disabled people starting disability enterprises are heavily rooted in negative motives. For example, the main reason for establishing disability enterprise is to generate household income, often at a subsistence level, to support themselves and their families. While unemployment and poverty remain fundamental problems affecting the majority of Korean disabled people and their families, this finding repeatedly indicates that families with at least one disabled member live in relative income poverty. Enterprise is frequently associated with the will to overcome a state of social marginality or economic discrimination (Godley, 2005). Moreover, 17.7 per cent of the respondents in the Biannual Survey reported that they were unable to work because non-disabled employers do not recognise their capabilities, and 15.8 per cent of the respondents were refused jobs because of their impairments. In particular, negative employer attitudes, assumptions and Confucian socio-cultural norms that view disability as a source of shame may impede workplace entry (Hwang and Brandon, 2012). These findings are similar to wider international research in which established impairments and financial problems are identified as the central motives for disabled people starting their own business (Blanck et al., 2000; DeMartino et al., 2011).

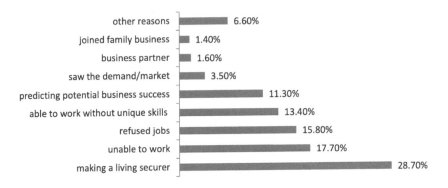

Source: SMBA (2011).

Figure 8.3   *Motivation for venturing into business*

There are positive reasons for disabled people establishing disability enterprises, such as the desire to be actively involved in economic activities, the desire to build successful businesses, and working with non-disabled people. Overall, however, evidence suggests that many disabled people who are economically marginalised from society often take the initiative of starting an enterprise because they have no alternative. When building sustainable employment strategies, the establishment of new businesses by disabled people is clearly a route to economic security for some disabled people in Korea (see Larsson, 2006).

Hardships in obtaining capital, sluggish sales and lack of business training are reported as the top challenges facing disability enterprises (Van Niekerk et al., 2006; Walls et al., 2001). These reflect the general challenges faced by new business ventures (Harding, 2006). The Biannual Survey highlights that disability enterprises generally start with a relatively small amount of seedcorn money. The difficulty in obtaining capital and loan guarantees are identified as one of the main barriers encountered by disabled people when considering starting a business. In total, 65.7 per cent of the respondents in the survey started up their own business with self-funding. This obviously is the main difficulty to overcome for any business in order to become sustainable. Following Korean disability employment policy and PDEA imperatives, financial agencies have extended their maximum support in the form of incentives, loans and schemes. But the findings also show that disabled entrepreneurs are not given full information on all the types of financial assistance available from these agencies.

DISABLED PEOPLE AND ENTERPRISE: FUTURE DIRECTIONS

The Korean government has made a considerable commitment to increasing the employability of disabled people in order to provide greater income, social inclusion and independence. However, the investment is not yet at a satisfactory level where disabled people can fully participate in their business activities, and several important issues are faced. The definition and scope of disability enterprises in the PDEA is too narrow, and unclear as to what counts as self-employed small and micro business. If this definition included disability enterprises, the number of enterprises would increase to about 220 000. Moreover, although the PDEA prohibits discrimination against disabled people in businesses, the Act does not provide any specific guidelines on the duties, liabilities and remedial procedures. The policy and legislation relating to disability employment and enterprises are still based on the medical model of disability, so disabled entrepreneurs are still perceived as non-participants in the economy and have been socially and economically marginalised. De Vries (2003: 1) argues that 'many disabled people are protected from the world of economics, politics and a social order, which excludes them from the mainstream'.

In neoliberal economic discourses, the disability employment problem transfers the responsibility from the state to the individual in terms of access to and survival within the labour market (Anderson and Galloway, 2012: 95). As Pavey (2006: 219) argues, this constructs the issue on a 'deficit-based model of disability' that has to accommodate individual functional limitations. In Korea, disability has traditionally been associated with impairment, shame and stigma (Hwang and Brandon, 2012). This in turn means that disabled people are often blamed for being less functional, and having lower incomes, less education and wider social capital. This in turn perpetuates the construction of disabled people as 'unproductive' (Gleeson, 1998). As a consequence, disabled people experience economic, cultural, educational and social marginalisation. Such institutionalised discrimination and prejudice excludes them from diverse social roles, especially from having an active role in the labour market. Services for disability enterprise should be tailored toward individuals' particular needs. The lack of both paternalist and neoliberal policy to change deep-seated attitudes limits disabled people's economic activity in both paid employment and enterprise.

Reflecting the wider literature (Mathis, 2003; Noakes, 2006), disabled people in this analysis have plenty to gain from running their own business, such as a good source of income for maintenance, flexibility and resourcefulness. As with disability enterprises, disabled people can be helped to get decent jobs and to boost their income, not relying on benefits. But there is a question about the sustainability and efficiency of disability enterprises. The competitive nature of marketing could turn disabled enterprises into a hidden disadvantage when they face competition from others. One reason is that they are often regarded as having competitive disadvantages because of additional labour costs (for example, the need to hire a person to carry merchandise instead of carrying it oneself, additional transportation costs, slower production). It is undeniable that it is difficult for disabled people to match the productivity of non-disabled employees in the market (Graffam et al., 2002). For this reason, there have been public procurement policies to purchase products made by disability enterprises. However, the Korean procurement programme is based on voluntarism and not enforcement. Also, disabled entrepreneurs rarely have previous self-employment experience. Enterprise training is central to disabled people managing capital, marketing and management skills in establishing and developing small businesses (Anderson and Galloway, 2012). However, employment support does not currently extend to training, technical consultation and counselling programmes to support disabled people into potential microenterprises in Korea (Walls et al., 2001). Mathis (2003) argues that entrepreneurship training should be made available for disabled people, even for some disabled people to whom entrepreneurship does not appeal, because disabled people can either take the necessary steps toward entrepreneurship or they can return to conventional employment as a means of self-sufficiency. Disability enterprises are still segregated in employment situations and are subject to lower incomes and conditions than other businesses.

The Korean government has been attempting to develop a unique enterprise service delivery system for disabled people. In reality, this system has resulted in a lack of cooperation between ministries – the Ministry of Employment and Labour, Ministry of Health and Welfare, Ministry of Patriots and Veterans Affairs, and the SMBA – and the duplication of services (Won et al., 2009). While disability issues are addressed by the Ministry of Health and Welfare, all small business developments are the remit of the Ministry of Employment and Labour and the SMBA. This means that disability enterprises are not classified as disability employment or a vocational rehabilitation programme. As a result, specific employment and rehabilitation programmes are designed for disabled people, but self-employment or enterprise is not considered as an employment support service option. Moreover, the local governmental system in Korea is still immature. Local authorities have a limited effective system to support the disability enterprise (Kim et al., 2011). Therefore, comprehensive and systematic collaboration between the central and local government bodies need to be established so that a variety of services can reach disabled people in the community.

CONCLUSION

Most research on disability enterprises has focused on economic outcomes and success, but this chapter has shown that disability enterprises offer an opportunity for disabled people's lives to be fashioned by what they can do, instead of what they cannot do. However, disability enterprises are more likely than others to be home-based and micro, and many of them have been pushed into starting up business because their disability practically disqualifies them from other forms of employment. So, they are not absorbing many of those who cannot prosper in paid employment. This chapter shows that the biggest hurdles of disability enterprises may be the misconceptions about disabled people's capabilities as business owners. In policy terms, the limited impact of the paternalist quota and sheltered employment schemes, overlaid with rather dilute legal rights contained in the Korean DDA, leaves disabled people undersupported in both mainstream employment and enterprise development. The need to further support enterprise access and sustenance – for example through finance, training, market advantage, take-off incentives/subsidies and human resource expertise – have all been absent from much policy support for Korean disabled small business ventures. The macro-level policy limitations and the lack of micro-level support, overlaid with Confucian attitudes towards disability, present continued major hurdles for disabled people, especially young disabled females, in contemporary Korea.

In spite of the obstacles, the positive relationships between disabled people's firms, employability and economic growth should be acknowledged. Especially, we argue that the success of disability enterprises needs to be reconsidered not only in terms of income and profits, but also considering independence, participation and inclusion in society, engaging meaningful work, and increasing well-being. It is important to recognise that simply encouraging disabled people to start business will have little effect. What is needed is policy that considers accessibility to and the sustainability of self-employment enterprises. Policy should also avoid assumptions that such activities are a fallback option from paid employment, as this perpetuates a deficit approach and fails to address access to both self-employment and paid contractual employment.

REFERENCES

Ablenews. 2013. 'Problems of Disability Employment Services'. (In Korean.) 12 July.
Allen, S., and C. Truman. 1993. *Women in Business: Perspectives on Women Entrepreneurs.* London: Thomson.
Anderson, M., and L. Galloway. 2012. 'The Value of Enterprise for Disabled People'. *International Journal of Entrepreneurship and Innovation* 13 (2): 93–101.
Arnold, N., and C. Ipsen. 2005. 'Self-employment Policies: Changes through the Decade'. *Journal of Disability Policy Studies* 16 (2): 115–122.
Berthoud, R. 2006. *The Employment Rates of Disabled People.* Department of Work and Pensions Research Report No. 298. London: Department of Work and Pensions.

Blanck, P.D., L.A. Sandler, J.L. Schmeling, and H.A. Schartz. 2000. 'The Emerging Workforce of Entrepreneurs with Disabilities: Preliminary Study of Entrepreneurship in Iowa'. *Iowa Law Review* 85 (5): 1583–1670.

Boylan, A., and T. Burchardt. 2003. *Barriers to Self-employment for Disabled People.* London: Small Business Service.

Burchardt, T. 2005. *The Education and Employment of Disabled Young People.* Bristol: Policy Press.

Canguilheim, G. 1991. *The Normal and the Pathological.* New York: Zone Books.

Cho, M. 2013. 'Legislative Challenges on Disability Employment System in Korea'. *Quarterly Journal of Labor Policy* 13 (1): 71–100.

Choo, K. 2011. 'Need an Incubating Support for Establishing Disability Enterprise'. (In Korean.) *Ohmynews*, 21 October.

Chung, J., and G. Cho. 2007. 'A Study on the Employment Discrimination of the Person with Disability in the Labor Market'. *Education Journal for Physical and Multiple Disabilities* 49: 477–499.

Clark, K., and Stephen Drinkwater. 2000. 'Pushed Out or Pulled In? Self-employment among Ethnic Minorities in England and Wales'. *Labour Economics* 7 (5): 603–628.

Cole, A., A. Lloyd, B. McIntosh, M. Mattingley, P. Swift, R. Townsley, and V. Williams. 2007. *Community Based Day Activities and Supports for People with Learning Disabilities: How We Can Help People to 'Have a Good Day'.* London: Social Care Institute for Excellence.

Cooney, T. 2008. 'Entrepreneurs with Disabilities: Profile of a Forgotten Minority'. *Irish Business Journal* 4 (1): 119–129.

DeMartino, R., W.S. Atkins, R.J. Barbato, and V.J. Perotti. 2011. 'Entrepreneurship in the Disability Community: An Exploratory Study on the Deaf and Hard of Hearing Community (Summary)'. *Frontiers of Entrepreneurship Research* 31 (4). Accessed 20 December 2013 at http://digitalknowledge.babson.edu/fer/vol31/iss4/5.

De Vries, L. 2003. 'Workforce Development: The Case of Disabled People towards Economic Empowerment and Entrepreneurship'. Presented at 48th ICSB World Conference, Belfast, 15–18 June.

Employment Development Institute. 2011. *Panel Survey of Employment for the Disabled.* (In Korean.) Seoul: EDI.

European Commission. 2005. 'The New SME Definition'. Accessed 20 December 2013 at http://ec.europa.eu/enterprise/policies/sme/files/sme_definition/sme_user_guide_en.pdf.

Gleeson, B. 1998. *Geographies of Disability.* London: Routledge.

Godley, A. 2005. *The Emergence of Ethnic Entrepreneurship.* Princeton, NJ: Princeton University Press.

Graffam, J., K. Smith, A. Shinkfield, and U. Polzin. 2002. 'Employer Benefits and Costs of Employing a Person with a Disability'. *Journal of Vocational Rehabilitation* 17: 251–263.

Greer, G. 1999. *The Whole Woman.* London: Doubleday.

Grinker, R.R. 2007. *Unstrange Minds: Remapping the World of Autism.* New York: Basic Books.

Hall, E., and R. Wilton. 2011. 'Alternative Spaces of "Work" and Inclusion for Disabled People'. *Disability and Society* 26 (7): 867–880.

Harding, R. 2006. *Social Entrepreneurship Monitor.* London: Foundation for Entrepreneurial Management.

Hwang, S.K., and T. Brandon. 2012. 'A Comparative Examination of Policy and Models of Disability in Korea and the UK'. *Language of Public Administration and Qualitative Research* 3 (1): 47–64.

KIHASA (Korean Institute for Health and Social Affairs). 2011. *2011 The National Survey on People with Disabilities.* (In Korean.) Seoul, Korea: Ministry of Health and Welfare.

Kim, C. 2011. 'Comparative Perspectives on Disability Employment Policy'. *International Review of Public Administration* 15 (3): 27–35.

Kim, J.W., and A. Davis. 2006. 'Korean Disability Employment Policy: What is It Offering People with Learning Disabilities?' *Social Policy and Society* 5 (3): 409–419.

Kim, S., S. Song, and J. Won. 2011. 'Importance–Performance Analysis on Business Environment and Support Policy of Disability Firm'. (In Korean.) *Management Education Review* 15: 141–151.

Larsson, S. 2006. 'Disability Management and Entrepreneurship: Results from a Nationwide Study'. *International Journal of Disability Management Research* 1 (1): 159–168.

Lim, M., S. Yang, H. Kim, and E. Kim. 2011. *2010 The Survey of Economic Activity Status for the Disabled.* (In Korean.) Sungnam, Korea: Employment Development Institute.

Lim, T. 2002. 'Korea, the Nation to Venerate Che-Myon'. (In Korean.) In *Jeong, Chemyon, Yonjul and the Human Relationship of Korean*, edited by T. S. Lim, 101–128. Seoul, Korea: Han-Na-Rae.

Lorenzo, T., L. van Niekerk, and P. Mdlokolo. 2007. 'Economic Empowerment and Black Disabled Entrepreneurs Negotiating Partnerships in Cape Town, South Africa'. *Disability and Rehabilitation* 29 (5): 429–436.

Marlow, S. 2002. 'Women and Self-employment: A Part of or Apart from Theoretical Construct?' *International Journal of Entrepreneurship and Innovation* 3 (2): 83–91.

Mathis, C. 2003. 'Disability and Entrepreneurship: A Formula for Success'. Accessed 20 December 2013 at www.ntac.hawaii.edu/downloads/products/.../EB-Vol4-Iss02-Success .doc.

Ministry of Government Legislation. 2005. 'Statute: Promotion of Disabled Persons' Enterprise Activities Act'. (In Korean.) Accessed 1 October 2013 at www.law.gov.kr/ lslnfoP.do?lsiSeq=122443.

Ministry of Health and Welfare. 2012. *Survey on the Current Status of Disabled People.* (In Korean.) Gwacheon: MoHW.

Mont, D. 2004. 'Disability Employment Policy'. Social Protection Discussion Paper Series. Ithaca, NY: Cornell University Press.

National Human Rights Commission of Korea. 2013. *Human Rights Statistical Yearbook 2012.* (In Korean.) Seoul: National Human Rights Commission of Korea.

Noakes, P. 2006. *Disability in Great Britain: Results of the 1996/7 Disability Follow-up to the Family Resources Survey.* Social Research Division. London: Department of Work and Pensions.

OECD. 2003. *Transforming Disability into Ability.* Paris: OECD.

Office for National Statistics. 2012. *Labour Force Survey.* London: ONS.

Oh, K., D.A. Rosenthal, J. Kim, and J.W. Lui. 2005. 'Vocational Rehabilitation in South Korea: Historical Development, Present Status and Future Direction'. *Journal of Rehabilitation* 71 (1): 49–55.

O'Reilly, A. 2007. *The Right to Decent Work of Persons with Disabilities.* Geneva: ILO.

Pagán, R. 2009. 'Self-employment among People with Disabilities: Evidence for Europe'. *Disability and Society* 24 (2): 217–229.

Park, J. 2007. *The Study of Encouraging Disabled Women for Participating in Economic Activities.* (In Korean.) Seoul: EDI.

Park, J. 2010. 'Analysis of the Relationship between Employers' Perceptions and Employing Disabled People'. (In Korean.) *Journal of Korean Social Welfare Administration* 12 (1): 151–175.

Pavey, B. 2006. 'Human Capital, Social Capital, Entrepreneurship and Disability: An Examination of Some Current Education Trends in UK'. *Disability and Society* 21 (3): 217–229.

Raheim, S. 1996. 'Micro-enterprise as an Approach for Promoting Economic Development in Social Work: Lessons from the Self-employment Investment Demonstration'. *International Social Work* 39 (1): 69–82.

Robb, A., and R. Fairlie. 2009. 'Determinants of Business Success: An Examination of Asian-owned Businesses in the USA'. *Journal of Population Economics* 22 (4): 827–858.

Roulstone, A., L. Gradwell, J. Price, and L. Child. 2003. *Thriving and Surviving at Work: Disabled People's Employment Strategies*. Bristol: Policy Press.

Roulstone, A., and S. Prideaux. 2012. *Understanding Disability Policy*. Bristol: Policy Press.

Scotch, R. 2001. *From Good Will to Civil Rights: Transforming Federal Disability Policy*. Philadelphia, PA: Temple University Press.

Shane, S. 2008. *The Illusions of Entrepreneurship*. New Haven, CT: Yale University Press.

Small and Medium Business Administration (SMBA). 2011. *2011 Biannual Nationwide Survey of Disability Enterprises*. (In Korean.) Seoul: KODDI.

Stafford, B. 2005. 'New Deal for Disabled People: What's New about New Deal?' In *Working Futures: Disabled People, Policy and Social Inclusion*, edited by A. Roulstone and C. Barnes, 17–28. Bristol: Policy Press.

Stanley, K., L. Asta-Lohde, and S. White. 2004. *Sanctions and Sweeteners: Rights and Responsibilities in the Benefits System*. London: IPPR.

Sung, S. 2003. 'Women Reconciling Paid and Unpaid Work in a Confucian Welfare State: The Case of South Korea'. *Social Policy and Administration* 37 (4): 342–360.

Van Niekerk, L., T. Lorenzo, and P. Mdlokolo. 2006. 'Understanding Partnerships in Developing Disabled Entrepreneurs through Participatory Action Research'. *Disability and Rehabilitation* 28 (5): 323–331.

Waddington, L. 1996. 'Reassessing the Employment of People with Disabilities in Europe: From Quotas to Anti-discrimination Laws'. *Comparative Labour Law Journal* 18: 62–101.

Walls, R.T., D.L. Dowler, K. Cordingly, L.E. Orslene, and J.D. Greer. 2001. 'Microenterprising and People with Disabilities: Strategies for Success and Failure'. *Journal of Rehabilitation* 67 (2): 29–35.

Watson, N., A. Roulstone, and C. Thomas. 2012. *The Routledge Handbook of Disability Studies*. London: Routledge.

Wickham, M. 2013. *Self-employment in London*. London: GLA Economics.

Won, J.H., S.J. Song, and K.S. Kang. 2009. 'A Study on the Policy for Competitive Advantage of Disability Firm'. (In Korean.) *Journal of Korea Safety Management and Science* 11 (2): 27–32.

World Health Organization and World Bank. 2011. *The World Report on Disability*. New York: WHO and World Bank.

Yu, D. 2008. 'Effects of Job Placement Services for People with Disabilities on Quality of Work'. (In Korean.) *Disability and Employment* 18 (1): 5–21.

9. Designing public policy to support entrepreneurial activity within the disabled community in Ireland

Thomas M. Cooney

INTRODUCTION

People with disabilities are disproportionately inactive in the labour market, and their incomes are much lower than for people without disabilities (OECD, 2014). Furthermore, given that impairments vary in terms of type, severity, stability, duration and time of onset, as well as that individuals may suffer from multiple conditions and impairments (Berthoud, 2008), experiences of impairment will be unique for every person with a disability, as will be their personal experience of disadvantage in terms of labour market activation. However, there is some evidence to suggest that rates of entrepreneurial activity differ little between people with and without disabilities (Pagán, 2009; OECD, 2014), although disabled entrepreneurs are often less likely to create sustainable ventures (Renko et al., 2016). Cooney (2008) suggested that successful self-employment within the disabled community can expedite active economic and social participation; enable greater control by people with disabilities over their workload, work hours and work location; and provide greater flexibility in coping with their disability than is normally found within paid employment.

An Organisation for Economic Co-operation and Development (OECD, 2014) report highlighted that there is a large variation in self-employment rates for people with disabilities across European Union (EU) Member States. The self-employment rates of people with disabilities are relatively low in many north-eastern EU countries and higher in southern EU countries. For example, the self-employment rates for people with disabilities in Bulgaria, the Czech Republic, Denmark, Germany, Estonia, Latvia, Lithuania, Slovenia and Slovakia were below the 5 per cent level in 2007; while the rates exceed the 15 per cent level in Greece, Italy, Cyprus, Poland, Portugal and Romania. The data shows that in Ireland people with disabilities have a slightly higher rate of self-employment than people without disabilities. It should be noted that caution is needed when interpreting the data from the different countries, because the differences in self-employment rates across countries are influenced by a variety of factors, including: (1) variation in the definition of disability used in collecting the statistics; (2) the level of disability benefits and the ease of accessing them; (3) the extent to which people with disabilities are included in or excluded from society and education; (4) employer discrimination; (5) demographic factors; and (6) the incidence of severe disabilities. However, the overall data does offer interesting insights into the rate of entrepreneurial activity in different countries and how these are influenced by local economic and social stimuli.

In the United States, a major report was delivered by the Presidential Task Force on Employment of Adults with Disabilities (2000) which revealed that in 1991, people with disabilities had a higher rate of self-employment (12.2 per cent) than people without disabilities (7.8 per cent), with approximately 40 per cent of the disabled self-employed having home-based businesses. By the time of the 1994 national census, the number of people with disabilities who were self-employed had risen to 14 per cent. The United States Census Department (2011) stated that approximately 15 per cent of people with disabilities who are working are self-employed, versus less than 10 per cent of people without disability who are entrepreneurs. A major report in the United Kingdom (UK) on self-employment for people with disabilities (Boylan and Burchardt, 2003) found that of those in paid work, 18 per cent of disabled men and 8 per cent of disabled women were self-employed (compared to 14 per cent and 6 per cent of non-disabled men and women, respectively). Boylan and Burchardt analysed the data on self-employed disabled people to build a greater understanding of their characteristics, and found that both disabled self-employed men and disabled self-employed women were older, on average, than their non-disabled counterparts (49 years old compared to 43 for men, 45 compared to 42 for women). The report also identified that a higher proportion of disabled self-employed men and disabled self-employed women had no educational qualifications (20 per cent and 12 per cent, respectively) compared to non-disabled self-employed (13 per cent and 10 per cent, respectively), while a smaller proportion of disabled self-employed people lived in households containing children, compared to non-disabled self-employed people (this is partly due to the different age profile of the two populations). The report additionally found that disabled men and women had been self-employed longer (13.1 years on average for men, 8.4 years for women) in comparison to non-disabled men and women (11.3 years for men, 7.9 years for women), although this finding was partly explained by the fact that disabled self-employed people are also older on average. The number of hours worked by disabled self-employed men (42.8) was lower than for non-disabled self-employed men (48.6), and similarly the number of hours worked by disabled self-employed women (29.5) was lower than for non-disabled self-employed women (33.3). The research also found that disabled self-employed people were more likely than non-disabled self-employed to be unable or unwilling to report their earnings, while disabled men and women were less likely to be in professional occupations (this finding would be related to lower educational qualifications). People with disabilities bring lower human capital to their employment than non-disabled people, and self-employed disabled men report lower incomes from self-employment than their non-disabled counterparts. Nearly 80 per cent of the self-employed with disabilities have no employees, compared to 74 per cent of those without disabilities and non-work-limited disabled men.

While business creation and self-employment are not suitable for everyone with a disability, there are several ways in which policy-makers can improve entrepreneurship support for this community. An OECD (2014) report recommended that policy-makers should introduce the following policy measures: (1) Increase awareness about the feasibility of entrepreneurship; (2) develop entrepreneurship skills; (3) support the development, acquisition and use of assistive technologies; (4) ensure access to appropriate financial support; and (5) continue to improve Internet and information technology accessibility. The OECD recommendations are based on research of policy offerings in OECD countries, and are typical of what is required in many economies. However, there is little coherency across the five recommendations, and each is offered as a distinctly separate measure. Furthermore, research has found that intensive, tailored, one-to-one or small group support provision is likely to produce the most successful outcomes (Arnold and Ipsen, 2005; Enabled4Enterprise, 2009; EMDA, 2009; Dotson et al., 2013), but such approaches are highly resource-intensive, they target a relatively small group of people, and they are not integrated into other initiatives or measures. Overall, the system of support is quite disconnected and offers no clear pathway for a person with a disability in their journey towards becoming self-employed.

THE SITUATION IN IRELAND

According to the Central Statistics Office (CSO) Census (CSO, 2016), a total of 643 131 people in Ireland stated that they had a disability, accounting for 13.5 per cent of the population. Of this number, 311 580 people (48.4 per cent) with a disability were male, while 331 551 (51.6 per cent) were female. There were 130 067 people with a disability aged 15 and over at work, accounting for 22.3 per cent of the total disabled working population of 584 045. This compares with 53.4 per cent for the overall population aged 15 and over who were at work. To support the inclusion of people with disabilities into Irish society, the government launched a National Disability Strategy in 2004 that sought to tie together law and policy in the area of disability. The Comprehensive Employment Strategy for People with Disabilities (2015–2024) was published by the government in 2015 as a mechanism to address the significant gap that existed in the rates of employment between people with and without disabilities. One of the key strengths of the strategy was that it ensured a coordinated approach to supporting people with disabilities with their ambition to progress into employment; but little attention was given in the strategy to self-employment as a potential career option. In 2017, the National Disability Inclusion Strategy (2017–2021) was launched, which comprised eight themes: (1) equality and choice; (2) joined-up policies and public services; (3) education; (4) employment; (5) health and wellbeing; (6) person-centred disability services; (7) living in the community; and (8) transport and access to places. In January 2020, the government approved the Mid-Term Review of the National Disability Inclusion Strategy, and stated that the focus for 2020 and 2021 would be on the implementation of the United Nations Convention on the Rights of Persons with Disabilities.

According to the CSO (2016) census, there are 17 654 people in Ireland with disabilities who are self-employed and have employees (13 118 male, 4536 female),

Table 9.1   *Self-employment and people with disabilities*

Nature of Disability	Self-Employed with Employees			Self-Employed with No Employees		
	Total	Male	Female	Total	Male	Female
Disabled Persons	17654	13118	4536	34461	26198	8263
Blindness or a serious vision impairment	1645	1201	444	2980	2242	738
Deafness or a serious hearing impairment	5034	4086	948	8696	7167	1529
A difficulty that limits basic physical activities such as walking, climbing stairs, etc.	7373	5147	2226	14381	10397	3984
An intellectual disability	334	256	78	766	635	131
A difficulty with learning, remembering or concentrating	2651	1927	724	5408	4071	1337
A psychological or emotional condition	1447	978	469	3763	2628	1135
A difficulty with pain, breathing or any other chronic illness or condition	8158	5854	2304	16040	11973	4067
Difficulty dressing, bathing or getting around inside the home	3329	2188	1141	6915	4811	2104
Difficulty going outside the home alone to shop or visit a doctor's surgery	4037	2568	1469	8404	5585	2819
Difficulty working at a job, business or attending school or college	3890	2693	1197	8312	6157	2155
Difficulty participating in other activities, for example leisure or using transport	5379	3632	1747	10727	7538	3189

Source: CSO (2016).

plus there are 34 461 people with disabilities who are self-employed and have no employees (26 198 male, 8263 female). It is interesting to note that the ratio of male to female is approximately 3:1, which contrasts with the rate of 1.6:1 found in the GEM Ireland study (2019) for the general population. Table 9.1 provides a detailed breakdown of the rates of self-employment by the nature of disability.

A report by Cooney and Aird (2020) on entrepreneurship for people with disabilities in Ireland identified a range of barriers that persons from the community might face when seeking to establish their own business. The principal barriers identified included accessibility of information and support, the low expectations of support providers, and the inflexibility of the benefits system. The barriers also included: (1) fear of loss of income from social security benefits or supplemental disability programmes; (2) difficulties in obtaining start-up capital due to poor credit ratings; (3) lack of access to appropriate support, or training not tailored to their individual needs; (4) lack of assets to use as collateral due to difficulties in finding suitable employment; and (5) psychological issues such as self-confidence, mindset and fear of failure. Furthermore, many could not 'see themselves' in the marketing material for self-employment training and opportunities and therefore could not envisage themselves as an entrepreneur. The report noted that there are no dedicated or specifically tailored measures provided by government or its enterprise support agencies for people with disabilities in Ireland to develop their entrepreneurship skills, access finance, or identify with role models or the beneficiaries of targeted policies. It is understood by government that all people should be treated equally with regard to enterprise support, and some officials would argue that providing separate supports in business is contrary to the United National Convention on the Rights of People with Disabilities.

To encourage people in receipt of welfare benefits to start their own business, the Department of Employment Affairs and Social Protection offers some benefits that temporarily cover the loss of state income supports if a person is currently, or has recently been, in receipt of welfare benefits. The Back to Work Enterprise Allowance (BTWEA) encourages people receiving certain social welfare payments to become self-employed. The people receiving the Back to Work Enterprise Allowance can keep a percentage of their social welfare payment for up to two years. Additionally, people who are earning low income due to self-employment may be entitled to Jobseeker's Allowance or Supplementary Welfare Allowance. It should be noted that the supports available for self-employment are open to the general population and not just targeted at people with disabilities. People with disabilities may be entitled to other welfare benefits, but that would be dependent upon being means tested and how they might satisfy the eligibility criteria. The Reasonable Accommodation Fund is available for the employment of people with disabilities, comprising the Workplace Equipment and Adaptation Grant, the Personal Reader Grant, the Job Interview Interpreter Grant and the Employee Retention Grant. The Department also provides access to a Disability Awareness Support Scheme which provides funding for private sector employers to arrange and pay for disability awareness training for staff who work with a colleague who has a disability. These grants are excellent supports for businesses who wish to employ a person with a disability, but they generally cannot be accessed a person with a disability who wishes to become self-employed. The welfare system is supportive of people with disabilities in terms of providing benefits, and it is also supportive of people in receipt of welfare benefits who wish to start their own business. Unfortunately, it offers no customised benefits for people with disabilities who wish to start their own business and so 'the welfare benefit trap' remains a considerable challenge in Ireland. The lack of a national policy to support people with disabilities has been highlighted by a variety of reports (e.g. Cooney and Aird, 2020), but identifying what approach might be most appropriate remains open to debate.

THE CHALLENGES OF DESIGNING TAILORED SUPPORT

One of the key questions that is frequently asked within this topic area is, 'Why is tailored support needed for people with disabilities who wish to start their own business? Can they not use the same supports that are available to the general population?' It could be suggested that the same argument could be made regarding other underrepresented communities in terms of entrepreneurial activity, such as women entrepreneurs. However, the dedicated unit created by Enterprise Ireland to support women entrepreneurs in Ireland has been widely acknowledged as being very successful, and led to the publication in January 2020 of the Action Plan for Women in Business. Creating tailored supports for people with disabilities who wish to start their own business is critically important as it will shine a light on self-employment as a career opportunity that is available to them. Furthermore, an OECD (2014) report found that:

- People with disabilities are disproportionately inactive in the labour market in all EU Member States.
- Evidence exists to suggest that people with disabilities who participate in the labour market are just as likely as those without disabilities to be self-employed.
- Self-employment can facilitate active economic and social participation and give control to the individual over their levels of participation.
- Self-employment allows flexibility in workload, work hours and work location, providing more elasticity in coping with disability than can be often found in paid employment.
- Policies need to support entrepreneurs with diverse impairment characteristics in different ways and over varying timescales.

It is broadly agreed that business creation and self-employment are not suitable for all people with disabilities, but there are several ways in which policy-makers can improve their support for those people who wish to become self-employed. Tailored supports also recognise and respect the additional and distinctive challenges faced by people with disabilities when starting their own business. Boylan and Burchardt (2003) sought to identify ways in which support agencies could help people with disabilities to establish their own business, and identified the following key considerations:

- Ensure that self-employment is offered as a positive choice rather than a last resort.
- A national scheme for start-up grants and loans for disabled entrepreneurs should be overseen by experienced business advisers with disability awareness training.
- Business support providers should actively market their services (in accessible formats) to socially excluded groups, and implement disability awareness training for all advisory staff and assessors.

Doyel (2000) argued that in the development of an entrepreneurship programme for people with disabilities, some key components would be essential to its success. These components include a careful selection process for entrepreneurs with disabilities (including a demonstration of commitment by the participant), tailored entrepreneurship education and training, financial assistance for the business, and support for the business after start-up. Any entrepreneurship programme for people with disabilities should also fit the diverse range of people that it serves. The programme must also be open to everyone, regardless of the type and severity of their disability, and while this may take time to achieve, nevertheless it should be the ambition of the programme from the time of its original design.

Policy-makers face several barriers when designing and implementing support for aspiring disabled entrepreneurs. The first is making people with disabilities aware of self-employment and business ownership as a possible paid work option for them. Disabled people, like the non-disabled, face general barriers to labour market participation, but they also face specific barriers to entrepreneurship due to the nature of their disability. Difficulties in obtaining capital are accentuated because many people with disabilities either have low-paid jobs or are unemployed with little disposable income, and they frequently have poor credit ratings. Consideration of the specific barriers to entrepreneurship faced by disabled people includes:

- Making information accessible to as wide a range of people as possible: any information provided must take diversity of impairment into account (type, severity, fluctuation, time of onset). Furthermore, many people with disabilities who are in business for themselves never receive help from official institutions, due to the nature of the supports on offer (Harper and Momm, 1989).
- The provision of appropriate and sensitive business support, and tackling unhelpful attitudes of business advisers: sensitivity of support providers to the target audience must be addressed in terms of overcoming support provider prejudice and their low expectations of people with disabilities running a sustainable business.
- Providing flexible benefits to enable transition to self-employment: benefits should not be reduced too quickly on transition to entrepreneurship, or discriminate unfairly against those people with disabilities who chose to become entrepreneurs (OECD, 2014). Policy-makers might consider 'bridging schemes' that enable access to benefits while earning low self-employment incomes.
- Developing relevant business knowledge and skills: people with disabilities bring lower human capital to their employment than non-disabled people.
- Developing confidence and overcoming limited aspirations: aspiring disabled entrepreneurs often lack the self-belief that they can start and operate a business successfully, particularly among those with mental health issues (EMDA, 2009).

The characteristics of a person's disability will influence their individual capacity and willingness to become entrepreneurs (Kašperová et al., 2018), and various studies have highlighted concerns about access to social welfare benefits as a barrier to self-employment (Boylan and Burchardt, 2003; Doyel, 2002; Pavey, 2006; Enabled4Enterprise, 2008; EMDA, 2009). Some individuals might be able and willing to take up self-employment as a paid work option, but this is unlikely to be sustainable for many without extensive and/or long-term support (Kitching, 2014). Therefore, outreach work and partnerships might be needed to increase the profile of self-employment, while reimagined approaches to social welfare payment could reduce the 'welfare benefit trap' (EMDA, 2009). In designing and implementing support initiatives, policy-makers face a trade-off between providing generic advice to large numbers of disabled recipients, and providing intensive, tailored support to highly targeted subgroups (Kitching, 2014). The extensive approach reaches greater numbers, but arguably with limited success in terms of sustainable businesses. The intensive approach provides tailored support to a limited number of businesses with, potentially, a higher probability of sustaining the businesses supported.

The primary research enabled a novel policy model to be designed that combines extensive and intensive forms of support, while being considerate of the distinctive challenges faced by aspiring disabled entrepreneurs, sensitive to the diversity of impairment conditions, and cognisant of government resource constraints.

THE FUNNEL APPROACH

The research methodology comprised a variety of approaches, including primary and secondary research, drawing on qualitative and quantitative data. The research design provided an opportunity for a broad range of stakeholders to contribute to the design of entrepreneurship policy for people with disabilities in Ireland. The different research methods employed were: (1) review of existing literature; (2) analysis of good practice internationally; (3) in-depth interviews with key stakeholders; and (4) a seminar attended by 87 people in June 2019. The multiple information collection points ensured that a detailed understanding of the principal issues and potential solutions was possible, plus a wide array of perspectives on the topic was gathered. The analysis of the research data and the contributions from seminar participants led to the adoption and fine-tuning of a Funnel Approach relating to the introduction of new policies supporting entrepreneurship for people with disabilities. The first version of this model was presented by Cooney et al. (2018).

The Funnel Approach (see Figure 9.1) begins with a broad awareness campaign to inform people with disabilities of entrepreneurship as a potential career option. This should be targeted at the total community and related stakeholders (for example, advocacy organisations, enterprise agencies, care support personnel), and might involve modest resourcing. If people wish to learn more, then they will go to a dedicated website that provides links to relevant programmes and supports, provides resources to evaluate business ideas and develop business plans, and offers relevant information in one location for a person with a disability who is a potential, nascent or existing entrepreneur. Once they have learned more about starting a business, they may then wish to participate in a generally available 'Start Your Own Business' programme. These programmes are not tailored for people with disabilities but are available to the general population and so are no additional cost to the organisation, agency or government department leading the initiative. After completing the Start Your Own Business programme, the business idea will be evaluated by a review panel who will determine whether it has merit in being developed further. If the business idea has merit, then mentoring support will be provided (assuming that the proposer of the idea still wishes to go ahead with the business). Following mentoring, if the business is to start then some soft loan financing would be made available through ring-fenced funding. Through self-selection by aspiring disabled entrepreneurs (in terms of deciding whether to opt in or opt out of the process), and business idea elimination by review panels or enterprise support agencies, participants work their way through the funnel stages, with fewer participants at the later stages where the resource implications are much greater. Finally, it is the ambition of this concept that eventually a network of entrepreneurs with disabilities will be established in each country (as in the UK and other countries), and that members of this network will act as role models and advocates for others to follow.

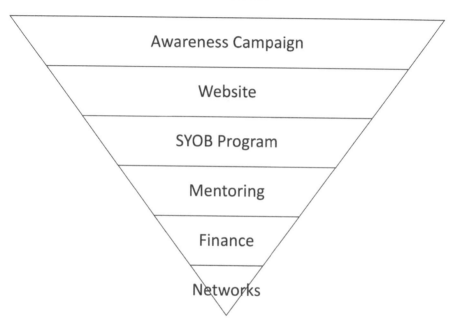

Figure 9.1   *The Funnel Approach*

When examining the international examples of good practice, it was clearly evident that long-term sustainability was a critical issue for these initiatives. The more successful initiatives had one-to-one mentoring for every participant, and maximising the number of business start-ups was a regular goal. However, providing one-to-one mentoring and appropriate financial support for every participant who starts a programme was hugely resource-intensive and made the initiatives difficult to sustain on a long-term basis. Many of these initiatives also introduced tailored Start Your Own Business programmes, which were expensive as the training and content all needed to be customised. The initiatives were generally targeted at a small pocket of people with disabilities and therefore did not build broad awareness campaigns concerning the positive values of entrepreneurship for people with disabilities. Neither did they link with existing supports at national level, but instead focused generally on local collaboration. The Funnel Approach is designed to: (1) generate broad awareness; (2) utilise existing supports; (3) minimise the use of the most expensive resources; and (4) be inclusive of any person with any form of disability. The Funnel Approach enables interested individuals to self-select their participation, but it also acts as a filter on business ideas and entrepreneurial desire. The number of people using the services will automatically be reduced in moving down the funnel as people drop out, either because they no longer wish to participate or because their business idea is unlikely to be sustainable. The Funnel Approach has long-term viability because it utilises existing resources and programmes, and it also acts as a quality control filter for people and their business ideas.

The Funnel Approach proposes that the initial phase is macro policy based, in terms of creating a change of culture towards encouraging people with a disability to become entrepreneurs through an education and promotional awareness campaign. As the funnel narrows, policy delivery becomes micro-oriented in terms of offering mentoring and financial assistance. This is unusual, as policy initiatives are generally either macro or micro in approach. The Funnel Approach is novel as it is not currently offered in academic literature as a delivery mechanism for enterprise policy. It also allows an inclusive approach, initially to all members of the targeted community, but focuses the most expensive resource elements towards the locations where fewer participants will be involved. Moreover, it allows a variety of stakeholders to be involved in the process and to contribute resources to the delivery of supports. It would not be possible to offer this approach to the general population, because the large number of participants would make the latter stages of the funnel unworkable. However, this Funnel Approach could potentially be adopted for similar types of initiatives within other minority communities.

CONCLUSION

Initial research findings highlighted that customised initiatives should seek to be inclusive of all people regardless of their disability, since it is impossible to predict who might wish to start a business or who might benefit most from support. Clearly, the more ambitious the objectives for tailored entrepreneurship programmes, the higher the level of resources needed to achieve them. Policy-makers might feel that resources are better spent on those suffering most from social exclusion and requiring the greatest support. Alternatively, they might choose to focus support on 'low-hanging fruit', those most likely to produce successful outcomes quickly. The research additionally suggested that while policy-makers might recognise the need for tailored entrepreneurship programmes, any decision on the introduction of such initiatives will be influenced by available funding and political priorities.

There are three significant benefits to policy-makers of the Funnel Approach: (1) it is inclusive of all disabled people and offers each a pathway to business start-up; (2) it utilises support from the existing entrepreneurship ecosystem; and (3) it focuses the most expensive resources (mentoring, finance, networks) into the lower areas of the funnel where there are fewer support recipients. However, some ecosystems are stronger than others, so the model would need to be tailored for each country. Furthermore, the funnel approach is intended to increase the efficient and effective use of the limited available resources dedicated to entrepreneurship support for people with disabilities, by (where possible) tapping into existing initiatives for aspiring entrepreneurs in the general population. It also means that different stakeholders can be responsible for funding specific stages of the funnel (for example, enterprise agencies – Start Your Own Business programmes; banks – financing) and not require government to fund the full range of activities.

The design of public policy can derive from different approaches to the issue being addressed, and the goals that policy-makers are seeking to achieve. Bridge and O'Neill (2017) stated that approaches to achieving enterprise policy objectives can be divided into two categories: (1) addressing individuals and businesses; and (2) addressing the business environment. The Funnel Approach addresses both (environment initially; individuals and businesses later), while also offering the possibility of greater long-term sustainability than is currently available with existing models. Finally, the Funnel Approach is of value to: (1) researchers, due to the significant lack of academic literature on this topic; (2) policy-makers, who are seeking to introduce policy support measures without having access to relevant data regarding what works; (3) disability advocacy organisations, who wish to offer guidance to the community they represent; and (4) disabled entrepreneurs, who are seeking tailored support to assist them to start and grow a business.

ACKNOWLEDGEMENTS

The author wishes to acknowledge John Kitching and Eva Kašperová who co-authored the original conference paper which forms the basis of this chapter. The author also wishes to acknowledge Brian Aird who co-authored the report which provided much of the additional content for the chapter. All have granted their permission for their work to be used in this chapter and the publications are referenced in the chapter.

REFERENCES

Arnold, N.L., and Ipsen, C. (2005). Self-employment Policies: Changes Through the Decade. Journal of Disability Policy Studies, 16(2), 115–122.

Berthoud, R. (2008). Disability Employment Penalties in Britain. Work, Employment and Society, 22(1), 129–148.

Boylan, A., and Burchardt, T. (2003). Barriers to Self-Employment for Disabled People. Small Business Service, London.

Bridge, S., and O'Neill, K. (2017). Understanding Enterprise: Entrepreneurs and Small Business. Macmillan International Higher Education.

Cooney, T.M. (2008). Entrepreneurs with Disabilities: Profile of a Forgotten Minority. Irish Business Journal, 4(1), 119–129.

Cooney, T.M., and Aird, B. (2020). Pathway to Entrepreneurship for People with Disabilities in Ireland. Technological University Dublin, Dublin.

Cooney, T.M., Kitching, J., and Kasperova, E. (2018). Policy Challenges in Supporting Entrepreneurs with Disabilities: A Funnel Approach. Babson College Entrepreneurship Research Conference. Waterford, 6–9 June.

CSO (2016). Census 2016. CSO, Dublin.

Dotson, W.H., Richman, D.M., Abby, L., Thompson, S., and Plotner, A. (2013). Teaching Skills Related to Self-employment to Adults with Developmental Disabilities: An Analog Analysis. Research in Developmental Disabilities, 34(8), 2336–2350.

Doyel, A.W. (2000). No More Job Interviews: Self-Employment Strategies for People with Disabilities. Training Resource Network, St Augustine, FL.

Doyel, A. (2002). A Realistic Perspective of Risk in Self-Employment for People with Disabilities. Journal of Vocational Rehabilitation, 17(2), 115–124.

East Midlands Development Agency (EMDA) (2009). Scoping Study into the Business Support Needs of Disabled Entrepreneurs in the East Midlands. http://webarchive .nationalarchives.gov.uk/20100113061153/http://www.emda.org.uk/uploaddocuments/dis abledentrepreneurScopingReport%202009.pdf.

Enabled4Enterprise (2008). Barriers and Opportunities: Equipping the Enterprise Sector to Deliver 'Disability Smart' Services. Online at: http://www.lcdisability.org/?lid=19899.

Enabled4Enterprise (2009). Project Report: Equipping the Enterprise Sector to Deliver 'Disability Smart' Services. Enabled4Enterprise.

GEM Ireland (2019). Entrepreneurship in Ireland 2019. Enterprise Ireland, Dublin.

Harper, M., and Momm, W. (1989). Self-Employment for Disabled People: Experiences from Africa and Asia. International Labour Office.

Kašperová, E., Kitching, J., and Blackburn, R. (2018). Identity as a Causal Power: Contextualizing Entrepreneurs' Concerns. International Journal of Entrepreneurship and Innovation, 19(4), 237–249.

Kitching, J. (2014). Entrepreneurship and Self-employment by People with Disabilities. OECD, Paris.

OECD (2014). Policy Brief on Entrepreneurship for People with Disabilities. OECD, Paris.

Pagán, R. (2009). Self-employment among People with Disabilities: Evidence for Europe. Disability and Society, 24(2), 217–229.

Pavey, B. (2006). Human Capital, Social Capital, Entrepreneurship and Disability: An Examination of Some Current Educational Trends in the UK. Disability and Society, 21(3), 217–229.

Presidential Task Force on Employment of Adults with Disabilities (2000). Getting Down to Business: A Blueprint for Creating and Supporting Entrepreneurial Activities for Individuals with Disabilities. US Department of Labor, Washington.

Renko, M., Parker Harris, S., and Caldwell, K. (2016). Entrepreneurial Entry by People with Disabilities. International Small Business Journal, 34(5), 555–578.

United States Census Department (2011). 2011 Disability Status Report: United States. Employment and Disability Institute at the Cornell University ILR School.

10. How entrepreneurs with physical and mental health challenges can benefit from an entrepreneurial ecosystems approach

Mirza Tihic, Gary Shaheen and Felix Arndt

INTRODUCTION

One in four United States (US) adults—61 million Americans—have a disability that impacts major life activities (Centers for Disease Control and Prevention, 2018). The number of people in the United Kingdom who reported a disability is estimated at 14.1 million (Vaughan, 2021). More than half of the people with disability (PWD) are of working age, yet they continue to experience a staggeringly high rate of unemployment, estimated at between 65 and 90 percent (US Department of Labor, Office of Disability Employment Policy, n.d.; World Health Organization, 2011). While much of the data associated with disability and unemployment remains insufficiently analyzed as to cause and effect, a few studies correlate the effects that individual barriers (micro), services and organizational barriers (meso), and societal, systems and policy barriers (macro) contribute concurrently to the exclusion of PWD from labor markets (Kitching, 2014). These factors, in turn, are complicated by predominant medical views of impairment and disability, with more attention given to overcoming basic barriers of mobility, symptomology and lifestyle, without addressing the individual, service-related and societal/systems-related factors that help PWD discover or recover valued life roles with full inclusion and integration into the community (Pagán, 2009; Shaheen, 2016).

The currently dominant segregated systems and societal stigma that PWD face contribute to their inordinately low rates of wage employment, and even lower rates of self-employment (Hughes and Avoke, 2010; Meager and Higgins, 2011). Thus, social entrepreneurs seeking to change these dynamics must become not only supporters of new venture creation, but also agents of systems change. With this in mind, this chapter has four main research aims, to understand: (1) how social entrepreneurs can facilitate new venture creation by PWD; (2) how the potential and ability of PWD, to start their own business ventures, can help them overcome micro-, meso-, and macro-level challenges; (3) the perspectives on the services and systems that require change in order to support social entrepreneurship through new venture creation by PWD; and (4) implications for policy and practice improvements based upon the outcomes illustrated in the case examples. We illustrate these critical interfaces and their implications with two examples. We suggest that social entrepreneurs should embrace an integrated, holistic perspective to overcome these shortcomings and enable the establishment of more ventures owned and operated by PWD. We conclude the chapter with suggestions for remediation and future study.

SOCIAL ENTREPRENEURSHIP AS "FORCE MULTIPLIER" FOR SYSTEMS CHANGE

Social entrepreneurs use business methods, including the creation of social enterprises, to address employment inequalities among PWD. The success of social enterprises is measured in terms of both social impact and business viability (Rotz et al., 2015; Dees et al., 2001; Warner and Mandiberg, 2006). New venture creation aligned with social purposes can represent a valid and transformative response to economic, human rights, and ecological concerns (Aggestam, 2017). Current scholarship and practice add environmental impact as a third bottom line when social entrepreneurship focuses on improving ecological conditions as a component of their business model.[1] Double or triple bottom line considerations necessarily mean that social entrepreneurs must negotiate, leverage resources, and ultimately positively influence ecosystems other than those directly related to business planning, sales generation, and economic viability of the ventures. In essence, social entrepreneurship is concerned with effecting positive, transformative social and economic change among PWD. Social entrepreneurs and the enterprises they create can also facilitate systems change leading to the development of new paradigms about what it means to have a disability. The positive outcomes generated by social enterprises can include the generation of new policies, partnerships and resources that ensures their rights, societal inclusion and economic stability.

Efforts that mobilize multiple social and economic systems towards the goal of ensuring jobs at a living wage in integrated employment settings are necessary for PWD to achieve the lives they wish to lead in their preferred communities. An over-reliance upon the medical model of disability that deems people with disabilities as "not ready" for work has been disproven by evidence-based employment practices that support rapid access to mainstream employment (Bond et al., 1997). While practices have evolved from an emphasis upon providing employment for PDW in segregated and sheltered workshops, the continued low rate of integrated, competitive employment cited above suggests that new approaches for providing jobs and careers at living wages, including new venture creation, should be considered. Social entrepreneurship is a global phenomenon, as enterprising venture creators leverage knowledge, skills, and resources to help people with disadvantages and/or disabilities to generate the income necessary to sustain themselves and their families (Dees et al., 2001). An early proponent of creating businesses addressing social purposes is the Nobel laureate Muhammad Yunis, who pioneered microcredit for venture creation in his native country of Bangladesh and other countries throughout the world (Yunis, 2007).

The business case for social entrepreneurship is that it can create jobs through social ventures, add to the economic health of communities, and make communities better places to live. That is because more people, otherwise unemployed or relying on public assistance, produce value and improve their economic stability (Yunis, 2007; Nicholls, 2008). Social enterprises also add value as an aid to recovery for PWD, since employment can be positively correlated to recovery outcomes (Bond et al., 1997; Bond, 1998; Marrone and Boeltzig, 2005). The positive outcomes of social enterprise creation are most often felt in the geographical areas where businesses are located by improving job opportunities for PWD who are employed by the venture. Emerging research suggests the effectiveness of social enterprises in meeting the double (or triple) bottom line (Maxwell et al., 2015). However, their impact, while often very consequential for those having jobs, can have localized but not systemic results if ventures are not scaled up.

The future challenge for the field of social entrepreneurship is for it to become the "point of the spear" for social, civic, and economic inclusion among whole communities of persons who face economic disenfranchisement, including PWD, within and across countries (Dees et al., 2001; Yunis, 2006; Ng et al., 2020; Arndt et al., 2021). Creation of social enterprises is an important step towards these goals. However, another valid approach is to "seed and upscale" the economic inclusion of these persons within and across communities by helping them to start and operate their own business ventures (Yunis, 2007). This entails not only a "retail strategy" (creation of one or more social purpose ventures providing employment for some individuals) but also a "wholesale strategy" (systems change that enables widespread economic inclusion and employment of PWD as a required component of civil society) (Shaheen, 2016; Shaheen and Tihic, 2010). When systems and perceptions of disability change, as PWD are provided opportunities to become business owners contributing economic value to their communities they can feel more empowered to face the future with hope and expectation of better lives (Shaheen, 2011; Ng and Arndt, 2019). The intersection of social entrepreneurship with systems change is a poorly explored area that this chapter intends to address.

RELEVANCE OF SOCIAL ENTREPRENEURSHIP TO SYSTEMS CHANGE

Numerous publications have examined the correlation and outcomes of systems change that have relevance for understanding the micro–meso–macro intersectionality of social entrepreneurship. Christens et al. (2007) discussed how systems change must consider an integrated focus on systems and their constituent individuals, and how they interact continuously to shape each other. Kreger et al. (2007) echoed the necessity of considering intersectionality of systems change, including events and trends, patterns of interaction, context, and cultural or social models, and the inherent attributes of the systems themselves. Weber et al. (2012: 1037) noted that "for realizing long-term transformative change, more is needed than individual product or process innovations at firm level, but comprehensive system innovations, i.e. novel configurations of actors, institutions and practices that bring about a new mode of operation of entire sectors or systems of production and consumption."

As social entrepreneurs such as Muhammad Yunis and others have demonstrated, social entrepreneurship can be focused on boutique-scale social purpose businesses, but also can catalyze widescale changes in systems, resource allocations, and societal attitudes that validate transformative methods used to establish dual-purpose social ventures (Yunis, 2007). Such methods can include upscaling the number of entrepreneurs with disability (EWD) operating in the regular economy to address societal inclusion and/or economic inequality. These transformative methods also include strategic planning that employs the use of success stories, educational materials, formal presentations, white papers, and issue briefs, among other methods, to demonstrate that the social entrepreneurship initiative has achieved its outcomes and to make the case for upscaling and replication.

An example of these methods for promoting dialogue and demonstrating social entrepreneurial outcomes includes the US Center for Medicaid Services grant-funded Medicaid Infrastructure Grant (MIG) implemented in New York State (NYS) from 2009 to 2012. Although the intent of the MIGs was primarily to improve access to wage-based employment for PWD, NYS expanded upon its StartUP NY project, implemented statewide Entrepreneurship Learning Dialogues and conference presentations, and issued numerous briefs, white papers, and toolkits in an effort to increase awareness and disseminate best practices for supporting entrepreneurship for PWD (Cornell University, 2021).

Fundamentally, the goal is to create social entrepreneurship initiatives which demonstrate outcomes that are potentially sustainable and replicable. Our two case studies analyze two fundamentally different scenarios. The first case study demonstrates an effective approach to inclusive entrepreneurship (Shaheen and Tihic, 2010) that has led to a system change with sustainable outcomes for individuals, agencies and institutions. The second case study describes a social venture that identifies and leverages the distinct resources of an entrepreneur with severe disabilities. This social venture has demonstrated social and inclusive impact by scaling the idea around the world. In essence, these case examples illustrate how venture creation by individuals with disabilities can improve their lives and the communities in which they live.

CASE EXAMPLE 1: STARTUP NY AS A SOCIAL ENTREPRENEURSHIP INITIATIVE

Individual entrepreneurship presents a potentially valid employment outcome for some PWD. Research demonstrates that PWD can be successful small business owners when provided with the opportunities, training, and support (Walls et al., 2001; Tihic and Hadzic, 2019). From 2007 to 2010, the US Department of Labor Office of Disability Employment Policy (ODEP) provided funding for three national demonstration projects to test and research effective methods for improving self-employment among PWD. One of these projects, StartUP NY, was implemented in New York State by Syracuse University and its Burton Blatt Institute through the auspices of the Onondaga County Department of Social Services.

The inclusive entrepreneurship goals of StartUP NY extended across micro, meso, and macro levels. Embedding improved opportunities for PWD to become self-employed was a major program goal, including strategies for sustaining and scaling up the initiative after the end of the three-year grant. StartUP NY proposed to train at least 150 PWD and help 50 of them to launch their own revenue-generating businesses over the three-year project period. StartUP NY served people with diverse disabilities, and the only criteria for enrollment were: (1) people had to have a documented disability of any type; (2) they had to have a commitment to entrepreneurship; and (3) they had to reside within the counties served by the project grant. By the end of the project, StartUP NY had trained over 250 people and assisted over 60 of them to start and operate revenue-generating business (Shaheen and Killeen, 2010; Killeen et al., 2010). That number had since grown to over 100 businesses in operation by the end of 2014 (Syracuse University, 2014).

StartUP NY took an integrative, ecosystems approach to social entrepreneurship. At the micro level, it worked directly with prospective EWD by helping them develop their inherent gifts, skills, and vision for venture creation. This effort was enabled both through traditional business feasibility and planning assistance, but also through regular networking luncheons where entrepreneurs shared insights, helped one another to overcome business creation hurdles, and supported one another as their own "community of practice." As the initiative increased the number of EWD, generating revenue independent of their public assistance resources, it not only provided financial motivation but also helped them develop self-empowering perspectives, improved social capital, and economic power as purchasers and sellers in the marketplace. With increased self-reliance and reduced reliance on disability services systems as "a way of life—not an aid to life," new business owners articulated that they felt more confident and hopeful for their futures. Entrepreneurs gained practical skills (market research, networking, developing a budget, bookkeeping, and so on) delivered by business counselors and partner agencies that helped them to develop new skills in starting, operating, and financing their businesses in ways that helped them to compete effectively in their marketplaces. In essence, they viewed themselves not as disabled persons with disability-focused services occupying so much of their time and lives, but rather as business owners in their communities whose time was well taken up in making their ventures succeed.

StartUP NY, as part of an inclusive entrepreneurship model, also sought to improve the ways that public and private agencies helped to make services and resources more available for self-employment services by PWD (meso level). This included identifying and partnering with a community credit union and local foundation to make business seed capital available to StartUP NY entrepreneurs, that was customized with financial literacy training. This in turn drove development of a new business start-up revenue stream. Integration across organizations that provided disability as well as generic business training and incubation was pursued by regular attention to partnership development. Tuition-free business planning training was provided by the local Small Business Development Center (SBDC).[2] Organizations were regularly convened in forums to strategize new policies and methods that their public funding authorities could consider in promoting entrepreneurship when organizations felt less empowered to do so. Outcomes of these efforts were often realized when disability service providers began to ask people if they were interested in self-employment as well as wage employment, when such an option had been rarely or not ever presented by counseling staff.

To influence system change, the program regularly developed and published training and informational resources. Public and private agencies, including public business development incubators, learned of, and began to use, inclusive entrepreneurship practices through development of "primers," white papers, and toolkits.

The New York State Department of Vocational Rehabilitation Services (ACCES-VR)[3] can provide business start-up financial assistance and/or business planning counseling for entrepreneurs with disabilities, when entrepreneurship is an approved service. They often receive requests for assistance by PWD to start their own businesses, but find that while they may have a desire to be self-employed, they often lack business planning skills (Kitching, 2014; Tihic, 2019). Nationwide, VR agencies have success serving a miniscule number of their customers in self-employment (Revell et al., 2009; West, 2012). Consequently, the local ACCES-VR office was extremely skeptical of StartUP and was reluctant to refer its customers to the program. However, after acknowledging the program's success, referrals from VR and a closer relationship occurred.

An important strategy facilitating systems change was the decision to integrate inclusive entrepreneurship within a new, New York State, federal Center for Medicaid Services-funded initiative to improve employment outcomes for PWD across the state. While that initiative was primarily focused on wage employment, it brought entrepreneurship to the attention of senior State Agency officials who were regularly briefed on its progress. Perhaps one of the most salient outcomes of this effort to promote entrepreneurship occurred as public and private agencies shifted their perspective on the validity of self-employment as a career option, based upon observing the successful creation of new start-up ventures among clientele that they served.

StartUP NY and its inclusive entrepreneurship focus demonstrates how using social entrepreneurship principles and practices can help to change societal attitudes; enable and empower people with barriers to social, civic, and economic inclusion; challenge public misconceptions and paradigms related to these populations; and improve policies and programs within and across systems so that they can become more accessible and inclusive of PWD. Social entrepreneurship in its most generous sense is about addressing intersectionality of these elements through social and economic means, and achieving systems change. This change would enable more individuals with employment barriers to achieve greater financial stability and independence. The case examples that follow are perhaps the best testimony that social entrepreneurship can achieve demonstrable individual, services, and systems change.

How a Social Purpose Venture Helps Sam to Become an Entrepreneur

Sam is an African-American male in his mid-fifties who lives in the suburbs/rural area of Syracuse, NY. He is a veteran soldier. He experienced a traumatic head injury when he was a young man serving in the military. The doctors told him that he would be a "vegetable" for the remainder of his life. However, he worked hard to relearn everything, including how to speak, and eventually became a home caregiver for his parents and his in-laws. Sam lives with his extended family, which includes his parents, in-laws, his wife, and children, in one house. Taking care of the elderly in his house for more than seven years required him to drive to all their medical-related appointments. Recognizing this need that the elderly had, and his joy in providing transportation services, Sam started dreaming about owning his own transportation services business. The idea of the business was his "happy place" in his struggle to overcome the accident and lack of support by his doctors who called him a "vegetable."

Throughout his life, Sam had to prove to himself and others that he could be more than the type of person that he was labeled by his doctor. While he works hard at changing perceptions of those around him, he also admits that it is difficult to overcome his own, internal perceptions about the limitations that his disability can produce: "I'm trying to get myself to a point that I want to think bigger than that. I don't want to think like I'm slow, I need help and this and that … It's just sometimes I've got the stuttering problems. Sometimes I got the speech problems."

Micro Level: Unleashing Sam's Entrepreneurial Spirit

Sam joined StartUp in 2007 and with its assistance started his transportation services company in 2009. Conscious of his disability, he did not speak much, yet he showed up to every event and class that was offered and/or promoted by the StartUp efforts and initiatives.

Start-UP was more than learning about business planning for Sam; it was a chance to be recognized by staff and his peers as an aspiring entrepreneur first, and a person with disabilities second. He has been navigating his internal barriers and external misconceptions by leveraging the resources and social capital he gained from StartUp and maintaining his positive attitude. Sam talks about how having the chance to articulate and realize his entrepreneurship dreams in a "no stigma zone" helped him to succeed in his continuing education, his business start-up, in marketing his business, and even in his personal life.

StartUp helped participants recognize their strengths and limitations with the goal of enabling them to leverage their strengths while minimizing their limitations. Sam realized that his passion or strength was that he enjoyed interacting with people. However, he had no other skills and/or knowledge of business start-up.

Working with a StartUp business navigator, Sam discovered that marketing is his passion, because it enables him to take charge, influence others to support his venture, and makes him go out in the community and interact with people and different constituencies, with new and growing confidence. He was a shy person with a disability before StartUP, but was transformed after gaining confidence from his accomplishments, into an outgoing, self-directed entrepreneur with a smile. He now believes that establishing a great conversation is key for success in his business.

By marketing and talking to clients and potential clients, Sam has established relationships with medical services providers to gain support related to the business. For example, his new confidence around sharing his perceived weaknesses and limitations (including that he does not know how to schedule appointments properly) enabled him to get assistance from medical services provider support staff, who pitch in to assist in managing those facets of his work. Further, his family stepped up and helped him to develop a support team, who address other weaknesses and shortcomings he has identified throughout the entrepreneurial discovery process of StartUp.

StartUp also provided the platform for Sam to create both peer and professional social capital. The professional social capital includes not only small business services providers, but also disability service providers. He only talked about good experiences with the agency providing disability-related services. For example, he must report his Social Security Disability Income (SSDI)[4] benefit and has had a "good feeling" in his interactions to do with SSDI.

Overall, his experiences are directly linked to his emotions. He maintains and leverages the social capital which provides him with "good feelings." Moreover, he accessed those services which eventually provided him support and assistance to access and leverage the resources available to him. As result, Sam perceives disability as something good. Apart from his negative experiences with doctors as a young man, he does see a benefit in having a disability and disclosing it.

Since becoming an entrepreneur, Sam has exhibited changes in his ideas and values. When asked about his identity, he identifies himself as just as an entrepreneur, rather than an entrepreneur with disability, and when he introduces himself he says, "My name is Sam. I'm an entrepreneur." Sam perceives entrepreneurship as a means of empowerment to overcome his disability-related challenges, sharing that entrepreneurship has been a "booster" for him to overcome the negativity he experienced from doctors and others thinking of him as something less than he is. Moreover, he has shifted the conversation from him and his disability to his business: "Instead of talking about me, talk about my business."

Meso Level: Addressing the Business Infrastructure

StartUp assisted prospective entrepreneurs to develop their business infrastructure by leveraging and adapting the "4 Stage Entrepreneurship Model" (Morris et al., 2012). A key model enhancement was the creation of new partnerships that could leverage their resources and talent to support aspiring entrepreneurs by accessing their subject matter expertise, and in some cases, for the financial resources they could provide to the business.

In Stage One, the entrepreneurial awareness or discovery phase, Sam worked one-on-one with the StartUp business navigator at the Syracuse University's South

Side Innovation Center (SSIC),[5] a business incubator that became the physical hub of StartUP. Here, the business navigator helped Sam to understand his business development challenges, and to develop his support team to provide both social support and encouragement, but also tangible help with the business, and by connecting him to relevant service providers in the community that could provide additional personal and business counseling.

In the US, PWD who want to return to work or start a business often fear the effects that making money will have on their public assistance allowances. Social Security Administration (SSA) Disability Insurance (SSDI) is often crucial for PWD to access daily living stipends and medical insurance that might be jeopardized if the recipient starts earning too much money. Unlike entrepreneurs who are not receiving social security benefits, those who do must also get assistance in managing their benefits as they start earning business-related income. StartUp connected Sam with a benefits advisor who walked him through the SSDI needs and requirements, and connected him with the point of contact at the agency providing SSDI. Because StartUP also secured the participation of a benefits planner who worked as a team with his business navigator, Sam was able to maintain his benefits as his business income increased. He leveraged the increase in income to buy new vehicles and hire drivers, and was able to leverage new money needed to pursue his core entrepreneurial vision.

In this stage, he also received financial literacy training and access to an Individual Development Account[6] (IDA) matching funds saving program, worked with a benefits advisor to maintain his SSDI, and attended more than 40 hours of small business-related training at the SSIC. Once he established his social support, completed the financial literacy training, opened an IDA account, and developed his business feasibility model, he graduated from Stage One and the business navigator connected him to the Small Business Development Center (SBDC) at Onondaga Community College (OCC) for Stage Two of the venture creation process.

In Stage Two, Sam worked with the SBDC on developing his formal business plan and completed the Syracuse Entrepreneurship Bootcamp, a six-week entrepreneurship training facilitated by Syracuse University. He maintained his IDA account and continued working with both his benefits advisor and his StartUp business navigator. After completing his business plan, he had his internal operating and external marketing processes fleshed out and was ready to proceed to Stage Three: the implementation of his business plan. Here, Sam became a new small business tenant at the SSIC, leveraged his IDA to purchase a vehicle, and continued taking classes at SSIC. During this stage, Sam focused on the particulars of bringing his products to market and generating revenue. The business navigator also ensured that he could receive ongoing troubleshooting and technical assistance by connecting him with a mentor from SCORE.[7] SCORE is a US-based national network of volunteer, expert business mentors. By the end of Stage Three, Sam was well on his way towards operating a viable, well-organized business, and ready to scale up the venture in Stage Four.

As Sam progressed in Stage Four, his business gained more customers, he remained engaged with StartUp's network and his business navigator, and maintained his social security benefits, while earning business income. Sam also received technical assistance from students enrolled in Syracuse University's Whitman School of Mangement consulting class. Here, five students worked directly with Sam over the course of a semester on creating tools, processes, and procedures to sustain and grow his business.

The availability of business counselors, mentors, and access to business planning services helped Sam to create a viable business operational structure. Sam's involvement in StartUP helped him to establish his entrepreneurial vision, self-confidence, and confirm that owning a business would be a feasible and meaningful career. But without such infrastructure and technical support, he would not have been able to translate his dreams into an operating reality, including learning about and using financial accounting techniques, marketing tools, profit/loss projections, and other aspects necessary to running any business successfully.

Macro-Level Systems and Environmental Considerations

StartUP sought to launch successful ventures, but also to create environmental, attitudinal, and systems change benefitting future entrepreneurs with disabilities. A number of these positive changes are referenced below.

The SBDC already served prospective entrepreneurs with disabilities, but in their words: "they often never followed through." After their involvement in StartUP and experience with its model, the business advisor at SBDC developed "Simply Speaking: Inclusive Entrepreneurship Guidelines for SBDC Advisors," and disseminated it to all SBDC advisors in New York State (NYS) at an annual NYS SBDC gathering. The guide laid out a plan for SBDC counselors to follow in working more effectively with entrepreneurs with disabilities.

Additionally, both the South Side Innovation Center and the Women Business Center in Syracuse, NYS recognized the value of StartUp, since many of their clients were also part of the StartUp project. They adapted the Inclusive Entrepreneurship tools and curriculum that was used by the StartUp business navigator for use within their own organizations and found them to be effective in serving their "harder to serve" clients.

Sam's work with ARISE[8] and Social Security Administration advisors helped to demonstrate how the model could be used successfully with individuals with disabilities. Consequently, their appreciation of the process led to several referrals to StartUp, and helped to change the misgivings that these disability service providers previously had about recognizing entrepreneurship as a viable employment option for PWD.

In summary, development as an entrepreneur has helped Sam to conceptualize and realize his dreams of independence. In his personal life, the friends and acquaintances he met through his entrepreneurial journey help to maintain his positive mindset, encourage him, and are happy for him and his business. He keeps in touch with other entrepreneurs from StartUP, leverages his family members in his business, and has removed himself from people who were negative towards him and his business.

Summary: Challenges and Cautions

Sustainability and scalability are achievable for social entrepreneurship by addressing accessibility, opportunity, resource leveraging, and partnerships as not only processes but also outcomes. However, visionary leadership and nurturing a commitment to developing cross-sector partnerships over time is key to long-term success. Support for systems transformative social entrepreneurship can be affected by changes in leadership, resources, and the political and economic climate, and if left unattended can atrophy in much the same way that a social enterprise can experience when it loses business contracts.

StartUP NY encountered resistance to change among service providers, business incubators, and even its sponsoring university. However, by diligently nurturing collaborative relationships and drawing inspiration from entrepreneurs who overcame significant personal, systemic, and societal barriers to start their own businesses, these methods are proven to work with all of the customers that its host business incubator enrolls, including those without disabilities. Self-employment is increasingly viewed by public and private agencies in New York as a potentially valid career preference, not as an alternative to consider only when wage employment is unsuccessful. Even so, public seed financing, and ongoing consultation for prospective EWD, is not yet widely available. Neither is access to the government Minority and Women Owned Business purchasing preference certification, by virtue of having a disability. Consequently, not only business creation, but scalability and extending employment in these ventures to others with disabilities, is difficult to achieve.

These examples demonstrate both the staying power and the fragility of social entrepreneurship directed towards sustainable systems change and scalability. Aspiring social entrepreneurs who intend to foster, sustain, and grow systems improvements must consider the sustainability factor. Like single social enterprises, positive return on investment is possible in local communities by addressing the double bottom line. For self-employment, that means more businesses are created and economically viable, and more PWD who were previously unemployed or underemployed can increase their economic stability. The challenge for social entrepreneurs working to transform systems is how to ensure that even while individual gains are made, gains in transforming systems and embedding support for self-employment become established over the long term.

CASE EXAMPLE 2: NIGHT MARATHON

Night Marathons are popular running events that take place in the late evening, that are staged across Europe. Runners have the option to run different distances, there is a wheelchair competition, volunteers help making these events happen. They are typical large-scale running events. Each runner is charged a fee. The profit from each event is collected for a trust that is dedicated to researching a cure for paralysis.

The events came to life through the initiative of Angela, who created the inclusive idea of the Night Marathon after having an accident that paralyzed her and created more challenges in addition to the blindness she was living with before the accident. Night Marathon was well promoted as a way to provide inclusive fitness and social experiences for all individuals, regardless of the presence or absence of a disability, and became one of the most popular running events in Europe and subsequently worldwide. Today, Night Marathon competitions are held regularly on several continents. More than 2 million runners have participated in these events worldwide, and they regularly attract several thousand runners to each run.

The initiative not only brings together people from all walks of life in one "universally accessible" event, but has also generated millions of dollars of funding that supports research with the aim of curing disabilities. Angela was able to make this series of events happen by leveraging her own personal social and collegial network, developed while undertaking a series of adventurous trips after she became blind. For example, she travelled to the North Pole.

Micro Level: Putting Things Together

Angela lost her eyesight in one eye at an early childhood age. Despite this, she became a passionate sportswomen and adventurer. She engaged in kayaking and competed successfully on the international level even after losing her eyesight completely when she was in her early twenties. Among other accomplishments, she walked to the North Pole. This became a flagship event with much publicity that helped her to build a large social and professional network in the area of adventure sports. In 2010, she had a traumatic accident that left her paralyzed. Since then, she has been confined to a wheelchair, and needs support to navigate both her blindness and her paraplegia. Among other life setbacks occurring from the accident, she was forced to sacrifice some of her independence and initially moved back into her parents' home. Unwilling to accept being unable to walk, she developed a personal life mission devoted to curing paralysis. All of her efforts and most of her daily routines are aimed at collecting funds to further research in this area, to enable more people with disabilities to regain independence. Of course, this event and the purpose behind it (curing paralysis) is also an entrepreneurial venture that requires a network of sponsors, helpers, organizers, researchers, and so on. While Angela unites many of the marketing resources to promote this event and give it an identity, pulling off any event of this size requires a well-organized entity behind the scenes, consistent with developing a meso-level strategy.

Meso Level: Building the Entrepreneurial Infrastructure Supporting the Greater Cause

Night Marathon does not stand in a vacuum, but leverages, feeds into, and impacts larger movements. It is a socially directed venture that, just like any business, must address a market need by providing a needed service. A running event, particularly in

Europe, leverages tradition in the region in which regional and local running events are featured as often as on a weekly basis. It fits with a health movement for more sport, better food, and so on. Europe has a culture of giving for personal challenges with the aim of sponsoring social causes. Europe has also one of the most progressive legislation and social support for inclusion. Consequently, the Night Marathon social venture incorporates and fits very well into the cultural setting. It is no surprise that across the Commonwealth and beyond in many developed and developing countries, the concept has attracted much attention and support.

Having a "head" like Angela, who embodies so many of the ideals and spirit of this event, is both an attribute of the social venture and a marketing resource that can be leveraged. Sports are integrative mechanisms in society with a long tradition across many cultures. By locating the venture within this context, the running events demonstrate and promote the validity of this integrative mechanism and become part of the internal operational features of the enterprise. In addition, its business plan of channeling the surplus after expenses for the greater good, with a clear purpose that is communicated to its "buying publics," is an additional element that enables the success of this event series as a social entrepreneurship example.

Macro Level: Taking a New Perspective

Night Marathon seems to be a metaphor that is open to continual interpretation, depending upon one's perspective. As a sports competition, Night Marathon incorporates a friendly and competitive spirit. It encourages everyone to train to stay healthy. It is inclusive and does not limit running to the abled. It encourages both participants and spectators to challenge held beliefs by developing new perspectives on disability; facilitated by Angela's example as one of the main stakeholders and participants who overcomes both blindness and paraplegia. The act of running also serves as a metaphor that encourages people not to stand still, but to be moving and dynamic. The event encourages all runners to contemplate the experience of what it means to overcome disability by stepping into someone else's shoes (for example, the darkness/blindness of Angela as a symbol for this), but equally leverages people's public perceptions of the disability of blindness for a good purpose.

Summary

Night Marathon is an event series built by Angela who is both blind and paralyzed. Angela has shown exceptional motivation to overcome some of the hardships she has experienced by creating a socially driven initiative that satisfies her personally; is operated with full awareness of its "market position" and with plans and strategies in place to deliver her "product"; and is building awareness and changing the social perceptions of what it means to have a disability. In essence, Angela has translated her hardship into in exceptional fundraising opportunity that aligns her personal agenda of promoting the greater good.

DISCUSSION AND POLICY IMPLICATIONS

In this chapter, and its two diverse case studies, the integration of the micro level (individual), meso level (operational infrastructure), and macro level (systems and societal) of entrepreneurship comprise an entrepreneurial ecosystem. Social entrepreneurship that addresses each of these elements concurrently has enabled two entrepreneurs to overcome their challenges, created two social purpose-directed ventures, and contributed to improved systems and public perceptions. Contemplating and addressing each of these ecosystem elements can engage and help social entrepreneurs to create impactful organizations and contribute to society. We suggest that the three levels cannot be looked at in isolation, but need a holistic approach to enable people to convert their challenges into personal success stories. Social entrepreneurship initiatives addressing each level can enable individual EWD to develop their personal vision and plans, bring their vision to market through venture creation, and demonstrate a return on investment for society by demonstrating their success.

One reoccurring element of high importance across each case example context was the building and leveraging of networks. The networks were important to each entrepreneur on a personal level, to share experiences and improve their confidence. The networks provided a source for financial and resource leverage to strengthen the entrepreneurial ventures. The two social purpose ventures in our case studies sought to work for the greater good, as well as to operate effectively. The entrepreneurs were thereby able to mobilize additional networks and resources as self-reinforcing mechanisms.

The existence of both of our exemplary social ventures were great antecedents to strengthen the motivation of individuals to get involved with them, and to build persistence over time to achieve their impact. Each venture has distinct, but very detailed understandings of leveraging the resources that were needed to achieve their impact: mobilizing space, knowledge, finances, networks, and institutions at the right time and in the right, complementary manner. Both were the result of several years of planning and implementation which enabled progression and learning.

In addition to the enterprising nature of both social ventures, addressing the well-being of their participants was a common factor that was central to each of the entrepreneurs' visions. While each venture's ultimate goal was to achieve their own individual goals, both social ventures went beyond this to achieve higher purposes through collective efforts at mobilizing their stakeholders.

Visionary leadership seems to be a core factor that enabled both types of socially directed venture to be founded, to persist, and to establish the necessary ecosystems, without which the purposes could not have been achieved and sustained. Visionary leadership was necessary to put together the available resources in synergistic ways that enabled each venture to make improvements across all three levels of the ecosystem.

CONCLUSION

In summary, social entrepreneurship fits into today's political climate of inclusion, respect for individualization, and promotion of independence, and self-help. In this sense, the above case studies underscore how entrepreneurship can be life- and income-empowering for PWD, who often struggle with achieving economic and social equity with non-disabled members of their communities. Social entrepreneurship that privileges individual venture creation can leverage the political climate supporting inclusion in unique ways that both challenge and incentivize disability services organizations to address their organizational goals of promoting recovery and income equality. But for these goals to be realized, social entrepreneurs must factor in strategies that leverage the combination of accessibility, opportunity, resource leveraging, and partnerships in unique ways to overcome the myriad individual (micro), services (meso), and environmental (macro) challenges faced by many EWD. We show that recognizing and addressing the interplay of these factors, in addition to addressing the mechanics of starting and operating a business, enables EWD to individualize their experiences and overcome the challenges that society often raises along the path to civic, social, and economic inclusion.

NOTES

1. Retrieved from http://www.american.edu/americantoday/campus-news/20120321-Social
   -Enterprises-Have-a-Triple-Bottom-Line.cfm.
2. Small Business Development Center (SBDC) is a US Small Business Administration funded service. The SBDC provides free marketing, financing, and business-related activities to local entrepreneurs.
3. In the United States, the federal Rehabilitation Services Administration promotes employment of people with diverse disabilities by funding Departments of Vocational Rehabilitation (VR) in all states and territories.
4. Social Security Disability Insurance (SSDI) is a payroll tax-funded federal insurance program of the United States government. It is managed by the Social Security Administration and designed to provide supplemental income to people who are physically restricted in their ability to be employed because of a notable disability.
5. South Side Innovation Center (SSIC) is a community-based microenterprise incubator operated by the Whitman School of Management at Syracuse University.
6. An Individual Development Account (IDA) is a bank savings account geared towards low-income individuals to assist in building assets to achieve financial stability and long-term self-sufficiency.
7. SCORE is a US Small Business Administration-funded service. SCORE is the nation's largest network of volunteer, expert business mentors, focusing on providing mentoring services to entrepreneurs.
8. ARISE is a non-profit Independent Living Center that provides disability services for people of all ages and abilities in Syracuse and Central New York.

REFERENCES

Aggestam, M. (2017). Social entrepreneuring: "what's good for society is also good for business." In P. Meising and M. Aggestam, *Educating Social Entrepreneurs From Idea Generation to Business Plan Formulation.* New York: Business Expert Press.

Arndt, F., Ng, W., and Huang, T. (2021). Do-it-yourself laboratories, communities of practice, and open innovation in a digitalised environment. *Technology Analysis and Strategic Management*, 33(10), 1186–1197.

Bond, G.R. (1998). Principles of the individual placement and support model: empirical support. *Psychiatric Rehabilitation Journal*, 22(1), 11–23.

Bond, G.R., Becker, D.R., Drake, R.E., and Vogler, K.M. (1997). A fidelity scale for the individual placement and support model of supported employment. *Rehabilitation Counseling Bulletin*, 40, 265–284.

Centers for Disease Control and Prevention (2018). Disability and Health Data System (DHDS). Updated May 24, 2018; cited August 27, 2018. http://dhds.cdc.gov.

Christens, B.D., Hanlin, C.E., and Speer, P.W. (2007). Getting the social organism thinking: strategy for systems change. *American Journal of Community Psychology*, 39, 229. https://doi.org/10.1007/s10464-007-9119-y.

Cornell University (2021). *New York Makes Work Pay.* Ithaca, NY. https://register.yangtaninstitute.org/p-NYMakesWorkPay.cfm.

Dees, G., Emerson, J., and Economy, P. (2001). *Enterprising Nonprofits: A Toolkit for Social Entrepreneurs.* New York: John Wiley.

Hughes, C., and Avoke, S.K. (2010). The elephant in the room: poverty, disability, and employment. *Research and Practice for Persons with Severe Disabilities*, 35, 5–14.

Killeen, M., Adya, M., and Shaheen, G. (2010). *Inclusive Entrepreneurship-Final Project Report.* Syracuse, NY: Syracuse University.

Kitching, J. (2014). *Entrepreneurship and Self-Employment by People with Disabilities.* Project Report. Paris, France: Organisation for Economic Co-operation and Development.

Kreger, M., Brindis, C., Manuel, D., and Sassoubre, L. (2007). Lessons learned in systems change initiatives: benchmarks and indicators. *American Journal of Community Psychology*, 39, 301–320.

Marrone, J., and Boeltzig, H. (2005). *Recovery with Results, Not Rhetoric.* Paper 2. Boston, MA: Institute for Community Inclusion Publications. http://scholarworks.umb.edu/ici_pubs/2.

Maxwell, N., Rotz, D., and Dunn, A. (2015). *Economic Self-Sufficiency and Life Stability One Year After Starting a Social Enterprise Job.* Princeton, NJ: Mathematica Policy Research.

Meager, N., and Higgins, T. (2011). *Disability and Skills in a Changing Economy, UK Commission for Employment and Skills.* Briefing Paper Series. http://www.oph.fi/download/140962_equality-disability.pdf.

Morris, M., Schindehutte, M., Edmonds, V., and Watters, C. (2011). Inner city engagement and the university: mutuality, emergence and transformation. *Entrepreneurship & Regional Development*, 23(5–6), 287–315.

Ng, W., and Arndt, F. (2019). "I never needed eyes to see": leveraging extreme challenges for successful venture creation. *Journal of Business Venturing Insights*, 11, e00125.

Ng, W., Arndt, F., and Huang, T.Y. (2020). Do-it-yourself laboratories as integration-based ecosystems. *Technological Forecasting and Social Change*, 161, 120249.

Nicholls, A. (2008). *Social Entrepreneurship: New Models of Sustainable Social Change.* Oxford: Oxford University Press.

Pagán, R. (2009). Self-employment among people with disabilities: evidence for Europe. *Disability and Society*, 24(2), 217–229.

Revell, G., Smith, F., and Inge, K. (2009). An analysis of self-employment outcomes within the federal/state vocational rehabilitation system. *Journal of Vocational Rehabilitation*, 31, 11–18.

Rotz, D., Maxwell, N., and Dunn, A. (2015). *Economic Self-Sufficiency and Life Stability One Year after Starting a Social Enterprise Job*. Oakland, CA: Mathematica Policy Research, published through Roberts Economic Development Fund.

Shaheen, G. (2011). Inclusive entrepreneurship. In B. Kingma (ed.), *Academic Entrepreneurship and Community Engagement: Scholarship in Action and the Syracuse Miracle* (pp. 110–126). Cheltenham, UK and Northampton, MA, USA: Edward Elgar Publishing.

Shaheen, G.E. (2016). "Inclusive entrepreneurship": a process for improving self-employment for people with disabilities. *Journal of Policy Practice*, 15(1–2), 58–81.

Shaheen, G., and Killeen, M. (2010). A "primer" on the StartUP New York 4-phase Entrepreneurship Model. http://nymakesworkpay.org/docs/StartUP_New_York_4-Phase _Model.pdf.

Shaheen, G., and Tihic, M. (2010). Definition of inclusive entrepreneurship. https://en .wikipedia.org/wiki/Inclusive_entrepreneurship.

Syracuse University (2014). *SBA PRIME at SSIC. Final Report to the US Small Business Administration*. Syracuse, NY.

Tihic, M. (2019). Experiences of entrepreneurs with disabilities: a critical disability theory perspective. Dissertations - ALL. https://surface.syr.edu/etd/1028, Syracuse, NY.

Tihic, M., and Hadzic, M. (2019). Critical theory: when too critical becomes a barrier for aspiring entrepreneurs with disabilities. *Frontiers of Entrepreneurship Research*, 39, 313–318.

US Department of Labor, Office of Disability Employment Policy (n.d.). Disability Employment Policy Resources by Topic. Retrieved September 9, 2014 from http://www .dol.gov/odep/topics/research.htm.

Vaughan, M.A. (2021). Family Resources Survey: Financial Year 2019 to 2020. National Statistics, UK. https://www.gov.uk/government/statistics/family-resources-survey-financial -year-2019-to-2020.

Walls, R.T., Dowler, D.L., Cordingly, K., Orslene, L.E., and Greer, J.D. (2001). Microenterprising and people with disabilities: strategies for success and failure. *Journal of Rehabilitation*, 67(2), April–June.

Warner, R., and Mandiberg, J. (2006). An update on affirmative businesses or social firms for people with mental illness. *Psychiatric Services*, 57(10), October, 1488–1492.

Weber, K. Matthias, and Rohracherb, H. (2012). Legitimizing research, technology and innovation policies for transformative change: combining insights from innovation systems and multi-level perspective in a comprehensive "failures" framework. *Research Policy*, 41, 1037–1047.

West, Michael D. (2012). *Access to Public Self-Employment Opportunities and Resources for Individuals with Disabilities*. Virginia Commonwealth University.

World Health Organization (2011). *World Report on Disability*. Geneva: WHO.

Yunis, M. (2006). Social business entrepreneurs are the solution. In A. Nicholls (ed.), *Social Entrepreneurs: New Models of Sustainable Social Change* (pp. 39–44). New York: Oxford University Press.

Yunis, M. (2007). *Creating a World Without Poverty*. New York: Public Affairs.

11. The role of government policies in establishing a conducive entrepreneurial environment for disabled entrepreneurs in China

Tiansheng Yang, Shandana Sheikh, Shumaila Yousafzai and Xiangxin Yang

INTRODUCTION

There are an estimated 82.96 million disabled people in China, accounting for approximately 6.21 percent of the total population of China (CDPF, 2016). Despite this, there has been scant research on disabled people in China, a gap that needs to be addressed by both academic scholars and policy-makers. In recent years, an increase in entrepreneurship has been one of the most significant changes in European labor markets, with entrepreneurship becoming the main source of economic growth in industrialized and less-developed countries (Kritikos, 2014). In China, entrepreneurship has been increasingly present in the national consciousness, partially due to references by the Chinese government and in local newspapers, such as "local entrepreneur star," "entrepreneurial year," and "Chinese future stars." However, there is no information on disabled entrepreneurs, and it seems that disabled people have been generally overlooked in Chinese entrepreneurial activities. Previous research has widely identified that disabled people usually earn less money and have fewer opportunities to work than non-disabled people; are sometimes excluded from society; and are more likely to be self-employed because they have no alternative options (Leyland-Jones et al., 2005; Renko et al., 2016).

Entrepreneurship plays an important role in reducing social exclusion and economic discrimination, which are often found in relation to minority groups (Godley, 2005). In this context, self-employment can be important for disabled people, both in terms of different political perspectives and for the individuals concerned (Wennekers et al., 2005). Self-employment is likely to help disabled people out of underemployment, unemployment, and low income, which may improve their perceived social value and self-sufficiency (Blanck et al., 2000). Previous research shows high rates of self-employment among disabled people (Pagán, 2009), and such enterprises not only make an economic contribution, but also make a significant contribution in the provision of jobs for other disabled people (Blanck et al., 2000).

The relationship between an individual with disability and their environment is important. Despite disabled people having a broadly positive attitude towards entrepreneurship, the entrepreneurial environment can still cause extreme challenges for them. Compared to non-disabled people, disabled people may face greater obstacles in accessing entrepreneurial opportunities, placing them at a disadvantage (Cooney, 2008). For example, disabled people often face significant barriers when attempting to access critical resources such as key business information, financial support, and institutional and social support (Boylan and Burchardt, 2002; Harper and Momm, 1989; Lindsay, 2011). Besides, one of the major barriers to entrepreneurship among disabled people is a lack of human capital or educational attainment. For example, in China, 42 percent of disabled people of working age (over 18 years old) are relatively uneducated, with only 35 percent of them having completed primary education (World Health Organization, 2011). This may be due to physical disabilities that prevent them from accessing a higher level of education; or external factors, such as parents' preferences for the education of non-disabled children, the lack of special educational institutions for children with disabilities, and issues related to the accessibility of educational institutions. In addition to educational barriers, other barriers to entrepreneurship for people with disabilities include poor geographic mobility and workplace accessibility, a lack of help in management, discrimination against individuals, and personal confidence issues with regard to entrepreneurial abilities. These factors partly explain the low growth and poor performance associated with companies owned by disabled people.

Reflecting upon the impact of the environmental context and the influence that government policy can have on disabled entrepreneurs, this chapter aims to explore how the Chinese government impacts disabled entrepreneurs, and to evaluate current Chinese government policy. Adopting the entrepreneurial ecosystem framework (Isenberg, 2011), which explores the link between the entrepreneurial environment and the entrepreneur, this research analyzes the barriers in terms of current policy from the perspectives of Chinese disabled entrepreneurs. Accordingly, the findings inform current policy-makers and enterprise development policy and generate new insights in current entrepreneurial literature for disabled entrepreneurship. In light of the above, the objective of this research is to understand the role that the Chinese government plays in creating an entrepreneurial environment for disabled entrepreneurs in China. Specifically, this study aims to understand the lived experiences of disabled entrepreneurs in China to assess how government policies affect the entrepreneurial environment around them. The next section presents an overview of the Chinese entrepreneurial ecosystem and the role of government policies.

ENTREPRENEURIAL ECOSYSTEM IN CHINA AND THE ROLE OF CHINESE GOVERNMENT POLICY

Disabled Entrepreneurship in the Chinese Research Context

Although often overlooked in academic studies, the Chinese government maintains a strong concern for disabled people and makes efforts to provide fulfilling lives for them. Disabled people have always received special attention and development as a special human resource in Chinese society. The Chinese scholar Xiaotong (1985) mentions that:

> A disabled person needs to learn and work. Once a person with a disability has access to appropriate learning and employment opportunities, he or she often gets stronger than the general people because of their strong will. Their achievements benefit not only themselves but also other people in the community. If the society discriminates against disabled people and do not give them open study and employment opportunities, it will be a great waste of labor and intellectual resources.

Since the founding of the People's Republic of China, and especially since the recent reforms and opening up of society, the employment situation for disabled people has been greatly improved. The government has set out a series of positive legislative and administrative actions to improve the life conditions and social status of Chinese disabled population. The Disabled People with Protection Act, which came into force in 1991 and revised in 2008, concerns many issues including rehabilitation, welfare, cultural life, education, employment, access, and legal liability, and is of great importance in protecting the rights of disabled people. Additionally, the China Disabled Persons' Federation (CDPF, 2016) considers many aspects to help disabled people, such as safeguarding disabled people's rights, rehabilitation, social security, employment, education, public information, physical training, and international cooperation. Diversified employment methods have been established, such as concentrated employment, proportional employment, individual employment, and assistive employment.

Nevertheless, disabled people in China still have a serious problem in terms of self-employment. At the national level, many policies have been integrated to give them jobs and offer them more convenient lives, but a lot of specific and necessary work has been neglected. With 85 million people in China that are registered as disabled, only 0.75 percent (639 000) are self-employed (CDPF, 2016). Scholars have argued that government should play the leading role in supporting disabled people by formulating and improving support policies, and by implementing preferential policies for the establishment of disabled entrepreneurial organizations (Xu et al., 2015). Through policies such as simple approval procedures for business establishment and lower registered taxation, the barriers and risks for self-employment of disabled people can be reduced, improving the success rate of entrepreneurs. Furthermore, government, enterprises, and society should jointly provide entrepreneurial assistance for disabled people, and tackle the problems of entrepreneurship faced by disabled people by integrating social resources through non-governmental organizations. In order to realize the full employment and entrepreneurship potential of disabled people, it is necessary to balance the relationship between employment and market competition (Sun, 2006). The role of government is to increase education and training and develop human resources for disabled people; changing the social environment of discrimination and creating entrepreneurial support for disabled people would help disabled entrepreneurship (Chen and Mingxiao, 2010).

The Chinese Entrepreneurial Ecosystem

The entrepreneurial ecosystem (EES) approach to understanding entrepreneurship has gained popularity in recent years. It effectively combines individuals, businesses, and society to create social wealth and economic prosperity (Prahalad, 2005). While several definitions exist for EES in academic literature, we adopt Isenberg's definition, which defines the EES as a set of interconnected domains or factors (culture, finance, policy, markets, human capital, and social support), all of which independently but also collectively impact the entrepreneurial environment for entrepreneurs in a given context (Isenberg, 2011).

The EES approach is increasingly being used to support entrepreneurs and better understand entrepreneurship, and has also recently become a part of the disabled entrepreneurship literature. Many scholars claim that entrepreneurship supports economic development. This claim has generated increasing interest in the role of government policy in creating a conducive environment for entrepreneurship (Acs et al., 2008; Audretsch et al., 2007; Shane, 2007). This in turn is determined by the policies implemented by the government for entrepreneurs, ensuring no discrimination on the basis of gender, class, disability, and race. Accordingly, entrepreneurship policy has implications for disabled people who are at the margins of the labor market (Shier et al., 2009).

Many governments in the world have acknowledged that disabled entrepreneurship requires support. In China, most of the relevant government plans and policies are generalized to support all types of disabled entrepreneurs. However, due to the differences in disabilities, such as the type and severity of different disabilities, general policies cannot work for all disabled individuals. In prior research on disabled entrepreneurship it has been found that more targeted policies may be more effective, such as concentrated bespoke one-to-one or small group assistance (Arnold and Ipsen, 2005; EMDA, 2009; Dotson et al., 2013). Amongst the efforts on the policy front, over the past two decades the Chinese government has set out a series of positive legislative and administrative actions to improve the life conditions and social status of disabled people in China. In this regard, the Disabled People with Protection Act, which came into force in 1991 and was revised in 2008, addressing many issues including rehabilitation, welfare, cultural life, education, employment, access, and legal liability. The China Disabled Persons' Federation (CDPF, 2016), an initiative of the Chinese government, considers many aspects to help disabled people, such as safeguarding disabled people's rights, rehabilitation, social security, employment, education, public information, physical training, and international cooperation. Besides this, there are also some small organizations which aim to help disabled people by raising money for them. These small organizations are typically established by enthusiasts who have a passion for helping disabled people without a profit motivation.

To enhance the economic contribution of disabled people, the government of China has also made considerable efforts in improving the employment situation for disabled people, primarily through entrepreneurship and self-employment.

Entrepreneurship plays an important role in reducing social exclusion and economic discrimination, which can be frequently found in ethnic groups (Godley, 2005). It has been argued that people with disabilities are sometimes excluded from society, and that they are more likely to be self-employed because they have no alternative options (Renko et al., 2016). Furthermore, entrepreneurship has also been considered to be a pathway for enhancing the physical, financial, and emotional well-being of the disabled (Blanck et al., 2000). Yet, despite its key role in enhancing the economic participation of disabled people, the rate of entrepreneurship among this segment remains low, primarily due to the significant barriers that hinder disabled people from accessing entrepreneurship as a viable career choice.

Although 85 million people in China are registered as disabled, only 0.75 percent of these (639 000) are self-employed (CDPF, 2016). Disabled people often face significant barriers to access critical resources such as information, finance, institutions, and business and social support (Lindsay, 2011). For example, self-employed people often face problems in accessing institutional support, financial support, business and professional support, and informational support, and face discrimination from suppliers and customers (Boylan and Burchardt, 2003; Harper and Momm, 1989).

Considering the role of government policy in entrepreneurial activity, it has been widely recognized that disabled people face discrimination in the entrepreneurial environment compared to their non-disabled counterparts (Cooney, 2008). This fact partly explains the hypothesis of low growth and poor performance associated with companies owned by disabled people. Scholars in this area believe that the businesses of disabled people are not typically underperforming, but are suffering from constrained performance. Disabled people face restrictions not only because of their disability, but also because of their living environments, including the negative perspectives of other people in society (Hammel et al., 2008). Despite disabled people having a broadly positive attitude towards entrepreneurship, the entrepreneurial environment can still cause extreme challenges for them. Compared to non-disabled people, disabled people may face greater obstacles in accessing entrepreneurial opportunities, placing them at a disadvantage.

METHODOLOGY

The data for this study was collected by interviewing ten disabled entrepreneurs (five male and five female) from Shanghai and Suzhou through a purposive sampling strategy (Bryman, 2011; Yin, 2015). Shanghai, an international business city of more than 24 million people, is one of the largest cities in China. Hence, Shanghai provides opportunities for this research to select a useful sample in order to improve credibility and trustworthiness. In terms of economic strength, Shanghai is located in the east of China, has the largest harbor in business use, produces 1.92 trillion CNY (£0.22 trillion) per year, and has a gross domestic product per capita of 83 000 CNY (£9540). Known as the birthplace of entrepreneurship in China, it is easy for entrepreneurs to find business opportunities in Shanghai (Gu and Yi, 2004; Yan and Wang, 2017).

Therefore, it supports the research in improving its degree of generalization by presenting opportunities to meet many kinds of entrepreneurs.

Suzhou, a large city with a 3000-year history, has over 10 million inhabitants (Suzhou Municipality, 2012) and is an hour's drive from Shanghai. As Suzhou has a long history and is famous for Chinese silk, many people operate small-scale businesses there such as embroidery and engraving (Suzhou Municipality, 2012). Many county-level cities and districts of Suzhou, such as Wujiang, SIP, Mudu, and Zhangjia Gang, are well-developed areas. In particular, SIP hosts thousands of international companies, such as Bosch, Siemens, SEW, and Delphi Automotive (SIP, 2012). In addition, Kunshan, a part of Suzhou, is one of the most developed county-level cities in China (Xie et al., 2005). Therefore, Suzhou provides suitable resources and policies for entrepreneurs to expand their businesses (Tian, 2013).

In order to achieve diversity, this study considered interviewees of different ages, types of impairment, business types, years of business experience, and annual income. We ensured the sample's validity based on two important criteria: the interviewee had an impairment, and they were an entrepreneur. These criteria were justified by visiting their office (checking their names on their company's website if possible) and asking for certification of their disabilities. Table 11.1 provides a detailed description of sample characteristics.

Data was collected through a dialogical interview process (Stewart, 1998), following a semi-structured interview schedule. Respondents were asked open-ended questions, the answers to which would reflect how the government supports their businesses according to their experiences. In addition, the interviewees were asked for their opinion on the current government policies for disabled entrepreneurship. Interviews were voice recorded, which helped the authors to transcribe correctly (Gordon, 1980; Spradley, 1979). After each interview, the interview protocol was flexibly revised for subsequent interviews in order to achieve better results (Coulon, 1995). Data was translated first into English, then transcribed using ATLAS/ti in order to identify major themes (Strauss and Corbin, 1998). In addition, the interview transcripts were analyzed based on descriptive codes which were taken from those major themes. Furthermore, memo-writing was adopted, because it is a good analytical method which can produce short descriptive headings by identifying patterns in order to contextualize data (Bryman, 2011; Strauss and Corbin, 1998; Yin, 2015).

FINDINGS

Grounded in the entrepreneurial ecosystem framework and based on analysis of the interviews, the findings of this study suggest that disabled people in China face many barriers that challenge them in becoming entrepreneurial and sustaining their businesses. In line with the research objectives, the findings discuss the role of the Chinese government in creating a facilitating or constraining environment for disabled people.[1] This section will discuss these factors based on a theoretical framework of the entrepreneurial ecosystem (Isenberg, 2011) as shown in Figure 11.1.

Table 11.1   Demographic profile of interview respondents

No. (Pseudonym)	Gender (Age)	Impairment	Business (Years in business)	Education	Income (CNY)	Amount of living support (CNY)	Knowledge of government loan policy	Loan amount (CNY) (Release time in years)
1. Mary	Female (58)	Lost right leg	Logistic (1)	High school	3 500	2 000	Basic	0 (0)
2. Christina	Female (48)	Infantile paralysis	Community economy (3)	High school	20 000	720	Advanced	300 000 (3)
3. David	Male (33)	Hearing loss	HR management (5)	Bachelor	30 000	1000	Advanced	200 000 (2)
4. Jack	Male (32)	Lost two legs	Stock farming (3)	High school	3 500	0	Basic	0
5. John	Male (33)	Lost two legs	From street singer to community economy (8)	Primary school	5 000	0	Basic	0
6. Helen	Female (58)	Lost left leg	Embroidery (25)	Bachelor	10 000	2000	Basic	20 000 (2)
7. Lily	Female (48)	Lost eyesight	Massage shop (20)	Bachelor	500 000	1500	Basic	300 000 (3)
8. Richard	Male (52)	Lost right hand	Elevator tower (28)	Secondary school	500 000	0	Basic	0
9. Jessie	Female (54)	Lost left leg, spinal injury	Embroidery (8)	Secondary school	12 000	0	Basic	0
10. Tim	Male (65)	Lost left leg, spinal injury	Engraving (40)	High school	150 000	350	Advanced	0

Financial Support by the Government

Personal living expenses support (PLES)

Disabled entrepreneurs faced more barriers in the past because there were few official policies to support them: "At the start-up stage of my business, I did not gain any support from government policy because at that time there was no policy for disabled entrepreneurs" (Helen).

All the interviewees were, to varying degrees, in a poor financial situation before starting their businesses and were in receipt of personal financial support from the local CDPF branches. For example, Tim mentioned that, "with this amount of money I can only pay for breakfast for a few days, so what should I do for the rest of month?"

The purpose of such personal financial support is to help relieve the burden of living costs for disabled entrepreneurs. As Mary mentioned, "I walk to my office every day because I want to save money, and I would like to receive more financial

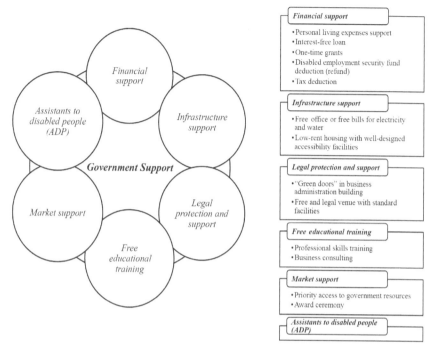

Source: Isenberg (2011).

Figure 11.1   Isenberg's model of an entrepreneurship ecosystem

support so that I can buy good food for my family without having to borrow money from relatives." The amount provided by the CDPF is largely dependent upon the district level of the CDPF that is in charge of the disabled person's region, as illustrated in Table 11.1. Additionally, this amount was in most cases not enough to support the living expenses. For example, Tim stated, "as a disabled person, in my area, I can receive 350 CNY [40 GBP] per month to support my personal life from the government, but I think this is nowhere near enough, and the minimum monthly wage in my area is about 3,500 CNY [400 GBP]." In addition, the amount of money can vary between different CDPF district levels. For example, Lily said, "I also receive 1500 CNY [200 GBP] per month from the government as personal financial support." Although she received more money than Interviewee 10, that amount of money is fixed and it is not enough for current living costs, as she mentioned: "At first, I thought this money was enough because living costs were not so high as they are now." However, some interviewees mentioned that the CDPF adjusts the extent of personal living expense support based on increases in living costs. As Interviewee 6 mentioned:

I have enjoyed this service for almost 6 years and the amount of money has been adjusted 3 times, from 500 CNY per month to 2000 CNY [250 GBP] per month. I feel very happy with this extra income and it is very stable because on the first day of each month I will receive the money.

Furthermore, Tim said, "I have received this support for almost 2 years and the disability assistance representative (assistant to disabled people) tells me that they will increase the amount of money, as I need to have rehabilitation treatment on my leg. This policy will to some extent relieve my financial stress."

Interest-free loans, security fund, and tax deductions

Financial support in the form of funding for entrepreneurship is a key to business start-up. Our findings reflect government efforts in this regard, where the government provides disabled people with interest free loans, one-time grants, and tax deductions. With regard to interest-free loans, the policy introduced in 2015 for disabled entrepreneurs facilitated disabled entrepreneurs to apply for loans ranging from 50 000 CNY to 500 000 CNY, which were payable within three years. However, the process for applying for such loans was perceived to be time-consuming and cumbersome. Moreover, strict evaluation and monitoring mechanisms were in place for recipients of such loans:

> yes, of course, when I had this business idea I applied for a three-year interest-free loan. I was told that applicants could have a loan ranging from 100 000 CNY to 500 000 CNY. It took me a month to compete all the documents, though luckily I received support on this paperwork from the assistant to disabled people and a clerk from the third party. I was informed after three weeks that I could have a 300 000 CNY loan, and I was so happy at the time. (Mary)

While some entrepreneurs had information about the interest-free loan policy of the government, many expressed that there was a lack of information about such financial support for their business:

> I didn't know that the Government had this policy to help us at the time. When my son went to senior high school, it cost 2000 CNY [250 GBP] per year. I borrowed 10 000 CNY from my relatives to set up a business and I tried to minimize the total fixed costs for starting my business. It was 11 km from my living area to my shop, and I walked every day to save money. It was a very hard life at the time. (Tim)

With regard to one-time grant policy, this was specifically targeted at disabled entrepreneurs in the nascent stage of business development, and could only be applied once. However, this grant, although disbursed as a one-time payment, was not repayable and thus encouraged disabled entrepreneurs to put in more effort for their business.

Tax deduction and security fund policies of the government further enabled and encouraged entrepreneurs in sustaining and growing their businesses while also supporting other disabled people. As regards tax refund policy, tax deductions were offered to companies employing more disabled people. Accordingly, this policy not only encouraged entrepreneurs to create more jobs for disabled people but also helped disabled entrepreneurs to reduce their companies' financial pressures: "officers working in the CDPF told me that if this company employed disabled people, it would receive a remission, and that it did not need to pay at all if the proportion of disabled people was greater than 1.5%. As such, I did not need to pay" (Lily).

The government provides disabled security funds to disabled people, where companies or entrepreneurs had to provide security to disabled people they employed in their business. This security was according to the proportion of disabled people wherein companies employing less than 1.5 percent the entrepreneurs had to pay this security "as my company grew (it now has 20 subsidiary companies) my accountant told me that we needed to pay towards the Disabled Employment Security Fund" (David).

Infrastructure Support

The findings suggest that support was provided by the government to set up businesses, primarily through infrastructure support. This was reflected in two aspects: rent-free office space and support in covering fixed costs associated with the business.

Free office space, or free electricity and water

This policy was specifically targeted to entrepreneurs who were aiming to set up small-scale businesses and did not have the funds to rent an office. Under this policy, entrepreneurs got access to free office space, and also refunds on bills in some cases. Accordingly, such government support assisted disabled start-up entrepreneurs who do not have enough funds for infrastructure. Normally, disabled entrepreneurs had three years of free office use and refunds on bills such as for electricity and water:

> my first office was provided by the CDPF and I still have this office because it is a milestone for me. I was working at my home before in order to save money because the rental fees in Shanghai are very high, and my dream was to have my own office one day. I applied for this policy with a lot of documents including my business plan, and I got an office with nice decoration in two weeks.

The provision of physical space provided immense confidence and encouragement to disabled entrepreneurs to operate their business, as Mary narrated:

> my office was also provided by the Government, and for the first five years I do not need to pay the rental fees. All the offices they provide are standard, but the Government will pay for the decoration and we can also ask for our own preferred style. I really like this policy and it motivated me to work harder.

Low-rent housing with well-designed accessibility facilities

Under this policy, the government provided low-rent housing opportunities to disabled entrepreneurs, which was perceived as a financial aid among most respondents since the rentals offered by the government were much lower than the market rate. The respondents also expressed positive opinion about the low-rent housing policy of the government in terms of accessible facilities for themselves, as Richard narrated: "I lived in a low-rent flat with 2 bedrooms which had well-designed accessibility facilities and the rental fees were affordable for me" (Richard).

In recent years, the price of a house has increased dramatically, especially in tier-one and tier-two cities. Even in Suzhou, a second-tier city, the cost of a home is approximately 20 times the average annual income of a resident. Especially in Shanghai, the rental fees have become a huge problem for disabled people:

> the rental fees in Shanghai are very high. I did not have money when I started my business, and I was living in a flat with one bedroom which was far from my office in order to save money. It took me two hours to return home and I could not have a good sleep every day because I had to sleep on the floor with my husband in order to let my kids sleep on the bed. (Christina)

Legal Protection and Support (Policy)

Provision of easy access through green doors

A significant area where disabled entrepreneurs face challenges is in terms of the ease of setting up the business, primarily due to their disability which puts them at a disadvantage as compared to other non-disabled entrepreneurs. The analysis of interviews suggests that the government provides support to disabled entrepreneurs by facilitating them through "green doors" which allow them priority access for their business needs, thus saving them time and energy. Moreover, the government also provides assistants to help disabled entrepreneurs in accessing public offices for their business needs. John narrated his experience of having priority access in a public facility:

> as our government wants to create a good and peaceful society for people, disabled people have the right to use public facilities and services. One day I was handing in my documents to commercial administration and I only had one hour left because I had another important meeting. However, the line was too long and I did not have enough time. One of the officers provided me with a "green door" entrance and I was told that according to the law disabled people have priority. I also found that each department had this rule. (John)

Provision of event spaces with standard facilities

There is evidence from the data that the government supports disabled entrepreneurs in organizing events by providing them with free space, but more importantly by legalizing and fully acknowledging their entrepreneurial efforts, regardless of how minor they may be. Two interviewees expressed that being previously buskers, they were not allowed to sing in public areas, and they had been asked to pay penalties. Nevertheless, they were supported by the CDPF and were able to access venues to organize concerts legally. This policy support enabled disabled entrepreneurs to run their businesses legally and safely. "One time I was updating my information in the

CDPF, and I received the information that we could have legal places to sing. Since then, my business has become stable and I have gained many lovely fans."

Free Educational Training (Human Capital)

Professional skills training

There is considerable evidence from the narratives of respondents for support in terms of human capital among disabled entrepreneurs. In this regard, findings suggest provision of free classes for disabled people by the district level of the CDPF, which enables them to learn skills before starting their businesses or applying for jobs (CDPF, 2016). These include professional skills training in areas of floriculture, embroidery, engraving, clock and watch repair, machinery maintenance, and interior design (CDPF, 2016): "The CDPF arranges a lot of free activities and classes for disabled people to learn skills such as computing, fixing watches, mechanics for cars or motorbikes, etc." (John).

Skills training provided opportunities to disabled people for taking up employment or starting a business. This policy was strongly appreciated by all respondents, who expressed its role in terms of helping them to start sustainable long-term businesses by providing them with the requisite knowledge and skills:

> Give a man a fish and he will eat for a day; teach him how to fish and he will eat for a lifetime … the CDPF arranges free classes regularly for disabled people and I am one of the teachers in this class as my skills are professional-level. I was invited by the CDPF to teach disabled people how to do … engraving and share my experience of how to set up a business with this skill. I treat this class like a warm group, and we become very close friends by the end. Some of them become my employees and set up their own businesses after working for several years with me. (Mary)

Business consulting

The findings reflect government support in areas of business consulting services for disabled entrepreneurs, which enables disabled entrepreneurs not only to expand their businesses on a commercial scale but also to improve their business efficiency. E-commerce is very popular in China and many entrepreneurs use online shops. Hence, support in the online presence of businesses run by disabled entrepreneurs enables them to become more competitive in their field while also helping them to improve their sales:

> I was told by one government officer about setting up online shops, which I was really interested in. He provided me with several successful cases, all running small businesses like mine. As I have physical disabilities I find it is very difficult to deliver my products by myself, and traditional trading is not suitable for me anymore. An online shop was a good idea, and they helped me to set up an online shop with a lovely website. I also shared the link with my consumers because it was easy for me to keep them updated with my work and my information. It also saved me a lot of time introducing, meeting, and delivering for consumers because this process is now all completed online. (Mary)

Market Support

Priority access to government resources

Most disabled entrepreneurs run small-scale businesses, and hence find it difficult to improve sales volumes, primarily because of lack of social capital. It is challenging for disabled entrepreneurs to access customers as compared to non-disabled entrepreneurs. Hence, the government supports them by connecting them to customers and other resourceful people who would help them to improve their business sales: "yes, when my business grew, and I became more well-known I tried to do business with the local government and they placed my order in a priority position. Also, the district level of the CDPF helped me to promote my company and I got more orders from other departments" (Jessie).

Award ceremonies

Rewarding and appreciating entrepreneurs for their business efforts is a significant way to enhance business growth. The findings suggest that the government plays a key role in rewarding disabled entrepreneurs through regular award ceremonies wherein recognition of business efforts by disabled entrepreneurs is given and awards are disbursed to them. This helps disabled entrepreneurs to expand their markets, because the awards not only attract many people to visit but also increase the appreciation of disabled entrepreneurs' professional skills and abilities: "I received a very important certification from the provincial CDPF: [providing certification for disabled people with relevant skills] ... of creative and cultural entrepreneurship in JiangSu province. This certification provided strong publicity for my company and me" (Jessie).

In addition, these awards boost self-confidence among disabled entrepreneurs, giving them a sense of ownership and achievement of their business: "I feel that the central government really cares about us. As a disabled person, my professional skills are highly appreciated by government, which makes me proud." They even feel more responsible for their business, like Mary mentioned, "My business's purpose is not only to earn money but also to disseminate culture."

Barriers Still Faced by Chinese Disabled Entrepreneurs and How They Might be Reduced

Increase monthly allowances (finance)

Although all the interviewees mentioned that they received monthly allowances, they noted that the amount of money is not sufficient for living expenses, especially in some areas which give small allowances. Shanghai is a high-cost city in China, as Mary mentioned: "4000 CNY (480 pounds) per month is the minimum living cost according to my experience. Therefore, I think the allowance is too little." Furthermore, Mary states that there is a big gap between actual minimum wage and allowance, "I can receive 350 CNY (40 pounds) per month to support my personal life from the government. But I think this is nowhere near enough, the minimum monthly wage in my area is about 3500 CNY (400 pounds)."

Make the interest-free loan more flexible (policy)

Some of the interviewees noted that they could only apply for this policy once. Once they had paid back the money, they were not allowed to apply again:

> Yes, I mentioned above that I received a 200 000 CNY loan which relieved the pressure on capital turnover. However, I was rejected when I applied for it again. I thought I had good credit since I had paid the entire loan back in advance. I hope this policy can be more flexible in the future. (Helen)

They also complained that the process was too long and complex. It seems that they would prefer a simpler and faster procedure to get the money as soon as possible:

> Yes, it is a good policy. I had a 300 000 CNY three-year interest-free loan. But the process was too long: it took me around 6 months. I hope the process can be made quicker. Also, I could only apply once: when I went to apply a second time I was rejected immediately. (Lily)

Improve the utilization rate of free offices and provide more options to applicants (support)

Although providing free offices is a good policy which helps disabled entrepreneurs to start businesses, some interviewees mentioned that they could not express preferences regarding their offices. For example, the location and style of decoration was determined by the CDPF:

> Also, I have been to the city-level CDPF and seen that many floors and rooms are empty. I think it is very important to manage the usage because many disabled people need an office when starting a business. I really like the area of the city-level CDPF, the location has convenient transportation and is perfect for disabled people like me to start businesses. However, they do not provide this for us. (Mary)

Lily also mentioned that the office should be free to be used not only as a classic office, as many disabled entrepreneurs are running different types of businesses. Flexible use of offices would improve efficiency:

> Also, the CDPF provided me with one big office and I planned to redecorate it as a massage shop. However, this plan was rejected as this room was only designed for office use. I found that many rooms were empty or were not being used properly. I tried to rent them instead and this was declined as well. If we could decide how to use these offices it would be better. I hope that this policy can be made more flexible.

Building up a competency-based instructing system (policy)

As the CDPF arranges free classes for disabled people to learn skills, some interviewees noted that the policy is helpful, but that it is important to stimulate disabled people's enthusiasm rather than just provide lessons. In addition, they mentioned that they faced greater barriers in the wider market because their skills were out-competed by non-disabled people:

These skills are designed for just survival-level existence, and when the course participants pass the test they will get a one-month internship with a wage of 35 CNY per day. Some of my friends told me that they lost their jobs after a month. I think it would be better for the government to take a more long-term view and provide more individualized lessons for disabled people. (Mary)

Improving efficiency of providing policy information to disabled entrepreneurs (policy)

The semi-structured interviews have shown that many disabled entrepreneurs do not know about the policies which are relevant to them. As some of the interviewees do not know how to use the Internet to check the CDPF's up-to-date policy database regularly, it is very important for the government to explore more ways to keep them updated. In addition, the CDPF has three levels: the central CDPF, the provincial CDPF, and the city-level CDPF. Normally, the central CDPF provides the strategic plan and the city-level CDPF provides detailed policy. The city-level CDPF has the responsibility not only to follow the strategic plan, but also to put it into action.

Improving the continuity of assistants to individual disabled people (human capital)

According to the interviewees, reliance on assistants to disabled people (ADPs) is significant, and the ADPs take on many responsibilities including visiting, listening, and solving problems. However, as most ADPs are volunteer staff, they cannot track disabled entrepreneurs efficiently, and it is also difficult for disabled people to have good service from them. In addition, ADPs are important connection between disabled people and all departments of government and the disabled reply on them more than any other officers from CDPF, according to interviewees' experience. Many interviewees saw different people every time they visited, making it difficult to build up a sustainable relationship. For example, Helen (Interviewee 6) mentioned: "However, most of the assistants are volunteers and they will not work in this job for very long. It is difficult for us to build up long-term relationships." In addition, most ADPs in the CDPF are also volunteers, and Lily mentioned that, "Some of volunteers working in the CDPF bring me gifts at each festival but I saw different people every time. I would prefer for one person to visit me regularly." The same situation was faced by Jessie (Interviewee 9): "When I was in the WuZhong district-level CDPF, every festival, an ADP would come and visit me and ask what I needed. I think they were volunteers and every time I saw a different face." However, Lily appreciates the regular greetings from government officers, "Yes, some of the officers from the government visit me regularly. I can feel their warm care which goes above and beyond that required by their duties."

Figure 11.2 sums up the suggestions for overcoming the barriers that disabled Chinese entrepreneurs are facing.

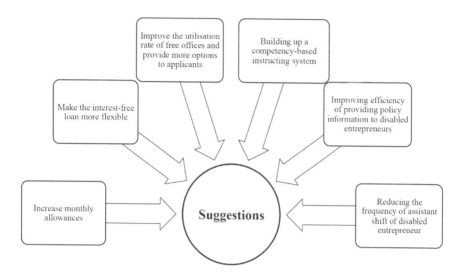

Figure 11.2   Suggestions for overcoming existing barriers

DISCUSSION

The Chinese government has made a significant commitment to encouraging disabled people to start businesses in order to help them to achieve greater incomes and social inclusion. However, according to the interviewees, some of the policies do not reach a satisfactory level whereby disabled Chinese entrepreneurs can fully concentrate on their businesses, and several issues are faced by these entrepreneurs as a result. This chapter sheds light on a range of interesting and unexpected issues which emerged from the thematic approach of the interview transcripts based on our research questions: (1) According to Chinese disabled entrepreneurs' life experience, how does the Chinese government support them when they start their business? and (2) From the perspective of current policy for Chinese disabled entrepreneurs, what barriers do they still face?

The CDPF provides various types of support to disabled entrepreneurs in terms of human capital, finance, policy and markets, both directly and indirectly. Previous literature has shown that other countries' governments also provide similar support (Isenberg, 2011). As the CDPF is a key bridge connecting disabled entrepreneurs to other government departments, disabled entrepreneurs rely on it heavily. The CDPF may need to develop a better ecosystem in terms of finance, culture, human capital and support (Isenberg, 2011). In the following sections we provide some suggestions.

Improving both Hard and Soft Support

Based on the findings, the types of government support can be categorized as "hard" and "soft" support (Colin-Thome, 2002; Ramsden and Bennett, 2005). Although previous literature has not considered the nature of support in the area of disabled entrepreneurship, research findings indicate that both types of support need to be improved in order to increase disabled people's entrepreneurial potential. Additionally, within the ecosystems, all the domains will influence each other: for example, when the government provides more financial support, it may relieve the pressure on families, thus increasing cultural support (Mason and Brown, 2014). This also applies to "hard" and "soft" support: for example, once the government reduces the social stigma for disabled people (soft support), less support may be needed from interest-free loans because they can access loans directly from banks.

Hard support may refer to financial or infrastructural support (Colin-Thome, 2002). Research findings indicate that disabled entrepreneurs need larger allowances to support their life expenses. The CDPF may need to adjust the sizes of monthly allowances according to local living standards. Additionally, the interviewees appreciated that the policy of interest-free loans supported their businesses, but some suggested that they would like to have continuous loans, and were even willing to pay interest, whereas the existing policy is designed for one-time loans. Finance is a key factor for a company's growth, and better financial systems give more methods of successful innovation and economic growth (King and Levine, 1993). In addition, the maximum size of the loan is 500 000 CNY (CDPF, 2016), but this policy is designed to help small-scale businesses, and so a policy which can offer more flexible loan amounts is needed.

Soft support may refer to cultural, educational, and social support (Kirby, 2006). Reducing social stigma for disabled people is necessary because it prevents them from reaching their potential (Shakespeare, 2013). Additionally, social stigma affects the promotional process for disabled people, which increases their proclivity for entrepreneurship (Renko et al., 2016). The government allocates some jobs for disabled people, but they face stigma, and it is essential to provide continuous care rather than just to give an individual a job. Furthermore, disabled people are a vulnerable group (Shakespeare, 2013). For example, it can be important to expand the systematic support of disabled people, though many disabled people do not need financial support such as subsidies. Providing a monthly allowance is important to them, but it is not a medicine. Therefore, the government should take responsibility to change people's attitudes to disabled people and to reduce social stigma. Furthermore, the CDPF should provide individualized training courses based on the talents of each disabled entrepreneur.

Building a Better Entrepreneurial Ecosystem for Disabled People

Redesigning these policies and increasing both hard and soft support will help China to have a stronger entrepreneurial ecosystem which provides a better business environment for disabled entrepreneurs. For example, if the government provides more financial support, disabled entrepreneurs may have greater chances to develop their businesses (Viriri and Makurumidze, 2014). If the government provides more cultural support, disabled entrepreneurs may face less discrimination and they may put more effort into their businesses (Hwang and Roulstone, 2015). If the Government provides more educational support, it may help disabled entrepreneurs to avoid business risks (Harris et al., 2014). Moreover, the different domains of entrepreneurial ecosystems may influence each other (Mason and Brown, 2014). For example, improving financial support may reduce stress for disabled people's families, and human capital may thus be improved automatically (Mason and Brown, 2014). Likewise, due to the improvement of cultural support and the reduction of social stigma, disabled people may apply for bank loans more easily and access better education, automatically improving the financial and educational aspects of the ecosystem.

These changes will build a better business environment for China, which means that China may have a stronger entrepreneurial ecosystem, and more disabled entrepreneurs will participate. This will also benefit other aspects in terms of economy, society, wealth creation, environment, family and individuals, and so on. For example, disabled entrepreneurs may contribute to the economy both directly and indirectly (Mohammed and Jamil, 2015; Hwang and Roulstone, 2015). The changes may contribute to the environment because some of the disabled entrepreneurs may found businesses which solve environmental problems. Additionally, most of the interviewees are social entrepreneurs and most of them have families, so the improvements will not only reduce family pressures but will also be good for the individuals.

CONCLUSIONS

This study demonstrates how the Chinese government supports disabled entrepreneurs in terms of finance, culture, human capital, markets, and policy based on the entrepreneurial ecosystem (Isenberg, 2011). Clearly, the Chinese government has expended a great deal of effort in helping disabled entrepreneurs and the CDPF attempt to update and redesign their policy according to the development of local economies. However, the existing entrepreneurial ecosystem in China still has room for improvement, and reducing social stigma is of great importance for disabled people. Furthermore, the research findings indicate that the Chinese government provides substantial hard support in terms of providing monthly allowances, interest-free loans, educational training, allocating jobs, free offices, and infrastructural equipment. However, disabled entrepreneurs need greater support from government because current hard support underestimates their requirements.

Implications

This exploratory study attempts to describe the existing entrepreneurial ecosystem in China by exploring how the government supports disabled entrepreneurs. Previous research describes how entrepreneurial ecosystems affect entrepreneurs (Isenberg, 2011), and this study indicates that disabled entrepreneurs are also affected by ecosystems, showing that the domain of policy is important because Chinese disabled entrepreneurs rely on the government more than non-disabled entrepreneurs. Furthermore, this study attempts to produce insights addressing a research gap, by employing ecosystems to explore the role of government policy in business environments (Renko et al., 2016).

Limitations and Future Research

This is an exploratory study in the context of China, and only two cities are considered, which may not represent the current situation of China. For future studies, researchers may examine how ecosystems are different in different regions or countries, and how ecosystems affect disabled entrepreneurs in different contexts. Furthermore, future research may explore which elements of ecosystems are most important for disabled people. As current literature indicates that different domains of ecosystems may affect each other, future research may study how the six domains (culture, finance, policy, markets, human capital, and social support; Isenberg, 2011) influence each other (Foss et al., 2019). Additionally, this research did not integrate gender considerations, and future research may involve a comparative study between male and female entrepreneurs. Research findings shows that women face more barriers than men. Therefore, some barriers relate to disability issues, whereas others relate to gender issues. Previous literature has studied female entrepreneurship, but few studies have considered disabled women's entrepreneurship. As this research only included ten interviewees, the small sample may not enable a high degree of generalization (Wallace and Wray, 2006; Guba and Lincoln, 1994). Future research may adopt a positivist approach with a larger sample by using surveys to determine what patterns emerge, and achieve a higher degree of generalization.

NOTE

1. The Chinese Disabled Person's Federation (CDPF) which has four levels: central, provincial, city, and district levels. The central level of the CDPF makes strategic policies and the provincial CDPF takes responsibility to implement these policies according to local disabled people's situation (CDPF, 2016).

REFERENCES

Acs, Z.J., Desai, S., and Hessels, J. 2008. Entrepreneurship, economic development and institutions. *Small Business Economics*, 31(3), 219–234.

Arnold, N., and Ipsen, C. 2005. Self-employment policies: changes through the decade. *Journal of Disability Policy Studies*, 16(2), 115–122.

Audretsch, D.B., Grilo, I., and Thurik, A.R. 2007. Explaining entrepreneurship and the role of policy: a framework. *The Handbook of Research on Entrepreneurship Policy*, Cheltenham, UK and Northampton, MA, USA: Edward Elgar Publishing, pp. 1–17.

Blanck, P.D., Sandler, L.A., Schmeling, J.L., and Schartz, H.A. 2000. The emerging workforce of entrepreneurs with disabilities: preliminary study of entrepreneurship in Iowa. *Iowa Law Review*, 85(5), 1583–1670.

Boylan, A., and Burchardt, T. 2002. Barriers to self-employment for disabled people. Report for the Small Business Services. London: Department of Trade and Industry.

Boylan, A., and Burchardt, T. 2003. Barriers to self-employment for disabled people. London: SBS Research & Evaluation.

Bryman, A. 2011. *Social Research Methods*, Oxford: Oxford University Press, pp. 1–809.

Chen, Xiaohong, and Mingxiao, Lu. 2010. Construction, problems and countermeasures of the entrepreneurial service system for disabled people. *Journal of Yunnan University of Finance and Economics*, 4, 129–132.

China Disabled Persons' Federation (CDPF). 2016. Statistical communique on the development of the work on persons with disabilities in 2016. Retrieved from http://www.cdpf.org.cn/.

Colin-Thome, D., 2002. The NHS plan: general practitioners with special interests. *British Journal of Cardiology*, 9(6), 359–360.

Cooney, T. 2008. The role of generativity in psychological well-being: Does it differ for childless adults and parents? *Journal of Adult Development*, 15(3), 148–159.

Coulon, A. 1995. *Ethnomethodology*. Thousand Oaks, CA: SAGE.

Dotson, W.H., Richman, D.M., Abby, L., Thompson, S., and Plotner, A. 2013. Teaching skills related to self-employment to adults with developmental disabilities: an analog analysis. *Research in Developmental Disabilities*, 34(8), 2336–2350.

East Midlands Development Agency (EMDA). 2009. *Scoping Study into the Business Support Needs of Disabled Entrepreneurs in the East Midlands*.

Fei, H.T., Fei, X., Hamilton, G.G., and Zheng, W. 1992. *From the Soil: The Foundations of Chinese Society*. California: University of California Press.

Foss, L., Henry, C., Ahl, H., and Mikalsen, G.H. 2019. Women's entrepreneurship policy research: a 30-year review of the evidence. *Small Business Economics*, 53(2), 409–429.

Godley, A. (2005). *The Emergence of Ethnic Entrepreneurship*. Princeton, NJ: Princeton University Press.

Gordon, C. (ed.). (1980). *Power/Knowledge: Selected Interviews and Other Writings 1972–1978 by Michel Foucault*. New York: Pantheon Press.

Gu, D., and Yi, Z. 2004. Sociodemographic effects on the onset and recovery of ADL disability among Chinese oldest-old. *Demographic Research*, 11, 1–42.

Guba, E.G., and Lincoln, Y.S. 1994. Competing paradigms in qualitative research. In N.K. Denzin and Y.S. Lincoln (Eds), *Handbook of Qualitative Research*, Vol. 2, pp. 163–194. Thousand Oaks, CA: SAGE.

Hammel, J., Magasi, S., Heinemann, A., et al. 2008. What does participation mean? An insider perspective from people with disabilities. *Disability and Rehabilitation*, 30(19), 1445–1460.

Harper, M., and Momm, W. 1989. *Self-Employment for Disabled People: Experiences from Africa and Asia*. International Labour Office.

Harris, D.J., O'Boyle, M., Bates, E., and Buckley, C. 2014. *Harris, O'Boyle & Warbrick: Law of the European Convention on Human Rights*. Oxford University Press, USA.

Hwang, S.K., and Roulstone, A. 2015. Enterprising? Disabled? The status and potential for disabled people's microenterprise in South Korea. *Disability and Society*, 30(1), 140–155.

Isenberg, D. 2011. The entrepreneurship eco-system strategy as a new paradigm for economy policy: principles for cultivating entrepreneurship. Babson Entrepreneurship Eco-system Project, Babson College, Babson Park: MA.

King, R.G., and Levine, R. 1993. Finance, entrepreneurship and growth. *Journal of Monetary Economics*, 32(3), 513–542.

Kirby, V. 2006. *Judith Butler: Live Theory*. London: A&C Black.

Kritikos, A. 2014. Entrepreneurs and their impact on jobs and economic growth. Productive entrepreneurs can invigorate the economy by creating jobs and new technologies, and increasing productivity. https://wol.iza.org/uploads/articles/8/pdfs/entrepreneurs-and-their-impact-on-jobs-and-economic-growth.pdf?v=1, accessed on June 19, 2020.

Leyland-Jones, B., Baselga, J., Latreille, J., Wardley, A., and Lennon, S. 2005. A novel loading regimen for trastuzumab in MBC: boost serum levels in early cycles. *Journal of Clinical Oncology*, 23(16 suppl.), 594–594.

Lindsay, S. 2011. Discrimination and other barriers to employment for teens and young adults with disabilities. *Disability and Rehabilitation*, 33(15–16), 1340–1350.

Mason, C., and Brown, R. 2014. *Entrepreneurial Ecosystems and Growth-Oriented Entrepreneurship*. Final report to OECD, Paris, 30(1), 77–102.

Mohammed, A.U., and Jamil, S.A. 2015. Entrepreneurial barriers faced by disabled in India. *Asian Social Science*, 11(24), 1–7.

Pagán, R. 2009. Self-employment among people with disabilities: evidence for Europe. *Disability and Society*, 24(2), 217–229.

Prahalad, C.K. 2005. *The Fortune at the Bottom of the Pyramid: Eradicating Poverty Through Profits*. Saddle River, NJ: Wharton School Publishing.

Ramsden, M., and Bennett, R.J. 2005. The benefits of external support to SMEs: "hard" versus "soft" outcomes and satisfaction levels. *Journal of Small Business and Enterprise Development*, 12(2), 227–243.

Renko, M., Parker Harris, S., and Caldwell, K. 2016. Entrepreneurial entry by people with disabilities. *International Small Business Journal*, 34(5), 555–578.

Shakespeare, T. 2013. *Disability Rights and Wrongs Revisited*. London: Routledge.

Shane, S.A. (ed.). 2007. *Economic Development Through Entrepreneurship: Government, University and Business Linkages*. Cheltenham, UK and Northampton, MA, USA: Edward Elgar Publishing.

Shier, M., Graham, J.R., and Jones, M.E. 2009. Barriers to employment as experienced by disabled people: a qualitative analysis in Calgary and Regina, Canada. *Disability and Society*, 24(1), 63–75.

SIP. 2012. *The 12th Five Year Plan for Energy Saving in SIP*. SIP Administrative Committee, Suzhou.

Spradley, J.P. 1979. *The Ethnographic Interview*. New York: Holt, Reinhart & Winston.

Stewart, A. 1998. *The Ethnographer's Method*. Vol. 46, Thousand Oaks, CA: SAGE.

Strauss, A., and Corbin, J. 1998. *Basics of Qualitative Research*. Thousand Oaks, CA: SAGE.

Sun, Xiande. 2006. Improvement of the employment security system for the disabled in China. *Scientific Socialism*, 3, 97–100.

Suzhou Municipality, 2012. *12th Five Year Planning of Circular Economy in Suzhou*. Retrieved January 4, 2015, from http://www.zfxxgk.suzhou.gov.cn/sxqzf/szsrmzf/201211/t20121107_165049.html.

Tian, X. 2013. Establishment of policy support system for college students' entrepreneurship in Suzhou. *International Journal of Emerging Technologies in Learning (iJET)*, 8(5), 27–31.

Viriri, P., and Makurumidze, S. 2014. Engagement of disabled people in entrepreneurship programmes in Zimbabwe. *Journal of Small Business and Entrepreneurship Development*, 2(1), 1–30.

Wallace, M., and Wray, A. 2006. *Critical Reading and Writing for Postgraduates*. Thousand Oaks, CA: SAGE.

Wennekers, S., Van Wennekers, A., Thurik, R., and Reynolds, P. 2005. Nascent entrepreneurship and the level of economic development. *Small Business Economics*, 24(3), 293–309.

World Health Organization. 2011. Summary: World Report on Disability 2011 (No. WHO/NMH/VIP/11.01). World Health Organization.

Xiaotong, Fei. 1985. *Disabled People Need to Learn and Work*. March Wind.

Xie, Y. et al. 2005. Socio-economic driving forces of arable land conversion: a case study of Wuxian City, China. *Global Environmental Change*, 15(3), 238–252.

Xu, Y., He, K., and Zhang, L. 2015. Discussing of mental rehabilitation of children with disability under ICF theory and practice. *Chinese Journal of Rehabilitation Theory and Practice*, 1447–1450.

Yan, C.M., and Wang, M.J. 2017. Prof. Baohui Han: make Shanghai Chest a window, a platform, and a business card for Shanghai Chest Hospital. *Shanghai Chest*, 1(5), 34–34.

Yin, R.K. 2015. *Qualitative Research from Start to Finish*. New York: Guilford Publications.

12. The need for an inclusive entrepreneurial ecosystem for women with disability in Pakistan

Shandana Sheikh

INTRODUCTION

Stephen Hawking famously said that 'disability need not be an obstacle to success'. This quote aptly captures the myriad opportunities that disabled individuals can access to improve their economic participation by employment or entrepreneurship, and thus become part of an inclusive society. Yet only a few people overcome their disability to live a normal life. One may reflect on differences among individuals who, despite their disability, live an independent life. Is it their self-motivation and passion to fulfil their aspirations, or is it the support that they receive from others, including family, friends and society, that enables them to live an independent and fulfilling life?

There are two principal theoretical models to explain the status of people with disability (PWD). First, the medical model of disability, also referred to as the deficiency model, views a disabled person as someone who is 'sick' or 'unhealthy' and needs to be fixed (Donoghue, 2003), thus putting responsibility of a person's disability entirely on themselves. By contrast, the social model of disability shifts the blame away from the individual and instead considers the social and environmental factors impacting on people with disability, therefore enabling an in-depth understanding of the disadvantages that PWD face from their environment (Siminski, 2003). Adopting the latter view, and considering the low rate of entrepreneurship among the disabled population across the globe, this chapter seeks to build an understanding of the factors (culture, policy, markets, social support, financing, and human capital) within the entrepreneurial ecosystem (EES) (Isenberg, 2011) that challenge or facilitate disabled entrepreneurs, specifically disabled women in a low-income country, Pakistan. Research on women entrepreneurs suggests that besides younger and older disabled people, ethnic minorities and those living in economically depressed areas, women typically find it extremely difficult to start businesses on their own and run them successfully (see, e.g., Mair and Marti, 2009). Accordingly, women's contribution to national economic growth and development is often disregarded.

In seeking to throw some light on this problem, the discussion in this chapter concerns the story of a disabled women entrepreneur in Pakistan, Tanzila Khan. With her disability, Tanzila breaks through the stereotypical public portrayal of the heroic, white, and non-disabled male entrepreneur. Tanzila had the determination and motivation to not let disability be a barrier in life, and she became an entrepreneur and an advocate for women with disabilities in Pakistan. The debate concerns the notion of whether being disabled justifies being excluded from entrepreneurship. I suggest that women with disability take the same opportunities in different ways; they are differently abled and operate within the constraints of their entrepreneurial environment, with resources they can access. In light of the above, Tanzila's story highlights the critical need to make disabled people a part of the mainstream agenda of inclusive development and growth, by better understanding the challenges they face.

DISABILITY AND ENTREPRENEURSHIP

Adopting the World Health Organization's definition, disability refers to 'the negative aspects of the interaction between an individual (with a health condition) and the contextual factors (environmental and personal factors)' (WHO, 2001: 213). This definition reflects the critical role of the disabled person's environment (Autio et al., 2014; Zahra et al., 2014) in enabling disabled people to become independent.

A significant pathway for empowerment of disabled individuals is entrepreneurship, defined as venture creation, which enables PWD to become self-sufficient but also contributes to economic development. Entrepreneurship is perceived by policy-makers as a solution for labour market disadvantage and social exclusion of the disabled (De Clercq and Honig, 2011). Despite its importance, research on disabled entrepreneurship remains scant, although disabled people are significantly part of the labour market as well as self-employment, thus reflecting their participation in paid work (Boylan and Burchardt, 2002; Cooney, 2008). Besides, research documents that entrepreneurship plays a key role in enhancing self-sufficiency of PWD and enabling them with increased security of life and yet the rate of entrepreneurship of PWD remains very low (Parker Harris et al., 2014). Given that all entrepreneurship is contextually embedded, a plausible explanation for this is the disadvantage and discrimination disabled people face in their entrepreneurial environment, which discourages them to undertake entrepreneurship as a career choice. Institutional issues include lack of funding for business start-up, fear of losing benefits/social security (Boylan and Burchardt, 2002), lack of confidence (Foster, 2007), and consumer discrimination (Jones and Latreille, 2011), among others. While non-disabled entrepreneurs may also face these constraints, the challenge is far greater for disabled individuals aspiring to become entrepreneurial (Ng and Arndt, 2019). Studies exploring disability and entrepreneurship have had an individualistic focus, where performance in entrepreneurship is attributed to individual attributes, disregarding the role of the context. Accordingly, the extent to which a disabled individual accumulates any resource – for example, social or human capital – is explained by the individual's ability, and not by the conditions of their entrepreneurial environment (Cooney, 2008). A critical factor explaining access to and accumulation of capital among disabled people is social inclusion, including social activities and employment (Williams et al., 2011). However, due to the various constraints faced by disabled people in accessing social activities (Williams et al., 2011), and in obtaining educational qualifications and employment (Burchardt, 2000, 2003; Pavey, 2006), the amount of capital that disabled people invest remains low.

Disabled entrepreneurs are treated as a homogenous group who are predominantly male, thus posing an issue of gender blindness in disability and entrepreneurship research (Ahl, 2002, 2006; Hamilton, 2013). Accordingly, when gender is included, research suggests that women face greater challenges in venture creation and in sustaining their enterprise, due to a number of factors, including the inferior public perception of female entrepreneurs. Thus, the environment for a disabled woman entrepreneur is, at best, typically unhelpful in supporting business start-up and growth. This is not because of the female entrepreneur's disability, but due to their perceived inability to enact a 'standard' entrepreneurial role, which is based on non-disabled individuals. Essentially, a one-dimensional view of entrepreneurship as strictly encompassing able-bodied individuals and disregarding other marginalized individuals, including transgenders and disabled entrepreneurs, leaves an inadequate understanding of the what, why, and how of entrepreneurship (Welter, 2011). Besides, limiting the definition of an entrepreneur to high-growth and profit-oriented businesses presents a bird's-eye view of the value generated from entrepreneurship, value that encompasses several levels including benefits accruing for the individual of value that spreads communally. Accordingly, in line with the goals of sustainable and inclusive development and the need to find value in everyday entrepreneurship (Foss et al., 2019), more research is required on entrepreneurship undertaken by PWD.

WOMEN AND DISABILITY, A DOUBLE JEOPARDY

Approximately 15 per cent of the world's population suffer from one or more recognized disabilities (WHO, 2011); 80 per cent of them live in rural and low-income countries. This issue has been aggravated in the recent global coronavirus pandemic, with PWD 6 per cent less likely to be employed compared with the general population, thus making PWD more susceptible to poverty (United Nations Economic and Social Commission for Asia and the Pacific, ESCAP). In Pakistan, 10–15 per cent of the total population are thought to be disabled (WHO; National Database and Registration Authority). Of these, 50 per cent are women and girls with disability. Despite a large proportion of women with disability (WWD), Pakistan remains far from being part of an inclusive society, and WWD are excluded from the mainstream agenda primarily due to their perceived inability to participate in economic and social activity.

Pakistan ranks at 151 in the Global Gender Gap Index. This ranking is the lowest in South Asia and reflects the high level of gender inequality prevailing in the country (Global Gender Gap Report, 2020). Various efforts have been made to close the gender gap under the United Nations (UN) Decade of Action for the attainment of the Sustainable Development Goals (SDGs). A key incentive here is that improved gender equality could enhance Pakistan's gross domestic product by approximately 30 per cent (Voluntary National Review, 2019). Accordingly, in an effort to 'leave no one behind', empowerment of women with disability has been a key goal of the Ministry of Human Rights in Pakistan. Efforts are being shifted away from the medical model of disability to a human rights perspective, one that enhances the capacity of WWD, increases public recognition, and reduces vulnerability and typical public stigma associated with disability. Key strategies initiated to improve the status of WWD include supporting women in accessing legal protection, financial inclusion, development of key skills, and providing them with an inclusive business culture. Here local companies are encouraged to sign up to Women's Empowerment Principles and promote gender-responsive procurement (UN Women, 2017).

Women are recognized as an integral component in the economic and sustainable growth of Pakistan (Voluntary National Review, 2019). Yet, despite women constituting more than half of Pakistan's population, their participation in economic output is minimal, with only 31.4 per cent of women being part of the workforce, compared with 68.6 per cent of men (Pakistan Economic Survey 2016/2017). A large proportion of women work in the informal sector, and without any legal protection (Bari, 2020). As a result, despite working for longer hours and simultaneously juggling work and family responsibilities, the contribution of these women is not accounted for in Pakistan's economic output. Accordingly, they are often unable to overcome poverty, and they continue to face discrimination and exploitation which restricts their potential as well as national economic growth. This problem partly explains the low-growth and underperformance hypothesis – a self-fulfilling prophecy – that is associated with women-owned ventures. Scholars suggest that it is not in fact underperformance, but constrained performance, that defines women's businesses. Therefore, while an individual's ability and attitude may be important in determining their intentions to become entrepreneurial, the role of the entrepreneurial environment may be more important in making this decision, as well as in the entrepreneur's subsequent success. Following from this, WWD often face greater barriers in accessing entrepreneurial opportunities compared with non-disabled women and men. Speaking to Tanzila Khan, a Pakistani disability rights activist, motivational speaker and founder of Girly Things PK, a mobile application which delivers sanitary napkins to women with disabilities, she highlights:

> Gender is a bigger barrier and disability only makes it worse. For example, with simple, everyday things, men can go to the bathroom anywhere, whether he has a disability or not. Women can't do that. And a woman with disability has a bigger checklist to go through to do anything in life.

WWD are deprived of access to basic human rights including education and employment, skills training, healthcare, transport facilities, and entrepreneurship. Moreover, WWD face safety and care constraints in everyday life owing to their inability to move around freely, but also due to lack of accessible infrastructure including even roads, transportation facilities specifically for women and the availability of female assistants. These infrastructural problems place further pressure on the family of the disabled, both financially and in terms of effort and time. Mothers who bear greater responsibility in caring for children and the home find it harder to divide their time between household work and caring for a disabled child. On the other hand, fathers have the responsibility to provide a living for the family and consequently need to spend a greater proportion of their income to care for a disabled child; disabled children may have greater and more precarious health care needs and they may require special education which may be more expensive than mainstream schooling. Furthermore, parents bear the responsibility of their disabled girl child all their life because marriage prospects for such girls, particularly in a society like Pakistan, are very low. People perceive girls with a disability as an abnormality and fear that it may transfer onto generations, thus rejecting such girls in marriage proposals.

Yet, despite the challenges faced by WWD, entrepreneurship and self-employment are considered to be a viable career option and a pathway for independence (Blanck et al., 2000). PWD have personal goals in life which suit their strengths, disabilities, family, self-worth, and environment (Doyel, 2000). PWD thus expect recognition of these goals, and consideration for the challenges they face to achieve these goals from their entrepreneurial environment. Hence, if their environment is supportive, entrepreneurial activity could significantly increase among disabled women.

ENTREPRENEURSHIP ECOSYSTEM FOR WOMEN WITH DISABILITY: TANZILA'S ACCOUNT

An individual's motivation and personal attitude are factors determining the extent of their empowerment in, and control over, their lives. These individual-level attributes are in turn influenced by various social factors within the individual's environment that influence the career pathway for any disabled person. For example, Tanzila's empowerment as a WWD was attributed to a blend of her personality and her thoughts about her own future that motivated her to become entrepreneurial and independent in life. A wheelchair user by birth, Tanzila did not take her disability as a constraint, but instead saw it as an opportunity:

> I was in 3rd or 4th grade and that was my first instance of becoming an entrepreneur; I started selling soap in my village to my family members … I have 7 uncles on my mother's side, so I have a lot of cousins. It was one summer that we were there in the village. I had a lot of 'Capri' soaps with me and my mother was like why you don't gift these to people here. I said no because I wanted to sell them and not gift them. So, I sold those tiny little toilet soaps to my cousin, a male guy. This was the first time I had a conversation other than those relating to you look nice and you look good. It was the first time I experienced this sort of negotiation. I had the authority of making a deal with the customer, even though it was my family. My uncles would joke and would tell me to reduce the price, but it was up to me to do that. It was something very minor, but I think it all started from there.

This trade was the first entrepreneurial encounter that Tanzila experienced in her life. Thereafter, she started her first business of 'friendship bands' in 5th grade in school:

> everyone expected that I would tie it to them [gift them], but I said no, I'll sell these to you. It was such a successful business that at the age of 12, I was selling friendship bands to all my class, and other classes started coming to my class and started asking for them. You know, when I started earning money from this, I started giving loans to my friends to buy lunch, cold-drinks, samosas.

Tanzila's experiences made her cognizant of the challenges women face, especially in a male-dominant society. Her aspiration to do something in life that would make her independent but also give back to her community led her to start Girly Things, an e-commerce website that offers female products tailored for WWD. Because of her own disability, Tanzila realized the need for better accessibility to basic needs, such as personal hygiene products and services. WWD tend to rely on male assistants primarily because they are physically stronger and can assist them in accessing various spaces, such as in helping to lift their wheelchairs. However, this dependence on males opens women to abuse and also strips them of their privacy, especially when it comes to basic needs, such as in accessing hygiene products and services. Tanzila realized that most shops in Pakistan were not accessible for women to go in person to buy sanitary napkins. Moreover, due to the societal taboo on menstruation in Pakistan, Tanzila came up with her business idea of delivering sanitary products urgently to women who need them. The 'urgent kit' includes a disposable undergarment, a sanitary pads pack and a blood stain remover. She recounted her feelings of becoming entrepreneurial:

> As a person with disability, this gave me that leadership feeling that made me feel that I was contributing something and giving something back to my school. And it was at this time that I realized that I can create magic with this life of mine and I didn't have to be dependent on anyone. That's what entrepreneurship taught me, the value of my own life. It taught me independence.

Besides motivation and self-determination, a conducive entrepreneurial ecosystem is critical to encourage WWD to become entrepreneurial and independent in life. For this, a significant factor contributing to empowerment of WWD is their social support ecosystem. This entails the involvement of family, friends and professional networks in playing a significant role in motivating WWD to think of their disability not as a disease but as an opportunity. Tanzila's mother played this role in her life and encouraged her to become an advocate for disability and to achieve everything she wanted in life. Despite being born in a patriarchal society, Tanzila did not think of her life as being restricted to her home due to her disability. Owing to familial support, she was able to attend a regular school, which enabled her to get access to the same education as other non-disabled students. In her opinion, this made all the difference in her life:

The schools did not have the capacity, even 1 per cent to accommodate me, but because of me, they had to do it. So, I like the idea that everyone gets access to one school. We have one world and we can't have two different worlds where one has access to ramps and sign language and all and the others do not. The school gives you all that. If you go to a school where other able-bodied people are also going, you get to learn so many other life skills, you learn to survive to operate in the world. You come across the same discrimination, same problems that all other students get.

Thus, access to education, primarily due to familial support, enabled Tanzila to build her human capital ecosystem and gave her an opportunity to understand life beyond her disability. Education also gave Tanzila the courage and confidence to interact with people who were not disabled. Human capital, which constitutes the knowledge and skills in individuals that are relevant to economic activity (OECD, 2008), is considered to be the most critical resource of entrepreneurs (Hitt et al., 2001). For people with disabilities, professional knowledge and business skills have been found to significantly unlock their potential and enhance their business start-ups (David and Hamburg, 2013; Hamburg and David, 2017). Yet WWD are vulnerable to exclusion from education opportunities and may therefore be at a greater disadvantage in employment and entrepreneurship compared with men with and without disabilities. Particularly in Pakistan's conservative society, access to education among women is constrained due to the strict confinement of gender roles, socio-cultural norms and institutional constraints, such as in transportation and in the phenomenon of female-only schools. These constraints become worse for WWD, who are perceived as a burden and a social stigma for their family and society. Accordingly, their participation in activities outside their home is perceived as a futile investment and a threat to their safety and honour. Speaking of the importance of education for WWD, Tanzila suggests the benefits that education may bring to the lives of WWD:

I grew up with ideas like honour killing; you will be shot if you talk to a man. The idea that women get is that they feel that they are a burden, and this really gets to them. I think education can change this mindset of a woman, if not of others. If a woman gets educated, there is a 90 per cent chance that she is going to get a job or start a business and make her own destiny. A slight access to education can change her slice of cake. Otherwise she is going to stay in her bubble and carry on with the fears she has acquired.

Beyond support from family, friends and their business network, a key factor determining entrepreneurial participation by WWD is their culture ecosystem. This entails positive attitudes and respect for women with disability and encourages WWD to move away from the margins and become part of mainstream economic activity. In Pakistan, there are vast additional challenges for women aspiring to become entrepreneurial. For example, socio-cultural and religious norms govern appropriate actions and behaviour for women and thus define their involvement in work outside their home. The local practices of *purdah* and *izzat* that perceive women's chastity as an honour constrain their mobility and thus their participation in public activities (Roomi and Parrott, 2008; Roomi et al., 2018). Accordingly, women are expected to fulfil responsibilities of home and family, which in practice becomes their only priority, while men are expected to be breadwinners for the family. In light of the male-dominant practices of Pakistani society, disabled women are extremely disadvantaged in accessing their basic rights in life. For example, mobility constraints can become doubly challenging for WWD due to the social stigma of disability, which compounds the stigma of women engaging in any activity outside their home. Additionally, parents of WWD are fearful of letting their daughters attend school because of these social stigmas. In Pakistan, marriage is considered to be the pinnacle of a woman's life, and having a disabled daughter at home means reduced marriage prospects for her. The presence of a disabled child also negatively impacts upon the prospects of their siblings. For example, males may not take a girl in marriage for fear of her having disabled children if even one of her family members suffers from a visible (physical) or invisible (mental) disability. Consequently, women not only bear the burden of their own disability but also carry the blame for affecting the lives of others around them. Speaking about this, Tanzila suggests the importance of a conducive culture ecosystem that generates positive attitudes towards WWD and recognition of their aspirations and efforts:

> The sensitive area is culture. Both genders face their own set of challenges that society throws at them. A double scoop of trouble is of course there for women. For a man with a disability, he is still a man and some things go in his favour, access to opportunities, moving outside the home. He has access to that lifestyle, being a father, a husband, and he can get married, and will have that respect. For women, half of these opportunities get cut because they are women at the end of the day. Even if they have a disability, men can have 10 men who can lift them up and assist them. For women, we have to first see and scan the men: Is he okay to come near me, will I be safe with him, is it even worth going in the building. And then they'd probably say no, I'd rather not go here.

Extending this to the context of entrepreneurship, being WWD and being entrepreneurs are two extremely rich and diverse areas which, when combined, can become a great success. Failure, however, beckons and is expected in Pakistan. Usually women are expected to do something 'soft', for example, fashion or beauty. WWD are perceived as incapable of doing even what would be expected of non-disabled women, primarily due to their visible disability and consequent disregard of their abilities. Dealing with feminine products, Tanzila realized that her business could only appeal to a small segment of the market, primarily due to the taboo associated with menstrual health in Pakistan, but also because she was a woman who was in a business that was targeted at women. Speaking about gender differences in access to entrepreneurial support, Tanzila said:

> Akshay Kumar, the famous Indian actor, made a movie called *Padman* about sanitary napkins. This movie is made by a man. And it is about sanitary napkins, a female product. It is not a big deal. No one invented the wheel. Even my dad can get me sanitary napkins if he wants to. Yet Akshay Kumar got so much claim for that.

This reflects the struggle of WWD, who face disadvantage in accessing support or appreciation for their business compared with their male counterparts. A man with disability would typically get more recognition for his efforts compared with a woman in the same business.

Non-availability of external finance is another major barrier for women entrepreneurs. Funding is the start-up seed for any business idea and plays a key role in assisting entrepreneurs to set up their business. Yet it has been widely discussed that women entrepreneurs face greater difficulty than their male counterparts in accessing financing for their business, including low financial skills, inability to fill out funding applications, lack of collateral, discrimination in lending practices, and inferior perception of their businesses, among others. Moreover, in Pakistan, women entrepreneurs face extreme discrimination in acquiring loans for their business due to stringent requirements, including their husband's signature on funding applications and the obligation under banking practices to disburse loans for the woman's enterprise directly to him. Moreover, lack of information about funding opportunities, including government and non-governmental sources, and the perception that only men would get funding, discourages women from accessing formal sources of finances. Instead, women primarily rely on informal sources of funds, including their family and friends, to set up and sustain their business. Extending this to WWD, their challenges become pressing due to the innate perception among society that disability is an inability of the mind, and hence an inability to perform any productive activity in life. Even if they get access to funding information and to financing institutions, WWD are discriminated in their access to funding, as Tanzila suggests:

> Conversations that happen in Pakistan really surprise you. I was pitching once for an investment and after the pitch was done, I asked them to download my app to give them a demo of what I was doing. The interview was over, but the Mic was still on and I could hear those men. And one person from amongst them said, what sort of app is she asking me to download, it's a family thing, it is so shameful. So, in fact he was judging my start-up, and these people are the ones we call mentors and coaches.

Several policy initiatives have been made to improve this destructive status of disabled people in Pakistan. For example, the Amendment to the Rights of Persons with Disability Act 2020, 'promotes, protects, and effectively ensures the rights and inclusion of persons with disabilities in the communities in line with the Islamic Injunctions and provisions of the Constitution of the Islamic Republic of Pakistan to advance efforts for recognition of their respect and dignity in society'. Within this Act, the government of Pakistan seeks to ensure the rights of PWDs, including women, children and transgender with disability, for protection against abuse and violence, accessibility and mobility, freedom of expression, equity in education, employment and health, amongst others. Besides government-led initiatives, private, non-governmental efforts to promote the interest of PWDs have also been initiated to improve the status of disabled people in Pakistan. For example, the Special Talent Exchange Program (STEP), a non-governmental organization, works towards empowering PWD, as well as in encouraging the public to adopt a rights-based approach to empower PWD. In its efforts to empower PWD, STEP in collaboration with other organizations has launched the disability job centre which provides skills development, mentoring, and coaching opportunities for PWD, while also helping them to find jobs in various sectors. Additionally, to help PWD in accessing better healthcare, initiatives such as the Sehat Sahulat Program of the Punjab government have been initiated, where underprivileged citizens as a whole can easily access healthcare. Additionally, Sehat Kahani, a tele-medicine platform which connects patients to female doctors by chat, audio, and video 24/7, has also been launched. This makes health services more accessible for PWD, who can get a consultation from home, such as during the global pandemic.

Yet, despite such efforts, there is a need to engage PWD and particularly WWD in the co-creation and co-production of policies that have been designed for them, as well as in the implementation of these policies. For example, the Pakistan government has introduced a policy specifically for WWD, but the need for that policy and its benefits can only be assessed by recipients for whom the policy was implemented. Tanzila expresses this view: 'Government is perhaps just doing guess work primarily because there may not be anyone in the government who is disabled. Hence, the government puts a ramp here and a ramp there without getting information whether it is actually needed there in that way or not.'

Despite the opportunity and access to study in non-disabled schools, Tanzila faced issues of mobility in certain parts of her school, which constrained her from taking advantage of certain facilities:

> Schools do allow you to come as a disabled person but sometimes even they can't do anything about certain things. Like for example, I didn't have access to a computer lab because there was no ramp there. My class in college used to be on the 2nd floor and I used to go up and down a lot. That helped me prepare for this world.

This problem highlights a significant aspect of policy intervention whereby both public and private educational institutions should have mandatory accessibility for PWD. Currently, only a few institutions in Pakistan are disabled-friendly, and this fact reflects the extent of inaccessibility to education among disabled people. The urgent need is to create accessible infrastructure for disabled people that allows them to access basic needs and opportunities in life.

THE FUTURE OF ENTREPRENEURSHIP AMONG DISABLED WOMEN

Acknowledging that entrepreneurship is a contextually embedded phenomenon and is shaped through the social order (Williams and Patterson, 2018; Chell and Baines, 1998; Kumra, 2010), the discussion presented here shifts the focus from the individual to the contextual, suggesting that WWD do not craft their life choices alone. Instead, the choices they make and are able to achieve in life are dependent on the broader entrepreneurial environment, which may support or constrain them, and thus affect their entrepreneurial potential. Accordingly, this chapter has explored a concern for a particular social group (women) at a 'neglected point of intersection' (disability) within 'a particular social setting' (entrepreneurship) (McCall, 2005: 1780).

There is a need for grass roots-level change to promote an all-inclusive environment for entrepreneurship among WWD. Firstly, WWD should not be perceived as a social burden. Instead, WWD are in fact individuals who are differently capable of contributing towards creating shared value in the economy. In Tanzila's view: 'Disability is not a minority. There are billions of people who have a disability. To make a difference, you need to have a contributing mindset and not a victimizing one.' In line with Hughes et al.'s (2012) call for researching non-traditional questions, by offering a context-based explanation and by adopting constructionist approaches to better understand entrepreneurship among the disabled, this chapter has suggested how the environmental context may influence disabled women entrepreneurs. Essentially, we have explored a particular social group (women) in a specific social setting (entrepreneurship) and at a point of intersection (disability). Reflecting on Tanzila's account of disability and entrepreneurship, this chapter sought to discuss the various factors that disabled women have to face in their entrepreneurial ecosystem.

Entrepreneurship undertaken by the disabled creates 'shared value' (Porter and Kramer, 2011) that entails economic value but also social value. For disabled entrepreneurs, social value constitutes individual and collective well-being derived from their business activity that they create in response to the unsatisfied needs of a large segment of the population (Austin et al., 2006). To unfold the potential of entrepreneurship and build entrepreneurial competencies among WWD, I have suggested why it is essential to create an inclusive entrepreneurial ecosystem, that is supported by:

1. institutional policies that address the social, economic and physical constraints of WWD;
2. the availability of finance for their start-ups; by their access to information on entrepreneurial opportunities and equal access to markets, skills and knowledge development from entrepreneurial education;
3. a supportive culture that promotes positive attitudes and motivation for entrepreneurship; and
4. social support from personal and professional networks; essentially, success in these areas requires an overall shift in the public's mind of WWD and their role in society.

In overcoming these multiple barriers, WWD need first to overcome the innate belief that they are a burden on others and are incapable of achieving what non-disabled women can achieve in life. In this chapter, Tanzila has shone a beacon on how WWD can overcome their social and economic barriers to success. Second, perceptions about WWD in society need to change, where positive attitudes towards WWD and their potential capabilities need to be inculcated. Here, media can play a significant role: in Pakistan, there is only very limited media coverage of disability. Where PWD are shown, they are portrayed as a social stigma to their families and society. This reinforces an already ingrained social view of PWD. The insensitivity of the media towards PWD has contributed to their invisibility and underrecognition in society. Consequently only a few WWD break through the barriers of perceived inability and lack of confidence to live independently and achieve their aspirations. Here again, Tanzila realized the underrepresentation and misconstrued image of PWD in Pakistani media, and produced her own film on this issue. In an effort to influence the broader narrative of disability as an inability to undertake normal activities in life, Tanzila played the lead role in *Fruitchaat*, a movie about a wheelchair-bound girl who, after failing to get a job because of her disability, became a fruit seller: 'To me, my disability is not about struggling with anything or a punishment: It is a lifestyle that nature has given me. It is a different state of the human body. People like me have fully-abled lives, but we are never shown accurately in the media.'

REFERENCES

Ahl, H. (2002). The construction of the female entrepreneur as the other. In B. Czarniawska and H. Höpfl (eds), *Casting the Other: The Production and Maintenance of Inequalities in Work and Organizations*. London: Routledge, pp. 52–67.

Ahl, H. (2006). Why research on women entrepreneurs needs new directions. *Entrepreneurship Theory and Practice*, 30(5), pp. 595–621.

Austin J.E., Stevenson H. and Wei-Skillern, J. (2006). Social and commercial entrepreneurship: same, different, or both? *Entrepreneurship Theory and Practice*, 30, pp. 1–22.

Autio, E., Kenney, M., Mustar, P., Siegel, D. and Wright, M. (2014). Entrepreneurial innovation: the importance of context. *Research Policy*, 43(7), pp. 1097–1108.

Bari, F. (2020). Women in the informal sector. https://www.dawn.com/news/1580309. Accessed on 19 May 2021.

Blanck, P.D., Sandler, L.A., Schmeling, J.L. and Schartz, H.A. (2000). Emerging workforce of entrepreneurs with disabilities: preliminary study of entrepreneurship in Iowa. *Iowa Law Review*, 85, pp. 1583–1668.

Boylan, A. and Burchardt, T. (2002). *Barriers to Self-Employment*. London: Small Business Service.

Burchardt, T. (2000). *Enduring Economic Exclusion: Disabled People, Income and Work*. York: Joseph Rowntree Foundation.

Burchardt, T. (2003). *Being and Becoming: Social Exclusion and the Onset of Disability*. London: London School of Economics.

Chell, E. and Baines, S. (1998). Does gender affect business 'performance'? A study of microbusiness in business services in the UK. *Entrepreneurship and Regional Development*, 10(2), pp. 117–135.

Cooney, T. (2008). Entrepreneurs with disabilities: profile of a forgotten minority. *Irish Business Journal*, 4(1), pp. 119–129.

David, A. and Hamburg, I. (2013). Integrating vulnerable and marginalized groups into vocational education and training through innovative solutions. *Problems of Education in the 21st Century*, 56, p. 42.

De Clercq, D. and Honig, B. (2011). Entrepreneurship as an integrating mechanism for disadvantaged persons. *Entrepreneurship and Regional Development*, 23(5–6), pp. 353–372.

Donoghue, C. (2003). Challenging the authority of the medical definition of disability: an analysis of the resistance to the social constructionist paradigm. *Disability and Society*, 18(2), pp. 199–208.

Doyel, A.W. (2000). No more job interviews: self-employment strategies for people with disabilities. St. Augustine: Training Resource Network.

Foss, L., Henry, C., Ahl, H. and Mikalsen, G.H. (2019). Women's entrepreneurship policy research: a 30-year review of the evidence. *Small Business Economics*, 53(2), pp. 409–429.

Foster, D. (2007). Legal obligation or personal lottery? Employee experiences of disability and the negotiation of adjustments in the public sector workplace. *Work, Employment and Society*, 21(1), pp. 67–84.

Global Gender Gap Report (2020). https://www.weforum.org/reports/gender-gap-2020-report-100-years-pay-equality. Accessed on 19 July 2021.

Hamburg, I. and David, A. (2017). Entrepreneurial education and skills in a changing society. In A. David and I. Hamburg (eds), *Entrepreneurship and Entrepreneurial Skills in Europe: Examples to Improve Potential Entrepreneurial Spirit*. Opladen: Verlag Barbara Budrich, pp. 12–31.

Hamilton, E. (2013). The discourse of entrepreneurial masculinities (and femininities). *Entrepreneurship and Regional Development*, 25(1–2), pp. 90–99.

Hitt, M.A., Ireland, R.D., Camp, S.M. and Sexton, D.L. (2001). Strategic entrepreneurship: entrepreneurial strategies for wealth creation. *Strategic Management Journal*, 22(6–7), pp. 479–491.

Hughes, K.D., Jennings, J.E., Brush, C., Carter, S. and Welter, F. (2012). Extending women's entrepreneurship research in new directions. *Entrepreneurship Theory and Practice*, 36(3), pp. 429–442.

Isenberg, D. (2011). The entrepreneurship ecosystem strategy as a new paradigm for economy policy: principles for cultivating entrepreneurship, Babson Entrepreneurship Ecosystem Project. Babson Park, MA: Babson College.

Jones, M.K. and Latreille, P.L. (2011). Disability and self-employment: evidence for the UK. *Applied Economics*, 43(27), pp. 4161–4178.

Kumra, S. (2010). The social construction of merit in a professional service firm: what is in and who is out? British Academy of Management Conference: Management Research in a Changing Climate, University of Sheffield, Sheffield, 14–16 September. Uxbridge: Brunel University.

Mair, J. and Marti, I. (2009). Entrepreneurship in and around institutional voids: a case study from Bangladesh. *Journal of Business Venturing*, 24(5), pp. 419–435.

McCall, L. (2005), The complexity of intersectionality. *Signs: Journal of Women in Culture and Society*, 30(3), pp. 1771–1880.

Ng, W. and Arndt, F. (2019). 'I never needed eyes to see': leveraging extreme challenges for successful venture creation. *Journal of Business Venturing Insights*, 11(June), e00125, pp. 1–10. DOI: https://doi.org/10.1016/j.jbvi.2019.e00125.

OECD (2008). *Gender and Sustainable Development. Maximizing the Economic, Social and Environmental Role of Women*. https://www.oecd.org/social/40881538.pdf. Accessed on 1 February 2019.

Pakistan Economic Survey (2016–2017). *Pakistan Economic Survey, 2016–2017*. https://www.finance.gov.pk/survey/chapters_17/Pakistan_ES_2016_17_pdf.pdf. Accessed on 19 May 2021.

Parker Harris, S., Renko, M. and Caldwell, K. 2014. Social entrepreneurship as an employment pathway for people with disabilities: exploring political–economic and socio-cultural factors. *Disability & Society*, 29(8), pp. 1275–1290.

Pavey, B. (2006). Human capital, social capital, entrepreneurship and disability: an examination of some current educational trends in the UK. *Disability and Society*, 21(3), pp. 217–229.

Porter, M. and Kramer, M. (2011). Creating shared value. *Harvard Business Review*, 89, pp. 62–77.

Roomi, M.A. and Parrott, G. (2008). Barriers to development and progression of women entrepreneurs in Pakistan. *Journal of Entrepreneurship*, 17, pp. 59–72.

Roomi, M.A., Rehman, S. and Henry, C. (2018). Exploring the normative context for women's entrepreneurship in Pakistan: a critical analysis. *International Journal of Gender and Entrepreneurship*, 10(2), pp. 158–180.

Siminski, P. (2003). Patterns of disability and norms of participation through the life course: empirical support for a social model of disability. *Disability and Society*, 18(6), pp. 707–718.

UN Women (2017). The power of procurement: how to source from women-owned businesses. https://www.unwomen.org/en/digital-library/publications/2017/3/the-power-of-procurement. Accessed on 20 June 2021.

Voluntary National Review (2019). Online. Available at https://sustainabledevelopment .un.org/content/documents/233812019_06_15_VNR_2019_Pakistan_latest_version.pdf. Accessed on 20 May 2021.

Welter, F. (2011). Contextualizing entrepreneurship – conceptual challenges and ways forward. *Entrepreneurship Theory and Practice*, 35(1), pp. 165–184.

Williams, B., Copestake, P., Eversley, J. and Stafford, B. (2011). *Experiences and Expectations of Disabled People – Executive Summary. A Research Report for the Office for Disability Issues*. London: Office for Public Management, and University of Nottingham.

Williams, J. and Patterson, N. (2018). New directions for entrepreneurship through a gender and disability lens. *International Journal of Entrepreneurial Behavior and Research*, 25(8), pp. 1706–1726.

World Health Organization (WHO) (2001). *International Classification of Functioning, Disability and Health*. http://apps.who.int/iris/bitstream/handle/10665/42407/9241545429 .pdf;jsessionid=A6B046CBF83B2D9FF04ED923BF8F94E3?sequence=1. Accessed on 20 June 2021.

World Health Organization (WHO) (2011). *World Report on Disability*. https://www.who.int/ teams/noncommunicable-diseases/sensory-functions-disability-and-rehabilitation/world -report-on-disability. Accessed on 20 August 2021.

Zahra, S.A., Wright, M. and Abdelgawad, S.G. (2014). Contextualization and the advancement of entrepreneurship research. *International Small Business Journal*, 32(5), pp. 479–500.

13. Disabled women entrepreneurs and microfinance: a road less travelled (for a reason)?[1]

Nadeera Ranabahu and Farzana Aman Tanima

INTRODUCTION

Development practitioners use microfinance as a tool to promote women's entrepreneurship in low- and middle-income economies. Institutions that provide microfinance services – microfinance institutions (MFIs) – often target women who own and operate businesses or have the willingness to engage in entrepreneurial activities (Ledgerwood and Gibson, 2013). A key reason for targeting women is to integrate them into mainstream economic activities, move them out of poverty and/or economically empower them by providing access to services such as loans, savings, insurance, leasing, remittance and business literacy development programmes (Armendáriz and Morduch, 2010; Ledgerwood and Gibson, 2013). However, certain groups of women, such as those with disabilities, are more vulnerable than others and often get excluded even from microfinance initiatives (Lewis, 2004; Paprocki, 2016). The mainstream pro-poor financial discourse, however, has largely ignored discussing issues faced by people/women with disabilities, or opportunities available for them to access microfinance for entrepreneurship. This chapter addresses this gap and aims to outline challenges faced by people/women with disabilities in accessing microfinance, opportunities associated with MFI services, and to explain how MFIs shape disabled women's entrepreneurial activities.

The main research questions this chapter intends to answer are: How does disability shape women's microfinance access and entrepreneurship experiences? How do MFIs shape entrepreneurial activities among women with disabilities? The study answers these questions by reviewing journal articles collected systematically, and outlining the patterns of use of microfinance by women with disabilities, opportunities they consider, and complications they face. Our intention is to synthesise available material and contribute to the disability and entrepreneurship literature by outlining whether use of microfinance, especially loans, for entrepreneurial purposes is considered 'a road less travelled', and if so, whether it is less travelled for a reason.

The reminder of this chapter is organised as follows. First, we provide an overview of the women entrepreneurs who use microfinance, and the reasoning for studying disabled women's access to finance. Next, we briefly outline the methods. After that we present our findings from the review, followed by the discussion. Finally, we end the chapter with conclusions.

WOMEN ENTREPRENEURS AND MICROFINANCE

Women and Microfinance Services

MFIs generally target women who own and operate (or have the intention of owning and operating) businesses, as they benefit more from access to finance. The basic premise here is that women are underrepresented in employment or self-employment, and through improving access to financial services they can be integrated into the mainstream economy (Armendáriz and Morduch, 2010). As a case in point, women are usually more credit-constrained than men, and MFIs provide an opportunity to initiate their own livelihood activities (Armendáriz and Morduch, 2010). Beyond economic benefits, women are responsible for household expenditure including children's education and health; hence, access to microfinance can have a social impact (Armendáriz and Morduch, 2010).

However, the development narratives that women are best poverty fighters, or that they are both 'vulnerable subjects and agents of economic change' (Khandelwal and Freeman, 2017: 49) have drawn criticisms (Maclean, 2017; Wilson, 2015). For example, with microfinance loans, women bear a triple burden of gendered roles (that is, productive, reproductive, and community labour) that include looking after dependent family members, and attending microfinance meetings while undertaking livelihood activities. Hindrances to conducting these gendered roles within patriarchal contexts can damage women's social standing in a community. Furthermore, MFIs and even joint liability groups, where three to five borrowers as a group are responsible for loan repayment, often put intense pressure on borrowers when recovering loans (Al-Azzam et al., 2012; Wright, 2006). These norms introduce new forms of domination on women and damage existing social ties and networks within a community (Ghatak and Guinnane, 1999). As women, in patriarchal societies, are often considered traditional custodians of family honour, they are fearful of any social sanctions which can damage their social network (Armendáriz and Morduch, 2010).

Microfinance and Women's Entrepreneurship

The mainstream claim in regard to links between microfinance and women's empowerment through entrepreneurial ventures is heavily critiqued and frequently debated within the gender and development studies literature (see Bateman, 2010). Anecdotal evidence, however, indicates that some women use microfinance services for business start-up or development activities. Microfinance loans provide a means, or capital, for women entrepreneurs to conduct business tasks (Ranabahu and Barrett, 2018). For example, loan money can be used to purchase assets or stock, upgrade existing equipment, extend business premises, or pay for marketing (Mahmood, 2011; Tundui and Tundui, 2020). Beyond direct investments of microfinance loans in a venture, women entrepreneurs also get other benefits through their links to MFIs, such as having an opportunity for entrepreneurial learning (Sigalla and Carney, 2012). Microfinance loans further provide opportunities to be strategic in entrepreneurial activities. That is, being a recipient of a microfinance loan adds complexity to entrepreneurs' decision-making where they need some form of planning, goal-setting, and calculating returns to obtain money and repay loans (Ranabahu and Barrett, 2020); these align with strategic behaviours of developing a business.

Nevertheless, enterprises financed by microfinance are considered to have limited growth potential. This is because of the limited specialisation of these ventures, where each usually offers common services already available, which in turn increases the probability of failure (Banerjee and Duflo, 2007). These businesses typically have no potential to scale up or to access formal commercial institutional funding (Alawattage et al., 2019; Karim, 2011; Weber, 2016). Therefore, these individuals are not considered as entrepreneurs in the full sense, and are referred to as 'perpetual entrepreneurs-in-waiting' (Alawattage et al., 2019: 55). This 'perpetual waiting' or lack of growth is partly due to the vulnerabilities associated with income risk, driving entrepreneurs to reject high-risk but high-yielding opportunities (Pearlman, 2012).

Among the disabled, these entrepreneurial concerns and issues are much more significant, as self-employment seems to be one (or the only) feasible option available for them in developing countries (Handicap International, 2006). But starting up a business is not an easy task in itself, especially for women with disabilities, as it requires self-confidence, motivation, business and financial literacy, networks and access to capital (Handicap International, 2006). In relation to access to capital, although obtaining microfinance loans seems to be an option, people with disabilities are highly underrepresented among the clients of MFIs (Handicap International, 2006). Our aim is to explore the reasons for such low representation by identifying the roles of microfinance amongst women with disabilities.

METHOD

This chapter is part of a broader systematic review conducted on vulnerabilities such as disability, age, sexuality, widowhood, forced displacement due to war or natural disasters, and how these vulnerabilities shape the use of microfinance and entrepreneurial activities (see Ranabahu and Tanima, 2021 for the full review). We used databases Scopus and EBSCOhost for the systematic review and extracted articles related to disability and microfinance for the period of 2000 to 2020 (see Ranabahu and Tanima, 2021 for full criteria on inclusion and exclusion). During the systematic review, we identified 21 articles related to microfinance and disability (note that these articles are marked with an asterisk, *, in the References section). Although not all articles included the term 'entrepreneurship', these articles gave indications of the way disability shaped business tasks. We reviewed these articles to identify key themes, synthesise results, and report on trends and patterns.

FINDINGS[2]

Our findings indicate that disabled people's reasons for the use (or non-use) of loans, and their experiences of microfinance for entrepreneurial purposes, are different to those of mainstream borrowers. Our findings also highlight that MFIs have a role in fostering entrepreneurship among caregivers, and microfinance could be used for rehabilitation leading to entrepreneurship. We also found challenges and barriers faced by disabled people in accessing microfinance for entrepreneurship. This section explains these findings in detail.

Use (or Non-Use) of Microfinance by Disabled People

The available literature indicates that people with disabilities are motivated for self-employment and use microfinance loans for business purposes (Beisland and Mersland, 2012). There are no significant differences in motivations for business start-up between persons with and without disabilities (Beisland et al., 2016). MFIs lend to disabled people, as long as the savings and other requirements are fulfilled; hence, Beisland and Mersland (2017) and Nuwagaba et al. (2012) explain that disability per se does not hinder disabled people's access to microfinance services. However, even among the MFIs that lend to people with disabilities, although disability prevalence is generally higher among the female population, Beisland and Mersland (2017) found that the borrower statistics do not reflect the overall population data. Hence, literature in this category points out that women with disabilities are considered more financially disadvantaged than males with disabilities (Beisland and Mersland, 2017; Lewis, 2004).

Studies also show that it is more common among people with disabilities to start ventures with their own money or family money, and then obtain money from MFIs later for business development purposes (Beisland and Mersland, 2012). The ability to start a business and earn money helps women specifically when they perceive that marriage is not a possibility due to their disability (Chaudhry, 2016). Thus, people with disabilities are considered an untapped market for microfinance services (Beisland and Mersland, 2014a; Mersland et al., 2009; Sarker, 2013).

Chaudhry (2016), using a critical disability feminist perspective, reports why disabled women are apprehensive about taking loans to invest in new enterprises. The author, using an ethnographic study, reveals that women with disabilities are disadvantaged in other ways, including by caste, class, impairment type, and not having familial/kinship support. Due to these additional disadvantages, disabled women in comparison to non-disabled women are not able to perform productive roles in the domestic sphere, or be mobile in local markets for entrepreneurial tasks. This, coupled with limited non-farm sector opportunities in general, and even fewer for people with disabilities, makes disabled women more apprehensive about accessing microfinance services.

Disabled microfinance clients, compared to others, have a high tendency to save (Beisland and Mersland, 2017), and women more frequently become members of savings groups than men (Beisland and Mersland, 2012). In some contexts, savings help them to develop some security (for example, to buy gold to secure their future), and they tend not to risk their life savings by investing in an enterprise where success is uncertain (Chaudhry, 2016). These decisions made by women reflect people's ability to make and act on their own life choices. At the same time, these studies reinforce the need for services other than loans for people with disabilities.

Alongside financial services, the literature identifies the need for other interventions to develop capacities of people (not just of women) with disabilities. These include skill development and financial literacy training programmes (Sarker, 2013). In some situations, training programmes on self-care are important even more so than livelihood support (Polu et al., 2015). These studies (Heeren et al., 2014; Polu et al., 2015) nevertheless indicate the need for these interventions to be conducted hand-in-hand with socio-economic rehabilitation programmes.

Use of Microfinance as a Tool to Facilitate Entrepreneurship among Caregivers

Within households, having a disabled family member can shape caregivers' self-employment or employment roles. As the majority of the caregivers are women, the task of caregiving takes up a significant proportion of their time (Nair et al., 2018). Although self-employment is considered a much better prospect for caregivers, the long-term nature of the illness and disability could have an added financial burden, the outcome of which could be continued poverty (Nair et al., 2018). Therefore, caregivers are willing to engage in home-based productive activities such as stitching, but they are unable or often unwilling to attend regular microfinance meetings due to caregivers' needs or stigma (Nair et al., 2018). In instances where caregivers attend microfinance meetings, they may have to accompanying their carers; however, this may not be feasible due to lack of infrastructure such as suitable transport, or not having wheelchair access to meeting locations.

Challenges and Barriers Faced by Disabled People in Accessing Microfinance for Entrepreneurship

Most studies in the area of disability and microfinance suggest that disabled people face challenges when accessing loans due to institutional norms and the existence of differing societal and community actors. At the individual level, women with disabilities have obstacles similar to women in general who access loans (for example, lack of collateral, fewer resources to business, lack of experience or training programmes). In addition to these general obstacles, disability shapes their experience, altering and intensifying these obstacles and adding others (Lewis, 2004).

The exclusion of people with disability, according to the available literature, stems from low self-esteem of disabled people themselves, exclusion by other members, exclusion by staff, and exclusion by service design (Cramm and Finkenflugel, 2008; Mersland et al., 2009; Thomas, 2000). Low self-esteem, which leads to self-exclusion, occurs due to repeated negative experiences (Mersland et al., 2009). For example, people with disabilities are usually considered as 'bad risks' for financial agencies, and considered inappropriate for microfinance loans or business services; hence, they are often referred to rehabilitation or charitable programmes (Lewis, 2004). Furthermore, people with visual and hearing impairment are more constrained than those with physical impairments, as they have a hard time following the discussions due to not having appropriate support (for example, Braille, sign language) (Nuwagaba et al., 2012). Attitudes such as 'microfinance is not for people with disabilities' also limit access (Nuwagaba et al., 2012). These negative discourses and societal norms lead to a loss of self-confidence and hinder women's decision-making capabilities.

Exclusion by members happens at joint liability groups. In these groups, borrowers decide and select who is in a group. This self-selection bias leads to exclusions of vulnerable people (Mersland et al., 2009). The stigmatisation and perceived risk associated with disabilities further worsen the self-selection bias. Stigma-related issues also cause discrimination regarding access to training programmes (Lewis, 2004). Therefore, Cramm et al. (2012) point out that people with disabilities prefer individual loans.

Exclusion by staff, due to conscious or unconscious biases, affects their assessment of creditworthiness and subsequently the entrepreneurial process. The evidence suggests that experienced loan officers perceive people with disabilities as high credit risks and, hence, neglect more vulnerable clients (Beisland et al., 2019; Beisland and Mersland, 2014b; Labie et al., 2015; Sarker, 2020). The rejection happens due to both prejudice and 'statistical discrimination', where staff members use an individual's disability as an indication of their entrepreneurial potential (Sarker, 2020). This could also be partly due to late payments, as late payments are found to be more common amongst disabled clients (Beisland and Mersland, 2017). Beisland and Mersland (2017) emphasise that reasons for these late payments could be because of having additional health-related expenses, not having enough money to make the repayments, MFIs providing standard loan products for people with disabilities, or a combination of any of these factors. To mitigate some of these staff-related exclusions, Sarker (2013) recommends recruitment of disability-friendly staff, having training programmes around these issues, and implementing policies outlining services for disabled people. Building strategic partnerships with organisations that support disabled people is also recommended (Sarker, 2013).

Exclusion by design happens due to the microfinance loan terms and conditions, such as compulsory savings requirements or weekly/monthly meetings. A key microfinance practice is the requirement for joint liability groups to meet weekly/monthly at a group member's house in the presence of a staff member. The primary function of this meeting is for the staff member to collect repayments. These meeting platforms are less accessible for people with disabilities, for reasons such as physical location of the meeting and lack of appropriate transport services (Lewis, 2004). Informational barriers, due to communication constraints (for example, verbal or written forms of information provided), can also exclude people from microfinance services (Lewis, 2004; Nuwagaba et al., 2012).

Furthermore, systematic failures or physical or informational barriers contribute to long-term exclusion of women with disabilities from MFIs. Girls with disabilities are frequently the last of families' priorities to be provided with education, which has long-term impacts on accessibility to financial services (Lewis, 2004). Loan officers, for example, perceive women with disabilities as unable to understand information or manage finances (Lewis, 2004). All these factors can hinder the participation of disabled women in economic activities, entrepreneurial investments, and their entrepreneurial actions.

Use of Microfinance for Rehabilitation Leading to Entrepreneurship

One less common theme identified from the review is the role of microfinance in post-rehabilitation efforts in poor and war-torn areas (Daher and Flessa, 2010; Fiasse, 2011). These services are relevant for both men and women, and reflect the agency to make decisions on their microfinance use. Due to low income or lack of basic welfare systems, patients who suffer from a walking disability or chronic lung diseases find it difficult to finance necessary healthcare equipment such as wheelchairs or oxygen concentrators (Daher and Flessa, 2010). This acts as a barrier for them to engage in income generation tasks. Hence, Daher and Flessa (2010) state that microfinance has the potential as a tool for financing medical devices.

DISCUSSION

In this chapter, our aim was to study how disability shapes women's microfinance access and entrepreneurial behaviours. We also explored the role of MFIs in reshaping these experiences. Using published peer-reviewed journal articles, we identified key usage or non-usage of microfinance, pathways that people/women with disabilities use to achieve entrepreneurial outcomes, and challenges that they face.

Our findings illustrate that both women with disabilities and caregivers of disabled people benefit from having access to microfinance (see Figure 13.1). Women with disabilities use microfinance services directly to increase entrepreneurial activities (see Beisland and Mersland, 2017; Nuwagaba et al., 2012). However, our findings reveal that women with disabilities are cautious when using or even considering microfinance for entrepreneurial activities due to lack of confidence, skills, and risks associated with business activities (see Chaudhry, 2016). Hence, individual-level capacity building programmes and skill development initiatives are required to understand their own capabilities and limitations.

As Figure 13.1 illustrates, another pathway which women with disabilities use to engage in businesses is to first use microfinance services for their rehabilitation needs; this then facilitates their ability to engage in livelihood activities (see Daher and Flessa, 2010). This indirect pathway of conducting entrepreneurial activities,

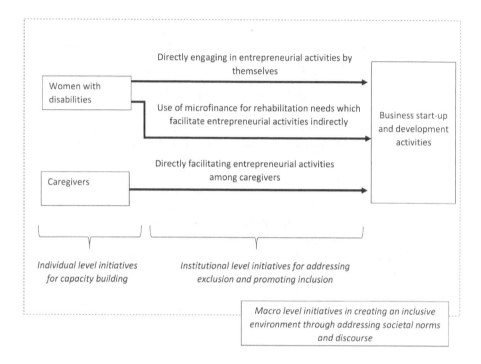

Figure 13.1   Pathways for entrepreneurship and support initiatives

however, requires MFIs expanding their lending criteria from livelihood-only loans to consumption-type loans which allow people to use the money for their health and wellbeing needs. If such lending flexibility is not feasible, MFIs could form partnerships with organisations which provide such rehabilitation support.

Our findings also illustrate that microfinance has the potential to enhance business activities of caregivers (see Nair et al., 2018). For caregivers, the main concern is that their daily tasks depend on the needs of the person they are looking after. Hence, they may not be able to adhere to strict joint liability group meeting requirements, nor attend any compulsory training sessions. This indicates that MFIs need to be flexible and monitor caregivers' loan usage and repayments using slightly different criteria.

In summary, MFIs need to assess their lending criteria, determine their strategies towards inclusiveness, and develop alternative routes for people to use microfinance and entrepreneurial services. This requires the institutions to look at all operational aspects of microfinance lending processes, including the role of solidarity groups where borrowers guarantee each other's loans, assessments of creditworthiness conducted by field-level officers, their incentives for incorporating women with disabilities, and prerequisites (for example, compulsory savings) associated with some of the microfinance schemes. The work of Lewis (2004), Mersland et al. (2009) and Sarker (2013) emphasises similar points. General infrastructure improvements such as having an office with wheelchair access, or conducting meetings at places easily accessible for disabled people, would also help in maintaining an inclusive atmosphere. Technology-enabled solutions such as digital financial services (for example, mobile money) could also help in lowering the financial access-related barriers.

At the same time, MFIs, as a part of their social marketing campaigns, could raise awareness about the issues faced by people/women with disabilities to create general awareness within the communities. Such efforts could help in reducing the stigma and increasing the acceptance of disabled people. In addition, industry associations and networks which MFIs are members of could be used for advocacy or collaborating with institutions such as Handicap International, and setting up inclusive standards across MFIs.

Our findings contribute to theory and practice related to disabled entrepreneurs in several ways. First, we outlined the role of microfinance in enhancing entrepreneurial activities among people/women with disabilities. The study sheds light on the need for modified versions of financial services, suggesting that loans may not be the only service that disabled people require to boost entrepreneurial activities. Next, we contribute by introducing a rudimentary conceptual framework (Figure 13.1). This framework, derived from our review, indicates pathways which can be used to enhance entrepreneurial activities for both disabled people and caregivers, and outlines areas of support that MFIs may have to consider. This framework could be used as a foundation to develop future studies; it needs further refinement using empirical studies, leading to development of testable propositions and hypothesis. This framework can also be used by MFIs and entrepreneurial service providers to identify focus areas when assessing inclusion criteria related to their service delivery. Finally, this study also outlines some practical strategies that MFIs could use to enhance entrepreneurial activities among women with disabilities.

CONCLUSION

In conclusion, we emphasise that MFIs need to consider both people with disabilities and caregivers, as self-employment may be one of the only income-generation activities available for them. As identified in this study, it will assist people with disabilities when directly engaging in entrepreneurial tasks or indirectly engaging in more livelihood-related tasks through fulfilment of their rehabilitation needs; and caregivers using microfinance to engage in economic tasks. Hence, we conclude that disabled people's use of microfinance for entrepreneurial tasks is still a road less travelled, but it is less travelled because of the road blocks (for example, lending design, joint liability group, or field officer-related exclusion), not having any road signs directing travellers (for example, institutional partnerships for rehabilitation needs), and not having any 'roadside' assistance for travel (for example, capacity-building programmes).

NOTES

1. This chapter extensively uses material published by authors in the journal article Ranabahu and Tanima (2021).
2. The 'Findings' section presented here, originally published in Ranabahu and Tanima (2021), is reprinted with the permission of the publisher. We have made minor changes to the original published version.

REFERENCES

Alawattage, C., Graham, C., and Wickramasinghe, D. (2019). Microaccountability and biopolitics: Microfinance in a Sri Lankan village. *Accounting, Organizations and Society, 72*, 38–60. https://doi.org/10.1016/j.aos.2018.05.008.

Al-Azzam, M., Carter Hill, R., and Sarangi, S. (2012). Repayment performance in group lending: Evidence from Jordan. *Journal of Development Economics, 97*(2), 404–414. https://doi.org/10.1016/j.jdeveco.2011.06.006.

Armendáriz, B., and Morduch, J. (2010). *Economics of Microfinance*, 2nd edn, MIT Press, Cambridge, MA, USA.

Banerjee, A., and Duflo, E. (2007). The economic lives of the poor. *Journal of Economic Perspectives, 21*(1), 141–168. https://www.jstor.org/stable/43189512.

Bateman, M. (2010). *Why Doesn't Microfinance Work? The Destructive Rise of Local Neoliberalism*, Zed Books, London.

Beisland, L.A., D'Espallier, B., and Mersland, R. (2019). The commercialization of the microfinance industry: Is there a 'personal mission drift' among credit officers? *Journal of Business Ethics, 158*(1), 119–134. https://doi.org/10.1007/s10551-017-3710-4.*

Beisland, L.A., and Mersland, R. (2012). The use of microfinance services among economically active disabled people: Evidence from Uganda. *Journal of International Development, 24*(1), S69–S83. https://doi.org/10.1002/jid.1720.*

Beisland, L.A., and Mersland, R. (2014a). Staff characteristics and the exclusion of persons with disabilities: Evidence from the microfinance industry in Uganda. *Disability and Society, 29*(7), 1061–1075. https://doi.org/10.1080/09687599.2014.902362.*

Beisland, L.A., and Mersland, R. (2014b). Income characteristics and the use of microfinance services: Evidence from economically active persons with disabilities. *Disability and Society, 29*(3), 417–430. https://doi.org/10.1080/09687599.2013.816625.*

Beisland, L.A., and Mersland, R. (2017). Exploring microfinance clients with disabilities: A case study of an Ecuadorian microbank. *Journal of Development Studies, 53*(11), 1929–1943. https://doi.org/10.1080/00220388.2016.1265946.*

Beisland, L.A., Mersland, R., and Zamore, S. (2016). Motivations for business start-up: Are there any differences between disabled and non-disabled microfinance clients? *Journal of International Development, 28*(1), 147–149. https://doi.org/10.1002/jid.3196.*

Chaudhry, V. (2016). Living at the edge: Disability, gender, and neoliberal debtscapes of microfinance in India. *Affilia, 31*(2), 177–191. https://doi.org/10.1177/0886109915622525.*

Cramm, J.M., and Finkenflugel, H. (2008). Exclusion of disabled people from microcredit in Africa and Asia: A literature study. *Disability, CBR and Inclusive Development, 19*(2), 15–33. http://hdl.handle.net/1765/79039.*

Cramm, J.M., Paauwe, M., and Finkenflügel, H. (2012). Facilitators and hindrances in the experiences of Ugandans with and without disabilities when seeking access to microcredit schemes. *Disability and Rehabilitation, 34*(25), 2166–2176. https://doi.org/10.3109/09638288.2012.681004.*

Daher, H., and Flessa, S. (2010). Microfinance as a tool for financing medical devices in Syria: An assessment of needs and a call for further research. *Journal of Public Health*, *18*(2), 189–197. https://doi.org/10.1007/s10389-009-0290-5.*

Fiasse, J. (2011). Impact of micro credit scheme for persons with physical disabilities in Herat, Afghanistan. *Disability, CBR and Inclusive Development*, *22*(1), 99–107. https://doi.org/10.5463/DCID.v22i1.8.*

Ghatak, M., and Guinnane, T.W. (1999). The economics of lending with joint liability: Theory and practice. *Journal of Development Economics*, *60*(1), 195–228. https://doi.org/10.1016/S0304-3878(99)00041-3.

Handicap International (2006). Good practices for the economic inclusion of people with disabilities in developing countries: Funding mechanisms for self-employment. Report. https://hdl.handle.net/1813/76549.

Heeren, M.-J.J., Ky, L., and van Brakel, W.H. (2014). Perceived needs related to social participation of people with Leprosy-related disabilities and other people with disabilities in Cambodia: A qualitative study. *Disability, CBR and Inclusive Development*, *25*(3), 24–44. http://doi.org/10.5463/dcid.v25i3.343.*

Karim, L. (2011). *Microfinance and Its Discontents: Women in Debt in Bangladesh*, University of Minnesota Press, Minneapolis, MN.

Khandelwal, M., and Freeman, C. (2017). Pop development and the uses of feminism. In Batman, M., and Maclean, K. (eds), *Seduced and Betrayed: Exposing the Contemporary Microfinance Phenomenon*, University of New Mexico Press, Albuquerque, published in Association with School for Advanced Research Press, Santa Fe, NM, 49–67.

Labie, M., Méon, P-G., Mersland R., and Szafarz, A. (2015). Discrimination by microcredit officers: Theory and evidence on disability in Uganda. *Quarterly Review of Economics and Finance*, *58*, 44–55. http://doi.org/10.1016/j.qref.2015.05.002.*

Ledgerwood, J., and Gibson A. (2013). The evolving financial landscape. In Ledgerwood, J., Earne, J., and Nelson, C. (eds), *The New Microfinance Handbook: A Financial Market System Perspective*, World Bank, Washington, DC, 15–48.

Lewis, C. (2004). Microfinance from the point of view of women with disabilities: Lessons from Zambia and Zimbabwe. *Gender and Development*, *12*(1), 28–39. http://doi.org/10.1080/13552070410001726496.*

Maclean, K. (2017). Microfinance and the 'woman' question. In Bateman, M., and Maclean, K. (eds), *Seduced and Betrayed: Exposing the Contemporary Microfinance Phenomenon*, University of New Mexico Press, Albuquerque, published in Association with School for Advanced Research Press, Santa Fe, NM, 251–264.

Mahmood, S. (2011). Microfinance and women entrepreneurs in Pakistan. *International Journal of Gender and Entrepreneurship*, *3*(3), 265–274. http://doi.org/10.1108/17566261111169340.

Mersland, R., Bwire, F.N., and Mukasa, G. (2009). Access to mainstream microfinance services for persons with disabilities: Lessons learned from Uganda. *Disability Studies Quarterly*, *29*(1), https://ssrn.com/abstract=1101701.*

Nair, S., Jagannathan, A., Kudumallige, S., Kumar, C.N., and Thirthalli, C. (2018). Need for micro-finance self-help groups among women family caregivers of persons with mental disability in rural India. *Mental Health and Social Inclusion*, *22*(1), 34–45. http://doi.org/10.1108/MHSI-10-2017-0039.*

Nuwagaba, E.L., Nakabugo, M., Tumukunde, M., Ngirabakunzi, E., Hartley, S., and Wade, A. (2012). Accessibility to micro-finance services by people with disabilities in Bushenyi district, Uganda. *Disability and Society*, *27*(2), 175–190. https://doi.org/10.1080/09687599.2011.644929.*

Paprocki, K. (2016). 'Selling our own skin': Social dispossession through microcredit in rural Bangladesh. *Geoforum*, *74*, 29–38. https://doi.org/10.1016/j.geoforum.2016.05.008.

Pearlman, S. (2012). Too vulnerable for microfinance? Risk and vulnerability as determinants of microfinance selection in Lima. *Journal of Development Studies*, *48*(9), 1342–1359. https://doi.org/10.1080/00220388.2012.693170.

Polu, W., Mong, A., and Nelson, C. (2015). Social and economic inclusion of people with disabilities: practical lessons from Bangladesh. *Development in Practice*, *25*(8), 1182–1188. https://doi.org/10.1080/09614524.2015.1078289.*

Ranabahu, N., and Barrett, M. (2018). Effectuation thinking and the manifestation of socio-cultural complexities in Sri Lankan female entrepreneurs' business decisions. In Yousafzai, S., Lindgreen, A., Saeed, S., Henry, C., and Fayolle, A. (eds), *Contextual Embeddedness of Women's Entrepreneurship: Going Beyond a Gender Neutral Approach*, Abingdon: Routledge, 139–153. http://dx.doi.org/10.4324/9781315574042-10.

Ranabahu, N., and Barrett, M. (2020). Does practice make micro-entrepreneurs perfect? An investigation of expertise acquisition using effectuation and causation. *Small Business Economics*, *54*(3), 883–905. http://dx.doi.org/10.1007/s11187-019-00157-6.

Ranabahu, N., and Tanima, F.A. (2021). Empowering vulnerable microfinance women through entrepreneurship: Opportunities, challenges and the way forward. *International Journal of Gender and Entrepreneurship*. http://dx.doi.org/10.1108/IJGE-01-2021-0020.

Sarker, D. (2013). Microfinance for disabled people: How is it contributing? *Research Journal of Finance and Accounting*, *4*(9), http://dx.doi.org/10.7176/RJFA/4-9-118.*

Sarker, D. (2020). Discrimination against people with disabilities in accessing microfinance. *Alter*, *14*(4), 318–328. http://dx.doi.org/10.1016/j.alter.2020.06.005.*

Sigalla, R.J., and Carney, S. (2012). Poverty reduction through entrepreneurship: Microcredit, learning and ambivalence amongst women in urban Tanzania. *International Journal of Educational Development*, *32*(4), 546–554. https://doi.org/10.1016/j.ijedudev.2012.02.011.

Thomas, M. (2000). Feasibility of integrating people with disabilities in savings and credit programmes in Bangladesh. *Asia Pacific Disability Rehabilitation Journal*, *11*(1), 27–31.*

Tundui, H.P., and Tundui, C.S. (2020). Performance drivers of women-owned microcredit funded enterprises in Tanzania. *International Journal of Gender and Entrepreneurship*, *12*(2), 211–230. https://doi.org/10.1108/IJGE-06-2019-0101.

Weber, H. (2016). Gender and microfinance/microcredit. In Steans, J., and Tepe-Belfrage, D. (eds), *Handbook on Gender in World Politics*, Edward Elgar Publishing, Cheltenham, UK and Northampton, MA, USA, 430–437.

Wilson K. (2015). Towards a radical re-appropriation: Gender, development and neoliberal feminism. *Development and Change*, *46*(4), 803–832. https://doi.org/10.1111/dech.12176.

Wright, K. (2006). The darker side to microfinance – Evidence from Cajamaru, Peru. In Fernando, J. (ed.), *Microfinance – Perils and Prospects*, Routledge, London and New York, 133–149.

14. A preliminary analysis of the impact of COVID-19 on the mental wellbeing of entrepreneurship students

Sylvie Studente, Filia Garivaldis and Wilson Ng

INTRODUCTION

The COVID-19 pandemic began at the end of 2019, and the virus was reported to be highly contagious (Liu et al., 2020). In order to decelerate the rapid spread of the virus, most countries brought in dramatic measures to restrict social congregation. These restrictions included bans on large events, the closure of schools and universities, and of places of worship (European Union, 2020). As a result, the public were advised to work from home where possible and limit travel (Mervosh et al., 2020). These global lockdown measures affected students in 142 countries worldwide as universities closed their classroom doors (Karalis and Raikou, 2020). Across the global higher education landscape, universities moved to a remote mode of teaching and learning immediately (Bisht et al., 2020; Crawford et al., 2020). The disruption caused to higher education by the pandemic has had a significant impact on the learning experience for students (Hill and Fitzgerald, 2020), which has been reported to have detrimental effects on students' social and psychological wellbeing (Prowse et al., 2020; Petillon and McNeil, 2020). Preliminary studies undertaken into the psychological wellbeing of students during the pandemic report that although some students have responded to changes in educational strategies, with resilience (Kelley, 2020), many have reported detrimental impacts to their mental health (Nania et al., 2020). It is likely that the closure of university campuses and the shift to remote teaching may have led to feelings of anxiety and loss of social integration for some students (Padron et al., 2021).

This chapter firstly reviews preliminary studies undertaken in the area, and reports upon a study conducted with entrepreneurship students at a London university with a largely international student base. Specifically, the study reported upon within this chapter examined the presence of a perceived impact of remote learning on students' social/psychological wellbeing, level of engagement, motivation with venture creation, social interactions, academic performance, 'university experience', and self-reported levels of depression and anxiety. This study supports the growing body of evidence on the impact of the pandemic on the student experience within higher education, and offers further insight by focusing upon entrepreneurship students seeking to build a foundation for entrepreneurial activities.

BACKGROUND MOTIVATION

University students ordinarily face a number of stressors under usual conditions. For example, first-year students transitioning to university life face the stresses of a new environment (Parker et al., 2004), international students face the stresses of acculturation (Smith and Khawaja, 2011), and there are general concerns regarding academic performance (Mikolajczyk et al., 2008). In the wake of the pandemic, these stressors have been exacerbated by the closure of university campuses, the shift to remote learning, and reduced opportunities for social integration with peers (Grubic et al., 2020). The following subsections discuss reported impacts of the pandemic upon students' psychological wellbeing, academic performance, social interaction and acculturation (in the case of interactional students).

Students' Psychological Wellbeing

Although the closure of university campuses and the mitigation strategy of remote learning has been necessary, current research reports worldwide trends in increased stress, anxiety and depression amongst university students (Liu et al., 2020; Rajab and Alkattan, 2020). Specifically, a number of studies have reported increased levels of depression, anxiety and stress (Elmer et al., 2020; Laher et al., 2021; Cao et al., 2020; Fu et al., 2021; Wang et al., 2020; Evans et al., 2021). These reported trends are not specific to the United Kingdom: a number of worldwide studies have also reported similar findings among students at international institutions (Fruehwirth et al., 2021; Faisal et al., 2021; Debowska et al., 2020). All of the studies mentioned here report a significant increase in depression and anxiety levels experienced by undergraduate students as the pandemic progressed. The study undertaken by Debowska et al. (2020) correlates these increases in anxiety and depression with social isolation and lack of integration due to remote learning and campus closures.

Research further purports that these aspects have also exacerbated pre-existing mental health conditions amongst university students, again correlated with the physical closure of campuses, restrictions on socialisation, and the loss of a daily routine (Young Minds, 2020). Additionally, levels of anxiety have been reported to have increased for students who have had little to no prior experience with distance learning (Piotrowski and King, 2020), and for those experiencing equipment problems with reliable internet access, availability of webcams and/or computers, for example (Bolatov et al., 2020).

Academic Performance

Academic performance has also reportedly declined as a consequence of the shift toward remote learning (Mudenda et al., 2020), as in some instances students have been struggling to focus upon their academic studies (Kecojevic et al., 2020). Research within the area reports that many university students have struggled to maintain motivation and engagement following the transition to remote learning

(Perets et al., 2020; Duraku and Hoxha, 2020). Academic performance is often judged by students in comparison to the performance of their peers. In normal learning settings this is done by observing how peers are contributing to the learning process, particularly within classroom-based debates and question-and-answer (Q&A) sessions. Judgements relating to effort and time spent learning can also be made through informal discussion among peers. However, in the remote delivery model, such opportunities have been significantly diminished.

Impact on Social Interaction

Studies conducted over the lockdown period reveal that many students have reported feeling socially isolated from their peers and lecturers (Boda et al., 2020). In particular, first-year students may feel that they have missed out on the experience of being able to form bonds and establish new friendships with classmates, as well as the overall 'university experience'. Reduced social interaction has specifically been detrimental to the wellbeing of students who live alone (Bolatov et al., 2020; Kawachi and Berkman, 2001). It is these reductions in social interaction coupled with feelings of loneliness which are associated with declines in student mental health (Wang et al., 2020), such as depression, anxiety, stress and loneliness (Elmer et al., 2020; Tambag et al., 2018). Upon further exploration, critical social dimensions for students' wellbeing include interaction, friendship, social support and co-studying. Social isolation in itself can lead to elevated anxiety and symptoms of depression (Hortulanus et al., 2006; Chaturvedi et al., 2020), which also has a knock-on effect on academic performance. This is because when students are socially engaged with peers, they are more likely to be motivated with their studies (Furrer and Skinner, 2003).

International Students

Preliminary studies have also focused on the impact of lockdown measures on international students who have had to return to their home countries and continue their university studies online. An example arises from Lai et al. (2020), who surveyed 124 international students who had returned home once lockdown measures were first announced. Findings indicate that 84.7 per cent of the students reported moderate to high stress levels, and 12.1 per cent of students reported symptoms of depression. Negative wellbeing was reported to be associated with the shift to remote learning, uncertainties regarding studies, and a general feeling of lack of social support.

METHODOLOGY

Drawing upon the background literature, the aim of the study reported in this chapter is to substantiate previous literature on the social and psychological impacts experienced by undergraduate students during the global lockdown. Participants included

40 undergraduate students who were enrolled on an entrepreneurship pathway at a London university with a largely international student base, and who engaged with their studies through remote learning during the lockdown period. The majority of participants (70 per cent, N = 28) had not engaged in remote learning previously. The research questions driving this study were as follows:

During the closure of university premises due to the government's imposed lockdown, do students report:
a) Increased symptoms of anxiety and depression?
b) Decreased motivation and engagement with entrepreneurial activities?
c) Feelings of having 'missed out' on their development, for example, as novice entrepreneurs?
d) A lack of social interaction with peers?

Students who participated in the study completed a ten-item online survey which was based around four key themes, as illustrated in Figure 14.1.

Figure 14.1   Data collection survey themes

FINDINGS AND DISCUSSION

The survey contained ten questions addressing each of the themes appearing in Figure 14.1. Overall, 39 of the 40 participants reported that the closure of university premises due to lockdown had a detrimental impact on their social and psychological wellbeing. A binomial test indicated that this proportion of participants (97 per cent) was significantly higher than the expected proportion by chance (50 per cent), p = 0.000 (2-sided). To unpack this further, the results from questions relating to each of social wellbeing and to psychological wellbeing are presented separately below.

Impact on Social Wellbeing

Universities are social hubs. Therefore, the closure of university premises is expected to reduce students' opportunities for social interaction. Indeed, 27 (67 per cent) participants in this survey reported the lack of opportunity for social interaction as a key concern during lockdown. A binomial test indicated that this proportion is significantly higher than what could be expected by chance alone (50 per cent), p = 0.000 (2-sided).

Moreover, the majority of participants (90 per cent) reported to have experienced feelings of loneliness and a lack of social support during lockdown. To the same extent, the majority of participants (95 per cent) indicated having 'missed out' on the 'university experience'. Despite this, or perhaps because of this, many participants (67.5 per cent) reported having collaborated/co-studied with peers in private settings. In all of the above cases, the majority proportions reported are significantly higher than chance, p = 0.000 (2-sided), p = 0.040 (2-sided), respectively. These frequencies are summarised in Figure 14.2.

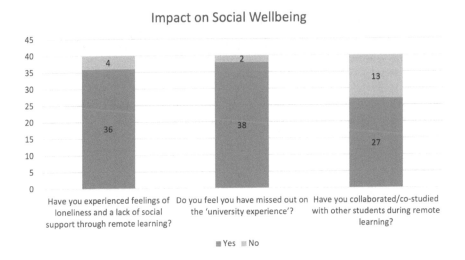

Impact on Social Wellbeing

Figure 14.2   Reported impact of closure of university premises on social wellbeing

Impact on Psychological Wellbeing

An overwhelming amount of research and evidence indicates that mental health and psychological wellbeing have suffered, particularly in young people, throughout the course of the COVID-19 pandemic (Petillon and McNeil, 2020; Wester et al., 2021; Prowse et al., 2020). The majority of participants in the current sample reported that during the period of remote learning, they have experienced both depression (67.5 per cent) and anxiety (85 per cent), significantly higher proportions than would be expected by chance, p = 0.040 and p = 0.000, respectively. Moreover, the majority of participants (90 per cent) also reported a lack of motivation to engage in study, p = 0.000. These frequencies are summarised in Figure 14.3.

Feelings and symptoms of depression can manifest as feelings of dejection, deflation, hopelessness and helplessness, and not surprisingly, a lack of motivation (Knutson and Wimmer, 2007). On the other hand, whilst anxiety shares an element of psychological distress, feelings of anxiety specifically among student cohorts are often attributed to the inability to meet study obligations, and expectations of

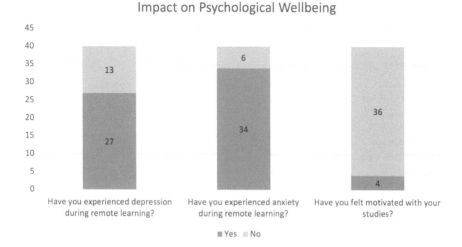

Figure 14.3   *Reported impact of closure of university premises on psychological wellbeing*

impending negative consequences such as academic failure (Higgins, 1987). Indeed, participants in the current sample (65 per cent) reported the lack of opportunity for academic performance as a key concern during lockdown, and only 50 per cent reported being able to independently engage with their studies during remote learning.

Relationships between Social and Psychological Wellbeing

A Spearman's correlation was conducted with the current data to identify relationships between survey items as a means of cross-validation of research. The correlation coefficients and p values for survey items that reached statistical significance in the survey are presented in Table 14.1.

The matrix in Table 14.1. reveals that participants were significantly likely to have collaborated and co-studied with other students if they have also been able to learn independently (p = 0.000). Perhaps working alone and working with others are behaviours that both involve the same resourcefulness in academic study in challenging conditions. Interestingly, neither working alone nor working with others was found to be related to study motivation (p = 0.304 and p = 0.151, respectively).

The matrix also reveals that feeling motivated to study is strongly and significantly negatively correlated with feelings of isolation and loneliness (p = 0.004), and feelings of depression (p = 0.002) and anxiety (p = 0.040). In other words, participants who were likely to report feeling motivated were unlikely to report isolation, depression and anxiety. This result suggests the importance of mental health in the context at least of our entrepreneurship students. Those students were nascent entrepreneurs

Table 14.1   *Relationships between survey items: cross-validation*

	1	2	3	4	5	6	7	8	9
During remote learning, have you been able to learn independently and engage with your studies?	-								
Have you felt motivated with your studies?	0.167	-							
Was the impact on academic performance a concern for you during lockdown?	0.000	-0.105	-						
Was the impact on opportunities for social interaction a concern for you during lockdown?	0.160	0.053	-0.509[b]	-					
Had you undertaken any online learning prior to lockdown?	0.218	0.145	-0.206	0.454[b]	-				
Have you experienced feelings of loneliness and a lack of social support through remote learning?	-0.167	-0.444[b]	-0.070	-0.053	-0.145	-			
Have you collaborated/ co-studied with other students during remote learning?	0.587[b]	0.231	-0.062	0.316[a]	0.221	-0.231	-		
Have you experienced depression during remote learning?	-0.160	-0.480[b]	0.050	-0.254	-0.361[a]	0.302	-0.026	-	
Have you experienced anxiety during remote learning?	-0.140	-0.327[a]	0.279	-0.142	0.122	0.327[a]	0.157	0.456[b]	-

Notes: [a] $p < 0.05$; [b] $p < 0.01$.

(approximately 70 per cent), who had studied course materials on venture creation but had no direct experience. The balance of the class were novice entrepreneurs with direct or indirect experience of venture creation, for example, typically by observing family entrepreneurs. The entrepreneurship activities of all students in the sample were based on their motivation in venture creation, in thinking through novel and potentially impactful ideas in teams allocated by the class facilitator.

DISCUSSION

Overall, our results suggest that poor motivation and isolation from collegial interaction impacted significantly on the entrepreneurship learning of the sampled students. We go on from our results to suggest that restrictions of physically undertaking entrepreneurial activities on-campus negatively impacted upon the interest in entrepreneurship of a large number of the sampled students. Accordingly, enforced absence from entrepreneurial activities produced a double negative effect on our entrepreneurship students. Firstly, absence from campus activities restricted their learning of entrepreneurial skills and techniques; and secondly, and potentially more gravely in terms of their development as entrepreneurs, the restriction of learning may have had the primary effect of reducing, and possibly extinguishing, an initial spark of curiosity about venture creation among a majority of students with a nascent interest in venture creation.

The second effect of enforced absence from collegial interaction and activities may therefore have reduced the number of novice entrepreneurs from the sampled class. A possible reason for this reduction follows previous studies of entrepreneurship students during economic crises 'cutting the losses' of their shortened, remaining time of their undergraduate degree post-crisis by concentrating instead on core subjects such as marketing, accounting and strategy that under constrained market conditions have provided better opportunities for graduate employment (McMurray et al., 2016).

As expected, the extent to which participants experienced depression during remote learning appears to be strongly and significantly related to the extent to which participants experienced anxiety (p = 0.003). Interestingly, however, experiences of depression were found to be negatively related to prior experience in online learning (p = 0.022). It could be that students who participated in online forms of learning in the past were already familiar with the challenges of this mode of learning, notably the risk of feelings of social isolation, and had strategies or means in place for addressing these challenges. This is reassuring as online learning becomes mainstream, as students begin to recognise the need to source and access additional means for social interaction, other than through their studies.

Furthermore, on the flipside of students reporting depression, a positive, interesting finding from our research is that at least a few entrepreneurship students appear to have sought alternative sources of knowledge to fuel their interest in entrepreneurship. Here, a further proposition could be that the challenges of access to knowledge of venture creation, and the absence of learning based on substantial, face-to-face opportunities for dissemination and discussion on-campus, may have inspired a few students to create their own entrepreneurial activities. For example, while up to four-fifths of our sample said that they experienced loneliness and/or depression, a significant percentage (67.5 per cent) collaborated with peers. As students reported collaborations exclusively in private, indoor settings, it may plausibly be suggested that discussions included ways in which course materials on venture creation could be drawn on to create opportunities out of the pandemic. This conjecture seems plausible, based on the effort that everyone needed to invest during lockdown to organise and prepare for any social activity, which was limited largely to online interaction. Follow-on research would flesh out the nature of opportunities created by a number of students, and the extent to which they sought to 'get ahead' of their entrepreneurship course by actively creating and developing ideas during lockdown, without being passively and negatively affected by their prolonged absence from campus.

It is important to remember here that the key purpose of university education is to facilitate independent thought and action, and as such the degree of scaffolding used for learning has to be proportionate with students' own activities to enable them to choose and develop entrepreneurial skills. Additionally, despite the negative impacts on student wellbeing during the lockdown, our findings also indicated that some of our entrepreneurship students responded to changes in the learning provision with resilience; an essential characteristic of nascent entrepreneurs. Follow-up research of entrepreneurship students in and beyond our research context would ascertain the extent of this resilience now that university campuses have reopened. However, our findings have suggested significant evidence of resilience in the collaborative activities of students during lockdown, where several students may have sought to overcome their sense of loneliness by organising and participating in online activities.

CONCLUSIONS

Overall, the results presented above support and validate research into the links between mental health, opportunities for social interaction and student performance, all of which come with physical access to a university campus. Based on these results, and in concert with the broader literature, the following recommendations can be made.

First, maintain social networking and interaction. Whilst avoiding university closures is beyond the control of universities themselves and of academic staff, continued access to social support networks during remote learning has a significant role to play in attenuating experiences of psychological distress. There is enough online education literature available from the last few decades that can inform academic leads and teaching staff on how to embed social networking opportunities within course structures and learning management systems (Adam, 2020).

Second, facilitate independent and collaborative learning resourcefulness. It appears that some students may have a proficiency in studying effectively when needed, making use of both social and personal resources to maintain motivation and academic engagement. It is certainly the case from the online education literature that some students are more capable of managing the challenges of this mode than others (Roddy et al., 2017). Leaving such differences unattended widens the inequalities that exist across students, and exacerbates the differences that come from diverse groups. Instead, course leaders could facilitate the application of skills and abilities needed for online education success, whether or not these involve effective communication, organisation and time management skills, through carefully considered and explicit learning and teaching practices and strategies. For example, staggered performance deadlines, one-on-one pastoral care provision, collaborative learning tasks and accessible study support resources (Chung and McKenzie, 2020) all aid to create inclusive learning and teaching environments.

Third, build future-focused student emotional resilience. The ability of entrepreneurship students, and young people more broadly, to develop emotional resilience is important. As our world and lifestyles are challenged by the pandemic and future climate crises, current and future generations of entrepreneurs require resilience to demonstrate unwavering pursuit in venture creation. Nascent and novice entrepreneurs, in a trial setting in class, need to overcome barriers to their self-sufficiency such that they can create ventures effectively, often and most powerfully out of severe economic and social challenges. The pandemic has created opportunities for entrepreneurship students to take a close and personal look at how they can draw on their enforced solitude to create opportunities, without merely being cowed into negative conditions of loneliness and depression. The extent to which entrepreneurship students may be able to overcome these conditions may depend upon authentic learning tasks that promote learning by doing.

Questions for Research

A number of interesting and potentially important research questions arise from our preliminary work in this chapter. A prominent question is the extent to which the positive and negative impacts on the education of entrepreneurial students during the pandemic has translated into the wider sector of higher education. An initial means of measuring this impact would simply be to consider the decrease or increase in the number of novice student ventures from the tail end of the post-lockdown onwards, compared with various periods before the lockdown.

For those students who responded to their mental challenges with a perhaps surprising degree of resilience, research could uncover any skills that students may have acquired out of their resilience to the pandemic, and explore how those skills may have assisted the actual process of venture creation.

The pandemic has also raised opportunities for scholarly research of the lockdown's positive and negative impact on higher education students, as we have suggested in our preliminary investigation in this chapter. Our context of entrepreneurship students seems a plausible way to start this international investigation, because of the need for entrepreneurship students to continue acquiring and practising skills outside the classroom with and without face-to-face interaction.

REFERENCES

Adam, E. (2020) No student is an island – students' perspectives of sense of community in online higher education. In S. McKenzie, F. Garivaldis and K. Dyer (eds), *Tertiary*

Online Teaching and Learning: TOTAL Perspectives and Resources for Digital Education (pp. 199–205). Singapore: Springer Nature.

Bisht, R., Jasola, S. and Bisht, I. (2020) Acceptability and challenges of online higher education in the era of COVID-19: a study of student's perspective. *Asian Education and Development Studies.* DOI: https://doi.org/10.1108/AEDS-05-2020-0119.

Boda, Z., Elmer T., Vörös, A. and Stadtfeld, C. (2020) Short-term and long-term effects of a social network intervention on friendships among university students. *Scientific Reports,* 10(2889): 1–12.

Bolatov, A., Seisembekov, T., Askarova, A., Baikanova, R., Smailova, D. and Fabbto, E. (2020) Online-learning due to COVID-19 improved mental health among medical students. *Medical Science Educator,* 31: 183–192.

Cao, W., Fang, Z., Hou, G., Han, M., Xu, X., et al. (2020) The psychological impact of the COVID-19 epidemic on college students in China. *Psychiatry Research,* 287(11298). DOI: 10.1016/j.psychres.2020.112934.

Chaturvedi, K., Vishwakarma, D. and Sing, N. (2020) COVID-19 and its impact on education, social life and mental health of students: a survey. *Children and Youth Services Review,* 121(105866). DOI: 10.1016/j.childyouth.2020.105866.

Chung, J. and McKenzie, S. (2020) Is it time to create a hierarchy of online student needs? In S. McKenzie, F. Garivaldis and K. Dyer (eds), *Tertiary Online Teaching and Learning: TOTAL Perspectives and Resources for Digital Education* (pp. 207–215). Singapore: Springer Nature.

Crawford, J., Butler-Henderson, K., Rudolph, J., Malkawi, B., Glowatz, M., et al. (2020) COVID-19: 20 countries higher education intra-period digital pedagogy responses. *Journal of Applied Learning and Teaching,* 3(1), 1–20.

Debowska, A., Horeczy, B., Boduszek, D. and Dolinski, D. (2020) A repeated cross-sectional survey assessing university students' stress, depression, anxiety, and suicidality in the early stages of the COVID-19 pandemic in Poland. *Psychological Medicine,* 1–4. DOI: 10.1017/S003329172000392X.

Duraku, H. and Hoxha, L. (2020) *The Impact of COVID-19 on Higher Education: A Study of Interaction among Student's Mental Health Attitudes towards Online Learning, Study Skills and Changes in Student's Life.* https://www.researchgate.net/publication/341599684.

Elmer, T., Mepham, K. and Stadtfeld, C. (2020) Students under lockdown: comparisons of students' social networks and mental health before and during the COVID-19 crisis in Switzerland. *PLoS ONE,* 15(7), e0236337. DOI: 10.1371/journal.pone.0236337.

European Union (2020) COVID-19 restriction measures. https://reliefweb.int/map/italy/european-union-covid-19-restriction-measures-dg-echo-daily-map-20042020.

Evans, S., Alkan, E., Bhangoo, J., Tenenbaum, H. and Knight, T. (2021) Effects of the COVID-19 lockdown on mental health, wellbeing, sleep, and alcohol use in a UK student sample. *Psychiatry Research,* 298(113819). DOI: 10.1016/j.psychres.2021.113819.

Faisal, R., Jobe, M., Ahmed, O. and Sharker, T. (2021) Mental health status, anxiety and depression levels of Bangladeshi university students during COVID-19 pandemic. *International Journal of Mental Health and Addiction.* DOI: https://doi.org/10.1007/s11469-020-00458-y.

Fruehwirth, J., Biswas, S. and Perreira, K. (2021) The Covid-19 pandemic and mental health of first-year college students: examining the effect of Covid-19 stressors using longitudinal data. *PLoS ONE,* 16(3), e0247999.

Fu, W., Yan, S., Zong, Q., Anderson-Luxford, D., Song, X., et al. (2021) Mental health of college students during the COVID-19 epidemic in China. *Journal of Affective Disorders,* February, 280(7–10). DOI: 10.1016/j.jad.2020.11.032.

Furrer, C. and Skinner, E. (2003) Sense of relatedness as a factor in children's academic engagement and performance. *Journal of Educational Psychology,* 95(1), 148–163.

Grubic, N., Badovinac, S. and Johri, A. (2020) Student mental health in the midst of the COVID-19 pandemic: a call for further research and immediate solutions. *International Journal of Social Psychiatry*. DOI: https://doi.org/10.1177/0020764020925108.

Higgins, E.T. (1987) Self-discrepancy: a theory relating self and affect. *Psychological Review*, 94, 319–340. DOI:10.1037/0033-295X.94.3.319.

Hill, K. and Fitzgerald, R. (2020) Student perspectives of the impact of COVID-19 on learning. *All Ireland Journal of Higher Education*, 12(2), 1–9.

Hortulanus, R., Machielse, A. and Meeuwesen, L. (2006) *Social Isolation in Modern Society*. London: Routledge.

Karalis, T. and Raikou, N. (2020) Teaching at the times of COVID-19: inferences and implications for higher education pedagogy. *International Journal of Academic Research in Business and Social Sciences*, 10(5), 479–493.

Kawachi, I. and Berkman, L. (2001) Social ties and mental health. *Journal of Urban Health*, 78(3), 458–446.

Kecojevic, A., Basch, C., Sullivan, M. and Davi, N. (2020) The impact of the COVID-19 epidemic on mental health of undergraduate students in New Jersey, cross sectional study. *Plos One*, September. DOI: https://doi.org/10.1371/journal.pone.0239696.

Kelley, S. (2020) Students face pandemic disruption with resilience. https://news.cornell.edu/stories/2020/04/students-face-pandemic-disruption-resilience.

Knutson, B. and Wimmer, G.E. (2007) Reward: neural circuitry for social valuation. In E. Harmon-Jones and P. Winkielman (eds), *Social Neuroscience: Integrating Biological and Psychological Explanations of Social Behavior* (pp. 157–175). New York: Guilford Press.

Laher, S., Bain, K. and Bemath, N. (2021) Undergraduate psychology student experiences during COVID-19: challenges encountered and lessons learnt. *South African Journal of Pscyhology*, March. DOI: 10.1177/0081246321995095.

Lai, A., Lee, L., Wang, M., Feng, Y., Lai, T., et al. (2020) Mental health impacts of the COVID-19 pandemic on international university students, related stressors, and coping strategies. *Frontiers in Psychiatry*, November. DOI: 10.3389/fpsyt.2020.584240.

Liu, Y., Kuo, R. and Shih, S. (2020) COVID-19: the first documented coronavirus pandemic in history. *Biomedical Journal*, 43(4), 328–333.

McMurray, S., Dutton, M., McQuaid, R. and Richard, A. (2016) Employer demands from business graduates. *Education + Training*, 58(1), 112–132.

Mervosh, S., Lu, D. and Swales, V. (2020) See which states and cities have told residents to stay at home. *New York Times*. https://www.nytimes.com/interactive/2020/us/coronavirus-stay-at-home-order.html.

Mikolajczyk, R., Maxwell, A., El Ansari, W., Naydenova, V., Stock, C. and Ilieva, S. (2008) Prevalence of depressive symptoms in university students from Germany, Denmark, Poland, and Bulgaria. *Social Psychiatry and Psychiatric Epidemiology*, 43(2), 105–112.

Mudenda, S., Zulu, A., Phiri, M., Ngazimbi, M., Mufwambi, W., et al. (2020) Impact of coronavirus disease 2019 (Covid-19) on university students: a global health and education problem. *Aquademia*. 4(2), ep20026.

Nania, T., Dellafiore, F. and Caruso, R. (2020) Risk and protective factors for psychological distress among Italian university students during the COVID-19 pandemic: the beneficial role of health engagement. *International Journal of Social Psychiatry*, July. DOI: https://doi.org/10.1177/0020764020945729.

Padron, I., Fraga, I., Vieitez, L., Montes, C. and Romero, E. (2021) A study on the psychological wound of COVID-19 in university students. *Frontiers in Psychology*, January. https://doi.org/10.3389/fpsyg.2021.589927.

Parker, J., Creque, R., Barnhart, D., Harris, J., Majeski, S., et al. (2004) Academic achievement in high school: does emotional intelligence matter? *Personality and Individual Differences*, 37, 1321–1330.

Perets, E., Chabeda, D., Gong, A., Huang, X., Fung, T., et al. (2020) Impact of the emergency transition to remote teaching on student engagement in a non-STEM undergraduate chemistry course in the time of COVID-19. *Journal of Chemical Education*, 97, 2439–2447.

Petillon, R. and McNeil, S. (2020) Student experiences of emergency remote teaching: impacts of instructor practice on student learning, engagement, and well-being. *Journal of Chemical Education*, 97(9), 2486–2493.

Piotrowski, C. and King, C. (2020) COVID-19 pandemic: challenges and implications for higher education. *Education*, 141, 6–66.

Prowse, R., Sherratt, F., Abizaid, A., Gabrys, R., Hellemans, K., et al. (2020) Coping with the COVID-19 pandemic: examining gender differences in stress and mental health among university students. *Frontiers in Psychology*. DOI: https://doi.org/10.3389/fpsyt.2021.650759.

Rajab, M. and Alkattan, K. (2020) Challenges to online medication education during the COVID-19 pandemic. *Cureus*, 12(7), e8966.

Roddy, C., Amiet, D., Chung, J., Holt, C., Shaw, L., et al. (2017) Applying best practice online learning, teaching and support to intensive online environments: an integrative review. *Frontiers in Education*, 2(59). http://doi:10.3389/feduc.2017.00059.

Smith, R. and Khawaja, N. (2011) A review of the acculturation experiences of international students. *International Journal of Intercultural Relations*, 35, 699–713. DOI: 10.1016/j.ijintrel.2011.08.004.

Tambag, H., Turan, Z., Tolun, S. and Can, R. (2018) Perceived social support and depression levels of women in the postpartum period in Hatay. *Nigerian Journal of Clinical Practice*, 21(11), 1525–1530.

Wang, Z., Yang, H., Yang, Y., Liu, D., Li, Z., et al. (2020) Prevalence of anxiety and depression symptom, and the demands for psychological knowledge and interventions in college students during COVID-19 epidemic: a large cross-sectional study. *Journal of Affective Disorders*, 275, 188–193.

Wester, E., Walsh, L., Arango-Caro, S. and Callis-Duehl, K. (2021) Student engagement declines in STEM undergraduates during COVID-19 driven remote learning. *Journal of Microbiology and Biology Education*, 22(1). DOI: 10.1128/jmbe.v22i1.2385.

Young Minds (2020) *Coronavirus: Impact on Young People with Mental Health Needs*. https://youngminds.org.uk/media/3708/coronavirus-report_march2020.pdf.

15. The hidden entrepreneurs: disability and entrepreneurship in Kazakhstan

Shumaila Yousafzai and Yerken Turganbayev

For a disabled person, the most important issue is the social and psychological adaptation to the renewed living conditions in society. While disability is inherent in every society equally, many people are at loss when faced with a person with disabilities, they feel uncomfortable and may even offend them with a careless statement. In public places, disabled people often need help, which again, unknowingly, ordinary people cannot provide them. Every able person needs to know that people with disabilities are a valuable part of our society, and we must make their difficult life easier. The hardest part is not being able to show your potential in a society with limited opportunities. While I have witnessed the success of my fellow disabled entrepreneurs whose lives have changed and they are living up to their full potential, nevertheless, our society is not yet ready to accept people with disabilities. We need to understand that no illness or accident can take away the kindness and warmth in your heart. There is no greater disability in the world than the cruelty of the human heart. After all, it's not our disability but the inability of the environment to accommodate our needs and people's attitudes that make us disabled. We are all members of one society, so we have the right to work, to have access to education, cultural and sports facilities. (*Astana Aqshamy*, 2013: interview with Dina Yerdildinova)

INTRODUCTION

Born into a large working family in the village of Ushkarasu in the Kostanay region of Kazakhstan, Dina Yerdildinova became an award-winning entrepreneur whose story offers a glimpse into the lives of disabled Kazakh entrepreneurs.

After completing high school in her village, Dina went on to pursue her childhood dream of becoming a teacher. In 1997, a spinal injury resulted in permanent disability and Dina had to discontinue her employment. With the aim of raising the status of disabled people like herself, Dina and a group of like-minded people founded an organization, Dos Centre for Independent Living, in 2005. In 2011, she started her first entrepreneurial venture through a limited liability partnership, a wheelchair repair centre called Tauelsizdik-D. Dina's idea was to use the income from this entrepreneurial venture to further the cause of disabled people, and today the partnership has licences and its own permanent professional partners. Dina's journey resonates with optimism and enthusiasm about the potential lying dormant in the disabled population of Kazakhstan. Her journey also describes the need for a changing attitude in Kazakhstan's non-disabled population, respect for people with disabilities (PWD), and encouragement for them to move away from the margins and become part of mainstream economic activity.

The United Nations Convention on the Rights of Persons with Disabilities (UNCRPD), established on 13 December 2006, is recognized as one of the most comprehensive human rights treaties in terms of putting disability back on the international agenda, even if it does not always result in enhancing the lives of PWD (Duell-Piening, 2018; Williams et al., 2018). Article 27 of the UNCRPD, which addresses work and employment, is arguably one of its most impactful components for PWD because the opportunity to earn a living in an environment that is open, inclusive and accessible enriches their independence and participation as valued members of society. Among other things, Article 27 calls for promoting opportunities for self-employment, entrepreneurship and the development of co-operatives for PWD. In addition, Sustainable Development Goal (SDG) 8 calls for promoting sustainable and inclusive economic growth, with productive employment and decent work for all.

Constituting one of the world's largest minority groups, with population assessments surpassing 1 billion people – about 15 per cent of the world's population – PWD are globally disadvantaged both socially and economically, experiencing significantly lower educational attainment than persons without disabilities, along with poorer health, higher rates of unemployment and poverty, and limited opportunities to participate in social and political life (WHO, 2021). Addressing the occupational and social needs of this group is a public policy and managerial concern of global significance.

In the wake of the break-up of the Soviet Union in 1991, Kazakhstan declared itself an independent republic with a goal of progressing towards joining the world's 30 most developed economies by 2050. Kazakhstan was among the first signatories of the UNCRPD; an expression of its enthusiasm for following the basic principles of international policy on PWD. The UNCRPD enacts for its signatory states a number of commitments to ensure the fulfilment of the rights of PWD. In January 2015, Kazakhstan ratified the UNCRPD as part of the Kedergisiz Keleshek (Future without Barriers) programme, which was launched by the ruling Nur Otan party to ensure accessibility and equality for its PWD (*Astana Times*, 2013). Since its inception, the constitution of Kazakhstan has ensured that every citizen, including PWD in any disability group, has equitable access to work and the same rights as able citizens do, and that no discrimination is imposed on the basis of disability (Ministry of Justice, 2015). Furthermore, since the ratification of the UNCRPD, Kazakhstan's government and civil society have striven to bring the country's regulations closer to the required standards, and to provide an equitable and inclusive environment for its PWD. According to Birzhan Nurymbetov, Minister of Labor and Social Protection of Population, 'Ensuring the rights and social protection of persons with disabilities is one of the most important tasks in the activities of the government' (www .primeminister.kz, 2020). For example, Kazakhstan's National Plan 2025 aims to ensure the rights of PWD by focusing on seven areas: disability prevention, access to inclusive education opportunities, providing accessible infrastructure and eliminating physical barriers, employment, effective rehabilitation, social services, and raising public awareness of and positive attitudes towards PWD.

Nevertheless, ratification and the National Plan 2025 has had little impact so far on the everyday lives of PWD in Kazakhstan. For example, 12.6 per cent of Kazakh children with disabilities still lack access to proper education and are home-schooled (*Astana Times*, 2018). The UN Special Rapporteur on the Rights of PWD, Catalina Devandas, highlighted that the country's efforts to include PWD in the educational system are still at the pilot stage and need to be scaled up (UN, 2018). Highlighting the need for the civil society and non-governmental organizations to join hands with the government, Zhadrasyn Saduakassov, an expert at the Kazakhstan Confederation of Disabled People, notes:

> The realization of Kedergisiz Keleshek can potentially have a profound impact on the lives of PWD in Kazakhstan. The ratification of [the UNCRPD] can be the start of a new era of real action. In this journey a great deal of onus rests on nongovernmental organizations, including the Confederation of Disabled People. We need new research on disability issues and investments to sustain prevailing initiatives to provide inclusive, equitable and accessible vocational options for PWD. (cited in Witte, 2017)

This chapter reports on the progress towards inclusion and the challenges faced by entrepreneurs with disability (EWD) in Kazakhstan, a nation that aspires to develop while using expertise from the former Soviet Union period. The chapter provides an analysis of the country's readiness for an inclusive environment for EWD. The narratives provided suggest that, despite impediments to their full participation, Kazakh EWD not only empower themselves but also extend the benefits of their entrepreneurial activity to the wider society. Therefore, obstacles confronted by PWD are disadvantageous to society as a whole, and equitable inclusion is central to the country's ability to realize the goal of growth and prosperity for all.

DEFINING DISABILITY

Disability is a multifaceted phenomenon that describes an interaction between a person's body and the society in which they operate. In its simplest form, disability refers to the imposition of restrictions on an individual's physical or mental impairment that substantially limits one or more major life activities, as a result of which the individual is excluded from participation in the society (ADA, 1990). The World Health Organization (WHO) refers to disability as 'the negative aspects of the interaction between an individual (with a health condition) and that individual's contextual factors (environmental and personal factors)' (WHO, 2001: 213).

In the disability literature, the definitions of disability are shaped by two contrasting ideologies. The medical model of disability associates disability with individuals and their impairment, and the resulting limitations that prevent them from participating in the economy as people without impairments do (Oliver, 1996). For example, historically, in the Soviet bloc, most PWD were unseen and not assimilated into the society, and a stigma about the inabilities of PWD persisted (Dunn and Dunn, 1989). Disabled children and adults were rarely seen in public. They had minimal contact with the outside world, as either they were dispatched to special schools or institutions, or physical obstacles precluded them from going outside their homes. A well-known incident centres on the reply from the Soviet Olympic representative when he was asked whether the United Socialist Soviet Republic (USSR) would take part in the first Paralympic Games: 'There are no invalids in the USSR' (Fefelov, 1986). With the term 'disability' legislatively tied to incompetence, and the amount of social payments contingent on the category of the disability, the USSR government's policy towards PWD focused on assistance, but not reintegration and adjustment (McCagg and Siegelbaum, 1989).

Under the socialist system, it was a common belief that disability can be 'prevented' by medical treatment. The medical model and charitable ideology shaped the Commonwealth of Independent States (CIS) countries' legislation, policies and programmes for PWD. For instance, even today, in the official policy of Kazakhstan, the term 'disabled' does not refer to the barriers that limit the ability of PWD to participate fully and effectively in society on an equal basis with others; instead, it focuses on using medical terms with negative connotations that refer to physical disorders of the human body (injury, defects). Such a mentality degrades dignity and contributes to a 'charitable' approach towards PWD, rather than an inclusive, equitable and human rights-based approach.

In contrast to the medical model, the social model of disability contends that an individual being disabled is the result of the society, rather than the individual person or that person's impairment (Oliver and Barnes, 2006). According to this view, the society is considered to have failed in its responsibility for including individuals with impairment, thus rendering them disabled. According to Oliver (1996: 33), 'disability is all the things that impose restrictions on disabled people; ranging from individual prejudice to institutional discrimination, from inaccessible buildings to unusable transport systems, from segregated education to excluding work arrangements, and so on'.

The major distinction between the two schools of thought – medical and social – rests on the extent to which disability is defined in terms of being internal to the individual, or external as a result of the environment in which they operate. In the medical model of disability, an individual is termed disabled as a result of internal factors, such as personal impairment, which prevent the individual from participating in the usual activities of the economy. The social model, on the other hand, explains the onset of disability as being the result of external factors, including the society, that are responsible for the social and economic wellbeing of the impaired individual: deficiencies in the society such as barriers to inclusion of individuals with certain impairments, negative attitudes and discrimination in the society towards individuals with impairments, and policies that fail to promote inclusion of individuals with impairments in the economy.

STATUS OF PEOPLE WITH DISABILITY IN KAZAKHSTAN

In Kazakhstan, approximately 4 per cent of the population (696 464 people) are registered as PWD, 56 per cent of whom are male, and 94 000 of whom are children under age 18 (Committee on Statistics of the Ministry of National Economy of Republic of Kazakhstan, www.inva.gov.kz). Following the USSR's system of categorizing PWD, Kazakhstan classifies disabilities according to the severity of impairment (Phillips, 2009). Disability statistics in Kazakhstan are carried out in the context of three categories: age (disabled children under 16 years old, disabled since childhood, disabled children from 16 to 18 years old, and disabled adults), sex (men and women) and residence (urban and rural). This practice is not in line with the WHO's principles of the International Classification of Functioning, Disabilities and Health (ICF), where functioning and disability are understood as a dynamic interaction of an individual's personal health condition with environmental and contextual factors (WHO, 2021). The United Nations (UN) convention Article 1 defines persons with disabilities as those who have long-term physical, mental, intellectual or sensory impairments that, in interaction with various barriers, may hinder their full and effective participation in society on an equal basis with others (UNCRPD, 2006). The difference between the definitions of 'disabled' and 'disability' in the Convention on the Rights of Persons with Disabilities (UNCRPD) and the law of Kazakhstan on the protection of the rights of PWD demonstrates the conceptual difference in approaches to the perception of PWD and attitudes towards disability.

Individuals who have a disability tend to feel oppressed, and secluded from the rest of the society, including the labour market. According to Kazakhstan's Ministry of Labor, in 2018 most of the 1609 university graduates with various degrees of disability experienced difficulties in finding work opportunities (UNDP, 2021). In Kazakhstan, approximately 2.5 per cent of PWD are of working age, but only a quarter of them are employed, and most PWD work in temporary jobs with no stable earnings or social protection (UNDP, 2021). While these figures are comparable to the figures from the United States, where 17.9 per cent of PWD were employed in 2020 (DOL, 2021), they are significantly lower than the average in Organisation for Economic Co-operation and Development (OECD) countries, where the figure is 40 per cent or more. In industrialized countries, 50–70 per cent of PWD of working age are employed (UN, 2021).

The reasons for high unemployment rates among PWD can be attributed both to personal preferences to remain unemployed, and to social and economic barriers and stigmatization, leading to low self-image (Ashley and Graf, 2018; Link and Phelan, 2001). PWD face challenges not only as a result of their impairment but also from the broader environment in which they operate. For example, about 80 per cent of facilities in Kazakhstan are inaccessible to PWD, and 20 per cent can be considered only partially accessible (CABAR, 2021). According to Miras Irgebayev, official representative of the Foundation for the Development of Social Projects Samruk-Kazyna Trust:

people with disabilities are often dependent on circumstances. Due to the lack of ramps, elevators, sign language interpreters and other necessary conditions, many people are forced to self-isolate and close themselves off from society. But they have the same potential, and most of them want to work and be free in financial terms. (cited in CABAR, 2021)

The President of Kazakhstan, Kassym-Jomart Tokayev, acknowledged that the accessibility of infrastructure in Kazakhstan is unacceptable:

We even introduced the administrative liability for non-compliance with accessibility requirements, but the current standards are still being violated everywhere. In practice, people with limited mobility do not always have an opportunity to leave their home and go outside on their own, not to mention to get to any facility and move around inside. This alarming and unacceptable situation needs to be urgently changed. (Fifth meeting of the National Council of Public Trust on 25 February 2021. (cited in CABAR, 2021)

DISABILITY AND ENTREPRENEURSHIP IN THE CONTEXT OF KAZAKHSTAN'S ENTREPRENEURIAL ECOSYSTEM

Entrepreneurship, an 'economic panacea' (Anderson et al., 2009), is viewed as an engine for the growth and development of a healthy economy (Swedberg, 2000). One of the ways PWD have countered their limited occupational opportunities is through entrepreneurship (Pagán-Rodríguez, 2012). Entrepreneurship can be a significant source of income and wealth creation for PWD, enabling them to support and maintain themselves, and making them a self-sufficient and productive part of economic progress (Anderson and Galloway, 2012; Baldridge and Neubaum, 2008; Harris et al., 2013, 2014). Entrepreneurship also offers advantages such as accommodation of impairment-related requirements and a flexible working schedule (Jones and Latreille, 2011; Schur, 2003); greater independence, range of choices and level of self-determination (Anderson and Galloway, 2012; Lorenzo and Motau, 2014); and more job satisfaction (Pagán-Rodríguez, 2015). Nevertheless, research suggests that PWD face greater challenges in accessing such key resources as informational, financial, institutional, training, business and social support for their business start-ups, and entrepreneurial activities and initiatives for PWD are still lagging behind those of other people because of discouraging governmental financial structures (Hwang and Roulstone, 2015; Renko et al., 2016), lack of support from vocational rehabilitation counsellors (Ashley and Graf, 2018; Halabisky, 2014), inaccessibility of the built business enterprise environment (Vick and Lightman, 2010), and discrimination from suppliers, customers, and financial and formal institutions (Jones and Latreille, 2011; Pagán-Rodríguez, 2015). Therefore, although entrepreneurship could be a route to achieving self-sufficiency, security and empowerment for PWD (Harris et al., 2014), rates of entrepreneurship among PWD remain low.

The entrepreneurial ecosystem (EES), a framework that connects entrepreneurship and disability research, is a model for gauging an environment's entrepreneurial activity. Isenberg (2011) and the World Economic Forum (WEF, 2013) define EES as constituting six factors: facilitating policies, a conducive culture, availability of finance, the acquisition and development of human capital, market opportunities and access, and institutional and infrastructural support. The EES establishes the social structure's position in allowing and restricting entrepreneurship with the implicit assumption that everyone has impartial access to opportunities and support, and a fair chance of prospering. However, access varies across contexts, particularly for PWD, who face more barriers to acquiring resources than their non-disabled counterparts do. While such an ecosystem may be supportive of non-disabled entrepreneurs, exploring the validity of the framework and its individual domains for disabled individuals may reveal rich insights into the mechanisms that hinder entrepreneurial activity in PWD. For example, even when PWD have viable entrepreneurial ideas or the intention to start a business of their own, the tools for testing and implementing the idea are seldom available and accessible (Shaheen, 2016).

To describe the life of entrepreneurs with disabilities in the context of Kazakhstan's EES, we present narratives from two Kazakh EWD. Theses narratives are based on interviews published in Kursiv.kz by Lonkina (2021), and an article in informburo. kz by Ruzmatova (2017).

BOX 15.1 BIRZHAN KUZHAKOV FROM URALSK, KAZAKHSTAN

In February 2001, at the age of 30, Birzhan lost his legs during his shift as a highway police officer in Uralsk when, on a freezing evening with temperatures at -40, the electricity went out in his guard trailer, along with the only source of heat. He could not leave his post and had to wait for the shift change. He lost his legs to frostbite, but did not lose hope, courage or perseverance. Birzhan is the founder of a company called Gibadat, which manufactures furniture and home decor in ethnic Kazakh style. His company also manufactures medical standing frames for children with Down's syndrome and cerebral palsy. This narrative highlights Birzhan's valuable contribution to society, to his business and to the disabled people in Kazakhstan. Birzhan's narrative is a testament to the research which suggests that entrepreneurship undertaken by the disabled creates 'shared value', entailing not only economic value but also social value (Porter and Kramer, 2011). For disabled entrepreneurs, social value constitutes the individual and collective wellbeing derived from the business activity they create in response to the unsatisfied needs of a large segment of the population (Austin et al., 2006).

After Birzhan's accident, his brother gave him an old piece of furniture from which he built a small locker, which he sold immediately. This experience made him think, 'Aha! I'll be a furniture maker.' In 2002, after registering his furniture business, Birzhan got his first major order to build beds, lockers and seats for a dormitory in a workers' camp. With the US$1331 he earned from that order, he bought new machine tools. At the same time, his funding proposal to a business incubator run by a local oil company was successful, and he was granted a free space in which to expand his product line with small kitchen tools in ethnic Kazakh style. While the space assisted him in sustaining his business, it still was not profitable. He knew he needed a big order, so he approached the city's *Akim* (Mayor) and offered to make furniture for him. Initially, the *Akim* was uncertain that he could rely on Birzhan's ability to deliver the order, but the *Akim* gave Birzhan a trial order and was satisfied with the product he delivered. From that time on, Birzhan did not look back, and has been delivering furniture to satisfied clients in schools, kindergartens and dormitories. Eventually, Gibadat furniture became renowned for its excellent artisanship and design throughout the region, including in Uralsk, Atyrau, Aktobe and Mangystau.

In his interview, Birzhan noted that it had been almost impossible for a PWD to find a job several years before. However, since the adoption of new laws, every organization is required to employ PWD. Birzhan proudly notes that, 'I hired disabled people long before it became a law. I know very well that invalids cannot survive without a job.' Birzhan currently provides employment to 35 people, 21 of whom are disabled.

Birzhan is also pleased with how his business is serving PWD through his products: 'When I met a mother of a child with cerebral palsy, I learned that this type of disability requires a standing frame called a verticalizer to help the disabled child sit and stand.'

After doing some research, Birzhan found that a verticalizer imported from Russia costs around $3400, so he decided to produce them on his own. After examining the various components of Russian-made verticalizers and consulting with orthopaedists, he made a version that cost only $280. Even then he decided to donate most of the verticalizers to the poor and needy. As a result, 75 per cent of the children with cerebral palsy in Uralsk have verticalizers, and the others are waiting for them.

The unavailability of external finance is a major barrier for EWD. Like other EWD, Birzhan faced greater difficulty than his non-disabled counterparts in accessing financing for his business. Barriers such as lack of collateral, discrimination in lending practices, and perceptions of their businesses as inferior are some of the hurdles that Birzhan faced in his journey. These challenges become pressing because of the perception in society that disability is an inability of the mind and therefore an inability to perform any productive activity in life. As Birzhan noted:

> It is not an easy task to establish and grow a business without financial leverage. In all these years, I have not received any assistance from the government except for a grant from the Damu Foundation, from which I acquired a laser machine for my business. EWD like me cannot rely on financial loans from commercial banks since they avoid lending to PWD because a court would support the disabled person, not the commercial bank, in any dispute.

The COVID-19 pandemic hit his business hard, and he had to lay off some of his employees. In spring 2021 he succeeded in a bid to manufacture furniture for a school, but the unexpected 50 per cent increase in the price of materials meant that he had to complete that order with almost no profit. Nevertheless, he is optimistic:

> I will bring life back to my business and extend the product line. If PWD like me were successful in securing a loan for their businesses, it would be wonderful, but I have come to realize that there are no exemptions for entrepreneurs with disabilities in Kazakhstan. Even if you have no legs, you should work as any other healthy man does because a customer needs a result. I do not mind working with no benefits, but I don't want additional obstacles, and there are a lot of obstacles for PWD in Kazakhstan.

BOX 15.2   ABLAIKHAN ASYLBAY FROM SEMEY, KAZAKHSTAN

In 1997, Abylaikhan Asylbay sustained severe injuries and was placed in Group 1 of disability, as the result of an accident with a construction crane in Semey. Despite the doctor's negative verdict, Abylaikhan was adamant that he would never use a wheelchair. During his recovery, he was thinking about his future career plans when he saw a programme about Darkembay Chokparov, a famous Kazakh expert in traditional crafts. For the next several years, Abylaikhan trained with the master. Then he started making archery equipment and jewellery from bones, leather, wood and metal. Over the next 20 years, he perfected his skills so much that his work was exhibited at the 2017 Astana Expo.

Despite his disability, Abylaikhan showed that, through entrepreneurship, he could not only support his family financially and be prosperous, but also fight for the rights of all Kazakhstanis with disabilities. Abylaikhan noted that, 'It is very difficult for a disabled person in our country to break through, both in business and in everyday life. It is different in big cities such as Almaty and Astana, where invalids are respected, but in other regions they are completely forgotten.'

Abylaikhan is a fierce supporter of uplifting the living standards for PWD in Kazakhstan. In his own capacity, he is providing valuable skill training to children with hearing impairments from a local boarding school. He notes:

> We are not invited to any meetings; they don't provide any help. I have long dreamed of opening a large workshop and teaching people like me, disabled people, so they do not sit at home but benefit society. Without help, I cannot do this. I turned to the akimat and to the deputies, but there's no point. They only promised, but they didn't do anything.

Social Support and Cultural Factors in the EES

A conducive EES is critical to encouraging PWD to become financially independent through entrepreneurship. As is evident from Abylaikhan's and Birzhan's narratives, a significant factor in the empowerment of PWD is their social support ecosystem: that is, the involvement of family, friends and professional networks in motivating

PWD not to think of their disabilities, but of their opportunities. Beyond support from family, friends and their business networks, another key factor in determining entrepreneurial participation by PWD is their cultural ecosystem.

As Alexandra Sharonova, accessibility expert and co-author of a report titled 'The Accessible Kazakhstan Project', notes, Kazakhstan society's views towards disability are changing: 'Now, the society understands that disability is not a medical problem but a social problem. If there were no barriers for people with disabilities, they could independently move around in public spaces, receive information, and do whatever they want' (CABAR, 2021).

Similarly, Zhadrasyn Saduakassov, an expert at the Kazakhstan Confederation of Disabled People, notes:

> I remember that before when I used to go to work there were these six stairs in front of me that I needed to climb with my wheelchair, and nobody would try to help me. While people of older generations still avoid us, the younger generation is different. They are not afraid to extend their help. The situation is beginning to change, and the attitude of ordinary people towards disabled persons is improving. (cited in Witte, 2017)

In 2008, to acknowledge PWD who are playing an active role in Kazakhstan's society, Zhanat Omarbekova, President of the Kazakhstan Confederation of Disabled People, initiated a yearly international award called Zhan Shuak. Describing her organization's role in changing people's attitude towards PWD, Zhanat observes:

> Attitudes are slowly changing. Today in Kazakhstan, people with disabilities lead an active social life and participate in events such as talks on making amendments to legislation concerning the position of people with disabilities in the society. However, we are making only the first steps, and we cannot say we have changed the situation completely. Kazakhstan's disabled population has been slowly coming out of hiding since independence. I think the point is that people see us through the media. (cited in Witte, 2017)

Lyazzat Kaltayeva, head of the Shyrak Association of Women with Disabilities, notes that, even in terms of infrastructure, attitude and inclusivity matter: 'The installation of ramps alone will not solve the problem. We need to cultivate a tolerant attitude towards people with disabilities from childhood. In doing so, maybe construction developers in pursuit of profit and deadlines will not overlook the needs of the disabled' (*Astana Times*, 2013).

Policy Factors in the EES

Ratification of the UNCRPD requires the signatory countries to revise their national legislation to come into line with the provisions of the convention. In October 2021, Kazakhstan announced the National Project for the Development of Entrepreneurship for 2021–2025 (primeminister.kz, 2021). One of the aims of this project is to increase the entrepreneurial activity among PWD by providing grants to citizens who are in socially vulnerable groups. In addition, within the framework of the task, 'Supporting entrepreneurs through the organization of subsidized jobs and the development of skills for the needs of entrepreneurs', Kazakhstan's government plans to subsidize 60 000 EWD by 2025 (primeminister.kz, 2021).

Currently, the Tax Code of the Republic of Kazakhstan provides for significant benefits that encourage PWD to engage in entrepreneurship and encourage employers to employ PWD (Tax Code, 2017). According to the Tax Code, enterprises of disabled people are defined as organizations in which the number of employed PWD for the tax period is at least 51 per cent of the total number of employees, and the cost of remuneration of disabled people for the tax period is at least 51 per cent of the total cost of wages. The benefits for such employers include a reduction in the taxable income of the enterprise; a reduction in corporate income tax; exemption from value-added tax on the sale by public associations of PWD of most types of goods, works, and services; exemption from excise taxes on passenger cars specially designed for PWD; a reduction in social tax for organizations that employ PWD with musculoskeletal disorders, loss of hearing, speech, or vision; and exemption from land tax and payment of state duties and property registration fees (Tax Code, 2017). Furthermore, PWD themselves have personal benefits for various types of taxes and payments (income tax, transport tax, land tax, property tax). In addition, the law on public procurement provides for the possibility of purchasing goods and services from a single source (that is, without competition) if the goods, works and services are purchased from public associations of PWD or organizations created by public associations of PWD (Public Procurement Law, 2015). Table 15.1 summarizes the policy initiatives by the government and non-governmental institutions in support of entrepreneurial activities of PWD in Kazakhstan.

With initiatives such as those listed in Table 15.1, it is evident that Kazakhstan's government understands the urgency in directly assisting PWD in their entrepreneurial activities. In June 2021, the government took a broader perspective by introducing the Law on Social Entrepreneurship, through which social enterprises in Kazakhstan will receive state support such as provision of infrastructure, grant financing, subsidized loan rates, property support, tax incentives, training and information support, and assistance in finding business partners and developing through acceleration programmes (inform.kz, 2021; Social Entrepreneurship Law, 2021). To obtain the status of a social enterprise, the business must fulfil one of several prerequisites: create high-quality jobs for socially vulnerable categories of citizens by employing PWD to at least 50 per cent of the total number of employees; produce goods intended for socially vulnerable segments of the population, the income from the sale of which must be at least 50 per cent of the total income of the enterprise; or provide social services and services in the fields of healthcare, education, upbringing, culture and sports. The Ministry of National Economy and a regional commission will administer and determine the legitimacy of these social enterprises.

Table 15.1   *Policy initiatives by government and non-governmental institutions in support of entrepreneurial activities of PWD in Kazakhstan*

No.	Initiator	Policy document (Year of adoption)	Initiatives for entrepreneurs with disabilities
1.	Government	Law on Social Protection of Disabled People (2005)	Creation of additional jobs for PWD through the development of individual and small and medium-sized businesses as one of the measures to ensure their employment.
	Government	United Nations Convention for the Rights of Disabled People (2008)	Kazakhstan became a signatory of the Convention on the Rights of Persons with Disabilities and its Optional Protocol on 11 December 2008. In doing so, Kazakhstan demonstrated its commitment to introducing human rights-based reforms in the domain of disabilities, reflecting the principles of dignity, full and equitable involvement, and accessibility for its citizens with disabilities.
2.	Nur-Otan Party	Kedergisiz Keleshek (Future without Barriers) Program (2013)	Supporting PWD in terms of creating conditions for inclusive education, employment, as well as maximum coverage of available infrastructure.
3.	Better Lives for People with Disabilities Project	Entrepreneurship Development Fund DAMU (2014)	Program launched in collaboration with the Shyrak Association of Women with Disabilities and BG international Ltd.
4.	Government	Public Procurement Law (2015)	Possibility of purchasing goods and services from a single source (without competition) if the goods, works and services are purchased from public associations of PWD and/or organizations created by public associations of PWD.
5.	Business Road Map (BRM) 2025	Entrepreneurship Development Fund DAMU – Komek Program (2017)	Creation of conditions that encourage PWD to conduct entrepreneurial activities as the basis of material wellbeing and professional growth. Assistance in improving the qualifications of disabled entrepreneurs through distance business training. Its website offers a video tutorial about the basics of running your own business, distance access to entrepreneurial training programmes and a section on laws, regulations and incentives for EWDs. The website also contains an online bulletin board that helps to connect PWD who need help in starting or running a business with sponsors who can provide financing, equipment and other resources for the business. DAMU works closely with the associations for PWD to promote the website to potential entrepreneurs. In 2018, the website received 2431 requests for help from EWD and found sponsors for 2068 requests. The sponsorships included providing sewing equipment, computers and office equipment, and equipment for shoemaking and furniture production.

No.	Initiator	Policy document (Year of adoption)	Initiatives for entrepreneurs with disabilities
6.	Government	Tax Code (2017)	Reduction in the taxable income of an enterprise.
			Reduction in corporate income tax.
			Exemption from value-added tax on the sale of most types of goods, works and services by public associations of disabled people.
			Exemption from excise taxes on passenger cars specially designed for disabled people.
			A reduction in social tax for organizations that employ PWD with musculoskeletal disorders or loss of hearing, speech and vision.
			Exemption from land tax and payment of state duties and property registration fees.
			Personal benefits for disabled people on income, transport, land and property taxes.
7.	Government	National Plan 2025 (2021)	Disability prevention.
			Access to inclusive education opportunities.
			Providing accessible infrastructure and eliminating physical barriers.
			Employment.
			Effective rehabilitation.
			Social services.
			Raising public awareness of and positive attitudes toward PWD.
8.	Government	Social Entrepreneurship Law (2021)	Infrastructure provision.
			Grant financing.
			Subsidized loan rates.
			Property support.
			Training and information support.
			Assistance in finding business partners.
			Acceleration programmes.
9.	Government	National Project for the Development of Entrepreneurship for 2021–2025 (2021) (primeminister.kz, 2021)	Grants to citizens from socially vulnerable groups. Organization of subsidized jobs and the development of skills for the needs of entrepreneurs (60 000 people in 5 years).
10.	Government	National Project 'Quality Education' Educated Nation	Creating conditions for inclusive education in schools and institutions of higher education.

THE WAY FORWARD

While research and information on policy support for EWD in Kazakhstan is limited in terms of the information available on the initiatives and the economic and social impact of such support programmes, the information provided in this chapter and the narratives of Kazakh entrepreneurs with disabilities show a clear recognition in

Kazakhstan of the potential for entrepreneurship among PWD. Kazakhstan's government has initiated and implemented several policies to support entrepreneurial activity among PWD, but gaps in the scope of the support provided to EWD remain. Being a PWD or EWD in Kazakhstan still means significant hardship in terms of physical infrastructure, access to education, training, finance, and other social and psychological barriers. In Kazakhstan's public spaces and workspaces, one rarely encounters a person in a wheelchair, with a white cane, with a guide dog, or with Down's syndrome or cerebral palsy.

Although some support is available, comparatively few people use it, and funding for EWD relies largely on negotiating separate agreements with banks for charitable contributions. EWD would benefit if publicly funded information services and support, online and offline, are made more accessible and visible. In addition, a strengthened set of entrepreneurship support initiatives should be considered for PWD. Furthermore, loan financing is offered to this group of entrepreneurs, although they are likely to face difficulty in accessing formal financing channels. Financial institutions should support PWD initiatives that promote sustainable social inclusiveness and entrepreneurship through affordable credit.

Attention should also be paid to ensuring that potential EWD get access to mainstream entrepreneurship support by, for example, ensuring that the frontline staff in entrepreneurship support centres are sensitive to the needs of EWD and offer them adapted support and services. Institutions of higher education, vocational training colleges and schools can offer training and education to improve entrepreneurial knowledge among PWD. For example, these institutions offer no PWD-focused entrepreneurship training courses, and the support for EWD does not include financing. In general, the initiatives reported in Table 15.1 do not provide integrated packages of support that combine skill development, advice and mentoring, access to finances, and networking, all of which could increase their effectiveness. In addition, a range of dedicated mentoring and training services could be developed for EWD, and sensitivity training could be provided to staff on how to adapt mainstream business advisory and other services to serve the specific needs of EWD. Finally, there is a need to improve institutions' capabilities with respect to entrepreneurship, disability, and inclusion to motivate and inspire PWD to choose an entrepreneurial career.

REFERENCES

ADA (1990). Americans with Disability Act. Available at: https://adata.org/learn-about-ada. Last accessed: November 2021.

Anderson, A.R., Drakopoulou Dodd, S. and Jack, S.L. (2009). Aggressors; winners; victims and outsiders, European schools' social construction of the entrepreneur. *International Small Business Journal*, 27(1): 126–136.

Anderson, M. and Galloway, L. (2012). The value of enterprise for disabled people. *Entrepreneurship and Innovation*, 13(2): 93–101.

Ashley, D. and Graf, N.M. (2018). The process and experiences of self-employment among people with disabilities: a qualitative study. *Rehabilitation Counseling Bulletin*, 61(2): 90–100. doi:10.1177/0034355216687712.

Astana Aqshamy (2013). Interview with Dina Erdildinova, 'The warmth of the heart is enough for everyone.' Available at: https://www.astana-akshamy.kz/zhurek-zhyluy-barine-zhetedi/ & https://best-people.info/medicine/47-erdildinova-dina.html. Last accessed: November 2021.

Astana Times (2013). Gov't seeks ways to support citizens with disabilities. Available at: https://astanatimes.com/2013/06/govt-seeks-ways-to-support-citizens-with-disabilities/. Last accessed: November 2021.

Astana Times (2018). Kazakhstan develops new national plan for people with disabilities. Available at: https://astanatimes.com/2018/10/kazakhstan-develops-new-national-plan-for -people-with-disabilities/. Last accessed: November 2021.

Austin, J., Stevenson, H. and Wei– Skillern, J. (2006). Social and commercial entrepreneurship: same, different, or both? *Entrepreneurship Theory and Practice*, 30(1): 1–22.

Baldridge, D.C. and Neubaum, D. (2008). A model of entrepreneurial intentions within the persons with disabilities population. *Frontiers of Entrepreneurship Research*, 28(5).

CABAR (2021). How accessible is Kazakhstan for people with disabilities? Available at: https://cabar.asia/en/how-accessible-is-kazakhstan-for-people-with-disabilities. Last accessed: November 2021.

DOL (2021). Disability Employment Statistics. Available at: https://www.dol.gov/agencies/ odep/research-evaluation/statistics. Last accessed: December 2021.

Duell-Piening, P. (2018). Refugee resettlement and the Convention on the Rights of Persons with Disabilities. *Disability and Society*, 33(5): 661–684.

Dunn, Stephen P. and Dunn, Ethel (1989). Everyday life of people with disabilities in the USSR. In William O. McCagg and Lewis Siegelbaum (eds), *People with Disabilities in the Soviet Union: Past and Present, Theory and Practice* (pp. 199–234). Pittsburgh: University of Pittsburgh Press.

Fefelov, Valerii (1986). V SSSR invalidov net! (There are no invalids in the USSR!) London: Overseas Publications Interchange.

Halabisky, D. (2014). Entrepreneurial activities in Europe – Entrepreneurship for people with disabilities. *OECD Employment Policy Papers*, No. 6, OECD Publishing, Paris. http://dx .doi.org/10.1787/5jxrcmkcxjq4-en.

Harris, S.P., Renko, M. and Caldwell, K. (2013). Accessing social entrepreneurship: perspectives of people with disabilities and key stakeholders. *Journal of Vocational Rehabilitation*, 38(1): 35–48.

Harris, S.P., Renko, M. and Caldwell, K. (2014). Social entrepreneurship as an employment pathway for people with disabilities: exploring political-economic and socio-cultural factors. *Disability and Society*, 29(8): 1275–1290.

Hwang, S.K. and Roulstone, A. (2015). Enterprising? Disabled? The status and potential for disabled people's microenterprise in South Korea. *Disability & Society*, 30(1): 114–129.

inform.kz (2021). *A Helping Hand: The Role of Social Entrepreneurship in Creating an Inclusive Society in Kazakhstan* (in Russian). Available at: https://www.inform.kz/ru/ article/3853151. Last accessed: November 2021.

Isenberg, D. (2011). The entrepreneurship ecosystem strategy as a new paradigm for economic policy: principles for cultivating entrepreneurship. Institute of International and European Affairs, Dublin, Ireland, 12 May, 1–13.

Jones, M. and Latreille, P. (2011). Disability and self-employment: evidence for the UK. *Applied Economics*, 43(27): 4161–4178.

Law on Social Protection of Disabled People (2005). Law of the Republic of Kazakhstan 'On Social Protection of Disabled People in the Republic of Kazakhstan', no. 39. Available at: https://adilet.zan.kz/rus/docs/Z050000039_. Last accessed: November 2021.

Link, G. and Phelan, C. (2001). Conceptualizing stigma. *Annual Review of Sociology*, 27: 363–385.

Lonkina, E. (2021). How a man with disabilities built his own business in Uralsk. Available at: https://kursiv.kz/en/news/biznes/2021-09/how-man-disabilities-built-his-own-business-uralsk. Last accessed: November 2021.

Lorenzo, T. and Motau, J. (2014). A transect walk to establish opportunities and challenges for youth with disabilities in Winterveldt, South Africa. *Disability, CBR & Inclusive Development*, 25(3): 45–63.

McCagg, William O. and Siegelbaum, Lewis (eds) (1989). *People with Disabilities in the Soviet Union: Past and Present, Theory and Practice.* Pittsburgh, PA: University of Pittsburgh Press.

Ministry of Justice (2015). Labour code of the Republic of Kazakhstan. Available at: https://adilet.zan.kz/eng/docs/K1500000414. Last accessed: November 2021.

Oliver, M. (1996). *Understanding Disability: From Theory to Practice.* St Martin's Press. https://doi.org/10.1007/978-1-349-24269-6.

Oliver, M. and Barnes, C. (2006). Disability politics: where did it all go wrong. *Coalition*, 8–13. Manchester: Greater Manchester Coalition of Disabled People.

Pagán-Rodríguez, R. (2012). Transitions to and from self-employment among older people with disabilities in Europe. *Journal of Disability Policy Studies*, 23(2): 82–93. doi:10.1177/1044207311422232.

Pagán-Rodríguez, R. (2015). Disability, training and job satisfaction. *Social Indicators Research*, 122(3): 865–885. http://www.jstor.org/stable/24721580.

Phillips (2009). There are no invalids in the USSR! A missing Soviet chapter in the new disability history. *Disability Studies Quarterly*, 29: 3.

Porter, M.E. and Kramer, M.R. (2011). Creating shared value: redefining capitalism and the role of the corporation in society. *Harvard Business Review*, 89(1/2): 62–77.

Primeminister.kz (2020). Kazakhstan implements National Plan for Ensuring Rights and Improving Quality of Life of Persons with Disabilities until 2025. Available at: https://primeminister.kz/en/news/kazakstanda-mugedek-zhandardyn-kukygyn-kamtamasyz-etu-zhane-omir-suru-sapasyn-zhaksartu-zhonindegi-2025-zhylga-deyingi-ulttyk-zhospar-iske-asyryluda-b-nurymbetov-2114836. Last accessed: November 2021.

Primeminister.kz (2021). *National Project for the Development of Entrepreneurship for 2021–2025*. Official Resource of the Prime Minister of the Republic of Kazakhstan. Available at: https://primeminister.kz/ru/nationalprojects/nacionalnyy-proekt-po-razvitiyu-predprinimatelstva-na-2021-2025-gody-159610. Last accessed: November 2021.

Public Procurement Law (2015). Law of the Republic of Kazakhstan 'About Public Procurement', no. 434-V 3PK, Republic of Kazakhstan (2015). Available at: https://adilet.zan.kz/rus/docs/Z1500000434. Last accessed: November 2021.

Renko, M., Harris, P. and Caldwell, K. (2016). Entrepreneurial entry by people with disabilities. *International Small Business Journal*, 34(5): 1–24.

Ruzmatova, M. (2017). Special businessmen. How people with disabilities become entrepreneurs. Available at: https://informburo.kz/stati/osobye-biznesmeny-kak-invalidy-delayut-dengi-v-kazahstane.html. Last accessed: November 2021.

Schur, L. (2003). Employment and the creation of an active citizenry. *British Journal of Industrial Relations*, 41(4): 751–771. doi:10.1046/j.1467-8543.2003.00297.x.

Shaheen, G.E. (2016). 'Inclusive entrepreneurship': a process for improving self-employment for people with disabilities. *Journal of Policy Practice*, 15(1–2): 58–81.

Social Entrepreneurship Law (2021). Law of the Republic of Kazakhstan 'About Changes and Additions in Some Legislative Acts of the Republic of Kazakhstan on Entrepreneurship, Social Entrepreneurship and Compulsory Social Health Insurance', no. 52–VII (2021). Available at: https://online.zakon.kz/Document/?doc_id=33046086&pos=2;-68#pos=2;-68. Last accessed: November 2021.

Swedberg, R. (2000). The social science view of entrepreneurship: introduction and practical applications. In R. Swedberg (ed.), *Entrepreneurship: The Social Science View* (pp. 7–44). Oxford: Oxford University Press.

Tax Code (2017). Code of the Republic of Kazakhstan 'On Taxes and Other Obligatory Payments to the Budget', no. 120-VI 3PK (2017). Available at: https://adilet.zan.kz/rus/docs/K1700000120. Last accessed: November 2021.

UN (2018). Report of the Special Rapporteur on the Rights of Persons with Disabilities on her Mission to Kazakhstan. Available at: https://digitallibrary.un.org/record/1473376?ln=en. Last accessed: November 2021.

UN (2021). *Disability and Employment, Fact Sheet.* Available at: https://www.un.org/development/desa/disabilities/resources/factsheet-on-persons-with-disabilities/disability-and-employment.html. Last accessed: October 2021.

UNCRPD (2006). *UN Convention on the Rights of Persons with Disabilities.* Available at: https://www.un.org/development/desa/disabilities/convention-on-the-rights-of-persons-with-disabilities.html. Last accessed: November 2021.

UNDP (2021). UNDP and UNV held an online conference on the employment of persons with disabilities. Available at: https://www.kz.undp.org/content/kazakhstan/en/home/presscenter/news/2021/august/undp-and-unv-held-an-online-conference-on-the-employment-of-pers.html. Last accessed: November 2021.

Vick, A. and Lightman, E. (2010). Barriers to employment among women with complex episodic disabilities. *Journal of Disability Policy Studies*, 21(2): 70–80.

Williams, V., Tarleton, B., Heslop, P., Porter, S., Sass, B., et al. (2018). Understanding disabling barriers: a fruitful partnership between disability studies and social practices? *Disability and Society*, 33(2): 157–174.

Witte, M. (2017). Kazakhstan making strides in disability access, acceptance. Edge Kz. Available at: https://www.edgekz.com/kazakhstan-making-strides-in-disability-access acceptance. Last accessed: November 2021.

World Economic Forum(WEF) (2013). *The Global Gender Gap Report 2013.* Available at: https://www.weforum.org/reports/global-gender-gap-report-2013/.

World Health Organization (WHO) (2001). *International Classification of Functioning, Disability and Health.* Geneva: WHO.

World Health Organization (WHO) (2013). *A Practical Manual for using the International Classification of Functioning, Disability and Health (ICF).* Available at: https://www.who.int/classifications/drafticfpracticalmanual.pdf. Last accessed: November 2021.

World Health Organization (WHO) (2021). *Disability and Health.* Available at: https://www.who.int/news-room/fact-sheets/detail/disability-and-health. Last accessed: November 2021.

16. Inclusive entrepreneurship in Palestine: context and prospects of people with disabilities

Wojdan Omran and Leila Farraj

INTRODUCTION

According to the World Health Organization, an estimated 1 billion people world-wide are reported as people with disabilities (PWDs) (WHO, 2021). PWDs are more prevalent in developing countries and are at a higher socio-economic risk due to "less education, poorer health outcomes, lower levels of employment, and higher poverty rates." This is because the relationship between poverty and disability is commonly cyclical in nature, such that poverty increases the chances of disability through limited access to necessities such as food, healthcare, safe water, and education; whereas disability can lead to increased rates of poverty as a result of limited education and employment opportunities (World Bank, 2021).

In the context of Palestine, colonialism and occupation have placed the Occupied Palestinian Territories (OPT) in a rather bitter top ranking among countries with the highest percentages of PWDs in the world (Snounu et al., 2019). Socio-political unrest affects virtually every segment of Palestinian society, further marginalizing at-risk communities that are already isolated from disparate and underdeveloped support ecosystems. This is especially true for PWDs as they are far too often underrepresented in the development process, with relief efforts falling short of fully addressing their immediate and long-term needs (Handicap International, 2020). Needs that are exacerbated by their prevalence in middle to low standard-of-living homes, highlighting a clear link between poverty and disability (Giacaman and Mitwalli, 2021). These factors have created a situation where Palestinians today are contending with inherent structural inequalities resulting in an underdeveloped market economy, along with severe restrictions limiting the movement of people and goods, which has led to staggering unemployment rates across the board (Handicap International, 2020). Recent statistics report an unemployment rate in Palestine at a staggering 27 percent overall (41 percent for youth) as of the third quarter of 2021 (Trading Economics, 2021). As for Palestinian PWDs, the unemployment rate has been estimated at an alarming 87 percent among the almost 130 000 PWDs living in Palestine (Abuasi, 2021; ARCO, 2021). These issues leave much work to be done towards addressing the immediate and long-term socio-economic needs of Palestinians in general, let alone marginalized groups such as PWDs in particular.

Palestinian PWDs have been systematically overlooked in policy-maker agendas, further reducing their economic capabilities and potential contributions.

In addition to these statistics, it is also crucial that the specific needs of PWDs are taken into consideration when formulating strategic and inclusive interventions that promote entrepreneurship amongst marginalized communities. An important insight from the numbers provided by the Palestinian Central Bureau of Statistics (PCBS, 2020) relates to trends in education by those affected by either disabilities or difficulties. With sparse enrolment in schools, illiteracy amongst Palestinian PWDs is at 31.6 percent (46.3 percent amongst females, and 19.9 percent amongst males). Levels of education are reflected in labor force participation rates amongst Palestinian PWDs, with the vast majority of this population being economically inactive, as indicated by their steep unemployment rate (87 percent) (ARCO, 2021). For females, it is reported that only 9 percent are active, while half of them are unemployed at 45.4 percent; for males, 47.0 percent are active in the labor market, with 37.5 percent unemployed. Of those who are active in the labor market, 50.4 percent of PWDs are regular wage employees, 22.7 irregular wage employees, 19 percent are self-employed, 7 percent are employers, and 2 percent are unpaid family members (PCBS, 2020).

Ultimately, these numbers are indicative of systemic shortcomings on the side of the Palestinian education system and its inherent inability or inaction to meet the needs of children with disabilities, which affects their long-term economic prospects, leading to further marginalization and exclusions from the labor market. With governing institutions that are inherently discriminatory against PWDs, accessing quality education, which is the foundation for sustainable employment opportunities in the future, becomes untenable at best (Handicap International, 2020).

The aim of this chapter is to provide contextual insights into the potential of the entrepreneurial environment for Palestinian PWDs. An integral part of this conversation is an understanding of the unique environmental circumstances that have exacerbated the inequities and exclusion faced by Palestinian PWDs. To this end, this chapter illustrates the ongoing adversities they face in the pursuit of equity and dignity, with regard to not only labor market opportunities in particular, but also living life in general. A notable observation highlighted in the process is the intersectional marginalization of women as PWDs in terms of institutional constraints, demonstrating the exponential obstacles they must overcome as aspiring entrepreneurs. Finally, this chapter ends with exclusive insights on the entrepreneurial ecosystem in Palestine and what lies ahead for PWDs in that respect. The following section begins with a discussion on the segment of society which is held to superhuman standards in providing selfless care and attention, while most often being on the receiving end of inequity: women.

THE DOUBLE-EDGED SWORD OF GENDER AND DISABILITY

Women make up nearly half of Palestine's 5.10 million population and head over one-tenth of Palestinian households (PCBS, 2020). Furthermore, enrolment rates for young women in school is at 91 percent; a rate considerably higher than that amongst men, at 71 percent. Despite greater enrolment rates in secondary and higher education institutions, which for women are at 91 and 60 percent, respectively, compared to their male counterparts which are at 71 and 40 percent, respectively, women's participation rates in the labor force remain disproportionately lower (women at 18 percent, men at 70 percent). In terms of PWDs, the numbers are extremely discouraging: for women with disabilities, these numbers are as low as 4 percent, compared to 24 percent amongst men with disabilities (PCBS, 2020).

There are several factors that affect women's dismal status in the labor force. First, there are the political (for example, occupation, colonialism) and socio-cultural (for example, patriarchal society) constraints which have severely inhibited all aspects of Palestinian life, resulting in a mismatch between the quality of education and growing labor market needs, ultimately limiting women's access to work opportunities. Making matters worse is the horizontal segregation of women in the labor force. This refers to the relegation of women's labor to sectors which lack growth potential (service and agriculture), while they remain mostly absent from the more productive sectors such as construction and transportation. This has resulted in the misrepresentation and inadvertent oversight of their contributions, ultimately leading to a lack of demand for women's labor. Another important factor is women's almost exclusive social position as caregivers. For the most part, this high burden role in Palestinian society is "mandatorily voluntary" for women in caring for not only household members but also extended family. Along with the existing factors previously mentioned, women must contend with additional challenges that relate to domestic violence, emotional and psychological distress, and domestic responsibilities (Hatuqa, 2021). For women branching out as aspiring entrepreneurs, limited access to support services, training opportunities, and credit have restricted their ability to establish viable enterprises, home-based or otherwise (Al-Botmeh, 2013). It is worth noting that, on a social level, women active in informal home-based enterprises are not perceived as labor market participants; rather, this is viewed as an extension of their domestic roles supporting their families financially (ILO, 2018). This puts a strain on women's ability to effectively branch out from their household role to become active labor market participants, leading to further marginalization as active participants on a socio-economic level (Giacaman, 2001). Women with disabilities have taken on multiple tedious roles as caregivers and providers with great tenacity when provided with just some of the access to resources and support necessary to function and thrive as an entrepreneur. One such example follows:

> Samya Rjoub is a 30-year-old woman entrepreneur with a physical disability in her left hand and leg. Samya lives with her eight siblings and her parents in a small house in Dura

village (Hebron). She only completed her secondary school education. Disability issues did not limit Samya from aspiring to pursue her goals and ambitions of being a successful female entrepreneur and an active member of her community. Samya volunteers and participates in many organizations such as The Palestinian General Union of people with disabilities in Hebron, Dura Association for people with disabilities, YWCA in Bethlehem and Hebron, and Bethlehem Arab Society for Rehabilitation. Samya also runs a small- scale business of dairy production with her mother. She owns six sheep and sells dairy products such as milk, yogurt, and butter. She had 15 sheep before, but seven sheep died after grazing in fields where pesticides were used.

Samya participated in the financial training provided by Asala, which took place from January 6 until January 9 2020 in Dura village (Hebron). The training has significantly enhanced Samya's skills and competence to manage her business financially and more efficiently. For instance, through the training, Samya has improved her financial skills such as budgeting, calculating profit/loss, and the importance of saving. As Samya implied, she used to receive external help with the financial matters related to her business, but now she manages her business finances on her own without any additional help. She became more self-reliant and independent in this regard. In addition, the training has helped her to separate her personal and business finances.

Samya aspires to grow her business and expand it. She needs to increase the number of her sheep, and fix the sheepfold to protect the sheep. (Asala, 2021)

EVENTS THAT HAVE EXACERBATED THE SITUATION OF PWDs IN PALESTINE

Examining the realities faced by thousands of Palestinians with disabilities cannot be taken in isolation from the ongoing occupation and colonization that has disabled them not only physically, but also economically, socially, and psychologically. Strict control over natural resources, the isolation of communities, limited mobility, and disproportionate violence has only exacerbated the plight of Palestinians and their challenges of self-preservation, leaving those with disabilities with a multitude of struggles to overcome.

During the first Intifada which began in 1987, then Israeli Defence Minister Yitzhak Rabin ordered Israeli soldiers to break the arms and legs of Palestinian protesters as a strategic deterrence method (Hass, 2005). The act has since come to be known as the the "broken bones policy," and led to the injury and disablement of a large number of children and young adults (Giacaman, 2021). The active use of violence aimed to disable and subjugate the masses throughout the West Bank and Gaza, and to further advance the Israelis' geopolitical interests throughout the territories (Puar, 2015). It can be inferred that there is a correlation between exposure to political violence and disability (Giacaman and Mitwalli, 2021). PWDs in Palestine are not exempt from Israeli violence; quite often, the disabled are directly targeted (Hass, 2005).

With the intent to protect and support PWDs, the Palestinian Disability Law of 1999 proved to be ineffective in countering the intense impact of political and socio-cultural constraints on their overall well-being (economic and otherwise). The reason is that this law focused on disability in medical and charitable terms, without addressing the environmental factors that led to the disability. To put this in perspective, over the course of the March of Return (2018–2019) alone, 7500 Palestinians were injured by Israeli ammunition, 87 percent of whom suffered from limb injuries and amputations; injuries inflicted during a series of eminently non-violent demonstrations protesting the siege of Gaza (Giacaman and Mitwalli, 2021). Technically, this law would not address those injured under such circumstances; ironically so, these are circumstances which represent the quintessential setting of Palestinian daily life. Further to this, the 1999 Law did not address women's or children's rights, a major shortcoming to national efforts to inclusively address the needs of PWDs (Giacaman, 2021). Even with the United Nations Convention on the Rights of Persons with Disabilities (CRPD), the Israeli occupying authorities would continue to disregard the rights of Palestinians in the Occupied Palestinian Territories and their obligations under international humanitarian law (Al Haq, 2020).

The health sector in Palestine is anchored by underdeveloped health facilities, combined with a lack of sustainable financing strategies and budget allocations towards social support services for PWDs. Furthermore, considerations for PWDs are mostly absent from mainstream legislation, national plans, and programs due to a predominant focus on medical rehabilitation in a rather general sense (World Bank, 2016). It is the donor-funded civil society organizations, non-governmental organizations, and the private sector which are the main providers of social and employment services for PWDs in Palestine. This is rather disconcerting, as donor aid continues to run short, especially with funds being diverted towards covering a budget deficit projected at US$1.2 billion as well as towards COVID-19 measures, taking priority over PWD needs in the process (UNCTAD, 2021).

Thus, it is apparent that there are inherent challenges within government legislation and policy-making when it comes to addressing the immediate and long-term needs of PWDs in Palestine. A strong reliance on donor-funded aid to support disability programs is unsustainable, as the inflow of aid remains inconsistent amidst local, regional, and global instability and crises.

ENTREPRENEURSHIP AND DISABILITY

It is clear that there are fundamental institutional (for example, socio-cultural, political, economic) constraints that have profoundly inhibited the provision of tailored care and support that would better equip PWDs to make notable contributions to society, particularly as part of the labor force. It is important to acknowledge that a viable and valuable alternative to being an employee is that of contributing as an entrepreneur. In fact, some studies report higher rates of self-employment in European Union countries with higher rates of PWDs (Kitching, 2014; Pagán, 2009). With regard to Palestine in particular, the promotion of entrepreneurship is essential, especially as micro, small and medium-sized enterprises (MSMEs) make up 99 percent of the economy and 80 of the labor force (Rajab, 2015). Ultimately, this reveals that self-employment, whether based in the home or otherwise, can provide a positive outlet for PWDs to become economically active and achieve a sense of socio-economic self-autonomy. For this to be an effective and practical option, access to customized quality support is crucial.

For Palestinian PWDs, lower labor market participation rates are a direct result of the minimal level of support services available to them, in which accessible education is a major factor (Grammenos, 2011). Not only do low participation rates affect PWDs themselves, but from a national standpoint the implications entail the "loss of productive output, increased welfare payments, and for society in terms of the impact of social exclusion and discrimination on civic participation and public life" (Kitching, 2014). In light of this, self-employment (or entrepreneurship) has been promoted as a rehabilitative tool for PWDs to become economically active (Arnold and Seekins, 2002).

However, a major thorn in the side of the aspiring PWD community is the lack of a conducive public policy to foster equitable and inclusive growth in entrepreneurial activity. Making matters worse is that even where there are attempts at inclusive legislation, tenuous implementation and limited efforts by local Disabled People Organizations (DPOs) continue to unwittingly dismiss women with disabilities and mothers of PWDs (ARCO, 2021). Furthermore, the ability of women to become entrepreneurs is constrained by traditional familial dynamics whereby women's agency is limited and subordinated to others. Collectively, these factors have relentlessly affected women's ability to embrace entrepreneurship as a viable means to address long-term unemployment challenges, which has only led to the perpetuation of labor market inequalities. Thus, despite efforts to challenge the status quo, persistent disparities among men and women remain, and the systemic marginalization of women with disabilities prevails (ILO, 2018).

An uplifting development with respect to the future of PWDs in Palestine is the rapid growth of the Palestinian entrepreneurial ecosystem, alongside a number of initiatives that have provided a platform for budding entrepreneurs to access the support services needed to fulfil their ambitions. This is apparent in the establishment of many public and private sector affiliated high-scale incubators, accelerators, co-working spaces, and capacity-building programs. As such, the most marginalized of Palestinian PWDs can benefit from improved access to the labor force via entrepreneurial measures that can help them to access the resources, networks of support, and knowledge needed to start and sustain their businesses, as well as to facilitate and provide incentives for investment in businesses in the Occupied Palestinian Territories (ILO, 2018).

When given the opportunity and proper facilities, PWDs can make the most impactful of contributions to their marginalized communities as well as greater society. One such example is illustrated:

> In Palestine, special needs children face daily difficulties within their communities and in schools due to the lack of appropriate social and educational support. In 2007, local social entrepreneur Nurreddin Amro – who is afflicted with 98 per cent blindness – launched the pioneering Siraj Al-Quds School and Society for the Blind and Special Needs. The

organization aims to promote and improve the educational, social and familial networks for visually impaired and marginalized children in Jerusalem and beyond. Since opening its doors, the school has served thousands of children and has offered formal education to those aged 4 through to 13, accepting students demonstrating the most financial need. Operated thanks to project funding, donations and minimal tuition fees, the organization is also helping to reduce the stigma surrounding blindness and disabilities in Palestine. "Visually challenged and special needs people suffer from a variety of difficulties and challenges during their education and lifetime. These problems stem from the absence of appropriate educational environments, lack of assistive technology and scarcity of life opportunities," Amro said. (Buller, 2019)

Thus, promoting entrepreneurship amongst PWDs would not only provide a gateway for their own enhanced economic activity, but would also foster the development of PWDs as contributors to society (ARCO, 2021). Enabling PWDs to create impactful social enterprises that may address some of the most pressing challenges faced by their own and other marginalized communities would not only create jobs in a rather adverse labor market, but would also serve on a broader, long-term scale by fostering meaningful progress towards socio-economic inclusion and institutional reform.

REFERENCES

Abuasi, N., 2021. Disability in Palestine is intertwined with poverty. The Borgen Project. https://borgenproject.org/disability-in-palestine-is-intertwined-with-poverty/.

Action Research for Co-development (ARCO), 2021. Promoting inclusive business and social entrepreneurship in Palestine. https://www.arcolab.org/en/portfolio/inclusive-business/.

Al-Botmeh, S., 2013. Barriers to female labour market participation and entrepreneurship in the Occupied Palestinian Territory. Birzeit, Palestine: Centre for Development Studies – Birzeit University and the YWCA of Palestine.

Al Haq., 2020. Palestinian disability and human rights groups submit to the UN Committee on the rights of persons with disabilities for its list of issues on Israel's initial report. https://www.alhaq.org/advocacy/17185.html.

Arnold, N.L. and Seekins, T., 2002. Self-employment: a process for use by vocational rehabilitation agencies. *Journal of Vocational Rehabilitation*, *17*(2), pp. 107–113.

Asala, 2021. Success stories: Samya Rjoub. https://asala-pal.org/success-stories/492.html.

Buller, A., 2019. A social entrepreneur seeks to reduce stigma of disabilities in Palestine. *Arab News*. https://www.arabnews.com/node/1580756/middle-east.

Giacaman, R., 2001. A community of citizens: disability rehabilitation in the Palestinian transition to statehood. *Disability and Rehabilitation*, *23*(14), pp. 639–644.

Giacaman, R., 2021. Disability under siege. Conceptual Frameworks of disability in the Occupied Palestinian Territory with a focus on the Palestinian legal and health systems. https://disabilityundersiege.org/wp-content/uploads/2021/03/Conceptual-Frameworks-of-Disability-in-OPT-Literature-Review-FINAL.pdf.

Giacaman, R. and Mitwalli., 2021. Disability in the occupied Palestinian Territories (West Bank and Gaza) Analysis Report. Analysis Central Bureau of Statistics Census Results 2017. Disability Under Siege.

Grammenos, S., 2011. IDEE: Indicators of Disability Equality in Europe, ANED 2011, Task 4.

Handicap International, 2020. The mandate of HI in Gaza and throughout the Palestinian Territories is to improve the daily lives of the most vulnerable including people with disabilities. https://hi.org/en/country/palestine.

Hass, A., 2005. Broken bones and broken hopes. *Haaretz*, November 4. https://www.haaretz.com/1.4880391.

Hatuqa, D., 2021. Women, work and COVID-19 in Palestine. Relief Web. https://reliefweb.int/report/occupied-palestinian-territory/women-work-and-covid-19-palestine.

International Labour Organization (ILO), 2018. The Occupied Palestinian Territory. An employment diagnostic study. ILO Regional Office for Arab States. https://www.un.org/unispal/wp-content/uploads/2018/04/ILOSTUDY_040418.pdf.

Kitching, J., 2014. Entrepreneurship and self-employment by people with disabilities. OECD. https://www.oecd.org/cfe/leed/background-report-people-disabilities.pdf.

Pagán, R., 2009. Self-employment among people with disabilities: evidence for Europe. *Disability and Society*, 24(2), pp. 217–229.

Palestinian Central Bureau of Statistics (PCBS), 2020. *Characteristics of Individuals with Disabilities in Palestine: An Analytical Study Based on the Population, Housing and Establishments Census 2007, 2017*. Ramallah, Palestine.

Puar, J.K., 2015. Inhumanist occupation: Palestine and the "right to maim." *GLQ: A Journal of Lesbian and Gay Studies*, 21(2), pp. 218–221.

Rajab, R.W., 2015. Enhancement of the business environment in the southern Mediterranean. https://pfesp.ps/uploads/Assessment_of_Palestinian_Policies_to_Facilitate.pdf.

Snounu, Y., Smith, P. and Bishop, J., 2019. Disability, the politics of maiming, and higher education in Palestine. *Disability Studies Quarterly*, 39(2).

Trading Economics, 2021. Palestine unemployment rate. https://tradingeconomics.com/palestine/unemployment-rate.

United Nations Conference on Trade and Development (UNCTAD), 2021. Report on UNCTAD assistance to the Palestinian people: developments in the economy of the Occupied Palestinian Territory. https://unctad.org/system/files/official-document/tdbex71d2_en.pdf.

World Bank, 2016. West Bank and Gaza. Disability in the Palestinian Territories: assessing the situation and services for people with disabilities (PWD). https://documents1.worldbank.org/curated/en/501421472239948627/pdf/WBG-Disability-Study-Final-DRAFT-for-Transmission-Oct-31.pdf.

World Bank, 2021. Disability inclusion. https://www.worldbank.org/en/topic/disability#1.

World Health Organization (WHO), 2021. *Fact sheets: Disability and Health*. https://www.who.int/news-room/fact-sheets/detail/disability-and-health.

PART III

THE IDENTITY AND CONTRIBUTION OF DISABLED ENTREPRENEURS

17. The making of a (dis)abled entrepreneur: an entrepreneurial identity perspective

Mukta Kulkarni and Yangerjungla Pongener

INTRODUCTION

Entrepreneurial identity is described as the set of claims about who the entrepreneur is (Navis and Glynn, 2011). It is not a static property of the founder, but is a discursively negotiated outcome where the individual is in a state of becoming (Essers and Benschop, 2007) based on evolving self and social feedback (Demetry, 2017). Past research on entrepreneurial identity has examined how identities materialize (Demetry, 2017; Gill and Larson, 2014), are negotiated in the case of multiple social identities (Essers and Benschop, 2007; Swail and Marlow, 2018), and the implications of entrepreneurial identity on outcomes such as investor judgments (Navis and Glynn, 2011) or on venture creation and growth (Alsos et al., 2016; Cardon et al., 2017; Fauchart and Gruber, 2011). This research has adopted a relatively functional stance focusing on the transitions to and within entrepreneurial work and the associated role identity (e.g., Demetry, 2017), and on the outcomes of identity (e.g., Fauchart and Gruber, 2011). Alternatively, an interpretivist approach to the identity-making of entrepreneurs with a disability remains an underexamined research concern (cf. Jammaers and Zanoni, 2020).

We examine the identity-making of entrepreneurs with a disability and extend prior conversations about entrepreneurial identity in the following ways. First, the identity emergence literature has noted that identity can be a confluence of internal and external influences (Demetry, 2017; Gill and Larson, 2014). We take a step back and outline how these influences interact to inform identity-making of the entrepreneur with a disability. Second, and relatedly, we examine the intersectionality of the two identities – that of being an entrepreneur and an individual with a disability – as it informs ongoing identity-making during the entrepreneurial process. This is important because there is a contradiction between the neoliberal view of the able-bodied successful entrepreneur, and the view of disability based on dependence and inability or weakness (Jammaers and Zanoni, 2020).

Entrepreneurship and Identity

Identity is a subjective understanding of who individuals think they were, are, and wish to become, and is reflected in questions such as "who am I?" and "how should I relate to others?" (Brown, 2019). Identity is not static, it is instead a constant and conscious struggle, a way of understanding oneself and what one stands for, as shaped by linguistic and social forces (Sveningsson and Alvesson, 2003). Along these lines, entrepreneurial identity is a set of claims about the founder, the venture (Navis and Glynn, 2011), and comprises the entrepreneur's cognitions and emotions about their work as a founder, shaped in part by extant cultural stereotypes and life episodes (Kisfalvi, 2002; Watson, 2009).

Prior research which has examined the construction of entrepreneurial identity suggests that individuals draw upon context-specific discourses to portray themselves as a certain type of entrepreneur (Gill and Larson, 2014). Identity construction and emergence is also associated with the adoption of new roles which are expressed through verbal justifications of activities and are validated by external stakeholders (for example, one's justifications and others' validations of one's move from hobby-driven dabbling to corporate venturing) (Demetry, 2017). Further, verbal practices such as the use of clichés (for example, risk and bravery) are also known to help create the entrepreneurial identity, albeit a weak one, so that it can be discarded should it become unsuitable (Down and Warren, 2008). Such research on identity-making as informed by the self and others is minimal, and the flexible nature of entrepreneurial identity and the process of identity emergence remains understudied (Demetry, 2017).

Research has also focused on identity negotiation, that is, the negotiation of tensions or stresses associated with multiple social identities. This research indicates that when faced with dichotomies and stereotypes (for example, local versus foreign, female versus entrepreneur), entrepreneurs employ context-specific strategies, such as downplaying one identity to favor another one based on the audience (Dy et al., 2017; Essers and Benschop, 2007). Ascribed characteristics and associated social identities indeed influence the achievement of entrepreneurial potential, and the social position of the entrepreneur may require negotiation even in online environments (Dy et al., 2017).

Research has further focused on the outcomes of the entrepreneurial identity for the venture, stakeholders, and the entrepreneur. For example, identity influences the decision to create a new venture (Shepherd et al., 2019) by shaping decisions about market segments, customer needs, and resources and capabilities to be utilized to produce offerings (Fauchart and Gruber, 2011). Entrepreneurial identity also has consequences for external stakeholders (for example, a criterion for investor judgments) (Navis and Glynn, 2011). Finally, identity can be important for the entrepreneur's psychological functioning and well-being (Shepherd and Patzelt, 2018). Taken together, entrepreneurship is closely associated with identity, and perceptions of who one is and wants to be influence how individuals may identify, evaluate, and exploit a potential opportunity (Shepherd et al., 2019).

Entrepreneurship, Disability, and Identity

More recently, the entrepreneur's health has been a focus area in entrepreneurship research (Shepherd and Patzelt, 2018). This research has examined why people with disabling conditions turn to entrepreneurship, outcomes of entrepreneurship for such individuals, the barriers these entrepreneurs may face, and how these may be overcome.

Persons with disabilities may turn to entrepreneurship as they sense obstacles within traditional employment spaces (Cooney, 2008; Wiklund et al., 2016, 2018), because their health condition may allow them to identify and exploit opportunities in unique ways (for example, a lawyer with an acquired hearing impairment may be uniquely positioned to work on cases involving a disability) (Baldridge and Kulkarni, 2017), and because entrepreneurship affords control over work and life (for example, balance work and health-related constraints) (Baldridge and Kulkarni, 2017; Cooney, 2008).

Entrepreneurship may prove beneficial to persons with disability who are hyper-focused, as they may be able to persist given their extreme focus. Entrepreneurship may also be beneficial to those individuals who are impulsive, as they may dodge escalating commitments in the face of venture infeasibility (Wiklund et al., 2016). However, there are also disadvantages to entrepreneurship, which are caused by work overload leading to stress and anxiety (Wiklund et al., 2016), by unpleasant external interactions which can worsen the entrepreneur's mental disorder (Wiklund et al., 2018), and when stakeholders question their ability (Cooney, 2008; Renko et al., 2016). Finally, research indicates that barriers such as lack of access to social networks that can aid ventures (Anderson and Galloway, 2012) and difficulties in obtaining start-up capital can be reduced via tailored training programs (Cooney, 2008) and targeted stakeholder engagement (Anderson and Galloway, 2012).

We came across only one study (Jammaers and Zanoni, 2020) that has examined identity-making of entrepreneurs with a disability. The study found that such individuals take different positions to construct their identities: that of an archetypal entrepreneur (for example, being one's own boss), a unique entrepreneur (for example, creating disability-specific offerings), a fallback entrepreneur (for example, out of necessity), and a collective entrepreneur (for example, mutual interdependency with stakeholders) (Jammaers and Zanoni, 2020). We add to this research by examining how identities are discursively constructed by the focal entrepreneur.

RESEARCH APPROACH

Research Context

According to the most recent census report, disability is captured as broad deviations from some standard in terms of hearing, seeing, locomotor ability, or multiple disabilities, and there are 26.8 million persons with a disability in India (Dhar, 2013). Disability is understood broadly in terms of impairments, limitations in activities, and restriction in participation in various life spheres. Most persons do not fare well when it comes to conventional organizational employment, and 73.6 percent are out of the Indian labor force given poor access to education and social stigma (Shenoy, 2011).

To increase entrepreneurship in India, the Department of Empowerment of Persons with Disabilities launched the National Action Plan in collaboration with the Ministry of Skill Development and Entrepreneurship in 2015. This plan is aimed at imparting vocational skill training through seven National Institutes and through 21 Vocational Rehabilitation Centers across the country. Further, the National Handicapped Finance and Development Corporation, which is an administrative body under the Ministry of Social Justice and Empowerment, provides financial assistance at concessional rates of interest to persons with disabilities for self-employment, and reimburses total recurring cost of training programs to the training institutes (Department of Empowerment of Persons with Disabilities, 2015). Most loans are geared towards the creation of small establishments such as a tailoring shop, a provision store, an *agarbati* (incense stick) making unit, and so on. Loans range from a few thousand rupees up to a limit of 10 lakh rupees (National Handicapped Finance and Development Corporation, 2016). However, there are no exact indicators of how many persons with a disability start their own ventures. People with a disability are largely viewed as recipients of welfare more than as individuals with rights or as sources of talent (Kulkarni et al., 2017).

Within this context, to understand the identity-making processes of entrepreneurs with a disability, we engaged in purposive sampling and adopted a phenomenological stance. This approach was best suited given the understudied research area (Jammaers and Zanoni, 2020), and as we wanted to capture the entrepreneurs' everyday lived experiences (Watson, 2009) of identity-making. We conversed with 12 individuals (Table 17.1) who have a visible disability (for example, blindness, mobility problems) and who have founded ventures. Conversations ranged from 45 minutes to almost three hours. During the analysis, we tried to attenuate effects of any biases we may have had on data interpretations by sharing our interpretations with each participant. Hence, what we offer as the identity-making process is co-constructed with and learned from participants (cf. Rhodes and Carlsen, 2018).

Data Analysis

To capture the broad essence of the phenomenon of entrepreneurship, all interviews were transcribed and read several times to understand participants' experiences. For example, one transcript led us to understand unfortunate experiences within the college placement system which made the participant divert his focus towards entrepreneurship. Next, we developed a broad identity-specific storyline per participant. After that, we developed an understanding of specific happenings (for example, family calling the entrepreneur a "bum" for not holding a stable and conventional job) that influenced participants' thinking about their identity (for example, "stakeholders do not see me as an entrepreneur"). We also focused on the "why" of the experience, that is, why an individual experiences a phenomenon the way they do (for example, experiencing an inferior position in the society given unfortunate interactions with family or other stakeholders, and that leading to an entrepreneurial journey to so-called freedom).

Table 17.1   Participant details

Pseudonym, (gender), age	Disabling condition	Educational background	Type of venture
Bala (M), 49	Blind	Master's (Political Science)	Plastic manufacturing and packaging
Deepak (M), 53	Progressive muscular atrophy	Master of Business Administration	Assistive technology consulting
Gopal (M), 42	Polio	Master's (Computer Science)	Technology consulting
Manoj (M), 29	Blind	College dropout	Digital marketing consulting
Prateek (M), 51	Blind	Chartered Accountancy	Apparel showroom
Ramesh (M), 27	Blind	Master of Business Administration	Assistive technology consulting
Rucha (F), 54	Blind	Master's (Music)	Disability training agency
Sagar (M), 40	Polio	Chartered Accountancy	Accounting firm
Shubham (M), 26	Blind	Bachelor's (Mass Media)	Documentary and film-making agency
Tejas (M), 38	Blind	Master's (Law)	Law firm
Udit (M), 49	Paralyzed	Master's (Computer Science)	Machinery automation
Vignesh (M), 26	Cerebral palsy	College dropout	Solar energy mining

Following Watson (2009), we developed the analytical section keeping in mind prior literature and our broad aim of understanding identity-making. Thus, our themes are akin to insights or clusters of relevant meaning gained from analysis of the interview transcripts (Berglund, 2007; Van Manen, 2014). For example, we refer to a participant's lack of aggression in his venture growth, based on meaningful parts in his interview where he narrated that his focus was on helping others with a disability and on his everyday creativity, more than on aggressive venture growth. We thus captured experiences of all participants in the form of anecdotes which described incidences, and with a few quotations to illustrate lived experiences (e.g., Van Manen, 2014).

FINDINGS

Our study presented three broad findings which we describe in detail in the following subsections. First, participants seemed to question whether they were an entrepreneur. This was because they saw themselves as accidental or forced migrants to entrepreneurship, and could not always apply the entrepreneurial label to themselves. Venture and life goals did not always justify their entrepreneurial identity. We summarize this under the heading, "Am I an entrepreneur?" Second, participants seemed to question whether others (key stakeholders) thought of them as an entrepreneur. This was driven by a perception of uneven support from parents who nudged or actively dissuaded participants from entrepreneurship, or by a perceived lack of client faith in participants' entrepreneurial ability given their disability. We summarize this under the heading, "Do others think I am an entrepreneur?" Third, participants seemed to question whether being an entrepreneur made for an inferior self. This was driven by a perceived a lack of social acceptance of their entrepreneurial ability even after setting up and running a venture. We summarize this under the heading, "Does being an entrepreneur make for an inferior self?"

Am I an Entrepreneur?

Participants wondered whether they were really an entrepreneur, as they saw themselves as accidental or forced migrants to entrepreneurship, as their venture and life goals were a likely misfit with the conventional view of entrepreneurship, and as they equated entrepreneurship with everyday creativity and everyday giving. We describe each of these below.

Udit, for example, saw himself as an accidental entrepreneur. He was finishing his integrated Master's and PhD in Computer Science at a premier institution as his desire "was to get into teaching." Udit recalled a "life changing" event when, feeling unwell, he was riding his bike to his family home. He recalled his "utter confusion" as he tried to stop and give a passerby a ride but could not control his legs and thereby his bike. After months of fighting a spinal infection, Udit was permanently wheelchair-bound. Teaching, his dream, seemed impossible given his physical limitations and lack of accessibility across educational institutions. He thus decided to apply his knowledge and create his own venture:

> I didn't know what to do. So, I said the best would be to start something on my own. So, entrepreneurship was not something out of choice. It was more out of having no other choices ... I always wanted to get into teaching ... The whole reason for [entrepreneurship] was to keep me employed ... I never wanted to be a businessman. I never wanted to be an entrepreneur so that way I was very successful. It gave me a very good life. And maybe 40-50-60 people along with me as well.

Similarly, Tejas, who runs a law firm, recalled his experience in medical school as he lost his eyesight. He could no longer see slides or understand blood samples, and was ousted. Tejas recalled his "complete confusion" and explained that entrepreneurship was a "purely stupid accident." Soon after the ouster, he and his friends were loitering near a law school. In what was random banter, friends wondered whether Tejas should turn to law and start his own practice. Sure enough, Tejas entered an accidental, albeit rewarding, entrepreneurial journey which was initially fueled by "no logic." As another example, Ramesh—a blind accessibility technology consultant—set up a venture centered on digital accessibility for persons with disabilities because, despite top grades in his MBA program, no organization hired him given his vision loss.

Further, participants wondered whether their venture and life goals fit with the conventional view of entrepreneurship. This was specifically because they often curtailed venture growth. For example, Udit owns a multi-story office which houses 40 employees and boasts a swimming pool. Having reached this stage of what he terms entrepreneurial success, Udit does not want to grow the venture. Gopal, who has trouble walking because of polio, owns a technology consulting venture which affords a steady income. He stated that after he filed his first patent, the venture served more as a vehicle to maintain a certain lifestyle whereby he could afford small donations to the local temple that serves daily meals to poor children. Gopal noted that his success was more about "reaching out to people" than about venture growth. Gopal accepted but downplayed his entrepreneur identity by suggesting that faculty members like us were also "entrepreneurs," because we "continually evolve and add innovations to our thoughts and teaching styles."

Sagar also wondered about the fit between his venture goals and life goals. As a wheelchair-bound chartered accountant, Sagar struggled to maintain "quality control" as he faced "hardship" in commuting. He thus chose to curtail venture growth and instead spends his time and energy on disability causes. He explained, "even with those [venture-related] successes, if you ask me, I'm not at all aggressive." Apart from running his venture, Sagar is currently training those with a disability to become "chartered accountants like me" and stand on their own feet so that they do not spend time in a dark place like him, contemplating suicide. He is also financially "supporting one boy who doesn't have two arms, an amputee."

Finally, participants equated entrepreneurship with everyday creativity and everyday giving. Sagar explained that big wins were few and far between, and his daily wins mattered more. He recalled a courtroom incident which highlighted seemingly ordinary challenges that needed entrepreneurial thinking:

> I remember the first case that I got … I was not even sure whether the courtroom was accessible. The first thought that came to my mind was, why you had to take this case. Why you had to get into litigation at all … And I thought for a while, okay, buildings are not accessible, [but] people are there … And [on] the day of hearing, I found out how the building is. It was on the second floor, no lift. So, the challenge was there. But I remember how I dealt with the challenge. That was important. I hired one person who took me on his back to the floor. And I appeared.

Today Rucha trains and finds employment for others who are visually impaired like her. To her, the national awards she has received for her entrepreneurial work do not mean as much as ordinary joys such as when she can help someone with a beneficial disability scheme. She chided one of us during the interview conversation, telling us that any conversation about entrepreneurship awards was "drama" and we should instead focus on her daily experiences.

"Everyday giving" was particularly important to Ramesh given his experiences as a child. Ramesh recalled that no regular school would enroll him, and he ended up attending a boarding school which was less than inspiring, killed creativity, and told blind students to study easy subjects such as the arts. The hostel's questionable hygiene ensured continued illness. Eventually, his parents enrolled him in a small local mainstream school where he was teased, mocked, and where teachers could not fathom what to do with him. Such social ridicule inspired him to engage in entrepreneurship, whereby he could help others with a disability through "everyday giving" in the form of accessibility solutions.

Overall, participants questioned their entrepreneurial identity as they saw themselves as forced or accidental migrants to entrepreneurship, and as they pursued seemingly non-entrepreneurial goals.

Do Others Think I am an Entrepreneur?

Uneven support from key stakeholders made participants wonder whether others acknowledged them as entrepreneurs. While parents were supportive of education and in procuring disability-specific assistive technologies, they dissuaded participants from entrepreneurship. Family thus simultaneously served as an enabler of a professional identity, but a disabler of the entrepreneurial identity. For example, Ramesh's father spent money on screen readers and inclusive education, but he insisted that Ramesh should not think of entrepreneurship. He was in favor of a steady corporate job given his son's blindness, and Ramesh's interest in entrepreneurship seemed unfathomable to his father. Such experiences led to Ramesh feeling "alone" and that he had to somehow chart his own way.

Shubham, who is also blind due to macular dystrophy, spoke of an even more imposing father: "Two PhDs, one law degree ... a brilliant scientist." Though focused on good education, he refused to let his son travel beyond a 10 kilometer radius, which meant access to only certain local colleges and restricted subjects. Shubham enrolled into a course on mass media to set up a venture to make documentaries and films. His father suggested that this course would instead "help make better presentations in a corporate job." Selling his film-making venture plan was an uphill battle as Shubham's father "panicked" at the thought of a blind documentary and film maker. To the father, entrepreneurship was simply not an option.

Apart from parents, clients also seemed to wonder about dealing with an entrepreneur who had a disability. For example, Manoj who is blind due to retinitis pigmentosa, spoke of his "ridiculous" situation where he felt that he was "not supposed to give up" even when he was "beaten up at every juncture." For Manoj, negotiating with clients was especially strenuous as they seemed to react negatively to his blindness. He recalled:

> I lost a lot of clients when they came to know I am blind ... there were lots of times where I would go for meetings. They get in touch through Facebook or LinkedIn or Twitter or through my website. They say, let's meet. I don't have to disclose my disability to them. But after I met them I never got those deals. They were skeptical about it. Consulting was becoming very difficult because of my disability.

Overall, families were perceived by participants as being ambivalent and sometimes actively against their entrepreneurial pursuits. Participants also felt that clients were more focused on their disability than on their ability. Such experiences made participants wonder whether others acknowledged them as entrepreneurs.

Does Being an Entrepreneur Make for an Inferior Self?

Even after their ventures had gotten underway, participants perceived a lack of stakeholder acceptance of their entrepreneurial ability. Manoj recalled some upsetting experiences of training and investing in some of his "bright employees," only to have them leave. He speculated that good employees perceived his disability as causing slower or no venture growth. Such experiences made him wonder whether entrepreneurship cast him as an inferior collaborator.

Vignesh, who has cerebral palsy and dyslexia, and has founded a solar energy mining venture, wondered whether his disability elicited unwarranted roadblocks as well as praise. For example, he recalled his family labelling him a "bum" and an "ass" who failed through school, dropped out of college, and joined a call center which only "all drug addicts" join. He also experienced frustration when his immediate and extended family discouraged him from entrepreneurial activities, as he would always be "dependent," and because not even an "orphan girl" would marry a disabled entrepreneur who was bound to fail. Soon after his venture gained some recognition, the same family, he told us, did an about-turn to sing his praises. Vignesh concluded that "normal" people would not have experienced such undeserved extremes.

Another experience made Vignesh wonder whether entrepreneurship actually reinforced inequality in society. Specifically, he wondered whether his disability was an illusory and temporary advantage that reinforced some inferior social position. He recalled visiting an organization where he thought he was welcomed into the chief executive officers' (CEO) office only because he is a "very slight-figured person in a wheelchair." Would the CEO have given the same treatment to someone who did not look like him or elicit sympathy like him? Vignesh noted that he has attempted suicide thrice because of social marginalization. He is no longer in a dark place, and wishes to be recognized as an entrepreneur, and not as "a disabled entrepreneur." He pointed out that we did not publish our work stating our name and our non-disability status, while he is always referred to as "a disabled entrepreneur."

A position of inferiority was also reinforced by stakeholders such as clients and suppliers, according to Bala. Bala, who is blind, recalled experiences when his competence and authority were questioned in his absence, and often in his presence. Bala noted that clients heard him respectfully, but also checked the veracity of his statements with his father as if he were not in the room. He noted:

> Customers or suppliers hesitated a little bit to deal with me. Whether I am competent [to] deal with them or not, whether I was authorized to deal with them or not. So, sometimes they used to, after dealing with me … confirm, reconfirm it with my father or my brother … if I go somewhere or someone comes here, if someone is with me, whether it is my escort or my assistant, instead of talking to me, they prefer to talk to that person.

Bala resented such behavior and stated that blind did not mean deaf or stupid, as some of his stakeholders seemed to assume. He pointed to his degree in political science and how he had topped his Master's program. Why, he wondered, were clients going through the charade of talking with him if they were not really going to listen to him? To them, he speculated, the disability was more prominent than his entrepreneurial work, and their behavior suggested his inferiority more than his ability.

Deepak, a wheelchair-bound entrepreneur in the assistive technology space, also outlined struggles about bolstering and showcasing his work. Clients heard his pitch politely, but took flight as soon as he spoke about tangible partnerships; a surprise to him, as he has a degree from one of the most prestigious institutions in the country. He pointedly noted that if he asked for any partnership with our school, we would also dither and shield ourselves with bureaucracy. Clients and potential partners were seemingly polite and sympathetic, but such etiquette suggested to Deepak that his bodily deficiency sometimes assumed primacy over his entrepreneurial ability in the minds of certain stakeholders, which in turn made him wonder about himself.

Overall, perceived lack of stakeholder acceptance of their entrepreneurial ability made participants question whether entrepreneurship was a positive endeavor. Our participants suggested that social interactions reminded them of their bodily limitations.

DISCUSSION

Our data indicated that the entrepreneurial journey did not always imply a salient, constant, or a positive entrepreneurial identity for persons with a disability. Participants questioned their entrepreneurial identity as they saw themselves as forced and accidental migrants to entrepreneurship, and because they often curtailed venture growth towards seemingly non-entrepreneurial goals associated with their disability identity (for example, helping others in need). Participants also questioned whether others saw them as entrepreneurs. This was because of uneven support from key stakeholders such as parents and clients. Despite venture growth and monetary gains, participants perceived the entrepreneurial identity as sometimes causing them to feel inferior as a person. This was because entrepreneurship was experienced as an avenue through which society reproduced and reinforced a relatively inferior position of entrepreneurs with a disability. Taken together, the salience and valence of the entrepreneurial identity seemed to fluctuate, based on self-doubt and social feedback. We now explain how our findings advance the conversation about identity-making among entrepreneurs.

Who Creates an Entrepreneur?

Participants of our study often resisted the entrepreneurial path. When they did attempt the entrepreneurial journey, they were not always accepted as entrepreneurs by stakeholders such as family members and potential clients. Whether as vocation or avocation, the entrepreneur's choices and actions were thus not always acknowledged by those around them. For these entrepreneurs, sources of roadblocks were not only distal in terms of societal or stakeholder expectations, but also relatively more proximal in terms of fears and expectations within their own home and given their disability. These experiences make us question who or what it is that creates an entrepreneur, and who should be labelled as one.

As we examine everyday entrepreneurs who are heroes of their own lives and within certain contexts (Welter et al., 2017), we can extend studies in the field of entrepreneurship. Our participants' experiences indicate that performance, or even the very essence of entrepreneurship—creation of novelty, creation of wealth, putting food on one's table, attempts at inching into mainstream society—depends on the identities of entrepreneurs. Looked at more broadly, the entrepreneur's experience of "being" is the primary source of meaning, and entrepreneurial outcomes can be valued from that basis. An outsider's view, whether it is an economic or a socialized perspective, cannot then satisfactorily account for entrepreneurial activity.

Relatedly, at what point in the entrepreneurial journey do we start and stop identifying someone as an entrepreneur? For example, when Prateek first started selling bedsheets by walking door-to-door, was he merely putting a roof over his family's head, or was he an entrepreneur (with concomitant contributions to the local economy), or was he doing and being both? That is, at what level of experience should an individual be labelled as an entrepreneur? Vignesh's venture has gained recognition, and yet he is moving away from his entrepreneurial endeavor and identity to focus on becoming a public servant to influence the disability discourse in India. As we study venture emergence and exit from a functional perspective, we can also examine the (de)construction of venture-related identity.

While the experiences related in this chapter can be seen as extreme cases, we hope that by collectively focusing on diverse and relatively marginalized protagonists in stories of entrepreneurship we can animate conversations about who is an entrepreneur, how the entrepreneur is "made," and what entrepreneurship is in the eyes of disabled entrepreneurs and as experienced by them. Experiences noted in this chapter suggest that capturing the performance and constituents of entrepreneurship (Gartner, 1990), who is and who becomes an entrepreneur (Gartner, 1988; Stanworth et al., 1989), why (Gartner, 1985), and whose story this narrative is (Steyaert, 2007), should be asked, alongside "Who creates an entrepreneur in our contexts?" The implications of such a question are non-trivial. The label or the identity influences not only the entrepreneur directly (for example, a feeling of well-being) (Shepherd, 2015; Shepherd and Patzelt, 2018), but also relatedly the support of their venture (cf. Fisher et al., 2017).

Does Entrepreneurship Reproduce and Reinforce Societal Inequality?

Participant experiences noted in this chapter suggest that entrepreneurship can be experienced as an avenue whereby inequality is (re)produced and reinforced in society (for example, being heard only because of sympathy towards a disabled body). Said differently, entrepreneurship can be both simultaneously a pathway for emancipation (economic freedom) and for further shackling (client pity toward the entrepreneur), for certain types of entrepreneurs who may be seen as operating on the fringes of society or who do not fit societal images of conventional entrepreneurs. Are certain entrepreneurs celebrated because they are expected to fail or disappoint? The experience of entrepreneurship is not always a neutral and accessible endeavor (Ahl and Marlow, 2012), and cannot always be associated with the narrative of optimism that characterizes most entrepreneurship research (Verduijn and Essers, 2013). Entrepreneurs can be (dis)abled even when they are seemingly successful.

Research suggests that entrepreneurship serves as a vehicle to break free of social constraints (Goss et al., 2011; Verduijn and Essers, 2013). However, it would appear that for certain individuals, emancipatory processes are not so clear. For example, our participants' experiences of entrepreneurship as both emancipation and shackling imply a paradoxical co-occurrence, and defining the phenomenon of entrepreneurship as one that encompasses contradictions may become necessary. Therefore, there is a need for a more nuanced understanding of entrepreneurship (Verduijn et al., 2014). There are indeed wide variations among entrepreneurs and their ventures (Gartner, 1985), and we need to understand the phenomenon of entrepreneurship from the point of view of the entrepreneur to expand the scope of entrepreneurship research (Ahl and Marlow, 2012).

CONCLUSION

We acknowledge that stories of entrepreneurship are never complete on their own and are interpreted based on readers' imagination (Gartner, 2007), cultural frames (Steyaert, 2007), or cognitive and emotional reactions, and thereby "stretch" what is being (un)said (Fletcher, 2007). The same story can be taken at face value (Gartner, 2007), as an incomplete one (Steyaert, 2007), or as one that manages to omit certain voices (Ahl, 2007).

Going forward, readers of this chapter may see nested stories in the experiences we have outlined or perceive experiences differently than we did, and thereby stretch what we have noted. For example, researchers can utilize the literature on post-traumatic growth to understand how entrepreneurs make sense of their trauma, who they are post-trauma, who they can become in the future, and their assumptions and goals going forward (Maitlis, 2009). Whether examining bodily (Haynie and Shepherd, 2011) or venture-specific trauma (Ucbasaran et al., 2013), researchers can theorize nuances in the entrepreneurial journeys of entrepreneurs based on how they construct interpretations and narratives of traumatic events (Haynie and Shepherd, 2011; Kulkarni, 2020), and how dimensions of disadvantage can remain part of the entrepreneurial identity but lose their stigma in the process of entrepreneuring.

Researchers can also examine identity trajectories of entrepreneurs by viewing identity as a constant and conscious struggle to understand oneself and what one stands for (Sveningsson and Alvesson, 2003), in the face of seemingly contradictory social identities (Jammaers and Zanoni, 2020). To the extent that entrepreneurial identity waxes and wanes based on self and social input, future work can focus on types of identity work; that is, how entrepreneurs create, repair, uphold, or revise their social identities towards a sense of coherence and distinctiveness (Snow and Anderson, 1987; Sveningsson and Alvesson, 2003).

As a final example, researchers can utilize literature on the emancipatory potential of entrepreneurship to examine carefully why experiences of entrepreneurship are not always neutral (Ahl and Marlow, 2012) or positive (Verduijn et al., 2014; Verduijn and Essers, 2013). Whether examining emancipation from the power of the other (Rindova et al., 2009) or from one's own troubled past (Chandra, 2017), researchers can theorize nuances in why and how some entrepreneurs comply with, and others challenge, existing expectations of entrepreneurs or of entrepreneurship (cf. De Clercq and Honig, 2011).

Overall, we hope that this chapter serves as a nudge to render visible the experiences of entrepreneurial identity-making for those precariously positioned in society with regard to their social status. As we collectively focus on such experiences in entrepreneurship, we can complexify the phenomenon and continue our exciting academic "party" (Shepherd, 2015).

REFERENCES

Ahl, H. (2007). Sex business in the toy store: A narrative analysis of a teaching case. *Journal of Business Venturing*, *22*(5), 673–693.

Ahl, H., and Marlow, S. (2012). Exploring the dynamics of gender, feminism and entrepreneurship: advancing debate to escape a dead end? *Organization*, *19*(5), 543–562.

Alsos, G.A., Clausen, T.H., Hytti, U., and Solvoll, S. (2016). Entrepreneurs' social identity and the preference of causal and effectual behaviours in start-up processes. *Entrepreneurship and Regional Development*, *28*(3–4), 234–258.

Anderson, M., and Galloway, L. (2012). The value of enterprise for disabled people. *International Journal of Entrepreneurship and Innovation*, *13*(2), 93–101.

Baldridge, D., and Kulkarni, M. (2017). The shaping of sustainable careers post hearing loss: Toward greater understanding of adult onset disability, disability identity, and career transitions. *Human Relations*, *70*(10), 1217–1236.

Berglund, H. (2007). Researching entrepreneurship as lived experience. In Neergaard, H. and Ulhoi, J. (eds), *Handbook of Qualitative Research Methods in Entrepreneurship* (pp. 75–93). Cheltenham, UK and Northampton, MA, USA: Edward Elgar Publishing.

Brown, A.D. (2019). Identities in organization studies. *Organization Studies*, *40*(1), 7–22.

Cardon, M.S., Mitteness, C., and Sudek, R. (2017). Motivational cues and angel investing: Interactions among enthusiasm, preparedness, and commitment. *Entrepreneurship Theory and Practice*, *41*(6), 1057–1085.

Chandra, Y. (2017). Social entrepreneurship as emancipatory work. *Journal of Business Venturing*, *32*(6), 657–673.

Cooney, T. (2008). Entrepreneurs with disabilities: Profile of a forgotten minority. *Irish Business Journal*, *4*(1), 119–129.

De Clercq, D., and Honig, B. (2011). Entrepreneurship as an integrating mechanism for disadvantaged persons. *Entrepreneurship and Regional Development*, *23*(5–6), 353–372.

Demetry, D. (2017). Pop-up to professional: Emerging entrepreneurial identity and evolving vocabularies of motive. *Academy of Management Discoveries*, *3*(2), 187–207.

Department of Empowerment of Persons with Disabilities (2015). *Skill Development for PwDs*. http://disabilityaffairs.gov.in/upload/uploadfiles/files/NationalActionPlanforSkillDevweb siteversion.pdf.

Dhar, A. (2013). Census reveals only marginal increase in the differently-abled population. *The Hindu.* http://www.thehindu.com/news/national/census-reveals-only-marginal-increase-in-the-differentlyabled-population/article5516279.ece.

Down, S., and Warren, L. (2008). Constructing narratives of enterprise: clichés and entrepreneurial self-identity. *International Journal of Entrepreneurial Behavior and Research, 14*(1), 4–23.

Dy, A.M., Marlow, S., and Martin, L. (2017). A Web of opportunity or the same old story? Women digital entrepreneurs and intersectionality theory. *Human Relations, 70*(3), 286–311.

Essers, C., and Benschop, Y. (2007). Enterprising identities: Female entrepreneurs of Moroccan or Turkish origin in the Netherlands. *Organization Studies, 28*(1), 49–69.

Fauchart, E., and Gruber, M. (2011). Darwinians, communitarians, and missionaries: The role of founder identity in entrepreneurship. *Academy of Management Journal, 54*(5), 935–957.

Fisher, G., Kuratko, D.F., Bloodgood, J.M., and Hornsby, J.S. (2017). Legitimate to whom? The challenge of audience diversity and new venture legitimacy. *Journal of Business Venturing, 32*(1), 52–71.

Fletcher, D. (2007). "Toy Story": The narrative world of entrepreneurship and the creation of interpretive communities. *Journal of Business Venturing, 22*(5), 649–672.

Gartner, W.B. (1985). A conceptual framework for describing the phenomenon of new venture creation. *Academy of Management Review, 10*(4), 696–706.

Gartner, W.B. (1988). "Who is an entrepreneur?" is the wrong question. *American Journal of Small Business, 12*(4), 11–32.

Gartner, W.B. (1990). What are we talking about when we talk about entrepreneurship? *Journal of Business Venturing, 5*(1), 15–28.

Gartner, W.B. (2007). Entrepreneurial narrative and a science of the imagination. *Journal of Business Venturing, 22*(5), 613–627.

Gill, R., and Larson, G.S. (2014). Making the ideal (local) entrepreneur: Place and the regional development of high-tech entrepreneurial identity. *Human Relations, 67*(5), 519–542.

Goss, D., Jones, R., Betta, M., and Latham, J. (2011). Power as practice: A micro-sociological analysis of the dynamics of emancipatory entrepreneurship. *Organization Studies, 32*(2), 211–229.

Haynie, J.M., and Shepherd, D. (2011). Toward a theory of discontinuous career transition: Investigating career transitions necessitated by traumatic life events. *Journal of Applied Psychology, 96*(3), 501.

Jammaers, E., and Zanoni, P. (2020). Unexpected entrepreneurs: The identity work of entrepreneurs with disabilities. *Entrepreneurship and Regional Development, 32*(9–10), 879–898.

Kisfalvi, V. (2002). The entrepreneur's character, life issues, and strategy making: A field study. *Journal of Business Venturing, 17*(5), 489–518.

Kulkarni, M. (2020). Holding on to let go: Identity work in discontinuous and involuntary career transitions. *Human Relations, 73*(10), 1415–1438.

Kulkarni, M., Gopakumar, K.V., and Vijay, D. (2017). Institutional discourses and ascribed disability identities. *IIMB Management Review, 29*(3), 160–169.

Maitlis, S. (2009). Who am I now? Sensemaking and identity in posttraumatic growth. In Roberts, L.M., and Dutton, J.E. (eds), *Exploring Positive Identities and Organizations: Building a Theoretical and Research Foundation* (pp. 47–76). New York: Psychology Press.

National Handicapped Finance and Development Corporation (2016, November 1). Success stories. http://www.nhfdc.nic.in/success-stories.

Navis, C., and Glynn, M.A. (2011). Legitimate distinctiveness and the entrepreneurial identity: Influence on investor judgments of new venture plausibility. *Academy of Management Review, 36*(3), 479–499.

Renko, M., Parker Harris, S., and Caldwell, K. (2016). Entrepreneurial entry by people with disabilities. *International Small Business Journal*, *34*(5), 555–578.

Rhodes, C., and Carlsen, A. (2018). The teaching of the other: Ethical vulnerability and generous reciprocity in the research process. *Human Relations*, *71*(10), 1295–1318.

Rindova, V., Barry, D., and Ketchen Jr, D.J. (2009). Entrepreneuring as emancipation. *Academy of Management Review*, *34*(3), 477–491.

Shenoy, M. (2011, December). Persons with disability and the India labor market: Challenges and opportunities. *International Labour Organization*, *13*, 1. http://www.ilo.org/wcmsp5/groups/public/---asia/---ro-bangkok/---sro-new_delhi/documents/publication/wcms_229259.pdf.

Shepherd, D.A. (2015). Party On! A call for entrepreneurship research that is more interactive, activity based, cognitively hot, compassionate, and prosocial. *Journal of Business Venturing*, *30*(4), 489–507.

Shepherd, D.A., and Patzelt, H. (2018). *Entrepreneurial Cognition: Exploring the Mindset of Entrepreneurs*. Cham: Springer Nature.

Shepherd, D.A., Wennberg, K., Suddaby, R., and Wiklund, J. (2019). What are we explaining? A review and agenda on initiating, engaging, performing, and contextualizing entrepreneurship. *Journal of Management*, *45*(1), 159–196.

Snow, D.A., and Anderson, L. (1987). Identity work among the homeless: The verbal construction and avowal of personal identities. *American Journal of Sociology*, *92*(6), 1336–1371.

Stanworth, J., Stanworth, C., Granger, B., and Blyth, S. (1989). Who becomes an entrepreneur? *International Small Business Journal*, *8*(1), 11–22.

Steyaert, C. (2007). Of course that is not the whole (toy) story: Entrepreneurship and the cat's cradle. *Journal of Business Venturing*, *22*(5), 733–751.

Sveningsson, S., and Alvesson, M. (2003). Managing managerial identities: Organizational fragmentation, discourse and identity struggle. *Human Relations*, *56*(10), 1163–1193.

Swail, J., and Marlow, S. (2018). "Embrace the masculine; attenuate the feminine"—Gender, identity work and entrepreneurial legitimation in the nascent context. *Entrepreneurship and Regional Development*, *30*(1–2), 256–282.

Ucbasaran, D., Shepherd, D.A., Lockett, A., and Lyon, S.J. (2013). Life after business failure: The process and consequences of business failure for entrepreneurs. *Journal of Management*, *39*(1), 163–202.

Van Manen, M. (2014). *Phenomenology of Practice: Meaning-Giving Methods in Phenomenological Research and Writing*. New York: Routledge.

Verduijn, K., Dey, P., Tedmanson, D., and Essers, C. (2014). Emancipation and/or oppression? Conceptualizing dimensions of criticality in entrepreneurship studies. *International Journal of Entrepreneurial Behavior and Research*, *20*(2), 98–107.

Verduijn, K., and Essers, C. (2013). Questioning dominant entrepreneurship assumptions: The case of female ethnic minority entrepreneurs. *Entrepreneurship and Regional Development*, *25*(7–8), 612–630.

Watson, T.J. (2009). Entrepreneurial action, identity work and the use of multiple discursive resources: The case of a rapidly changing family business. *International Small Business Journal*, *27*(3), 251–274.

Welter, F., Baker, T., Audretsch, D.B., and Gartner, W.B. (2017). Everyday entrepreneurship—A call for entrepreneurship research to embrace entrepreneurial diversity. *Entrepreneurship Theory and Practice*, *41*(3), 311–321.

Wiklund, J., Patzelt, H., and Dimov, D. (2016). Entrepreneurship and psychological disorders: How ADHD can be productively harnessed. *Journal of Business Venturing Insights*, *6*, 14–20.

Wiklund, J., Yu, W., and Patzelt, H. (2018). Impulsivity and entrepreneurial action. *Academy of Management Perspectives*, *32*(3), 379–403.

18. The opportunity to contribute: disability and the digital entrepreneur
Tom Boellstorff

ELLIE'S BEST-SELLING BED

Summits of green-topped mountains peek over the walls of Ellie's store. It cannot rain, so ceilings are not needed. Ellie leads me room to room, showing me her merchandise: case studies in clever beauty, attentive originality. Furniture, from beds to desks and even swings for the yard, all with custom animations built right in. A shirt that can manifest in three or even five sizes for 100 lindens.

Of course, the reason it cannot rain, that a piece of furniture can have "animations" inside it, that a shirt can change its size at will, is because Ellie's store is in the virtual world Second Life. Here, commerce takes place in Linden Dollars (or "lindens"); the exchange rate is usually around 250 lindens for US$1. Ellie's 40 cent virtual shirt is typically priced. But Ellie has been crafting things long before discovering this virtual world: "Let me explain the way I was raised. We didn't have a dining room: we had a cutting board and three sewing machines ... I have always crafted; if I was watching TV I was crocheting something." This earlier crafting had sometimes represented a source of income; for instance, making miniature items for dollhouses: "you could take a box of colored paper clips, two round-nosed pliers, straighten out the paper clip and rebend it into a coat hanger, sell ten of them for $5. There were 100 [paper clips] in a package, so you'd make $50."

A worsening disability made work and crafting nearly impossible for Ellie. One day:

> I had tried to start my crocheting, and I could not hold onto my crochet hook, I kept on dropping it. I mean, I could not crochet at all ... And to me, that was just, okay, shoot me now, my life is over. A friend of mine came in and found me just bawling, I mean he thought if he couldn't calm me down he was going to have to take me to the hospital. And he goes, "okay, I'm going to take you somewhere, if you can hold onto the computer mouse." I said "yeah, but that gets boring, you know, because it's not crafty." He said "well, I'm going to take you somewhere where you can build, and you can make things."

This was Ellie's introduction to Second Life, where she not only reclaimed crafting but found opportunities to sell. This included the virtual furniture mentioned earlier; in particular, beds, one of Ellie's specialties. Ellie would purchase a basic bed shape that someone else had designed in a third-party program such as Maya or Blender. These basic shapes, known as "kits," could be imported into Second Life as three-dimensional objects. Ellie added textures, making the bed appear to be made of worn wood or fine-patterned fabric. She would add animations so that an avatar could sleep, read a book, or sit with legs dangling. As Ellie showed me around her store, she described the financial calculus involved:

> This bed we're sitting on. It costs me 2500 lindens to get the kit. I'm selling it for 200. So I'd have to sell 13 of them to break even. Well, no, 15 to break even, because you've gotta consider I put money into the textures and money into the animations, right? ... It costs about 3000 lindens to make this. So I'm going to have to be able to sell a good 15 of them to break even. This is my most popular selling bed. I've sold 5.

As Ellie herself noted, "people say 'why is your stuff so cheap?' ... I'm not trying to sell it for a profit." Indeed, because Ellie also paid a monthly fee for the virtual land on which her store stood, she had a negative cash flow of $50–$100 a month:

> This is my therapy. My shrink actually said that I should submit the bill to Medicaid ... You see, if I did not have this outlet for my creative side, they would have to have me on drugs to keep me from going totally wacko ... For me this is a four-part therapy, okay? I get my creativity release, which will build up and truly drive me insane if I don't. I get a place where I can talk to other people about my disability. I have a place where I can satisfy my need to be an instructor. The fourth is, my friends are here. Which is a big thing many handicapped people do not get. I gave up driving a long time ago. I can't drive. I can barely get out of the house, with help, right now.

How can someone who identifies as an entrepreneur have a "best-selling" bed only five people have purchased? How can such a person not seek to sell for profit; indeed, lose money? Is this false consciousness, someone duped by neoliberal capitalism? Or might there be a more complicated interplay of selfhood, labor, and ability in a digital context? This is the point of departure for my analysis. Disabled persons in Second Life such as Ellie are articulating something through languages and practices of entrepreneurship, something that challenges the ableist paradigms of structuring digital socialities and regimes of labor.[1]

DIGITAL TECHNOLOGY, LABOR, DISABILITY

This chapter is based on 14 years' research in Second Life, five years of which have focused on disability (e.g., Boellstorff, 2015; Davis and Boellstorff, 2016). This virtual world is owned by Linden Lab; during my research it had about 600 000 residents. There is no cost in obtaining an account, but one must pay to own virtual land. I gathered data using methods including in-world participant observation, physical-world and in-world individual interviews, and in-world group interviews. I got to know disability communities through my original fieldwork and built on those connections for this research. These disability communities are as diverse as in the physical world, including visual and auditory impairments, limb loss, autism, epilepsy, post-traumatic stress disorder, multiple sclerosis, and the effects of strokes, cancer, Parkinson's disease, and other illnesses. This diversity thus includes congenital disabilities, disabilities acquired later in life due to disease or accidents, and conditions whose status as "disability" is contested (for instance, deafness and autism). Most of my interlocutors were between 40 and 60, but some were in the 20–40 range, and a few were in their seventies, eighties, and even nineties.

From its origins in the early 2000s, Second Life was designed as a virtual world where most objects and experiences would be created by residents (Ondrejka, 2004). This model, known by terms such as "user-generated content" or "prosuming," is fundamental to platform capitalism, in that platforms are underdetermined: Facebook does not produce most of its posts; YouTube does not create most of its videos. In Second Life, user-generated content can be given away freely or sold for Linden Dollars; as noted above, these can be exchanged for US dollars.[2] Most commodities sell for the equivalent of 50 cents to $2, but there are many items in the $5–$20 range and a few for more than $50, $100, or even $1000 (see Au, 2017).

The open-ended design of Second Life means there are ample possibilities for content creation and sales, but some characteristics of the virtual world work against these possibilities, particularly for disabled persons. While Second Life accounts are free, the relatively high cost of renting land is a barrier. A full region ("sim") costs $600 to set up, with a monthly fee of $295. Regions can be shared, and it is possible to own smaller parcels (or rent parcels from larger virtual landowners) so that one has a monthly fee of $25 or less, but even this is prohibitive for some disabled persons. Without land, creating and selling objects is harder though not impossible (see the Second Life Marketplace discussed below).

Despite these barriers, throughout my fieldwork I have been struck by how often disabled persons in Second Life participate in content creation and sales. The exact number of such persons is not key: ethnographic analysis is not about establishing what is prevalent, but exploring what is possible. Demographic data are difficult to obtain because accounts can be obtained anonymously, and not everyone reveals their disability in-world. Morgan, a disabled entrepreneur, noted that:

> In our community, this is huge because we can choose how much anonymity we want. And for some of our members, that anonymity is key to their comfort zone of participation. And then, of course there are a lot of people who just, they don't tell people, period … They're just choosing to explore this world without the D-word attached to it. They're not trying to be able-bodied. They're just trying to kind of see what it's like to not have the Big D front and center.

With these limitations in mind, it was clear that most of my interlocutors lived in North America or Europe. Most had limited resources—for instance, an annual income under $15 000 in the United States—though some identified as middle class. (One indicator: the research project was to have a virtual reality component involving the purchase of virtual reality headsets for at least 16 participants, but it was only possible to do this for three participants because the rest did not own sufficiently powerful computers.) In line with surveys estimating that around 60 percent of virtual-world residents identify as female in the physical world (Pearce et al., 2015: 15), the majority of my interlocutors were women. I emphasize female narratives in this analysis, and address how gender intersects with disability in the domain of entrepreneurship. While not commonly emphasized by my interlocutors, it bears recalling that through their creative labor they were contributing to the profits of Linden Lab (analogous to the way that content creators are pivotal to the profits of Facebook, YouTube, Twitter, and so on) (see Ekbia and Nardi, 2017).

My ethnographic material speaks to a range of topics; everyday experience (online or offline) always involves multiple cultural domains. I seek to contribute to literatures on digital technology and labor; literatures on disability and labor; and the emerging body of work addressing all three of these domains (e.g., Friedner, 2015). I turn particularly to entrepreneurship. As a pivotal theme addressed by current research on technology and labor, entrepreneurship opens the analysis to questions of intersubjectivity and belonging—to how "contribution" as affect and social fact shapes intersections of disability and labor. This is important because many disabled persons do not work for wages: indeed, state and national laws often forbid income as a condition for benefits. Appreciating the contributions of disability experience to the question of digital technology and labor requires moving beyond "employment" as narrowly construed.

Scholars writing on entrepreneurship have noted its connection to aspects of selfhood in addition to gender:

> where work is coded as entrepreneurship, [workers] learn to imagine themselves as risk takers rather than laborers. Their cultural characteristics—such as gender, race, ethnicity, nationality, citizenship status, and religion—make it possible for them to succeed in mobilizing themselves or others like them as labor. (Tsing, 2009: 167)

This is a "gendered, racialized, and classed distribution of opportunities and vulnerabilities" (van Doorn, 2017: 898), which is a context where "age, gender, ethnicity, region and family income re-emerge ... and add their own weight to the life chances of those who are attempting to make a living" (McRobbie, 2002: 518). While these authors do not list ability, I am certain they would consider it relevant, given that "the concept of disability emerged alongside the rise of industrial capitalism ... disability came to be understood as a limit to one's ability to earn a living" (Ross and Taylor, 2017: 85). It is "because of the Industrial Revolution ... [that] disability emerged as both an analytical concept and lived way of experiencing the world" (Friedner, 2015: 121). At the same time, disabled persons have long been reworking non-medical technologies in unexpected ways (Williamson, 2012). An important analytical task is to explore whether and how such disability lifeworlds are changing in the contemporary digital era.

While my argument is informed by recent developments in online socialities, it is important to place these developments in historical context. The connection between technology and labor has been a concern since the ancient Greeks, and was central to Marx's critique of capitalism. For instance, in Chapter 15 of *Capital*, Vol. 1, Marx discussed how alongside lengthening the working day and compelling workers to labor harder, technology allows capitalists to produce surplus value and thereby profit at the worker's expense. Here, as elsewhere, Marx emphasized labor's embeddedness in society: "Technology ... lays bare [man's] mode of formation of his social relations, and of the mental conceptions that flow from them" (Marx, 1976 [1867]: 493).

For over a century, anthropologists have taken up these questions of technology and labor. Malinowski's (1922) classic *Argonauts of the Western Pacific* was "totally devoted to the analysis of economic relations" (Godelier, 1977: 15). Other work showed how ostensibly "primitive" peoples without money actually interweave economics and culture in a complex fashion: "they make their economic relationships do social work ... [and] in all primitive economic systems differ only in degree and not in kind from our own" (Firth, 1954: 22; see Bloch, 1983). By showing the cultural embeddedness of labor, anthropological scholarship in dialogue with feminist Marxism challenged the image of a universal proletariat (e.g., Harris and Young, 1981; Meillassoux, 1972; Nash, 1993; Ong, 1987; Taussig, 1980). More recent work has explored how, "like workers, capitalists are always constituted as particular kinds of persons through historically specific cultural processes" (Yanagisako, 2002: 5; see Dunn, 2017). Anthropology has thus contributed an analysis that "treats capitalist action as culturally produced and, therefore, always infused with cultural meaning and value" (Yanagisako, 2002: 6). How might it be that entrepreneurs are being constituted as particular kinds of persons through historically specific conjunctions of disability and digital technology? Anthropological approaches can explore how these conjunctions might act as forms of "dislocation" in which "both places and persons are reconfigured by the movements of capital" (Harvey and Krohn-Hansen, 2018: 10; see also Bear et al., 2015).

LABOR AS CONTRIBUTION

Although Second Life is designed around the user-generated content model, making content for profit is neither obligatory nor a universal goal. Most residents do not produce items for sale at all: they purchase what others make, or they obtain items for free. Those who create often do so for the pleasure of creating, perhaps giving copies of favorite items to friends.

For some, however, the work of creating leads to sales. This is usually done either through an in-world store, on the Second Life Marketplace website, or both. (An in-world store requires paying for the virtual land on which the store sits, unless one advertises one's wares inside someone else's store, in which case a fee is often paid. If listing on the Second Life Marketplace, Linden Lab charges a 5 percent commission.) A few residents make thousands of US dollars selling avatar clothing or managing virtual real estate, though job-hunting in Second Life is not necessarily easy (Au, 2018). Most residents, however, earn less money, and this pattern holds for disabled entrepreneurs as well. A few have earned what they consider significant income; for instance, from managing a series of rental estates covering almost 40 Second Life regions, with six paid employees. Often, however, the income is more modest. For instance, one disabled fashion designer usually priced clothing items at around 450 lindens, and sold approximately 500 items a month, giving a monthly income of around $1000. And often there is no significant income at all: recall that Ellie had sold five copies of her best-selling bed, earning about $5.

How do disabled persons understand these dynamics of virtual labor in the context of entrepreneurial selfhood? How might disability intersect with and transform expectations regarding such forms of selfhood, given that in the United States and elsewhere, entrepreneurship is promoted by state and other entities as a way to conceptualize disability self-employment?[3] How is entrepreneurship being framed as a modality by which one's inner self is revealed to oneself and the social world?

Morgan, whose thoughts on anonymity and the "Big D" I cited above, had a good number of disabled acquaintances. So many of them were successful entrepreneurs—or sought to become entrepreneurs—that she founded an organization for disabled persons already in Second Life interested in entrepreneurship. Sitting in my Second Life home one day, she explained that her goal was to help ensure that for "people who don't feel like they have any contribution to make, we get them to a place where they can see they have a contribution":

> No longer do we have to sit there and go "I have to make a certain amount of money a year". For most of us, the society we're in doesn't support that for us. Right? It looks at us, and it doesn't even give us the opportunity to contribute in that way. You know, when they see a wheelchair coming through the door, or somebody with a stick to guide them, or they hear that they need an animal on site, "no, we can't accommodate that", right? And so our opportunities become more limited, but it doesn't mean that our potential is gone. It's definitely critical for me to feel that I have something to contribute.

In the same way as my other respondents, experiences with employment, and unemployment in the physical world led Morgan to reflect on the implications of disability for virtual-world entrepreneurship. Particularly relevant for my analysis is her linking of selfhood with a sense of contribution: "Contributing something back to society takes us off the focus of our condition and its challenges, to this focus on this other thing that we're contributing ... That's what gives us that initiative." Furthermore, Morgan (like others) directly connected this initiative to entrepreneurship: "The definition of an entrepreneur is a person who organizes and manages any enterprise, usually with considerable initiative and risk ... 'I'm putting myself out there; this is what I do'."

Morgan's definition of entrepreneurship recalls scholarly definitions discussed below. I have given Morgan the first word to underscore her point that entrepreneurship can be collaborative. Entrepreneurs are, of course, always part of collectivities that can include funders, peers, and workers, but for Morgan and my disabled interlocutors more generally, the idea of nurturing members of a community was not beyond my definition of entrepreneurship. For instance, Morgan was aware of Ellie and her best-selling bed: "you know, I listen to Ellie say 'hey, I spend more than I make'. But actually, I'm guessing, with a few skill sets, Ellie could make more than she spends, because she's super-talented." These skill sets could include things such as learning programs outside Second Life helpful in content creation, or better marketing. But what already stands out in these data is that disability languages and practices of entrepreneurship are shaping cultural logics beyond the economic.

"ENTREPRENEUR" AS SUBJECT POSITION

There has been sustained interest in the entrepreneur as a culturally and historically specific subject position: a socially extant category of selfhood that can be occupied in various ways (that is, as individualized "subjectivities"; see Boellstorff, 2005). A classic theorization of the entrepreneur-as-subject position comes from Schumpeter's *The Theory of Economic Development*. Schumpeter was concerned with the role of "new combinations of means of production" in economic development: "The carrying out of new combinations we call 'enterprise', the individuals whose function it is to carry them out we call 'entrepreneurs'" (Schumpeter, 1949: 74).

With regard to digital capitalism, Schumpeter's idea that entrepreneurs are pivotal to economic recombination and thus social change has gained mythic status, as indicated by the mere mention of (male) names such as Jobs, Gates, Zuckerberg, and Bezos. However, a rich body of scholarship has explored how conceptions of entrepreneurship have expanded beyond this figure of the corporate titan. The metaphor for employee–employer relations has shifted from that of property, where workers own themselves as if "they were property that could be rented to an employer for a certain period of time" (Gershon, 2017: 2), to a metaphor where "people now think they own themselves as though they are businesses—bundles of skills, assets, qualities, experiences, and relationships, bundles that must be consciously managed and constantly enhanced" (ibid.). This newly dominant metaphor represents "new imaginaries of labor in which making a living appears as entrepreneurship" (Stensrud, 2017: 161). In this framework, "contemporary culture's benchmark of success is the figure of the entrepreneur" (Duffy, 2017: 2): it is assumed that "you are no longer a worker, with worker's rights. Instead, you're an entrepreneur, and entrepreneurs take risks (and suffer them too)" (Dewhurst, 2017: 21).

Social scientists have explored links between economic formations and selfhood since at least Weber's (1930 [1905]) *The Protestant Ethic and the Spirit of Capitalism*. At issue are the ableist forms these links take in digital contexts. I coined the term "creationist capitalism" in my analysis of user-generated regimes emerging online since the 2000s (Boellstorff, 2015: Chapter 8). With this neologism I sought to highlight how creativity was becoming construed as a form of labor, particularly in the context of digital socialities where the cost of producing, say, ten virtual chairs was not ten times the cost of producing one chair (as opposed to the cost of producing ten wooden chairs compared to one wooden chair). I also sought to highlight how the Christian metaphysics Weber identified as central to dominant capitalist formations of the nineteenth century remain, albeit transformed, in the twenty-first century. I identified the pivotal transformation as one in which "workers are not just sellers of labor-power, but creators of their own worlds" (Boellstorff, 2015: 209). Rather than worldly success indicating divine favor, in creationist capitalism it is creation that reveals one's inner self. Increasingly, this inner self is an entrepreneurial self (rather than, say, the self of kinship or wage labor).

We now have a constellation of terms alongside "creationist capitalism" that track these shifts in digital labor, including communicative capitalism (Dean, 2010), aspirational labor (Duffy, 2017), platform capitalism (Srnicek, 2017), platform labor (van Doorn, 2017), and venture labor, which is "the explicit expression of entrepreneurial values by nonentrepreneurs" (Neff, 2015: 16). The actions, experiences, and subjectivities of my disabled interlocutors in Second Life further develop Neff's insights: in addition to non-entrepreneurs expressing entrepreneurial values, the horizon of what counts as entrepreneurship is expanding across the terrain of the human. The binarism of "entrepreneur" and "non-entrepreneur" is becoming destabilized in favor of multiple inhabitations of the entrepreneur subject position (just as, for instance, one can inhabit the "teenager" subject position as a diligent "geek," athletic "jock," and so on).

My analysis here thus explores how a concept related to self-identity can be transformed in ways never expected at the time the concept was originally formulated. Disability experience in virtual worlds provides new perspectives on how reconfigurations of "entrepreneur" are emerging: notions of entrepreneurial selfhood that do not stand outside the dominant discourse, but cannot be reduced to it either. In other words, a working hypothesis which I derive from my ethnographic data is that a prototypical Silicon Valley "entrepreneur" and the disabled persons I discuss in this chapter differentially inhabit a shared subject position. At issue is not conflating different forms of selfhood, but recognizing how differing forms of selfhood can be informed by a shared cultural logic. This issue illuminates emerging contours of an "entrepreneurial subjectivity" that involves reconfigurations of self-presentation and self-understanding (Bröckling, 2016; Marwick, 2017). Such reconfigurations include new forms of "entrepreneurial citizenship" in which "entrepreneurialism is not only a project of the self, but a project that posits relations between selves and those they govern, guide, and employ" (Irani, 2019).

These are, in short, forms of "entrepreneurial living" (Lindtner, forthcoming) in which selfhood and citizenship are construed as an intertwined entrepreneurial project. The scholars cited above in this section are among those who explore the benefits and dangers in these new forms of selfhood. At stake in understanding these benefits and dangers is what human agency and equality will mean in the digital age. We need analytical tools for comprehending this expansion of the entrepreneur's subject position, such that people "increasingly define themselves as self-branding entrepreneurs rather than employees" (Robinson, 2017: 2018). Recalling Weber, it is remarkable that this can be at least partially delinked from the desire for wealth (see Weeks, 2011). Neff notes that, "When people think of their jobs as an investment or as having a future payoff other than regular wages, they embody venture labor" (Neff, 2017: 16). This is a culture of capitalism that "shifts content creators' focus from the present to the future, dangling the prospect of a career where labor and leisure coexist" (Duffy, 2017: 4).

My interlocutors, most of whom did not enter Second Life with entrepreneurship in mind, reframed these conceptions of laboring selfhood. Lila, for instance, got to know Second Life after a friend asked her to spend time there: she had been in-world for four years before being disabled by a significant chronic illness. She then became a creator of roleplaying clothing, avatar body attachments, and furniture. However, she emphasized: "I actually didn't want to deal with building when I wasn't sick ... I was crazy bored at home and I wanted to do more, something to make me feel productive even if I didn't sell many things." Like Ellie and many other disabled entrepreneurs, a sense of productivity was linked to creating, collaborating, and sharing, not sales. For instance, customers had purchased about 40 copies of one of Lila's signature pieces of furniture. Some months, she would sell enough to pay the rent for her in-world store (about $15), but not consistently. However, Lila's real motivation was: "I like the fact that someone else enjoys things I make. I get some sense of satisfaction for work done."

As I noted earlier, this kind of ethnographic analysis confronts the complex interplay of multiple cultural domains. Lila's experience, and that of many of my interlocutors, draws on notions of craftsmanship (Sennett, 2009), but is also gendered, reflecting how historically the work of women has often not been seen as real "labor," reassigned an emotional value, and conflated with a "domestic" sphere. Entrepreneurial selfhood is thus not external to a gendered logic in which "online technology allows workers to carve out strategies to cope with conditions that are highly intensified because they are taken to be individual rather than structural in nature" (Gregg, 2011: 3; see Hochschild, 2001). Gender and ability are both shaped by this dynamic, which means that "people increasingly ... have to do the work of the structures [such as the welfare state] by themselves ... which in turn requires intensive practices of self-monitoring or 'reflexivity'" (McRobbie, 2002: 518). It is in this context of intensification through individuation—making work more overwhelming by making it more personal—that my interlocutors' naming of collaboration as intrinsic to their conception of entrepreneurship is particularly revealing.

COLLABORATION AND CAPABILITY

In this section I focus on the question of collaboration. While certainly informed by gender, as noted above the ideal of collaborative labor is mobilized by other cultural characteristics, including disability. For my interlocutors the link between disability, digital entrepreneurship, and collaboration was often shaped by upsetting and economically devastating experiences of physical-world employment discrimination. Consider how one morning a group of disabled persons discussed labor in both Second Life (SL) and the physical world (often colloquially termed "RL" or "real life," but with an understanding that Second Life was real as well):

Rhonda:	wonder if anyone else is afraid to try to get a job in RL … I fear that if I am unable to do it, keep up with my work, or if I cannot understand or am too slow … then I'll get fired and I will have lost my benefits.
Jason:	I share that.
Ruby:	ughhhh
Sylvia:	I will start my teacher training in March, and just like any social work I am afraid I will burn out twice as hard.
Rhonda:	Sometimes I'm sick or just unable to do things for a month or so … I don't think they take that into account when they think we should try to work, but could lose our benefits. So I've got lots of fear of that happening.
Sylvia:	♥
David:	The last job I had in RL, I lost two days before my trial period was over. It was in a hotel, shift work. And they scheduled me to do the late shift, and then I'd have to do the early shift the next day after, which meant that when I got home and took my meds, it took me at least a couple hours to go to sleep. So I didn't get enough sleep, and it kept burning me out.
Sylvia:	Gotta love the retail type of jobs.
David:	When I asked my boss if they could accommodate me, because basically they have to by law here in France, he asked why, so I was open with him and said it's because I have bipolar disorder. And his face just turned, and he talked about how people with manic depression are unreliable and dangerous to have around.
Lila:	sighs
Michelle:	dang
Sylvia:	GRRRRRR
David:	So they let me go. And that was the last time I worked in RL. I'm on disability now, stable, and I find that I can make a little pocket money here in Second Life by making custom mesh [objects] for people, some cars and some little buildings, and I'm working on a big house. So thanks to Michelle and others for teaching me how to do it! But that's how I use Second Life, a little pocket money here and there.

Another interlocutor, Joseph, noted how:

> I was told I would lose medical benefits by working. If anything, I could work and have $1 deducted for every $2 earned, I cannot have more than $2000 in an account, and it can work out to earn an extra $30 a week … employment means a whole lot more than money. It means having a place to go every single day where I am (hopefully) wanted and needed.

In conversations like these, and in everyday practices of digital entrepreneurship, we find (as in David's statements above) a valuing of creativity, a de-emphasis on sales despite income precarity, and an emphasis on collaboration and learning. These responses to conflations of labor and self-worth extend beyond disability: "Work is crucial not only to those whose lives are centered around it, but also, in a society that expects people to work for wages, to those who are expelled or excluded from work and marginalized in relation to it" (Weeks, 2011: 2).

Morgan noted that:

> It is such a conflicting situation, of constantly facing barriers to what you are capable of doing. And constantly having these outside forces suggest you're not being honest about

your capabilities, and that you could do more ... [Disabled persons] are actually forced into the position of entrepreneurship ... You're going to have to have the initiative to prove that you can make that contribution.

Morgan indicates that the "opportunity" to contribute can be compulsive too. The intersection of disability and the digital reveals how the entrepreneur subject position is centered on a normatively ableist self. This is a self who ostensibly faces no barriers to work, particularly when vocational rehabilitation programs frame entrepreneurship as a paradigm of disability self-employment. Digital technologies are now commonly linked to that paradigm, as if they ensure that labor transparently reveals one's value. This is one way that such technologies have often furthered, not mitigated, exclusions of disabled persons from the workforce (Ross and Taylor, 2017). To recall one of the most enduring insights of technology studies, no technology has an inevitable social valence. Technology does not inherently "make things better."

The ableist self on which the entrepreneur subject position is centered is presumed to be constituted through risk and individual productivity. It is thereby part of a cultural framework that narrowcasts dependency, mutuality, and collaboration in terms of start-up or open-sourced "disruptions" of corporate capitalism (Lindtner, forthcoming). However, my analysis builds on the growing body of work showing how the dynamics in play involve inclusion as well:

> [D]isabled people are being produced as idealized "workers with disabilities" and included in neoliberal workplaces ... they provide added value through helping corporations rack up CSR [corporate social responsibility] "brownie points." They are also remaking the workplace as a more affective space for [able-bodied] coworkers who experience novel feelings of responsibility, inspiration, attachment, and love. (Friedner, 2015: 121)

Disabled persons in Second Life respond to these shifting dynamics of exclusion and inclusion when framing "entrepreneur" as a selfhood characterized by collaboration and contribution as well as initiative and risk. This construes ability as interpersonal, and entrepreneurship as a capability that cannot be slotted into a classic teleology of wealth accumulation or even full employment. It is an aspirational labor where one key aspiration is the opportunity to contribute itself; recalling capabilities approaches to human rights that focus on "what people are actually able to do and to be, in a way informed by an intuitive idea of a life that is worthy of the dignity of the human being" (Nussbaum, 2006: 70; see also Burchardt, 2004; Sen, 2005). For my interlocutors, Second Life enabled collaborative entrepreneurship not just because of mobility limitations, but because the affordances of virtual worlds included community and tools for creation. When describing her unemployment, Michelle once noted that "job situations don't accommodate mental unwellness very well. What I find in Second Life though is an opportunity to get some of the very positive rewards of 'working,' of being productive, of making a contribution to the wider world."

That this wider world includes a virtual world underscores how the internet is not a monolithic cultural entity. Affordances of various online socialities vary, with often unforeseen consequences. Morgan once noted that:

When you compare to Facebook, Facebook is a social media … there's nothing solid in it, right? There's no open mikes: any creative expression I post on Facebook can be potentially limited to those that I would allow to see it, and those who see it, they're not going to pay me a dime for it.

Morgan here emphasizes Facebook's form as a network. In contrast, Second Life is "solid": meaning not that it is physical, but that it is a place. It does not mediate between two locations of culture, but is a site of culture itself:

If I try to go out and be an entrepreneur in the real world, I got bankers telling me why they're not going to fund me, I got office buildings telling me why they're not going to rent to me, I've got all kinds of people telling me what they can't do. And I find in the virtual world there's very little of that. You have a whole lot of the opposite. Which is, "yeah, you should do that. Yeah. I know someone who knows how to do that. You should talk to this person"… I didn't think I'd be able to build. And the people who build were like magicians to me, and I would watch people—Ellie was one of the first people I watched build, and I was pretty sure she was a magician, because she can build anything in a few seconds … and I'm just like "that will never be me; I'm not capable or competent," but I have come to realize I am capable of things I never imagined.

Morgan summarized her experiences and those of her fellow disabled entrepreneurs: "Our lives aren't over, and here is a virtual world where we can express that, and how we choose to define success. That's why we don't define it by somebody who can support themselves off their linden dollars annually. That's not a valid measurement of success."

CONCLUSION: TOWARD AN ANTHROPOLOGY OF ABSENCES

One possible interpretation of my analysis in this chapter is that disability entrepreneurs in Second Life are duped by neoliberal capitalism. However, more careful ethnographic attention reveals persons who in a sense take rhetorics of entrepreneurialism at their word, yet forge visions of a better self and community. Recentering entrepreneurial selfhood on collaboration and simultaneously reframing what "collaboration" entails, disability entrepreneurs sideline rhetorics of productivity and challenge dominant logics of ableism. As Michelle noted, "Second Life has given me a way to feel once again like I am a contributing member of society. It has helped me reconstruct my sense of identity, in the wake of becoming disabled."

At a methodological level, my analysis illustrates how "ethnographic thick description can surely offer a way forward for rethinking the economy outside of a capitalocentric frame" (Gibson-Graham, 2014: S149). Beliefs and practices around disability entrepreneurship in Second Life do nothing less than rework the notion of value, but in ways that cannot be reduced to either complicity or opposition. The relation to dominant beliefs is not so unilinear. Recalling insights gained from earlier research in Indonesia, I might say that these Second Life residents are not "translating" dominant notions of ability and labor. Rather, they "dub" them like a movie is dubbed into another language, resulting in an ongoing juxtaposition where moving lips never quite match the new, dubbed voice, but meaning-making nonetheless occurs (Boellstorff, 2003).

While some anthropologists are understandably "uncomfortable with scholarly insistence that people with disabilities teach us something" (Kulick and Rydström, 2015: 16), ethnographic analysis contributes more than knowledge regarding the specific community studied. For instance, attention to disability entrepreneurs in virtual worlds speaks to emerging dynamics of digital labor, and the implications of platform socialities for personhood. Their forms of mutual support challenge individualistic tropes of the self-made genius. Their experiences of value creation challenge the binarism of "ability" versus "disability," suggesting that rubrics attentive to human capability might prove more effective. Such insights also broaden intersections of disability studies and digital studies. To date, disability scholarship addressing virtual worlds has highlighted opportunities for "information, socialization, and community membership" (Stewart et al., 2010: 254). These are all valuable topics, but foregrounding labor allows us to pose different questions regarding current contexts and future possibilities for disability inclusion.

The point, then, is not that disabled persons should be compelled to "teach us something," but that they have a place at the table of recognized ways of living a fully human life. In this sense, I might term my analysis an "anthropology of absences." This builds on Boaventura de Sousa Santos's (2004: 239) notion of a "sociology of absences … an inquiry that aims to explain that what does not exist is, in fact, actively produced as non-existent." He emphasized that one way such "non-existence" is produced is "non-productiveness," which applied to labor takes the form of presumptions regarding "discardable populations" (ibid.), and which can be countered by "recuperating and valorising alternative systems of production … hidden or discredited by the capitalist orthodoxy of productivity" (Santos, 2004: 240; see Mitchell and Snyder, 2010). In recuperating and valorizing the work of digital disability entrepreneurs, I respond to how disability can be made to appear absent in regimes of labor, and how some disabled persons in Second Life presence their ability through languages and practices of entrepreneurship. This is why income can be partially delinked from entrepreneurship: entrepreneurship is being used to make present ability and contribution.

I also respond to the reality that some contemporary digital scholarship actively produces virtual worlds as non-existent, particularly those virtual worlds not oriented toward children (such as Minecraft) or predominantly structured as games (such as World of Warcraft). I remain amazed by how often colleagues ask me some version of the question, "Is Second Life even around any more?" Yet, "for ethnographers today, no task is more important than to make small facts speak to large concerns, to make the ethical acts ethnography describes into a performative ontology of economy and the threads of hope that emerge into stories of everyday revolution" (Gibson-Graham, 2014: S147).

This is true despite the danger that the disability entrepreneurs I discuss in this chapter could be taken as "poster children" for virtual worlds (and capitalist markets to boot). The tendency for disability experience to be reduced to either catastrophe or "inspiration" (Rousso, 2013) does not disappear in the digital domain. The response to this tendency should be neither to marginalize disability experience nor to treat it as an instance of "technosolutionism" (Lindtner et al., 2016), but to engage with that experience in contributing to interdisciplinary conversations regarding the human condition.

Making the lifeworlds of disability entrepreneurs in Second Life present in our conceptual debates can contribute powerfully toward better understanding the emerging digital economies that already transform societies. It reframes disability as a form of social action irreducible to limitation or lack. In a contemporary moment when so much discussion of online socialities foregrounds surveillance, deception, and precarity, the lifeworlds of disability entrepreneurs in Second Life point to the real possibilities for connection and creativity. And it is in approaches founded in neither utopia or dystopia, however promising or fearful the future might seem, that we find the best hope of comprehending our unfolding present.

ACKNOWLEDGEMENTS

I thank my Second Life interlocutors for their generosity, patience, and truly extraordinary insights. I thank my co-investigator, Donna Z. Davis, for her camaraderie and intellectual support. I thank Gerard Goggin and Haiqing Yu for their encouragement and support. A draft of this chapter was discussed by the LaborTech group; for the invitation to participate I thank Winifred Poster, the group's organizer; for their comments during the discussion I thank Opeyemi Akanbi, Sareeta Amrute, Julie Yujie Chen, Laura Forlano, Seda Guerses, and Lilly Irani. Additional comments were provided by Ilana Gershon, Alice Krueger, Silvia Lindtner, Alice Marwick, and Winifred Poster. A documentary about this project, *Our Digital Selves* (Bernhard Drax, director, 74mn, 2018), is freely available at https://youtu.be/GQw02-me0W4.

NOTES

1. In this chapter, I employ "disabled persons" rather than "people with disabilities." Both are contested and imperfect, but I find person-first language less effective (see Sinclair, 2013 [1999]; Titchkosky, 2001; Broderick and Ne'eman, 2008). I received Institutional Review Board (IRB) approval for this research. No HIPAA (Health Insurance Portability and Accountability Act) related details of health status were obtained, and details of self-identified disabilities (along with other personally identifying details) have been altered. Physical world and screen names have been changed; quoted text chat has been altered to make it harder to find using a search engine.
2. By extension the money can then be converted to any currency, but Linden Dollars are directly exchangeable only into US dollars.

3.   See, for instance, https://www.dol.gov/odep/topics/SelfEmploymentEntrepreneurship
.htm (accessed March 6, 2018); https://www.colorado.gov/pacific/dvr/self-employment
(accessed March 6, 2018).

REFERENCES

Au, W.J. (2017, September 25). Open forum: What's the most you ever paid for a virtual item
in Second Life (besides land)? *New World Notes*. Retrieved from http://nwn.blogs.com/
nwn/2017/ 09/sl-virtual-item-sale.html.
Au, W.J. (2018, April 6). Virtual job hunting in second life about as daunting as job hunting
IRL. *New World Notes*. Retrieved from http://nwn.blogs.com/nwn/2018/04/virtual-job
-second-life. html.
Bear, L., Ho, K., Tsing, A., and Yanagisako, S. (2015, March 20). Gens: A feminist manifesto
for the study of capitalism. Theorizing the contemporary. *Cultural Anthropology* website.
Retrieved from https://culanth.org/fieldsights/652-gens-a-feminist-manifesto-for-the-study
-of-capitalism.
Bloch, M. (1983). *Marxism and anthropology: The history of a relationship*. Oxford:
Clarendon Press.
Boellstorff, T. (2003). Dubbing culture: Indonesian gay and lesbi subjectivities and ethnogra-
phy in an already globalized world. *American Ethnologist, 30*(2), 225–242. doi:10.1525/ae
.2003.30.2.225.
Boellstorff, T. (2005). *The gay archipelago: Sexuality and nation in Indonesia*. Princeton, NJ:
Princeton University Press.
Boellstorff, T. (2015). *Coming of age in second life: An anthropologist explores the virtually
human* (2nd edn, with a new Preface). Princeton, NJ: Princeton University Press.
Bröckling, U. (2016). *The entrepreneurial self: Fabricating a new type of subject*. Los
Angeles, CA: SAGE.
Broderick, A., and Ne'eman, A. (2008). Autism as metaphor: Narrative and counter-narrative.
International Journal of Inclusive Education, 12(5/6), 459–476.
Burchardt, T. (2004). Capabilities and disability: The capabilities framework and the social
model of disability. *Disability and Society, 19*(7), 735–751.
Davis, D., and Boellstorff, T. (2016). Compulsive creativity: Virtual worlds, disability, and
digital capital. *International Journal of Communication, 10*, 2096–2118. Retrieved from
http://ijoc.org/ index.php/ijoc/article/view/5099/1639.
Dean, J. (2010). *Blog theory: Feedback and capture in the circuits of drive*. Cambridge: Polity.
Dewhurst, M. (2017). We are not entrepreneurs. In M. Graham and J. Shaw (eds), *Towards
a fairer gig economy* (pp. 20–23). Oxford: Meatspace Press.
Duffy, B.E. (2017). *(Not) getting paid to do what you love: Gender, social media, and aspira-
tional work*. New Haven, CT: Yale University Press.
Dunn, C.D. (2017). Personal narratives and self-transformation in postindustrial societies.
Annual Review of Anthropology, 46, 65–80.
Ekbia, H., and Nardi, B. (2017). *Heteromation, and other stories of computing and capitalism*.
Cambridge, MA: MIT Press.
Firth, R. (1954). Orientations in economic life. In E.E. Evans-Prichard (ed.), *The institutions
of primitive society* (pp. 12–24). Oxford: Basil Blackwell.
Friedner, M.I. (2015). *Valuing deaf worlds in urban India*. New Brunswick, NJ: Rutgers
University Press.
Gershon, I. (2017). *Down and out in the new economy: How people find (or don't find) work
today*. Chicago, IL: University of Chicago Press.
Gibson-Graham, J.K. (2014). Rethinking the economy with thick description and weak theory.
Current Anthropology, 55(S9), S147–S153.

Godelier, M. (1977). *Perspectives in Marxist anthropology.* Translated by Robert Brain. Cambridge: Cambridge University Press.

Gregg, M. (2011). *Work's intimacy.* Cambridge: Polity.

Harris, O., and Young, K. (1981). Engendered structures: Some problems in the analysis of reproduction. In J. Kahn and J. Llobera (eds), *The anthropology of pre-capitalist societies* (pp. 109–147). London: Macmillan.

Harvey, P., and Krohn-Hansen, C. (2018). Dislocating labour: Anthropological reconfigurations. *Journal of the Royal Anthropological Institute, 24*(S1), 10–28. doi:10.1111/1467 -9655.12796.

Hochschild, A.R. (2001). *The time bind: When work becomes home and home becomes work.* New York: H. Holt.

Irani, L. (2019). *Entrepreneurial citizenship: Innovators and their others in Indian development.* Princeton: Princeton University Press.

Kulick, D., and Rydström, J. (2015). *Loneliness and its opposite: Sex, disability, and the ethics of engagement.* Durham, NC: Duke University Press.

Lindtner, S. (forthcoming). *Age of experimentation: Making as entrepreneurial living in China's new normal.*

Lindtner, S., Bardzell, S., and Bardzell, J. (2016). Reconstituting the utopian vision of making: HCI after technosolutionism. *Proceedings of the 2016 CHI Conference on Human Factors in Computing Systems (CHI '16)* (pp. 1390–1402). New York: ACM. doi:10.1145/2858036 .2858506.

Malinowski, B. (1922). *Argonauts of the Western Pacific.* New York: E.P. Dutton & Co.

Marwick, A.E. (2017). Entrepreneurial subjects: Venturing from alley to valley. *International Journal of Communication,* 11, 2026–2029.

Marx, K. (1976 [1867]). *Capital: A critique of political economy. Volume I: The process of capitalist production.* Translated by Ben Fowkes. London: Penguin Books.

McRobbie, A. (2002). Clubs to companies: Notes on the decline of political culture in speeded up creative worlds. *Cultural Studies, 16*(4), 516–531.

Meillassoux, C. (1972). From reproduction to production: A Marxist approach to economic anthropology. *Economy and Society, 1*(1), 93–105.

Mitchell, D.T., and Snyder, S.L. (2010). Disability as multitude: Re-working non-productive labor power. *Journal of Literary and Cultural Disability Studies, 4*(2), 179–194. doi:10 .3828/jlcds.2010.14.

Nash, J. (1993). *We eat the mines and the mines eat us: Dependency and exploitation in Bolivian tin mines.* New York: Columbia University Press.

Neff, G. (2015). *Venture labor: Work and the burden of risk in innovative industries.* Cambridge, MA: MIT Press.

Neff, G. (2017). Conclusion: Agendas for studying communicative capitalism. *International Journal of Communication,* 11, 2046–2049.

Nussbaum, M. (2006). *Frontiers of justice: Disability, nationality and species membership.* Cambridge, MA: Harvard University Press.

Ondrejka, C. (2004). Escaping the gilded cage: User created content and building the Metaverse. *New York Law School Law Review, 49*(1), 81–101.

Ong, A. (1987). *Spirits of resistance and capitalist discipline: Factory women in Malaysia.* Albany, NY: State University of New York Press.

Pearce, C., Symborski, C., and Blackburn, B.R. (2015). Virtual worlds survey report: A trans-world study of non-game virtual worlds—demographics, attitudes, and preferences. Corporate report. Retrieved from http://cpandfriends.com/wp-content/uploads/2015/03/ vwsurveyreport_final_ publicationedition1.pdf.

Robinson, L. (2017). Entrepreneuring the good life? *International Journal of Communication,* 11, 2017–2021.

Ross, A., and Taylor, S. (2017). Disabled workers and the unattainable promise of information technology. *New Labor Forum*, 26(2), 84–90. doi:10.1177/1095796017699812.

Rousso, H. (2013). *Don't call me inspirational: A disabled feminist talks back*. Philadelphia, PA: Temple University Press.

Santos, B. (2004). The WSF: Toward a counter-hegemonic globalization, Part I. In J. Sen, A. Anand, A. Escobar, and P. Waterman (eds), *The world social forum: Challenging empires* (pp. 235–245). New Delhi: Viveka Foundation. Retrieved from http://www.choike.org/2009/eng/informes/ 1557.html.

Schumpeter, J.A. (1949). *The theory of economic development*. Cambridge, MA: Harvard University Press.

Sen, A. (2005). Human rights and capabilities. *Journal of Human Development*, 6(2), 151–166. doi:10.1080/14649880500120491.

Sennett, R. (2009). *The craftsman*. New Haven, CT: Yale University Press.

Sinclair, J. (2013 [1999]). Why I dislike "person first" language. *Autonomy, the Critical Journal of Interdisciplinary Autism Studies*, 1(2), 2–3.

Srnicek, N. (2017). *Platform capitalism*. Cambridge: Polity.

Stensrud, A.B. (2017). Precarious entrepreneurship: Mobile phones, work and kinship in neo-liberal Peru. *Social Anthropology*, 25(2), 159–173. doi:10.1111/1469-8676.12395.

Stewart, S., Hansen, T.S., and Carey, T.A. (2010). Opportunities for people with disabilities in the virtual world of Second Life. *Rehabilitation Nursing*, 35(6), 254–259.

Taussig, M. (1980). *The devil and commodity fetishism in South America*. Chapel Hill, NC: University of North Carolina Press.

Titchkosky, T. (2001). Disability: A rose by any other name? "Person-first" language in Canadian society. *Canadian Review of Sociology/Revue Canadienne de Sociologie*, 38(2), 125–140.

Tsing, A. (2009). Supply chains and the human condition. *Rethinking Marxism*, 21(2), 148–176. doi:10.1080/08935690902743088.

van Doorn, N. (2017). Platform labor: On the gendered and racialized exploitation of low-income service work in the "on-demand" economy. *Information, Communication and Society*, 20(6), 898–914. doi:10.1080/1369118X.2017.1294194.

Weber, M. (1930 [1905]). *The Protestant ethic and the spirit of capitalism*. Translated by Talcott Parsons. London: Allen & Unwin.

Weeks, K. (2011). *The problem with work: Feminism, Marxism, antiwork politics, and post-work imaginaries*. Durham, NC: Duke University Press.

Williamson, B. (2012). Electric moms and quad drivers: People with disabilities buying, making, and using technology in postwar America. *American Studies*, 52(1), 5–30.

Yanagisako, S. (2002). *Producing culture and capital: Family firms in Italy*. Princeton, NJ: Princeton University Press.

19. Disabled entrepreneurs creating value in Iran's entrepreneurial ecosystem

Vahid Makizadeh, Shumaila Yousafzai, Siavash Aein Jamshid and Adel Mohebbi

INTRODUCTION

People with disabilities have increasingly preferred entrepreneurship as a career more than than persons without disabilities (Harris et al., 2013). Surprisingly, the focus of the disabled entrepreneurship literature is still on life challenges and negative motives such as the absence of opportunities (Blanck et al., 2000; Boylan and Burchardt, 2002; Gouskova, 2012; Pagán, 2009) as drivers of entrepreneurship activity, rather than strengths and personal advantages or favorable contexts (Miller and Le Breton-Miller, 2017). Beyond the negative motivations, there are positive reasons to start a business by disabled people, such as flexibility and overall job satisfaction (Cooney, 2008; Pagán, 2009; Gouskova, 2012). Nevertheless, disabled entrepreneurs have been overly seen as underperforming in the literature (Larsson, 2006). There is little research on the success or competencies of disabled entrepreneurs (Bagheri and Abbariki, 2017; Miller and Le Breton-Miller, 2017; Roni and Ribm, 2009). A crucial step before evaluating the performance of disabled entrepreneurs is to understand what success in business means to them within the socio-economic context in which they run their businesses.

Disability as a heterogeneous social construct is related to a diverse set of individuals (Renko et al., 2016). This diversity means that different disabled entrepreneurs have different needs and motives, and different perceptions about value creation. Policy and research could benefit from paying more attention to the diverse set of disabled entrepreneurs' perception of value creation. The focus of previous research has been to evaluate the outcomes of entrepreneurial activity in objective monetary terms, even for the disabled (e.g., Holt and Macpherson, 2010; Halabisky, 2014), ignoring that entrepreneurs may have their own perceptions of what success means to them. There are some recognitions that entrepreneurs' evaluations of success go beyond economic returns (Wach et al., 2016), and that success in business cannot be equated simply by financial rewards (Sarasvathy et al., 2013). We argue that entrepreneurial success is a subjective and multidimensional construct, and understanding of subjective measures of success seems to be essential for entrepreneurship research, specifically in the disabled people's context (Wach et al., 2016; Fisher et al., 2014).

Entrepreneurs might persist with underperforming firms as long as individual, non-financial aims are considered satisfactory (DeTienne et al., 2008). Paradoxically, in some situations, profitable firms may be disbanded if they do not accomplish personal goals (Reijonen and Komppula, 2007; Sarasvathy et al., 2013). A one-sided economic analysis restricts the contribution of entrepreneurial activity, which is commenced by disadvantaged and marginalized groups such as the disabled (Welter and Smallbone, 2011). However, these groups often create unique value far removed from the purely financial value (Sheikh et al., 2019). A disabled entrepreneur can contribute highly at multiple levels by generating a social value which extends beyond the surface level (Renko et al., 2016; Parker Harris et al., 2014; Harris et al., 2013). In the case of entrepreneurs with disability, early achievement, such as the creation of work and operating self-supporting micro-enterprises, can be perceived as a success, and high profitability is the next stage of growth (Walls et al., 2001).

The importance of studying entrepreneurship of disadvantaged people through the value creation lens seems to be helpful to understand how the businesses of disadvantaged people result in positive changes toward their families, societies, and other businesses (Sheikh et al., 2019). They broadly categorize value outcomes as value creation accruing through entrepreneurship at four levels: (1) the individual level (for example, self-esteem: Cooney, 2008; Martin and Honig, 2019); independence (Halabisky, 2014; Dhar and Farzana, 2017), empowerment (Falch and Hernæs, 2012), work–life balance (Dhar and Farzana, 2017; Jones and Latreille, 2011; Pagán, 2009); (2) the business level (for example, access to resources and access to networks); (3) the household level (for example, improvements in attitudes towards entrepreneurship and family welfare); (4) the community or society level: to hire persons with disabilities (Blanck et al., 2000), social impact (Rozali et al., 2018), and social inclusion of minority groups (Anderson et al., 2006; Pavey, 2006).

Thus, the aim of this study is to explore and identify these values, certainly in a context that is less researched, in order to enhance our understanding of the contribution disabled people's businesses make in different societies. It is also essential to start from the disabled person's conceptualization of business success, as this may substantially differ from the mainstream definitions in the entrepreneurship literature. Disabled people often create their particular values through their businesses, for instance, by the contribution their business operations make in reducing poverty levels and strengthening the economic growth of a country (Falch and Hernæs, 2012), or how well it contributes to the disability groups.

CONTEXTUALIZING DISABILITY AND DISABLED ENTREPRENEURSHIP IN IRAN

Contextualizing the process of entrepreneurship within disability is necessary to help us in understanding the nuances of the social context for entrepreneurship. This study aims to explore the value creation of disabled entrepreneurs in the developing-country context of Iran. By using the narrative accounts of three disabled entrepreneurs from Bushehr, Iran, we show how disabled people create value for themselves, their family, business, and society through entrepreneurship.

People with disabilities, as one of the most significant minorities in the country, constitute nearly 1.3 percent of Iran's population (Soltani et al., 2015). According to the Human Rights Council (2013), disabilities in Iran can be classified into five groups: (1) disabilities due to illnesses/accidents or by birth; (2) disabilities caused during the eight-year Iran–Iraq war; (3) disabilities caused as a result of gunshots by the security forces; (4) disabilities due to amputation as a legal form of Islamic punishment; and (5) disabilities due to an increase in the air pollution and its destructive effects on human embryos, and thus birth defects.

Research shows that people with disability experience more access challenges than people without disability. For example, public transportation, funding, and cultural problems are the main challenges of access for disabled people in Iran (Mobaraki and Zadehbagheri, 2003). The absence of awareness, and financial problems, further affect their access to healthcare services in Iran. Disabled people experience poorer health than those without disabilities. Furthermore, one of the significant challenges among people with disabilities is their low level of happiness. The prevalence of depression among different groups of the population in Iran is around 5.6 to 73 percent, and the rate of depression among people with disabilities is higher than for the general population (Soltani and Takian, 2018).

Like most countries in the world, different legislations and laws have been passed, which trigger eligibility to benefits for disabled people, and Iran is no exception. The State Welfare Organization provides welfare benefits to people with disabilities in society. According to Alaedini (2004), this organization defines just four significant types of disability: physical, mental, hearing, and visual. The Iran–Iraq War resulted in a newly disabled population, which constitutes nearly 400 000 of Iran's population. The government created the Janbazan Foundation to provide war veterans with special treatment (Alaedini, 2004). The government of Iran has ratified national and international protection treaties concerning the rights of disabled people, such as the Comprehensive Law on Protection of the Rights of Persons with Disabilities in 2004, the Convention on the Rights of Persons with Disabilities in 2008, the Convention on the Rights of the Child (CRC), and the commitment of General Comment No. 9 of the CRC Committee.

Obviously, like the legislation of many countries, the Disability Protect Act (2003) privides protection in areas such as public building access, education, housing, and finance. For instance, organizations receiving state funding are supposed to employ 3 percent of their human resources from the general disabled population. However, no monitoring or punishment system makes the law work to protect the majority of persons with disabilities in Iran. For example, most public transportation is not accessible to people with disabilities. Similarly, public buildings are not fully accessible to disabled people (Bahreini, 2007). Currently, there are more than 250 disability-related non-governmental ornanizations (NGOs), in Iran with different levels of activity. Despite the government acknowledgment of the crucial role of these NGOs, they have to face many challenges (Adib-sereshki and Salenhpour, 2011). One of the solutions offered by NGOs for many underprivileged families with financial problems and low incomes has been to provide pensions. Unfortunately, the low amount of pensions is not a dependable source of relief (Kamali, 2011).

The Iranian government has been unable to define disability as a social issue, and the efforts to remove the social barriers have been insufficient (Samadi, 2008). The lack of a well-established regulation system for people with disability faced serious problems with employment and workplace challenges, in Iran as in the rest of the world (e.g., Hwang and Roulstone, 2015 in South Korea; Jones and Latreille, 2011 in the United Kingdom; Namatovu et al., 2012 in East Africa). There are no exact statistics available on the total employment numbers of people with disabilities of working age in Iran. According to the last Census (2012), most disabled people are of working age (15–64 years), and about 21 percent of working-age people with disabilities are out of work (Ashtari, 2013). However, the employment situation in Iran is complicated. The Iranian nation's population is young, and the rate of unemployment is about 15 percent. The rate of unemployment for people with disabilities is estimated to be twice as high (Moore and Kornblet, 2011). Unemployed people with disabilities in Iran face serious challenges and barriers to gain employment. One of these challenges is the attitudes of people without disabilities towards them. Attitudes of Iranian parents towards their children with disabilities are influenced by factors such as education, religion, and the degree of severity of disability (Adib-sereshki and Salenhpour, 2011). Attitudes of employers also continue to be a significant issue for disabled people. An example is lack of trust in their quality of the work and their capabilities. It is generally believed that employers avoid using disabled people, either because of discrimination or because they think that their working capabilities are not sufficient to do the job as well as those without disabilities (Bagheri and Abbariki, 2017).

METHOD

This study adopts a narrative approach as a reliable research method in entrepreneurship studies, to understand the lived experiences of disabled entrepreneurs and to explore the unique forms of value that disabled entrepreneurs create through their entrepreneurial activity (Larty and Hamilton, 2011). The narratives reported in the following section are based on interviews with three disabled entrepreneurs conducted in July 2019 in the Bushehr province of Iran. Each interview took approximately 90 minutes to complete. The interviews were voice recorded and transcribed in Persian (the Iranian language) and later translated into English. The narrative accounts of the three disabled entrepreneurs were prepared after paraphrasing by the researchers. A purposive sampling strategy was applied to choose participants who vary in the age of their business, family characteristics, educational background, and the way of starting the business (Silverman, 2005).

NARRATIVES OF IRANIAN DISABLED ENTREPRENEURS

In this section, we present the narrative accounts of three of the disabled entrepreneurs who were interviewed, to illustrate the different levels of contributions. We focus on the four levels of contributions: individual, business, household, and social. The interviews touched upon a wide range of topics, such as entrepreneurial aspirations, family life, sources of business support, barriers, and opportunities. The narratives reveal how businesses of disabled people help them to create value at multiple levels.

BOX 19.1   FARAH (FEMALE, 34, MOTHER OF TWO DAUGHTERS, SEVEN AND TWO-YEARS OLD)

Farah is an entrepreneur with a hereditary disability: muscular dystrophy. She has a workshop for manufacturing and training in handicrafts and clothes. She also has some activities in a number of other fields, from bridal tiaras and accessories, bridal items and handmade leather products, to handmade decorative kitchen assessories and even layettes. Her disability can be attributed to her symptoms 15 years ago, at the worst possible time in the days after her marriage. She was diagnosed with muscular dystrophy, and at that time, she was subjected to additional psychological pressure. A year after that, she completely lost her ability to walk and her mental condition deteriorated, which led her to become depressed and isolated. She was even referred to an exorcist for treatment. However, things did not carry on in the same way:

> I told myself I'm creative. My oratory is good too. I have an idea too. So I have to stand on my own again. After that, I started researching what is good for me and what could I do. I do what to be successful and I can cope with the disease with it. Because the crafts were easier to make and I could do it with the least amount of tools, I first started making bridal essentials. I have been doing this for 12 years now, it has been 7 years I do it professionally and I have now reached the point of being able to manage 7 people all the way down.

She points out that the most important individual achievements are self-esteem, happiness, and then improving her financial condition:

> The first thing that this work brought me was self-confidence, then joy and happiness that came with it afterward. My financial situation has also improved and covered the cost of our lives and illness. Besides, I can help my family and donate to charity, which makes me feel good.

Changing Farah's attitude and future vision and hope for her life are other issues that have affected this business. She has been frustrated about her future sometimes, but has a plan for it, pushing forward with her positive thinking about work decisions, such as starting a new business:

> I used to think I'm a paralyzed woman and it's all over. I'd be disabled and then be back in the house for a while, but after work I would have a brighter future. Every time I made a new decision, I told myself: no, I'm getting better and starting a new job. Some would say it's difficult to have a child, but I didn't. I planned and I did it right. Now I want to say I am sick, but I'll be fine on the day. When I saw that I was making such a small contribution, I went to university this year to get more professional training and education.

In terms of improving her business status, Farah points out that with the help of managerial skills, she has also expanded her business relationships. In doing so, she has sought to gain better access to financial resources and newer providers, also increasing her bargaining power:

> As much as I could, I tried to reach out to others. I have the phone number of many influential people in the municipality and the city council, and I keep in touch with them on various issues. Whether to criticize the problems I see in the city or to set up exhibitions and seasonal markets. I am currently holding a training class under the supervision of the Municipality Cultural Department. Nowadays, I don't have financing problems, because I got from the Cultural Heritage Organization and the Ministry of Social Welfare, I could easily get my loan. At the recent general exhibition, I've got many orders. I was very successful in every field I've entered and now I work with many people in different places. I also buy raw materials, mainly from wherever costs would be lower. Now that we have increased our orders, the same wholesalers are coming to sell us materials.

Alongside these factors, the impact of Farah's entrepreneurship on her family is clear in several respects. She argues that the income from her business is a reliable source of money for the family. The family members' participation in the new business has also increased:

> We used to rent a house, but despite all the hardships, we now can buy a house and some lands. My husband was a regular employee at his workplace. I helped him pay his college tuition until he gets his bachelor's degree, then he has been promoted at his work. My husband also said, let's buy a fishing boat. We bought it and my husband rented it to fishers every year.

Also, the income from this entrepreneurship has often positively impacted upon the family's financial decisions and has changed her and her husband's positions in financial and non-financial decision-making: "It has changed the financial decision making. So, financial decisions are for me to take. Although we always consult with each other, many decisions are left to me." Farah has also helped other members of the family, such as her brother or sister, and improved their financial situation: "I even paid some of their debts and I was able to get them loans through my contacts."

According to Farah, her husband and children have also been influenced by her business. It has increased the happiness, joy, and confidence of the family members, and improved the self-belief and positive thinking in her family:

> The burden of my illness was all on my husband's shoulder. In fact, not all of the costs of this disease are due to medication. Part of that is the spirit. He used to be psychologically annoyed sometimes, but nevertheless, when he saw the success of a job, he was still passionate, tolerate it easily, and also tried harder himself. When my daughter was at kindergarten, her schoolmates called her "the crippled mom's daughter", because of my illness. She was very depressed. Then her dad told her to look at her mom. "She's an artist …" But now if you talk to my daughter, she'll proudly say that my mother is an artist. She has realized that I have succeeded in doing so and this has increased her confidence.

In addition, these abilities and the success of Farah as an entrepreneur have entirely changed the perceptions and expectations of her family members. Previous doubts, worries and sympathetic looks have turned into confidence, and has even led to the involvement of more family members in her business:

> It was like a while after I was sick at home. I was banished from my family, but now that things have changed, they are getting closer and closer. So even in their decisions, they ask my opinion. Now my success is one of the crucial parameters for my husband's family. These days they go out and advertise me efficiently and talk proudly of my success, but they hadn't had such a look before and had a pity at first.

Thus, she now has a more prominent place in the family decision-making and can be relied on as a consultative and personal partner, especially since her symptoms of disability have also recently begun to appear in her brother and sister. Also, she particularly cares about them:

> Well, I've earned so much knowledge and ability in this period. Many of my friends and family members who want to start a business get involved. When you succeed, others will trust you more. My family is now expecting me to support my brother and sister mentally because they know I can understand them better.

As previously mentioned, Farah's business is tied to social issues, especially charity. She emphasizes in her remarks: "I like to spend more on charity. I've seen hardship and poverty with my own eyes. So, I try to do whatever I can to charity." Her charitable activities include financial and non-financial donations:

> Our charity includes a series of activities. One is teaching handicrafts to disabled people and homeless women and victims of domestic violence. I even teach poor people who are introduced to me outside the institution. With my training, they were able to run a small business and change their lives.

What Farah points out at the end is that her success as a disabled entrepreneur has always had a positive impact on the motivation and ambition of the people around her:

> At the first meetings, there were so many people and even students that had questions on how I was able to get on with my job, but after a while I was no longer aware of my disability and it became normal for them. Even when they see me they get more motivation to get along.

BOX 19.2 ALBORZ (MALE, 29, SINGLE)

Alborz has shaking hands (a type of movement disorder) and struggles with his speech and gait, but has started a delicate business despite his congenital physical and movement disabilities. He started his career in information technology (IT) services and electronic systems repair eight years ago. He moved to Bushehr five years ago. According to Alborz, during this time, he was mentally better, happier, and his work success significantly increased his self-confidence. Besides, he has tried to improve his physical condition (walking and speaking clearly). Before he began, Alborz was a shy person, and somewhat introverted: "When I got started, I found I had to be in the community and this made me focus more on my behavior and movements. And by doing so, I was able to improve myself physically as well as mentally."

He says he has now become fully independent financially and a self-reliant person, and the financial situation has boosted his self-esteem: "It makes me feel strong not to have to get help from someone."

He also mentions his attitude towards the future. At first, he always expected others to help him, but after a while, his vision of the future and his perception of it changed in the post-business period: "I've always been waiting for someone to do something for me. Someone to come up with a miracle for me. Now I look to the future to do a miracle myself and take a step for myself."

In this business, Alborz believes, in addition to self-confidence, he has acquired the ability to take risks:

> I came here only for the reason that I had a strong attachment to my mother. One day I told myself how long I was going to be like this. I told myself I was going to Shiraz anyway so that I could completely stand on my own. And finally, in this city – Bushehr – I had a lot of hardship and loneliness to become independent.

The business skills that Alborz has learned with this successful entrepreneurship have had a significant impact on gaining the trust of his stakeholders, access to financial and non-financial resources, good communications, and increased bargaining power:

> Naturally, as it goes along, one proves himself to others. I need to prove myself in the community so that others can trust me. The first year that a customer who comes in,

would say to himself, he's paralyzed. Can he do my job? But now, customers come from elsewhere and even some of them come to me to do their jobs.

In addition to risk-taking, he has learned business skills such as marketing and customer service during this time:

> At the beginning, I only sold in Bushehr and Shiraz, but then I tried to advertise on the internet and I sent my product elsewhere. I think customer service is critical because I have to deal with people of different ages and behaviors, but I have always tried to keep my client satisfied.

Alborz is also well-versed in the job:

> I have proven myself to be a responsible person to wholesalers or a customer. In fact, work has taught me to be responsible. Nowadays, the situation is that some colleagues are calling and asking me how to do so and so. In the marketplace, I deal with different places, and if I see someone selling me the raw materials expensively, I would easily refuse and work with someone else. For example, a mortgage bank called Bank Maskan wanted to loan me 1 billion Rials. I had no guarantor. The real estate agent told me to tell the bank manager to take his business license as the loan voucher. The manager told him it can't be said. How can this pay off with his disability? Alborz has been my tenant for two years and he has never paid off late, he said. Now, besides I have paid the loan, I can borrow much more quickly.

Besides overcoming problems in the personal and commercial fields, the support, ideas, and expectations of the Alborz family in these eight years cannot be ignored. At first, the family doubted Alborz's ability to be independent. However, their skepticism has gradually changed into trust. Alborz is proud of the family, and is helping the family financially:

> Before coming here and starting my own business, my family was always cautious and worried about my job. But when it comes to financial independence, the limits are reduced, and their worries lessened … my mom says I'm sure if Alborz says he will do something or buy something, he can and he will do it. Somehow, she is proud of this, and now they all trust me very much. Now they don't care about having a disabled child.

Considering all these factors, Alborz is satisfied with his current status in society. He was not part of the community for a while, but today he feels different because his life has inspired others and he can sometimes help others to be happier and more hopeful:

> There are many who say we gain hope when they see me. The person I rented my house from supports me a lot. When I see my friends and colleagues sitting depressed and thoughtful, I'm going to kid and joke around to make them feel good. I'll tell them you're healthy. Have faith.

He has also helped other disabled people to change their mental state:

> There are people who tell me a family member of theirs with a disability has the same conditions as you but is mentally miserable. Then they came to film me, or sometimes they bring them to the workshop to talk to them. It had a great effect on their mental state. It also makes me happy to be able to help someone like me.

Another fact that Alborz points out is the change in the way the community sees him, especially the family and business people who no longer see him as a disabled person, as he has been able to change that view a little: "They may have had a little support from the beginning; but not now. It's all on my credit and I no longer be known only for my disability."

BOX 19.3   AMIR (MALE, 39, MARRIED, ONE-YEAR-OLD DAUGHTER)

Amir, a 39-year-old man, owns a marine handcraft workshop. He had a car accident 17 years ago when he was 22 years old. He had been lying on a bed for four years due to complications, which caused his knees to be paralyzed. At age 31, after a long period of depression, he encountered a disabled charity and it was the turning point in his life:

> There was a silent death situation for me and I was locked up in a room. I wasn't talking to anyone. I didn't think of anything outside my room. I wasn't even thinking about getting dressed someday … I was introduced to a charity. In there, they were giving various training to the disabled for free, which I chose marine handcraft. After a month because I had good talent, the coach told me you could start your work independently.

He now has a successful business with four employees, is married, and has a one-year-old daughter. Amir explains his most important business accomplishments as restoring his mental condition, financial independence, community acceptance, social communication, and improving his social skills:

> When I saw I was selling something I made, I was eager to work more. Making these handcrafts had a great impact on my mental condition. It made me financially better and being independent. Little by little, my relationship with my family members had gotten better and I got to know more people outside.

After this, his self-esteem has increased; as he says: "A disabled person sees himself as a burden, but when you have what you earn, you get self-confidence and it gives you self-confidence. When you work, others will count on you and accept you."

As a result, at the individual level, this business has changed his attitude and increased his hope for the future and his greater desire for life:

> I never participated in home decisions before. Nothing did matter to me at all because my life was so messed up and I had no hope of how long my life would last. I never thought I'd be able to get married or have a family. These successes made me be more with my family, getting married, having a baby, even hoping to be back in good health and want to do it again. I used to say I don't want to be fine at all and I don't want this life.

At the business level, this entrepreneurship has led to greater business relationships and access to more financial and non-financial resources for Amir:

> These relationships and privileges have made it easier for me to get a loan. I was introduced to the Cultural Heritage Organization and other cities' handicraft fairs and I found markets in other cities. They were delivering their orders to me, and now a large part of my sales are from organizations.

This entrepreneurship has further strengthened his performance. For example, his management skills such as decision-making, sales, innovation and marketing, and his communication skills have been improved:

> Well, I was no longer shy and bashful. I could talk everywhere and be more intimate with others. Another influence that this success has had on me has been the desire to work harder every day. I was doing newer work every month. Because after a while, others were working harder and improving in the market. As an owner here, when you enter the workplace, you face a variety of challenges that will make you respond. One day there is a problem with your business partner, another day with a raw material problem, some days with a sales problem and so on. All this needs management.

In spite of all this, his entrepreneurship for the family has, above all, resolved their past worries and concerns about his mental state: "My family was always upset and depressed before I started. But now I'm really happy that I was able to have a successful business. My wife always says that her only motivation to marry me has been my hard work."

In addition, Amir was able to create better welfare conditions for his family: "Everyone is counting on me financially, and if necessary I will help them because my financial situation is fine and I have no dependence on anyone."

He has become a supportive person for the family in terms of personality: "Well, they ask for my help in the discussions and decisions at home, and sometimes they talk to me if they have a mental problem."

In the social impact dimension, he points out that he has been able to change the attitudes of others toward disability in society to some extent: "I was only suffering from pity because of others' perspective and sometimes even with a blow with a word, but I suppose it has now been proven that disability is not an eternal issue and now they look at me with an artist label."

He also helps other people with disabilities since the success of his business. He has created a small community for the rights of people with disabilities:

> I was introduced to them or met them in different places. I think this relationship works well for them because their mental state has improved after this acquaintance. Especially since I gave some of them free training and now they are working. There were a few people with disabilities who came together to form a group to help with disability rights where needed. We are defending or pursuing the rights of people with disabilities.

VALUE CREATION THROUGH DISABLED ENTREPRENEURSHIP

The narratives of Farah, Alborz, and Amir indicate how disabled entrepreneurship can be the source of value creation at multiple levels. Findings revealed that the main advantage for disabled entrepreneurs' activity is the change of position from the viewpoint of the disabled person and their stakeholders. Regardless of the differences in the entrepreneurial narrative for the interviewees, each acquired a new distinct position that is the consequence of values created by them through entrepreneurship. The findings show that disabled entrepreneurs have their perceptions of what success means to them. The values created through their entrepreneurial experience can be grouped into four levels: individual, household, business, and society.

The first level of value which was identified in the narratives is the individual values. Entrepreneurial experience has enabled people with disabilities to make individual achievements. These achievements are expressed through autonomy, changing attitudes of stakeholders—including family, financial institutions, customers, suppliers, and employees—empowerment, and personal wellbeing. These findings are in line with other studies such as Pagán (2009), Falch and Hernæs (2012), Halabisky (2014), and Martin and Honig (2019). The increase in autonomy reflects how disabled entrepreneurs create value beyond the traditional constraints and challenges they face in society. The self-confidence disabled people gain in their entrepreneurial enterprise, enables them to perform activities attributed traditionally to people without disability. Each one of them experiences independence by engaging in entrepreneurship. Their independence shows in the social notion of change from a dependent position to an independent position, and also in substantive matters such as increased financial independence and willingness to take risks. This finding is generally in line with previous studies. It shows how disabled entrepreneurship shapes economic self-sufficiency and thereby increases the ability to make decisions on their investment (Dhar and Farzana, 2017; Martin and Honig, 2019).

Another individual value created by disabled entrepreneurship is changed stakeholders' attitudes. As revealed by the narratives of the participants, their entrepreneurial activity has positively changed the attitudes of various stakeholders toward disabled people. Disabled entrepreneurs have been able to make a significant impact on family decisions, and have experienced more positive attitudes toward the disabled. This changes the concept of disability from society's viewpoint.

Personal growth was another individual value that was created. Improvement in personal attributes such as responsibility and risk-taking, making substantial decisions such as going to university (in the case of Farah) and getting married (in the case of Amir), are signs of personal growth. Each narrative tells a story of increased personal wellbeing. For all of the interviewees, entrepreneurship was a career move towards self-fulfillment: they relate their happiness, their more advanced social skills, their improved mental state, their optimism about and hope for the future, and their wellbeing, to engaging in doing business. Indeed, establishing a business is often reported to benefit the disabled by enhancing their happiness, positive attitude to life, and satisfaction with their lives. Besides empowerment, becoming a supportive person could also contribute to personal growth. These underline the potential of entrepreneurship as a path for the disabled to live a life that is personally meaningful and motivating.

Beyond the value for the individual entrepreneur, a disabled entrepreneur's engagement in the entrepreneurial activity can also add value to the business domain. All interviewees reported a desired level of business performance. At the business level, entrepreneurship has led to the development of business relationships. By developing social support systems through social skills (Viriri and Makurumidze, 2014), disabled entrepreneurs are able to build solid networks that can help them to serve new markets and customers. In doing so, they have sought to gain more access to financial and non-financial resources. Entrepreneurial activities also strengthened the managerial skills of disabled entrepreneurs. For instance, management skills such as decision-making, marketing, and communication skills have been improved. Following the strengthening of the disabled business, their bargaining power with suppliers has also increased.

Value creation at the household level is a critical factor in explaining the disabled people's entrepreneurial development. The positive impact on the household members of increased income from the entrepreneurial activity can improve their overall welfare and quality of life, and improve their attitudes toward the disabled, so they are viewed as independent and entrepreneurial. A disabled person's engagement in entrepreneurship may also have a positive influence on attitudes in the household. Access to resources such as employment tend to be good predictors of the disabled person's participation in decision-making. Another area in which their engagement in entrepreneurial activities can potentially add value is in the disabled person's decision-making role in the household. Analysis of the narratives indicates that disabled entrepreneurial activity solidifies familial ties.

Furthermore, entrepreneurship can enhance the consultative role of the disabled person in the household and improve trust toward them. Creating a sense of pride among family members was another subjective value that interviewees highlighted. This emotion has helped to promote the overall position of their family. The entry of family members into the business was another consequence of disabled people's entrepreneurship. As we have seen, Farah, as a female, has more influence over family outcomes. Future studies could consider gender differences concerning value creation by disabled entrepreneurs at the family level.

The impact of disabled people's entrepreneurship at the societal level is another dimension of value created through their entrepreneurial activity. Synthesizing the life stories of the disabled entrepreneurs shows them as agents of social change. Social outcomes in this regard mainly pertain to changing society's attitude towards disability in general, and engaging in entrepreneurial activity by disabled people. More specifically, disabled entrepreneurs are a source of inspiration for others, especially other disabled people. They have a positive impact on the motivation and ambition of the people around them. Helping others, especially disabled people, via education and advice to start business and non-profit programs can be a significant source of services, thus contributing to value creation at the community level. Setting up a network to help each other (Zamore, 2014) and to protect the rights of the disabled is another social value created by our participants. Analysis of the narratives shows that entrepreneurs with a disability can act as role models for their community. Furthermore, they could be the enablers for other marginalized groups such as the disabled. These findings are in line with previous studies such as Martin and Honig (2019) and Rozali et al. (2018).

In summary, the narratives of three disabled Iranian entrepreneurs underscore that value creation of disabled entrepreneurship is multi-level, and is the story of changing positions from care-recipient to an independent person. The first dimension of subjective value includes individual value, pertinent to personal success indicators such as autonomy, self-confidence, and positive attitudinal change. The business domain is the next level of value creation. Entrepreneurship enables the disabled person to form a business network and have more access to resources. Strengthening management skills and bargaining power are other values at this level. Another level of value refers to the household. Findings show that the disabled person engaging in entrepreneurship activity, besides improving family welfare, has a profound impact on the internal dynamics of their family through improving attitudes toward the disabled person's participation in decision-making, and reinforcement of family relationships. Social values are the last component of subjective value. At this level, changing society's attitude towards disability is a critical outcome. Helping others to start a business, and protection of the rights of persons with disabilities, shape other social values created by disabled entrepreneurship. Future research could further study the interaction between individual, household, business, and social levels that impact and contextualize values for disabled entrepreneurs. Figure 19.1 summarizes the value creation perspective.

CONCLUSION AND POLICY IMPLICATIONS

The multi-level value creation that disabled people in Iran find through engaging in entrepreneurial activity provides a robust and substantial motive to keep putting effort into their businesses. In this study, we shed light on four dimensions of

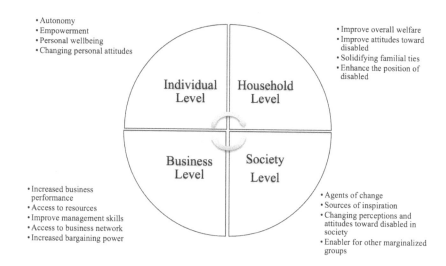

- Autonomy
- Empowerment
- Personal wellbeing
- Changing personal attitudes

- Improve overall welfare
- Improve attitudes toward disabled
- Solidifying familial ties
- Enhance the position of disabled

Individual Level | Household Level

Business Level | Society Level

- Increased business performance
- Access to resources
- Improve management skills
- Access to business network
- Increased bargaining power

- Agents of change
- Sources of inspiration
- Changing perceptions and attitudes toward disabled in society
- Enabler for other marginalized groups

Source: Adapted from Sheikh et al. (2019).

Figure 19.1   *Value creation perspective in disabled entrepreneurs*

subjective value with the experiences of disabled entrepreneurs. Such substantial, multidimensional values are revealed in the behavior of disabled entrepreneurs, who could thereby act as role models for their families and their local communities. Having a new position in society through entrepreneurship may indicate that entrepreneurship is a fruitful route for the disabled in society and enhances their potential to contribute to a country's economic growth (Falch and Hernæs, 2012).

However, this contribution also demonstrates the constraints that disabled people find in their entrepreneurial career while enacting the different values. Traditional attitudes about disabled people's role in society, and institutional problems in access to resources, could challenge the realization of their entrepreneurial goals and plans. Therefore, although this chapter highlights the importance of disabled value creation, it also emphasizes the need to consider the constraints on disabled value creation.

This study also has several policy implications. From our narratives, it was evident that formal and informal supports have played a substantial role in reinforcing the disabled people's position. For Farah and Alborz, it was family support, and for Amir it was a charity. Another implication is appropriate fit of the type of business and the condition of the disabled. All participants choose an entrepreneurial activity that was proportional to their abilities and financial status.

Hence, policy recommendations are equally disparate. The first recommendation is to invest in the education of disabled people. Education could lead to enhancing their empowerment. Hence, it also results in developing confidence and in changing the perceptions of disabled people and their stakeholders. These changes can lead to the resilience of disabled entrepreneurs in harsh times. The second recommendation is to develop initiatives for providing business consulting services. Such initiatives can have a critical influence on starting a desired entrepreneurial activity. A third recommendation is the need to make available and accessible loans to disabled entrepreneurs who have no savings, and access to collateral to facilitate business creation by them. Eventually, such a higher level of values is crucial to eliminating barriers for disabled people, providing them with multiple values that are inspiring to themselves. These findings help us to rethink the role of disabled entrepreneurship in society beyond financial issues.

REFERENCES

Adib-sereshki, N., and Salenhpour, Y. (2011). Disability and Iranian culture. Conference on Democracy, Diversity and Disability, Winnipeg, Canada.

Alaedini, P. (2004). *Training and Employment of People with Disabilities: Iran 2003 (An Ability Asia Country Study)*. Bangkok, Thailand: International Labour Office.

Anderson, R.B., Dana, L.P., and Dana, T.E. (2006). Indigenous land rights, entrepreneurship, and economic development in Canada: "opting-in" to the global economy. *Journal of World Business*, *41*(1), 45–55.

Ashtari, M. (2013). Disabled employment status. The Fifth Web Conference on Rehabilitation in Spinal Cord Injury. Tehran, Iran, July.

Bagheri, A., and Abbariki, M. (2017). Competencies of disabled entrepreneurs in Iran: implications for learning and development. *Disability and Society*, *32*(1), 69–92.

Bahreini, R. (2007). Understanding disability as a human rights issue. Gozaar: A Forum on Human Rights and Democracy in Iran. Message posted to http://www.gozaar.org/english/articles-en/Understanding-Disability-as-a-Human-Rights-Issue.html.

Blanck, P.D., Sandler, L.A., Schmeling, J.L., and Schartz, H.A. (2000). The emerging workforce of entrepreneurs with disabilities: preliminary study of entrepreneurship in Iowa. *Iowa Law Review*, *85*, 1583.

Boylan, A., and Burchardt, T. (2002). Barriers to self-employment for disabled people. Report for the Small Business Service, October.

Cooney, T. (2008). Entrepreneurs with disabilities: profile of a forgotten minority. *Irish Business Journal*, *4*(1), 119–129.

DeTienne, D.R., Shepherd, D.A., and De Castro, J.O. (2008). The fallacy of "only the strong survive": the effects of extrinsic motivation on the persistence decisions for under-performing firms. *Journal of Business Venturing*, *23*(5), 528–546.

Dhar, S., and Farzana, T. (2017). Entrepreneurs with disabilities in Bangladesh: an exploratory study on their entrepreneurial motivation and challenges. *European Journal of Business and Management*, *9*(36), 103–114.

Falch, R., and Hernæs, U.J.V. (2012). Disability, social identity, and entrepreneurship: evidence from a laboratory experiement in rural Uganda. Master's thesis.

Fisher, R., Maritz, A., and Lobo, A. (2014). Evaluating entrepreneurs' perception of success: development of a measurement scale. *International Journal of Entrepreneurial Behavior and Research*, *20*(5), 478–492.

Gouskova, E. (2012). Self-employment among people with disabilities: evidence from the current population survey. *SSRN Electronic Journal*. DOI: 10.2139/ssrn.2175687.

Halabisky, D. (2014). *Entrepreneurial activities in Europe – Entrepreneurship for people with disabilities*. Surrey, UK: OECD Publishing.

Harris, S. P., Renko, M., and Caldwell, K. (2013). Accessing social entrepreneurship: perspectives of people with disabilities and key stakeholders. *Journal of Vocational Rehabilitation, 38*(1), 35–48.

Holt, R., and Macpherson, A. (2010). Sensemaking, rhetoric and the socially competent entrepreneur. *International Small Business Journal, 28*(1), 20–42.

Human Rights Council (2013). Written statement submitted by Verein Sudwind Entwicklungspolitik, a non-governmental organization in special consultative status—the situation of persons with physical, motor and mental disabilities in the Islamic Republic of Iran. https://ap.ohchr.org/documents/dpage_e.aspx?si=A/HRC/22/NGO/62.

Hwang, S.K., and Roulstone, A. (2015). Enterprising? Disabled? The status and potential for disabled people's microenterprise in South Korea. *Disability and Society, 30*(1), 114–129.

Jones, M.K., and Latreille, P.L. (2011). Disability and self-employment: evidence for the UK. *Applied Economics, 43*(27), 4161–4178.

Kamali, M. (2011). An overview of the situation of the disabled in Iran. In A. Moore and S. Kornblet (eds), *Advancing the Rights of Persons with Disabilities: A US–Iran Dialogue on Law, Policy, and Advocacy* (pp. 15–20). Washington DC: Stimson Center.

Larsson, S. (2006). Disability management and entrepreneurship: results from a nationwide study in Sweden. *International Journal of Disability Management, 1*(1), 159–168. DOI:10.1375/jdmr.1.1.159.

Larty, J., and Hamilton, E. (2011). Structural approaches to narrative analysis in entrepreneurship research: exemplars from two researchers. *International Small Business Journal, 29*(3), 220–237.

Martin, B.C., and B. Honig (2019). Inclusive management research: persons with disabilities and self-employment activity as an exemplar. *Journal of Business Ethics, 166*(3). DOI:10.1007/s10551-019-04122-x.

Miller, D., and Le Breton-Miller, I. (2017). Underdog entrepreneurs: a model of challenge-based entrepreneurship. *Entrepreneurship Theory and Practice, 41*(1), 7–17.

Mobaraki, A., and Zadehbagheri, G. (2003). Comaparision of knowledge and attitude of mothers with mentally retarded children with those without mentally retarded children in Gachsaran. *Armaghan Danesh, 8*(31), 89–97.

Moore, A., and Kornblet, S. (2011). Iran and America: a dialogue on disability. In S. Moore and A. Kornblet (eds), *Advancing the Rights of Persons with Disabilities: A US–Iran Dialogue on Law, Policy, and Advocacy* (pp. 7–14). Washington, DC: Stimson Center.

Namatovu, R., Dawa, S., Mulira, F., and Katongle, C. (2012). *Entrepreneurs with disabilities in Uganda*. Research report.

Pagán, R. (2009). Self-employment among people with disabilities: evidence for Europe. *Disability and Society, 24*(2), 217–229.

Parker Harris, S., Caldwell, K., and Renko, M. (2014). Entrepreneurship by any other name: self-sufficiency versus innovation. *Journal of Social Work in Disability and Rehabilitation, 13*(4), 317–349.

Pavey, B. (2006). Human capital, social capital, entrepreneurship and disability: an examination of some current educational trends in the UK. *Disability and Society, 21*(3), 217–229.

Reijonen, H., and Komppula, R. (2007). Perception of success and its effect on small firm performance. *Journal of Small Business and Enterprise Development, 14*(4), 689–701.

Renko, M., Parker Harris, S., and Caldwell, K. (2016). Entrepreneurial entry by people with disabilities. *International Small Business Journal, 34*(5), 555–578.

Roni, N.N., and Ribm, M.M.U. (2009). Disabled entrepreneurship: a viable route of opportunity for the disabled. MMUBS Doctoral Symposium, August.

Rozali, N., Abdullah, S., Jamaluddin, J., Ramil, A.J., Hussin, N.S., and Ahmad, A.Z. (2018). Promoting social entrepreneurship among entrepreneur with disabilities in contribution for community. *MATEC Web of Conferences, 150*, 05101. EDP Sciences.

Samadi, S.A. (2008). Comparative policy brief: status of intellectual disabilities in the Islamic Republic of Iran. *Journal of Policy and Practice in Intellectual Disabilities*, 5(2), 129–132.

Sarasvathy, S.D., Menon, A.R., and Kuechle, G. (2013). Failing firms and successful entrepreneurs: serial entrepreneurship as a temporal portfolio. *Small Business Economics*, 40(2), 417–434.

Sheikh, S., Yousafzai, S., Sist, F., Aybeniz Akdeniz, A.R., and Saeed, S. (2019). Value creation through women's entrepreneurship. In S. Yousafzai, A. Fayolle, A. Lindgreen, C. Henry, S. Saeed and S. Sheikh (eds), *Women Entrepreneurs and the Myth of "Underperformance": A New Look at Women's Entrepreneurship Research* (pp. 20–33). Cheltenham, UK and Northampton, MA, USA: Edward Elgar Publishing.

Silverman, D. (2005). *Doing Qualitative Research: A Practical Handbook.* London: SAGE Publications.

Soltani, S., Khosravi, B., and Salehiniya, H. (2015). Prevalence of disability in Iran. *Iranian Journal of Public Health*, 44(10), 1436–1437.

Soltani, S., and Takian, A. (2018). Disability and happiness in Iran: what can we do? *Iranian Journal of Public Health*, 47(8), 1224–1225.

Viriri, P., and Makurumidze, S. (2014). Engagement of disabled people in entrepreneurship programmes in Zimbabwe. *Journal of Small Business and Entrepreneurship Development*, 2(1), 1–30.

Wach, D., Stephan, U., and Gorgievski, M. (2016). More than money: developing an integrative multi-factorial measure of entrepreneurial success. *International Small Business Journal*, 34(8), 1098–1121.

Walls, R.T., Dowler, D.L., Cordingly, K., Orslene, L.E., and Greer, J.D. (2001). Microenterprising and people with disabilities: strategies for success and failure. *Journal of Rehabilitation*, 67(2), 7–29.

Welter, F., and Smallbone, D. (2011). Institutional perspectives on entrepreneurial behavior in challenging environments. *Journal of Small Business Management*, 49(1), 107–125.

Zamore, S. (2014). Motivations for business start-up: are there any differences between disabled and non-disabled people? University of Agder, Master's Thesis. https://brage.bibsys.no/xmlui/handle/11250/220737.

20. The contribution of disabled entrepreneurs in the Sultanate of Oman
Eric V. Bindah

INTRODUCTION

Entrepreneurship is considered as a vehicle to economic growth, success and prosperity in today's modern era (Gree and Thurnik, 2003). Increasing attention has focused on entrepreneurship and new firm creation, and its potential for contributing to economic growth and job creation has been documented extensively in research (e.g., Fatoki, 2010). To stimulate entrepreneurship, it is imperative to understand the challenges that affect entrepreneurs in order to overcome them and to promote new policies and measures to create new business ventures. Challenges are not the same for all individuals in society. Although some obstacles are common to all people, some groups find specific obstacles, namely people with disabilities (Martins, 2004).

A few decades ago, disability and entrepreneurship were not even close to being linked. People would find it hard to believe that physically disabled persons could become entrepreneurs. Setting up a business is challenging enough, but those with mental and physical health issues often have to work even harder. A look at the literature on the subject indicates that this area of research has remained largely unexplored in both developed and developing countries. This is in comparison with the large number of studies conducted among abled entrepreneurs.

Generally speaking, individuals with physical and mental disabilities tend to forget the idea of becoming an entrepreneur, and this is due to many reasons such as the challenges of failure, stress, uncertainty, difficult conditions and experiences of discrimination, appropriate support, business networks and capital, to mention just a few. More recently, policy-makers realized that helping them would benefit the broader economy too, since it would reduce unemployment. Many initiatives by government agencies and other organizations have been undertaken in support of physically disabled individuals in the hope that they could take up the challenge to become entrepreneurs. These programmes and systems support physically disabled individuals to start up their own business.

The objective of this study is to understand disabled entrepreneurs' contribution, their motivations and challenges. As an exploratory study, this research is also aimed at identifying the potential factors which could affect their initiative to start their own business, and growth of the business. It also attempts to understand how challenges caused by disability contribute to motivate them to pursue entrepreneurship as a career. This led to the following research questions:

1. What are the obstacles disabled individuals face when they choose to become an entrepreneur?
2. What are the reasons that prevent disabled individuals from becoming an entrepreneur?
3. How to encourage disabled individuals to become an entrepreneur?
4. What are the solutions to remove obstacles they face in becoming an entrepreneur?

This study adopts the empowerment theory as its theoretical framework, because it offers value frameworks for promoting human empowerment, for example entrepreneurs living with disabilities. Empowerment theory is seen as one of the best in supporting the interests of people with disability (Budeli, 2010). Employing empowerment theory is to provide conceptualizations of social stratification and oppression, identify the personal and political barriers and dynamics that maintain oppression, offer value frameworks for promoting human empowerment and liberation, identify practical strategies for overcoming oppression and achieving social justice, and build on people's strength, resilience and resources (Robbins et al., 1998). Additionally, Robbins et al. (1998) wished for people with disability to realize their aspirations and strengths, and to engage themselves in actions that support their personal wellbeing and social justice. Empowerment theory acts as an agent of change in enabling communities to learn to recognize conditions of inequality and injustice, with the aim of taking action to increase the powers of those regarded as powerless (Budeli, 2010).

METHOD

The study is exploratory in nature, and both primary and secondary data was used. Considering the nature of the research, a semi-structured format was used in order to explore qualitative information. There are many reasons why researchers may find a qualitative research method appropriate for their study. Firstly, it can be reasonably argued that qualitative methods are sometimes more advantageous than quantitative methods, especially when exploring social phenomena (Kasl and Cooper, 1995). As this research on the experience of disabled entrepreneurs is still in the exploratory stage in Oman, there is little data and understanding of the phenomenon of disabled entrepreneurship. Under this circumstance, a qualitative method is appropriate in providing rich, deep data and achieving close involvement with the people being investigated. Secondly, it is difficult to find the exact figure of the total population of disabled entrepreneurs in Oman. Furthermore, willingness to respond to this research investigation has been reported (Burchardt, 2003). Thirdly, by conducting a face-to-face interview, the interviewer can try to make the interviewee feel at ease for the interview. According to Yin (1994), a face-to-face interview makes the interviewee more of an 'informant' than a respondent. The data collection method in this research allowed me to gain access to the 'spontaneous data' or general chat after the actual interview, which studies have found at times to be very useful and truthful when compared to the recorded data (Bryman, 2004).

Fourthly, regarding the defining terms of entrepreneurship development in the disadvantaged group, the research approach might discover new information and perspectives on disabled people's entrepreneurial motivations and challenges. As opposed to qualitative research, in quantitative research it is impossible to study the irrationality and various unpredictable actions that are common in individual human behaviour (Crotty, 1998). Quantitative research lacks the goal of understanding of description, control and prediction. Hence, this research aims to verify a version of reality which cannot be possible by conducting quantitative research.

Finally, qualitative research has usually been criticized for relying too much on the researcher's view about what is important and significant. It is often argued that qualitative study is difficult to replicate, because it is unstructured and often reliant upon the qualitative researcher's ingenuity (Blandford, 2013). It is suggested that the scope of the findings of qualitative investigations is restricted. In other words, it is hardly possible to know how the findings can be generalized to other settings or cases. However, it has also been stated that self-reflective assessment on the application of qualitative research methods in this research will avoid the bias of personal values that has been incorporated into the research process. It is crucial to pay attention to those points at which bias can occur.

The focus of this research is on the development of links between the experience of disabled entrepreneurs and their motivations, and barriers of entrepreneurship that are likely to also affect other disabled entrepreneurs. The theory will not be generalizable in a simplistic way, because no one can claim that all disabled entrepreneurs have exactly the same experiences. Therefore, this research aims to develop an understanding of the context in which individual operate, which will inform an understanding of other disabled people who are in business, those seeking to diversify, and disabled entrepreneurs' support services.

Nevertheless, it is not easy to examine disabled entrepreneurs in Oman. This is because although there are a large number of physically disabled people in the country, the number of individuals with physical disability who are entrepreneurs is relatively small. They are also hard to identify and a difficult sample to reach, as they are seldom seen in public running their own business venture.

It is not always the best approach to attempt to randomly sample the general population in hopes of finding a sample suitable for the research interest, and this is the case for disabled entrepreneurs. Given this difficulty, I employed the snowball sampling technique. I was lucky enough to have met a physically disabled person who started a business venture and was willing to take an active role in identifying other similar entrepreneurs. I was able to get in touch with a key informant during a workshop who was an active member of the association for the disabled and deaf club. This person became a key informant and made all first connections with other disabled entrepreneurs. Specifically, the informant reached out to as many as possible disabled individual members from the association who had tried their hand at venturing into small businesses and had an interest in entrepreneurship. Those individuals had on several occasions conducted discussions at the centre where the key informant regularly visited. Hence, the key informant was very much aware of the environment.

Communication with potential participants was made through emails, direct face-to-face contact with the person selected, or through communication with one family member who could get in touch with the targeted disabled individuals. When contacting other possible disabled individuals, the informant passed along information on the study, the contact information, and the potential schedule of when an interview could take place between myself and the disabled potential entrepreneurs. Individuals who were contacted were further instructed to pass along my call for an interview or meeting to other disabled individuals who they knew. In this way, the snowball sampling technique was used to gather the necessary data to conduct this research. However, one of my concerns was to acquire a decent sample size for this study. Since the study was qualitative and exploratory in nature, I expected a small sample size.

Key Informant

Key informant approaches utilize community members who are knowledgeable about the topic of interest and willing to share this knowledge. In this context, these are people who live and work in their local community, who have a social role through their vocation, and who therefore know the local context as well as the people about whom information is being sought (Gona et al., 2010). The use of a key informant was crucial for this research project.

I would have found it hard to connect with the disabled entrepreneurs without the help of a key informant. Unless someone expresses their interest and conducts regular discussions about their intention of becoming an entrepreneur, most people would not know who those individuals are. Even in my experience as a researcher, it never crossed my mind to look into this area of research prior to attending a workshop. How to reach out to the disabled entrepreneurs was also another great challenge, for many reasons, already elaborated in this study. I initially had no clue of how to find the disabled entrepreneurs. At first, I visited several business areas in the community with the intention of enquiring about the identity of these disabled entrepreneurs, but this attempt was unsuccessful and I could not identify any individuals who would fit the study. This stage was demotivating, and I considered abandoning the idea of conducting research in this area. However, when I met with the informant, more hope was built and I decided to proceed with the study. The key informant from the association played a key role in identifying and reaching out to the individuals involved in this research.

The key informant also played a key role in ensuring that individuals who participated in this study could by the means of this research make their voices heard and create awareness about the challenges, motivations and expectations disabled entrepreneurs faced. This research was expected to culminate in a report which would be made available to researchers, policy-makers and the public at large, to create awareness. It was considered a noble cause indeed. A trust was hence built between the key informant, participants and myself.

I also had to guarantee the participants that no mention of their names would be made in the report. While some participants were not so concerned about it, others did stress that they would prefer to retain their anonymity in the report. I chose not to enquire further on this matter, for fear of their refusing to participate in the study if their identity was revealed. Furthermore, I believe that anonymity was not an issue for this research, and on this basis decided to retain anonymity for all participants in this study. Hence, trust was built between all parties involved in this research.

Although it was imperative that I used a key informant for this study, there is also some hesitation when it comes to using an informant. Firstly, the biggest concern is whether or not the potential sampling frame would be biased. I was concerned that the informant may only contact those who had similar experiences, and therefore similar thoughts about the topics investigated. Secondly, the reach of the snowball would fully depend on those first contacted by the informant. Because of this, I understood that there was a possibility of missing out participants who might have participated in the study had they been contacted through the network that was created for this study. I discuss this limitation further in the next section, on the selection criteria.

Selection Criteria

Disability has been defined by the World Health Organization (WHO) as a dynamic multidimensional interaction between the key domains of impaired body structure and function, activity limitations, participation restrictions and contextual factors. The International Classification of Functioning, Disability and Health (ICF) puts more emphasis on function than on the condition or disease in terms of disability itself.

According to the Disabled Persons Act, 1992 a disabled person:

> means a person with a physical, mental or sensory disability, including a visual, hearing or speech functional disability, which gives rise to physical, cultural or social barriers inhibiting him from participating at an equal level with other members of society in activities, undertakings or fields of employment that are open to other members of society.

A physical disability is any type of physical condition that significantly impacts upon one or more major life activities. The types of physical disabilities, their causes, and the manner in which they impact upon a person's life are wide-ranging and virtually limitless. Physical disabilities can be the result of congenital birth issues, accidental injury, or illness. When we consider the huge number of possible causes of physical disabilities, we can quickly see how it is impossible to provide a comprehensive list naming each condition. Additionally, one physical condition might be considered disabling to one person but not another. The key aspect in defining physical disability is not whether a person has a specific condition, but how that physical condition impacts upon their daily life.

In this study, I interviewed participants with physical disability related to a past injury or birth injury alone. Unfortunately, I did not interview disabled entrepreneurs individuals with other forms of physical disability, due to several complexities in undertaking such interviews. For instance, in case of communication disability, I could not find an appropriate sign language interpreter, as at the time of conducting this research, I had very limited resources since the study was self-funded and no form of financial support was received from either public or private organizations. I was also concerned that if I attempted by myself to interpret the information from individuals who fell into other category of disability, the response could certainly be biased, as I did not possess the necessary expertise in sign language.

After each potential participant contacted me, they were screened to make sure that they fitted the selection criteria. Each respondent had to have a physical disability related to a past injury or birth injury. If the potential participant fitted these basic criteria, an interview was arranged.

Sample Demographics

Altogether, six disabled entrepreneurs who fitted the selection criteria were interviewed in this study. Gender-wise, four were males and two were females. During the interview, I observed that men tended to be more open to providing answers without hesitation, whereas females tended to be a little shy at the beginning in providing their responses. Nevertheless, as female participants became comfortable with the interviewer they provided very insightful information for this study. In terms of age composition, participants' ages were between 25 and 34 years old. The age group indicated that it was a good time to venture into their own business, since their energy level was high, and they had good ideas and self-motivation to run a business.

Four participants were married, and two were single. Those who were married did not hide the fact that they had difficulties in attaining a financially comfortable life. This was expected, however, as past studies showed that disabled individuals tend to be unemployed, and not have an appropriate or consistent source of income. In fact, participants who were married reported difficulties in finding a proper source of income as one of the reasons why they became an entrepreneur. On the other hand, participants who were single reported that they started a small business and were waiting for it to be profitable at certain point of time in the future. Once the business became profitable, they would then start thinking about getting married and forming a family.

Four respondents graduated from high school, while two participants attended high school but did not graduate. All participants had some vocational training, although it was not specified which kind of training participants had received in the past. I also asked participants whether they were self-employed, to confirm that the subjects matched with the definition of entrepreneurs. All six participants were self-employed.

Table 20.1   *Question guide used for interviews*

1.   What ignited the spark in you to think of starting up a new business venture?
2.   How do you generate ideas to start your own business?
3.   What would you say are the top skills needed to be a successful entrepreneur?
4.   Describe the society that you live in, how is your relationship with others?
5.   Does the society and culture have any kind of influence on you in your decision to be self-employed?
6.   What motivates you in life?
7.   What are your ideals?
8.   How can you prevent mistakes or do damage control when running a business?
9.   What challenges do you think disabled entrepreneurs may face in setting up their own business?
10. Do you think there are any sacrifices needed to become a successful entrepreneur? Can you elaborate on it?
11. Which factors do you think are most likely attributed to a disabled entrepreneur's success?
12. Do you believe there is some sort of pattern or formula to become a successful entrepreneur?

Semi-Structured Qualitative Interviews

Since this research did not attempt to generalize about disabled entrepreneurs' barriers to and motivations for running a business, and due to the fact that there has been little research on disabled entrepreneurship to identify key quantifiable measures, I decided to use qualitative semi-structured interviews for this research. Semi-structured interviews allow for a guide of set questions to be asked of participants, while also allowing for the interviewer to explore previously unidentified topics that participants bring up in their answers (Mertens, 2005). The technique was used to focus on the disabled entrepreneurs' challenges, their motivation, their perception towards the society they live in, how the society viewed them, and more. I used the question guide in Table 20.1 for this particular project.

Data Analysis

By using semi-structured interviews, the analysis had an inductive nature to it. In this approach I adopted an open mind without any preconceived ideas of what would be found. Some themes were apparent, given the nature of the questions asked; however, interviewing allowed for respondents to elaborate on each topic, which provided more in-depth answers but also themes not considered prior to the research.

To analyse the data, I reviewed all the responses to identify the emergent themes. I read through each interview twice, scanning for all pertinent themes. To do so, interviews were read to appropriately place each theme in a category that would best fit the response. Then, each segmented theme was read individually to achieve internal homogeneity, to verify that each theme contained quotes that were suited to that particular theme (Patton, 2002). External heterogeneity was achieved by re-reading all themes to make sure that each theme was distinct from the others (Patton, 2002). After this was complete, all interviews were read once more to verify that nothing was missed in the responses.

The process of categorizing the responses was challenging, because of the extensive answers received from the participants, as well as the observation of their attitudes towards the questions while responding to the interview.

KEY FINDINGS

Income and Life Satisfaction

One common theme which participants mentioned when asked about the main reason for their willingness to start up a new business was related to the potential of increasing their income. They felt the need to improve their life as they currently earned a low income which mainly covered their basic needs. They believed that by starting their own business they would be able to receive additional income which would help to improve their life, and that of their family. They felt that technology advancement and economic changes in the society had made life more expensive, and that they deserved the chance to start a business regardless of their physical disability. Participants also reported that self-motivation was a key factor in their quest to start up a business.

Idea Generation

Participants believed that careful observation and understanding of market needs was a key factor in generating ideas to start up a business. They generated ideas principally from the media, by reading the news, and following trends in the society and their immediate surrounding environment. One participant elaborated on some basic steps needed to begin the process of becoming an entrepreneur. She mentioned that once information is gathered, a careful plan is needed to explore the possibilities of putting the ideas into implementation. Idea generation, however, takes time and requires a lot of thinking, and can be demotivating at times due to the energy spent in the preparation, which is why participants believe that self-motivation as well as a high energy level is important in the process.

Skills Needed to be a Successful Entrepreneur

On this question, participants' responses were different, and this was expected. Most participants believe that individuals possess different skills and talents. Particularly, participants mentioned that patience was one of the qualities needed by disabled entrepreneurs. Having patience was an important factor for disabled entrepreneurs, because in many cases participants felt that the society does not give them enough chance to prove themselves. One participant reported that some people can be a bit condescending towards people with disabilities.

Participants also felt that acquiring knowledge was another important element to be able to start up a business. Indeed, studies have shown that education plays a significant role in entering and remaining in self-employment (Arum and Müller, 2004; Moriarty, 2007). But facts and figures from the national organization on disability show that only a small percentage of persons with mild or severe disability complete college degrees. Nevertheless, participants mentioned that there are many different methods of acquiring knowledge apart from obtaining a college degree. Among the methods mentioned was through the use of various media communications, and communication with peers and family members.

Participants mentioned that self-confidence was important attribute that disabled entrepreneurs should possess. Positive thinking, practice, and talking to other people were all useful ways to help improve or boost their confidence levels. Confidence comes from feelings of wellbeing, acceptance of the body and mind (self-esteem), and belief in one's own ability and skills.

Participants believed that communication skills were equally important if they wanted to start up their own business. The ability to communicate with others is critical to the operation of a small business. Fortunately, for a person with a disability, there exist many forms of technology which have over the years helped to improve the quality of life of disabled individuals, as well as to assist them to perform business functions. With their experience of disability, physically disabled entrepreneurs tend to do things differently according to their environment, which accommodates their disability.

Disabled entrepreneurs also believe that persuasion skills are important to become successful. Often they face the challenge of convincing others to support them in their entrepreneurial venture. In one case, the participant reported how he struggled to convince the bank manager to open a business account, because of his negative opinion of the disabled.

Stigmatization, Discrimination and Marginalization

People with disabilities are often stigmatized, discriminated against and marginalized in every facet of life. Participants reported that at times they felt socially excluded, stigmatized and even marginalized. This had negative consequences on their network ties and their cohesion in business circles, which were often weak. Most of the entrepreneurs living with physical disabilities reported that they have at least once felt they lacked confidence as a result of discrimination they experienced in some specific situation. For example, they said people thought that they were not competent because they were disabled.

Common Mistakes Made by Disabled Entrepreneurs

Respondents were asked to think of common mistakes that disabled entrepreneurs could make while venturing into a business start-up. Participants mentioned that it was pointless to pursue a business venture when a person does not possess the skills and interest in doing it. Participants also mentioned that it was important to be in control of the business, instead of appointing other people to manage the business.

Disabled entrepreneurs felt that if they could manage and control their business venture, they could derive a sense of self-satisfaction and pride, which would lead to more self-motivation and achievement orientation.

Common Challenges Faced by Disabled Entrepreneurs

Some of the common challenges faced by disabled entrepreneurs who wanted to start their own business venture included lack of disability laws and of awareness in the society about disability rights. They also mentioned a lack of qualified special needs trainers, or even the facilities or the right assistive technology tools that can help cater to the educational needs of individuals with disabilities and learning difficulties who would wish to start up their own business in the future.

Accessibility in buildings remains a big issue. There is an urgent need to make all buildings, offices and restaurants disabled-friendly. It is important for architects and policy-makers to make sure that all places, and all businesses, including beaches, offices, and restaurants, are more friendly, accessible and open to disabled people. Lack of accessibility features in buildings is a major challenge in workplaces for disabled people in Oman.

Physically disabled entrepreneurs said that most facilities for small business were not equipped to accommodate their conditions, as they lack proper equipment and machinery to assist them. Most of the entrepreneurs living with physical disabilities said that they lacked confidence as they have at least once experienced discrimination due to their disability.

People in business use broader networks to form business relationships that create opportunities all over the world. Most of the participants in the study said that they find it very hard to get involved in business networking activities, as their immediate environment does not allow them to do so. Getting capital to start a business is always a challenge for entrepreneurs. The majority of the participants said that this was an issue, mostly when they sought loans from financial institutions.

Study participants were not aware of the government support centres or initiatives to support businesses that are managed and operated by people with physical disabilities. Only a few said that they got support from the government. But the support they received was not enough to sustain them in running their ventures.

Sacrifices Made to Start Up Own Business Venture

Participants were also asked about the sacrifices they had to make in their lives before they could start up their own business. In this case, respondents mentioned several sacrifices which they made. Participants highlighted their ability to cope with different forms of pressure. They reported that the line between working life and personal life was sometimes blurred, as they had to think of their business ideas most of the time, even when the timing was not appropriate, and it is quite stressful. Participants also reported difficulty in preserving healthy sleeping habits, as they were often awake late at night, restless and thinking about their future.

Factors Attributed to Disabled Entrepreneurs' Success

Participants were asked about their opinion of which critical factors they believed were important to become a successful entrepreneur. Participants mentioned that having willpower is important if disabled entrepreneurs want to become successful. The ability to take responsibility and to remain committed to the tasks at hand was cited as an important success factor. Honesty was also another important element. Participants mentioned that being honest and true to themselves are important elements that would make others in the society trust them, and this was important for business as well. Building networks and professional relationship with the community was also cited as important by participants. By being in constant contact with the community, participants believe that this would allow them to communicate and deliver their ideas to the community much easier and faster.

PRACTICAL LESSONS LEARNED

This was the first time that I had engaged in a snowball sampling technique where a key informant was approached to conduct this research. During the course of conducting this research, there were many factors which I could not be in control of. For instance, the type of respondents chosen for the study was somewhat outside my control, as I mainly relied on the key informant to get in touch with participants to take part in this study. I was concerned that the sample could be biased in some way. Fortunately the key informant in this study was trustworthy and dedicated to the task.

I could only approach and interview participants with certain types of physical disability, and could not include all the categories of disabled individuals, due to the fact that more support and assistance was required to conduct such interviews and at the time this research was conducted I did not receive any form of support that could be useful to sample all the categories of disabled entrepreneurs. This research cannot therefore be generalized to the whole population of disabled entrepreneurs, because different categories of disabled entrepreneurs may face other forms of dilemma or have other motivations to start up their own business venture.

Following this research, I am of the opinion that there is still a need for a total social paradigm shift towards people living with disability, to avoid stigmatization of this community, through public awareness and the enactment of laws and regulations towards inclusivity and tolerance. Policy-makers need to undertake a dedicated review of policies that are meant to support people living with disabilities, to give them a better deal. Perhaps some old policies will need to be revamped, and new ones put in place where necessary. This must be done with a focus on critical areas such as education and skills development, start-up finance, and to influence the general environment to be more friendly towards people living with disabilities. As disabled entrepreneurs are role models in societies, it is imperative to provide support for business people living with physical disabilities, as these will open up new opportunities.

REFERENCES

Arum, R. and Müller, W. (2004). The reemergence of self-employment: comparative findings and empirical propositions. In: Arum, R. and Müller, W. (eds). *The Reemergence of Self-Employment: A Comparative Study of Self-Employment Dynamics and Social Inequality.* Princeton University Press, 426–454.

Blandford, A. (2013). Semi-structured qualitative studies. In: Soegaard, Mads and Dam, Rikke Friis (eds). *The Encyclopedia of Human–Computer Interaction,* 2nd edn. Aarhus: Interaction Design Foundation. https://discovery.ucl.ac.uk/id/eprint/1436174/2/semi-structured_qualitative_studies.pdf.

Bryman, A. (2004). Qualitative research on leadership: a critical but appreciative review. *Leadership Quarterly,* 15(6), 729–769.

Budeli, M. (2010). Understanding the right to freedom of association at the workplace: components and scope. *Obiter,* 31(1), 16–33.

Burchardt, T. (2003). Being and becoming: social exclusion and the onset of disability. CASEreports, 21. Centre for Analysis of Social Exclusion, London School of Economics and Political Science.

Crotty, M. (1998). *The Foundations of Social Research: Meaning and Perspective in the Research Process.* London: SAGE.

Fatoki, O.O. (2010). Graduate entrepreneurial intention in South Africa: motivations and obstacles. *International Journal of Business and Management,* 5(9), 87–98.

Gona, J.K., Mung'ala-Odera, V., Newton, C.R. and Hartley, S. (2010). Caring for children with disabilities in Kilifi, Kenya: what is the carer's experience? *Child: Care, Health and Development,* 37(2), 175–83. doi: 10.1111/j.1365-2214.2010.01124.x.

Gree, A. and Thurnik, C. (2003). Firm selection and industry evolution: the post country performance of new firm. *Journal of Evolutionary Economics,* 4(4), 243–264.

Kasl, S.V. and Cooper, C.L. (1995). *Stress and Health: Issues in Research Methodology.* John Wiley & Sons.

Martins, S. (2004). Barriers to entrepreneurship and business creation. Research paper, European Entrepreneurship Cooperation.

Mertens, D. M. (2005). *Research and Evaluation in Education and-Psychology: Integrating diversity with Quantitative, Qualitative, and Mixed Methods.* Thousand Oaks, London: SAGE.

Moriarty, M. (2007). Inclusive pedagogy: teaching methodologies to reach diverse learners in science instruction. *Equity and Excellence in Education,* 40, 252–265.

Patton, M.Q. (2002). *Qualitative Research and Evaluation Methods.* Thousand Oaks, CA: SAGE.

Robbins, S.P., Chatterjee, P., and Canda, E.R. (1998). *Contemporary Human Behavior Theory: A Critical Perspective for Social Work.* Boston, MA: Allyn & Bacon.

Yin, R. (1994). *Case Study Research: Design and Methods,* 2nd edn. Applied Social Research Methods Series, Volume 5. Thousand Oaks, CA: SAGE.

Index

Abylaikhan Asylbay 229
Action Plan for Women in Business 136
active labour market policies 100
ADEs *see* Australian Disability Enterprises
    (ADEs)
ADHD *see* attention deficit hyperactive
    disorder (ADHD)
ADPs *see* assistants to disabled people
    (ADPs)
Aird, B. 134
Alaedini, P. 281
Amendment to the Rights of Persons with
    Disability Act 2020 190
Americans with Disabilities Act 69, 120
anecdotal evidence 197
Ansberry, C. 70
anti-discrimination policies in Korea 120
anti-pull factors 44
anti-push factors 44
Antshel, K.M. 69
anxiety 208–10, 212, 213, 215, 249
Argonauts of the Western Pacific
    (Malinowski) 266
ARISE 152, 157
Arndt, F. 65, 78, 80–82
Arnold, N. 115
Article 13 of the PDEA 121
Article 27 of the UNCRPD 222
ASD *see* autism spectrum disorder (ASD)
Ashley, D. 9
Ashour, S. 103, 105, 106
Asmalovskij, A. 102
Asperger's syndrome 82
aspirational labor 269, 272
assistants to disabled people (ADPs) 174
Atkins, S. 7, 8
attention deficit hyperactive disorder
    (ADHD) 8, 69, 77, 81–3
Austin, R.D. 68
Australia 52–3
    Australian government disability
        employment programs 38
    disability in 37–8
    entrepreneurial journeys 40
    National Disability Insurance Scheme
        (NDIS) 38–9

people with disability 35
research design 39–40
secondary analysis disability
    employment statistics 40–51
Australian Bureau of Statistics (ABS) 37, 40
Australian Disability Enterprises (ADEs)
    38–9
Australian Disability Strategy (AND) 36
Australian government disability
    employment programs 38
Australian Human Rights Commission 43
Australian Research Council 36
autism spectrum disorder (ASD) 59–60,
    62–6, 70–72
    challenges and opportunities of
        entrepreneurship and 63–5
    different faces of entrepreneurship
        60–63
    individuals and entrepreneurship, pull
        factors for 68–72
    individuals and entrepreneurship, push
        factors for 65–8
award ceremonies 172

Back to Work Enterprise Allowance
    (BTWEA) 135
Bagheri, A. 8, 9
Baldwin, M.L. 65
barriers
    and challenges 46–9
    educational 161
    faced by disabled people 200–202
    financial access-related 204
    psychological 13, 16, 234
Barton, M. 103, 106
Baumol, W. 20, 21, 30
Beisland, L.A. 199, 201
beneficial disability scheme 253
benefits–tax ratio challenges 115
benefits to EwD 50–51
Biannual Nationwide Survey of Disability
    Enterprises 117, 121
Biannual Survey 124
Bidet, E. 101
Big Short (Lewis) 59
binomial logit model 91, 92

binomial test 211
Birzhan Kuzhakov 227–9
blind entrepreneur 26, 78, 80, 82
'blocked mobility' 35, 44
Bocelli, Andrea 23
Boylan, A. 132, 136
Bridge, S. 141
broad awareness campaign 138, 139
'broken bones policy' 241
BTWEA *see* Back to Work Enterprise
    Allowance (BTWEA)
Buhariwala, P. 102
Burchardt, T. 132, 136
Burry, Michael 59, 61, 68, 72
business consulting services 171, 294
business feasibility model 151
business management competences 16
business networking activities 306
business ownership 2, 137

Caldwell, K. 102
Canguilheim's formulation of social orders
    115
capitalist market economy 52
categorical variable coding 91, 92
causal reasoning approach 24
CDPF *see* Chinese Disabled Person's
    Federation (CDPF)
Centers for Disease Control and Prevention
    (2015) 63
Central Statistics Office (CSO) census 133
'challenge-based' model 25, 27, 78
Chart 77 Foundation 105
Chaudhry, V. 199
children with disabilities 161, 223, 239, 282
China, disabled entrepreneurs in 160
    better entrepreneurial ecosystem for
        disabled people 176–7
    competency-based instructing system
        (policy) 173–4
    entrepreneurial ecosystem and role
        of Chinese government policy
        161–4
    financial support by government 166–9
    free educational training (human
        capital) 171
    hard and soft support 176
    increase monthly allowances (finance)
        172
    individual disabled people (human
        capital) 174
    infrastructure support 169–70
        interest-free loan more flexible (policy)
            173
        legal protection and support (policy)
            170–71
        market support 172
        methodology 164–5
        policy information to disabled
            entrepreneurs (policy) 174
        utilization rate of free offices 173
Chinese Disabled Person's Federation
    (CDPF) 162, 163, 167, 169–78
Chinese disabled population 162
Chinese entrepreneurial activities 160
Chinese entrepreneurial ecosystem 161,
    163–4
Chinese government policy 161–4
Christens, B.D. 145
CIS countries *see* Commonwealth of
    Independent States (CIS) countries
civil society and non-governmental
    organizations 223
coding themes (or nodes) 40
collaborative entrepreneurship 272
collaborative labor 270
commercial entrepreneurship 87, 103
Commonwealth of Independent States (CIS)
    countries 224
communication disability 302
competency-based instructing system
    (policy) 173–4
Comprehensive Employment Strategy for
    People with Disabilities 133
Comprehensive Law on Protection of the
    Rights of Persons with Disabilities
    281
comprehensive system innovations 146
conducive culture ecosystem 189
conducive public policy 243
Confucian family obligations 118
Confucian socio-cultural norms 124
congenital disabilities 263–4
congenital impairments 82
Constitution of the Islamic Republic of
    Pakistan 190
contemporary digital scholarship 274
conventional organizational employment
    249
Convention on the Rights of the Child
    (CRC) 281
Cooney, T.M. 2, 6, 115, 121, 131, 134, 138
corporate capitalism 272
Cottle, Matt 66, 67, 70, 71

COVID-19 pandemic 8, 12, 228
Cramm, J.M. 201
CRC *see* Convention on the Rights of the Child (CRC)
'creationist capitalism 268, 269
creative endeavor 20, 30
Czech disabled people, responses of 107–8
Czech educational system 107, 109
Czech labour market 104
Czech Republic 99, 109–10
    definition and characteristics of European WISE 100–102
    methodological approach 104–5
    objective and research questions 104
    potential social entrepreneurs 105–7
    responses of Czech disabled people 107–8
    social enterprises and disabled people in labour market 102–3
    social entrepreneurship in 100
    university students as future social entrepreneurs 103
Czech social enterprises 100
Czech social policy 109
Czech WISE 100, 107, 110

Daher, H. 202
Davidsson, P. 61
DDA *see* Disability Discrimination Act (DDA)
Debowska, A. 209
De Clercq, D. 7
'deficit-based model of disability' 125
Defourny, J. 101, 102
Department of Empowerment of Persons with Disabilities 250
depression 209, 210, 213
    experiences of 215
    feelings and symptoms of 212
    loneliness and 217
    prevalence of 281
DES *see* Disability Employment Services (DES)
De Vries, L. 125
Dhar, S. 8
Diagnostic and Statistical Manual of Mental Disorders 63
digital capitalism 268
digital disability entrepreneurs 274
digital economies 275
digital entrepreneur, disability and 262
    anthropology of absences 273–5

    collaboration and capability 270–73
    digital technology, labor, disability 263–6
    'entrepreneur' as subject position 268–70
    labor as contribution 266–8
digital entrepreneurship 270, 271
Dipeolu, A.O. 69
disability advocacy organisations 141
Disability Awareness Support Scheme 135
disability-based model 27–8
disability business start-ups 43
disability communities 15, 263
Disability Discrimination Act (DDA) 120
disability discrimination legislation 120
disability employment
    and enterprises 125
    legislation in Korea 114
    policies in Korea 117, 119–21
    rate 121
Disability Employment Services (DES) 38–9
disability enterprises 115–17, 121–7
disability entrepreneurship 30, 39, 273
    in Australia 44, 52
    in Second Life 275
disability legislation 115
disability organisations 4, 39
'disability pride' 16
disability projects 28
Disability Protect Act 281
disability services organizations 157
disability services sector 36
disability social movement 37
disability-specific assistive technologies 254
disability statistics in Kazakhstan 225
Disability Support Pension 44
disabled community in Ireland 131–2
    challenges of designing tailored support 135–8
    funnel approach 138–40
    situation 133–5
Disabled Employment Security Fund 169
Disabled Enterprise Business Centre 121
disabled entrepreneurs 23, 70, 116, 121, 125, 126, 131, 137–9, 176, 251–6, 280, 285, 290–92, 294, 298, 300
    in China (*see* China, disabled entrepreneurs in)
    data analysis 250–51
    entrepreneurial activities among 77–83
    entrepreneurship, disability, and identity 248–9

entrepreneurship and identity 247–8
Iran's entrepreneurial ecosystem (*see*
      Iran's entrepreneurial ecosystem)
Korean 122
narratives of Iranian 283–90
physically 22, 31, 305, 306
research context 249–50
societal inequality 257–8
in Sultanate of Oman (*see* Sultanate of
      Oman, disabled entrepreneurs in)
value creation perspective in 293
disabled entrepreneurship 31, 66, 82, 163,
      165, 176, 183, 279, 294, 298, 303
in Chinese Research Context 161–2
in Iran 280–82
literature 279
value creation through 290–92
disabled-impaired entrepreneurs 84
disabled individuals, empowerment of 183
disabled microfinance clients 199
disabled people 69, 77, 80, 85, 90, 109,
      160–64, 169, 280
better entrepreneurial ecosystem for
      176–7
challenges and barriers faced by
      200–202
in Czech Republic (*see* Czech Republic)
discrimination against 65
economic activities 114
economic contribution of 163
empowerment of 81
and enterprise 116–17, 125–6
entrepreneurial challenges 88
entrepreneurial intentions of 86
entrepreneurship 291, 292
individual 174
Korean labour market context and
      117–19
in labour market 102–3
low employment rates 94
microenterprise in South Korea (*see*
      South Korea, disabled people's
      microenterprise in)
'mild or moderate' 119
self-employment of 116, 121, 162
in social entrepreneurship 108
social stigmas for 176
unemployment rate for 118
use (or non-use) of microfinance by
      199–200
in workforce 95
Disabled People Organizations (DPOs) 243

Disabled People with Protection Act 162,
      163
Disabled Persons Act 301
disabled women, entrepreneurship among
      191–3
disabled women entrepreneurs and
      microfinance 196
challenges and barriers faced by
      disabled people in 200–202
method 198
microfinance and women's
      entrepreneurship 197–8
use of microfinance as tool to facilitate
      entrepreneurship among
      caregivers 200
use (or non-use) of microfinance by
      disabled people 199–200
use of microfinance for rehabilitation
      leading to entrepreneurship 202
women and microfinance services 197
diversified employment methods 162
Doyel, A.W. 136
DPOs *see* Disabled People Organizations
      (DPOs)

ECHP *see* European Community Household
      Panel (ECHP)
e-commerce 171, 187
economic activities 3, 60, 109, 116, 118,
      124, 125, 188
Economic Activity Status for the Disabled
      Survey 2010 117
Economic and Social Changes: Facts,
      Trends, Forecast 100
economic and social empowerment 102
economic climate 90, 93, 115
economic contribution of disabled people
      163
economic principles 109
economic self-sufficiency 99
economic theory 43, 52
educational attainment 122, 161
educational barriers 161
educational level variable 93, 94
EES *see* entrepreneurial ecosystem (EES)
effectual reasoning 24
EMES 99, 100, 102, 109
emotional resilience 217
employee vs self-employment by disability
      group 41
Employment Act for the Relief of Recipients
      1961 119

Employment Development Institute 118
employment participation 39, 115
Employment Promotion and Vocational
    Rehabilitation Act for Disabled
    Persons 119
Employment Promotion for Disabled
    Persons 119
employment quota system 119, 120
empowerment 186
    of disabled individuals 183
    of disabled people 81
    economic and social 102
    of PWD 229
    theory 298
    women 197
    of WWD 187
enablers 49–50
entrepreneurial abilities 161, 251, 255, 256
entrepreneurial activities 27, 63, 82, 85, 88,
    93, 132, 208, 215, 223, 230, 255, 257,
    279, 280, 282, 290–94
    among disabled entrepreneurs 77–83
    government policy in]64
    of PWD 6, 232–3
'entrepreneurial alertness' 24
entrepreneurial aspirations 49
entrepreneurial assistance for disabled
    people 162
entrepreneurial behavior 89
'entrepreneurial citizenship 269
entrepreneurial competences 5
entrepreneurial ecosystem (EES) 5, 6, 12,
    15, 16, 39, 42, 143, 162–4, 176–8,
    182, 192, 226–7
    framework 161, 165
    Iran (*see* Iran's entrepreneurial
        ecosystem)
    Kazakhstan 226–33
    Night Marathons 153–5
    in Palestine 239, 243
    policy factors in 230–31
    social entrepreneurship as 'force
        multiplier' for systems change
        144–5
    social entrepreneurship to systems
        change 145–6
    social support and cultural factors in
        229–30
    StartUp NY as social entrepreneurship
        initiative 146–53
entrepreneurial education 42, 82
entrepreneurial endeavor 20, 21, 30, 59, 80

entrepreneurial environment 161, 163, 164,
    183, 185, 186, 191, 239
entrepreneurial experience 15, 71, 290
entrepreneurial idea 20, 21, 227
entrepreneurial identity 17, 247–59
entrepreneurial infrastructure 154–5
entrepreneurial intention 85–8, 93–5
entrepreneurial journeys 39–40, 42, 44, 152,
    252, 256–8
entrepreneurial learning 197
'entrepreneurial living' 269
entrepreneurial motivation 2, 9, 80, 82, 88,
    299
entrepreneurial narrative 290
entrepreneurial opportunities 23, 41, 60, 85,
    161, 164, 185
entrepreneurial organizations 61, 162
entrepreneurial parents 91, 94
entrepreneurial participation by WWD 188
entrepreneurial selfhood 267, 269, 270, 273
entrepreneurial skills and techniques 215
entrepreneurial students 217
'entrepreneurial subjectivity' 269
entrepreneurial success 59, 77, 82, 252, 279
entrepreneurial thinking 253
entrepreneurial tradition 15
entrepreneurship 60, 160, 186, 249, 258,
    291, 292, 297
    activities 214
    among disabled women 191–3
    challenge/necessity entrepreneurship 62
    development 5, 299
    within disability 280
    education 82, 88, 90
    emancipatory potential of 259
    entrepreneurship as spectrum
        phenomenon 63
    intentions 94
    learning 215
    policy 163
    potential of disabled people 162
    programme, development of 136
    research in Spanish university (*see*
        Spanish university research)
    strategic entrepreneurship 61
    and sustainability 87
Entrepreneurship 2020 Action Plan 85
entrepreneurship–disability field 69
Entrepreneurship Learning Dialogues 146
entrepreneurship students, mental wellbeing
    of 208, 216, 217
    academic performance 209–10

international students 210
methodology 210–11
psychological wellbeing, impact on
212–13
relationships between social and
psychological wellbeing 213–14
social interaction, impact on 210
social wellbeing, impact on 211–12
students' psychological wellbeing 209
entrepreneurs with disabilities (EWD) 2, 3,
6, 7, 9, 12, 13, 15, 16, 36, 39, 43, 44,
47, 48, 50–52, 139, 146, 147, 152,
157, 223, 234, 256
entrepreneurial identity formation of 16
in Hungary (*see* Hungary, entrepreneurs
with disabilities in)
in Kazakhstan 233
motivations of 14
potential motivations of 7
environmental social enterprises 107
Erickson, W.A. 66
Europe 2020 strategy 2
European Community Household Panel
(ECHP) 4
European Credit Transfer and Accumulation
System 89
European Disability Strategy 2010–2020 4
European labor markets 160
European Union (EU) 2
European WISE, definition and
characteristics of 100–102
evidence-based employment practices 144
evidence-based policy initiatives 36
EWD *see* entrepreneurs with disabilities
(EWD)
external finance, non-availability of 190
external heterogeneity 303

Falch, R. 290
Farzana, T. 8
female entrepreneurship 16
Fiet, J. 24
financial access-related barriers 204
financial institutions 234
financial literacy training 151
Flessa, S. 202
'forgotten minority' 2
formal commercial institutional funding 198
for-profit social enterprises 109
'4 Stage Entrepreneurship Model' 150
Franco, M. 103, 105
free educational training (human capital) 171

free electricity and water 169
free office space 169
funding opportunities 50
funnel approach 139–41

gender and disability, double-edged sword
of 240–41
gender inequality 184
George, Mary 24
Glaser, B. 27
Global Gender Gap Index 184
government resources, priority access to 172
Graf, N.M. 9
Greblikaite, J. 102
gross domestic product 185

Halabisky, D. 290
Hall, E. 102
Harris, Parker 2
Harris, S.P. 64, 70, 72, 102
Hawking, Stephen 182
health sector in Palestine 242
Heath, K.L. 9
Hernæs, U.J.V. 290
heterogeneous social construct 279
hidden entrepreneurs 221–2
defining disability 223–4
Kazakhstan's entrepreneurial ecosystem
226–33
status of people with disability 225–6
hinder entrepreneurial aspirations 46
Hitt, M.A. 61, 72
homogenous group 184
Honig, B. 7, 290, 292
Hosmer–Lemeshow statistics 93
Howard, T.L. 6, 8
Hughes, K.D. 192
human capital ecosystem 188
humanities-focused programmes 104
human resource management 64
Human Rights Council 281
Hungary, entrepreneurs with disabilities in
2–3, 14–16
methodology 9–10
motivations 6–9
people with disability 4–5
personal pull factors 11–12
personal push factors 13
social and economic environment as
pull factors 12
social and economic environment as
push factors 13

IDA *see* Individual Development Account
(IDA)
inclusive entrepreneurial ecosystem 183–92
inclusive entrepreneurship in Palestine
238–9
double-edged sword of gender and
disability 240–41
entrepreneurship and disability 242–4
situation of PWDs in 241–2
inclusive entrepreneurship model 87, 147
Inclusive Entrepreneurship tools and
curriculum 152
in-depth interviewees, typology of 57–8
India
disability discourse in 257
entrepreneurship in 250
persons with a disability in 249
Individual Development Account (IDA) 151
individual disabled people (human capital)
174
Industrial Accident Compensation Insurance
Act 1963 119
industrial capitalism 265
informal home-based enterprises 240
infrastructure support 169–70
innovative policies 101
integration social enterprises 100
intellectual disability 51
interest-free loan 168–9, 173, 176
internal homogeneity 303
International Classification of Functioning,
Disability and Health (ICF) 301
interview respondents, demographic profile
of 166
invisible disabilities 82
Ip, C.I. 103
Ipsen, C. 115
Iran's entrepreneurial ecosystem 279, 293–4
contextualizing disability and disabled
entrepreneurship in Iran 280–82
method 282
narratives of Iranian disabled
entrepreneurs 283–90
value creation through disabled
entrepreneurship 290–92
Ireland, disabled community in 131–2
challenges of designing tailored support
135–8
funnel approach 138–40
situation 133–5
Irgebayev, Miras 225
Isenberg, D. 8, 13, 226

model of an entrepreneurship ecosystem
167

Janbazan Foundation 281
Jobseeker's Allowance or Supplementary
Welfare Allowance 135
Johnson, T.D. 65
Johnson, W.G. 65
Jones, M. 62, 69
Joshi, A. 65
Joy Dew 71

Kaltayeva, Lyazzat 230
Kattouf, Pamela 71
Kazakh children with disabilities 223
Kazakhstan, disability and entrepreneurship
in 221–2
defining disability 223–4
Kazakhstan's entrepreneurial ecosystem
226–33
status of people with disability 225–6
Kedergisiz Keleshek programme 222
Kedmenec, I. 103, 105
Kim, C. 120, 122
Kireeva, N.S. 107
Konto Bariéry fundraising campaign 105
Korean cultural assumptions 115
Korean DDA 127
Korean disability employment policy 114,
120, 125
Korean disability enterprises 121–5
policy 119–21
Korean labour market 114, 117–19
Korean procurement programme 126
Korean quota system 120
Kreger, M. 145
Kummitha, R.K.R. 102

labor force 242, 243
Indian 249
participation 35
participation rates 239
via entrepreneurial measures 243
women's dismal status in 240
labor markets 2–4, 15, 16, 99, 100, 104,
107–10, 115, 118, 120, 125, 131, 143,
163, 183, 244
exclusion 101
inequalities 243
opportunities 44, 239
participation 3, 137, 243
Lai, A. 210

Latreille, P. 62, 69
law on public procurement 231
Law on Social Entrepreneurship 231
learning disorders 8
Le Breton-Miller, I. 8, 25, 62
legal protection and support (policy) 170–71
Lewis, C. 203
Lewis, Michael
    Big Short 59
liberal socio-cultural environments 78
Liga vozíčkářů 105
Linden Lab 263, 265, 266
loan financing 234
locus of control variable 86, 90, 93, 94
logistic regression analysis 86, 90, 91
Lonkina, E. 227
low labour market participation 2
low-rent housing policy 170
low-rent housing with well-designed
    accessibility facilities 169–70
low self-esteem 200

macro-level policy limitations 127
macro-level systems and environmental
    considerations 152
Malinowski, B.
    Argonauts of the Western Pacific 266
'mandatorily voluntary' for women 240
manual coding 40
March of Return (2018–2019) 242
market support 172
Martin, B.C. 290, 292
Marx, Karl 265, 266
Marxism 266
Mathis, C. 126
Medicaid Infrastructure Grant (MIG) 146
medical model 224
    of disability 144, 182, 223, 224
mental conditions, negative effects of 77
mental disorders 65
mental health 213
    and psychological wellbeing 212
mental wellbeing of entrepreneurship
    students 208, 216, 217
    academic performance 209–10
    international students 210
    methodology 210–11
    psychological wellbeing, impact on
        212–13
    relationships between social and
        psychological wellbeing 213–14
    social interaction, impact on 210

social wellbeing, impact on 211–12
    students' psychological wellbeing 209
Mersland, R. 199, 201, 203
meso-, and macro-level challenges 143
MFIs *see* microfinance institutions (MFIs)
micro, small and medium-sized enterprises
    (MSMEs) 242
microfinance 196
    disabled women entrepreneurs and (*see*
        disabled women entrepreneurs
        and microfinance)
    lending processes 203
    services 196
microfinance institutions (MFIs) 196–9,
    201–4
MIG *see* Medicaid Infrastructure Grant
    (MIG)
'mild or moderate' disabled people 119
Miller, D. 8, 25, 27, 62
Miller, Patricia 71
mobility constraints 189
model's variables 95
monthly allowances (finance) 172
motivations
    entrepreneurial 2, 9, 80, 82, 88, 299
    of EWD 14
    pull and push 16
    social push 15
MSMEs *see* micro, small and medium-sized
    enterprises (MSMEs)
musculoskeletal disorders 231

narrative approach 282
National Autistic Society 64
national demonstration projects 146
National Disability Inclusion Strategy 133
National Disability Insurance Scheme
    (NDIS) 36, 38–9
National Handicapped Finance and
    Development Corporation 250
National Plan 2025 222, 223
National Project for the Development of
    Entrepreneurship for 2021–2025 230
NDIS *see* National Disability Insurance
    Scheme (NDIS)
NDS *see* National Disability Strategy (NDS)
'necessity and opportunity' scholars 25
'necessity entrepreneurship' 25
Neff, G. 269
negative societal attitudes towards disability
    47
negative wellbeing 210

neoliberal capitalism 273
neoliberal economic discourses 125
neuro-cognitive conditions 61, 65–6, 72
neuro-cognitive disorders 59, 60, 62, 64, 65, 69, 72
neuro-developmental disorder 63
neuro-diverse individuals 66
neuro-diverse populations 65
neuro-diversity–disability–entrepreneurship link 60
neurological and psychological disorders 65
New York State Department of Vocational Rehabilitation Services (ACCES-VR) 148
Ng, W. 65, 78, 80–82
NGOs *see* non-governmental organizations (NGOs)
Night Marathons 153–5
non-disability market 51
non-disabled entrepreneurs 39, 81, 88, 116, 170, 172, 178, 183, 227
non-disabled people 3, 4, 114, 124, 132, 160–61, 164, 173
non-governmental organizations (NGOs) 85, 162, 190, 281
non-profit organizations 100, 109
non-profit social entrepreneurship organization 71
non-traditional funding 29
non-verbal communicative behaviors 63
not-for-profit social enterprises 109
novel policy model 138
Nurymbetov, Birzhan 222
Nuwagaba, E.L. 199
NVivo 40

Occupied Palestinian Territories (OPT) 238, 243
OECD *see* Organisation for Economic Co-operation and Development (OECD)
Oliver, M. 224
Omarbekova, Zhanat 230
O'Neill, K. 141
one-sided economic analysis 280
open labour market 101
    disabled people in 114
opportunity creation 24–5
opportunity-driven behavior 82
OPT *see* Occupied Palestinian Territories (OPT)

Organisation for Economic Co-operation and Development (OECD) 131–3, 136, 225
organizational behavior 64
outcomes and benefits 50–51

Pagán, R. 2, 4, 62, 65, 69, 290
Pakistan, women with disability in 182
    disability and entrepreneurship 183–4
    entrepreneurship among disabled women 191–3
    entrepreneurship ecosystem for women with disability 186–91
    women and disability 184–6
Palestine, inclusive entrepreneurship in 238–9
    double-edged sword of gender and disability 240–41
    entrepreneurship and disability 242–4
    situation of PWDs in 241–2
Palestinian Central Bureau of Statistics (PCBS) 239
Palestinian Disability Law of 1999 241
Palestinian education system 239
Palestinian entrepreneurial ecosystem 243
paraplegic entrepreneur 80
Park, J. 122
Parker, Eileen 67, 68, 70
Parker Harris, S. 8
Patel, P. 24
Pavey, B. 125
PCBS *see* Palestinian Central Bureau of Statistics (PCBS)
PDEA *see* Promotion of Disabled Persons' Enterprise Activities Act (PDEA)
people living with disabilities 307
People's Republic of China 162
people with disabilities (PWD) 2, 3, 6, 12, 13, 15, 35, 39, 43, 48, 51, 52, 61, 64, 88, 95, 102, 108, 110, 131, 132, 135–41, 143–8, 151–4, 157, 161, 164, 182, 183, 186, 188, 190–93, 196, 198–201, 204, 221–6, 229–31, 234, 244, 249, 250, 274, 279, 281, 290, 292, 298, 304, 305
    in ADEs 38
    in Hungary 4–5
    inclusive entrepreneurship in Palestine (*see* Palestine, inclusive entrepreneurship in)
    self-employment and 134
    unemployment for 282

people with diverse disabilities 147, 157
people without disability 35, 132 281, 290
people with physical disabilities 119, 122,
    306
personal pull factors 11–12, 16
personal push factors 13
person's disability, characteristics of 137
physical and mental disabilities 297
physical disabilities 62, 302, 307
    types of 301
physically disabled entrepreneurs 22, 31,
    305, 306
pilot study 26–8
Pisano G.P. 68
policy factors in EES 230–31
potential business services 8
potential social entrepreneurs 105–7
pre-coronavirus pandemic labour market 99
preliminary findings of pilot 28–9
Presidential Task Force on Employment of
    Adults with Disabilities (2000) 132
process-driven approach 24
professional skills training 171
Promotion of Disabled Persons' Enterprise
    Activities Act (PDEA) 115, 120, 121,
    123, 125
*The Protestant Ethic and the Spirit of
    Capitalism* (Weber) 268
psychiatric disabilities 88
psychological barriers 13, 16, 234
psychological distress 212, 216
psychological functioning and well-being
    248
psychological wellbeing of students 208
psychology-driven framework of attributes
    82
public administration bodies 108
public and private agencies 148
public decision-making processes 4
public policy, design of 141
public procurement policies 126
public seed financing 153
pull and push motivations 16
pull factors for ASD individuals and
    entrepreneurship
    ability to shape one's own
        accommodations 69–70
    hyperfocus and specialized skills 68–9
    motivated family and supportive
        networks 70–72
purposive sampling strategy 282

push factors for ASD individuals and
    entrepreneurship 65
    actual skill deficiencies and lack of
        preparation 67
    interviewing and selection 66–7
    systemic issues 67–8
PWD *see* people with disabilities (PWD)

qualitative research methods 298, 299
qualitative research techniques 27
quota system 119, 120

Rabin, Yitzhak 241
Ranabahu, N. 205
Reasonable Accommodation Fund 135
Reed, D.L. 9
Ren, L.R. 66
Renko, M. 7, 8
'retail strategy' 145
Richards, J. 65
risk tolerance 86, 90, 93
Rizzo, D.C. 6
Robbins, S.P. 298
Roux, A.M. 60, 64
Rozali, N. 292
Russinova, Z. 65
Ruzmatova, M. 227

Sadilek, T. 102
Saduakassov, Zhadrasyn 223, 230
Santos, Boaventura de Sousa 274
Sarasvathy, S. 24
Sarker, D. 201, 203
SBDC *see* Small Business Development
    Center (SBDC)
Schumpeter, J.A.
    The Theory of Economic Development
        268
Schur, L. 65
SCORE 151
SDG *see* Sustainable Development Goal
    (SDG)
secondary analysis disability employment
    statistics 40
    barriers and challenges 46–9
    enablers 49–50
    identity as self-employed or
        entrepreneurs 42
    motivations 44–6
    online survey 41
    outcomes and benefits 50–51
    Startup Muster® survey 42

types of businesses established 42–4
Second Life (SL) 263, 264, 266–70, 272, 273
   disability entrepreneurs in 275
   disabled persons in 272
security fund 168–9
Sehat Kahani 191
Sehat Sahulat Program 191
self-confidence 305
self-directed employment 6
self-employment 2, 3, 38, 65, 117, 118, 136, 148, 153, 160, 162, 186, 200, 204, 242, 243
   by disability group, employee vs 41
   of disabled people 116, 121, 162
   enterprises 127
   and entrepreneurship 40
   and people with disabilities 134
   and PWD 134
   services 147
self-reflective assessment 299
semi-structured interviews 9, 39, 174
   schedule 165
Shaheen, G.E. 102
Sharonova, Alexandra 230
Shier, M. 102, 107
Shore, Stephen 59
simple linear regression 91
skill development 44, 202, 234
SL *see* Second Life (SL)
Small and Medium Business Administration (SMBA) 117, 121
Small Business Development Center (SBDC) 148, 151, 152
SMBA *see* Small and Medium Business Administration (SMBA)
Smith, P. 102
snowball sampling technique 300, 307
social and economic environment
   as pull factors 12
   as push factors 13
social and solidarity economy 87
social benefits 4
social capital 150
social ecology of disability 52
social enterprises 99, 102, 145
social entrepreneurial intentions 103, 104
social entrepreneurial outcomes 146
social entrepreneurship 60, 61, 87, 99, 100, 102–5, 107–10, 143, 144, 153, 156, 157
   concept 103

disabled people in 108
initiative, StartUp NY as 146–53
initiatives 146
model 62
principles 105, 148
to systems change 145–6
social identities 248, 259
social interaction, impact on 210
social isolation 210
socialist system 224
social marginalization 255
social marketing campaigns 204
social model of disability 77, 78, 182, 224
social outcomes 292
social push motivations 15
social rehabilitation 101
Social Security Administration 152
Social Security Disability Income (SSDI) 150, 151
social security systems 94
social stigmas 65, 177, 188, 193
   of disability 189
   for disabled people 176
social support
   and cultural factors in EES 229–30
   networks 216
   systems 291
social values 292
social welfare benefits 137
social welfare payments 135
social wellbeing, impact on 211–12
socio-cultural and religious norms 188
South Korea, disabled people's microenterprise in 114–15
   disabled people and enterprise 116–17, 125–6
   Korean disability enterprises 119–25
   Korean labour market context and disabled people 117–19
South Side Innovation Center (SSIC) 150–51
Spanish university research 85
   determinants of entrepreneurial intentions 86–7
   entrepreneurship, education, and disability 88–9
   methodology 89–91
   results 91–3
   sustainability and entrepreneurship 87–8
Spear, R. 101

Special Act on the Preferential Purchase of
    Goods Produced 2008 121
Special Talent Exchange Program (STEP)
    190
SPSS *see* Statistical Package for the Social
    Sciences (SPSS)
SSDI *see* Social Security Disability Income
    (SSDI)
SSIC *see* South Side Innovation Center
    (SSIC)
'standard' entrepreneurial role 184
standard facilities, provision of event spaces
    with 170–71
Startup Muster® survey 39, 42, 43
StartUP NY 146–53
'Start Your Own Business' programme 138,
    139
State Welfare Organization 281
'statistical discrimination' 201
Statistical Package for the Social Sciences
    (SPSS) 39
STEP *see* Special Talent Exchange Program
    (STEP)
stigma-related issues 201
Stolman, L. 67, 71
strategic deterrence method 241
Strauss, A. 27
'stubborn' entrepreneurship 21
student mental health 210
students' entrepreneurial intentions 89
students' psychological wellbeing 209
student wellbeing 216
Sultanate of Oman, disabled entrepreneurs
    in 297
    common challenges faced by 306
    common mistakes 305–6
    data analysis 303–4
    factors attributed to disabled
        entrepreneurs' success 307
    idea generation 304
    income and life satisfaction 304
    key informant approaches 300–301
    method 298–300
    sacrifices 306
    sample demographics 302–3
    selection criteria 301–2
    semi-structured qualitative interviews
        303
    skills 304–5
    stigmatization, discrimination and
        marginalization 305
survey items, relationships between 214

Survio 105
sustainability and entrepreneurship 85
sustainability-related entrepreneurship
    approach 85
Sustainable Development Goal (SDG) 184,
    222
sustainable employment strategies 88, 124
Syracuse Entrepreneurship Bootcamp 151

tailored entrepreneurship programmes 140
Tanima, F.A. 205
Tanzila Khan 182, 185–93
Tax Code of the Republic of Kazakhstan 231
tax deductions 168–9
tax refund policy 168
technology-enabled solutions 204
technology-related industries 44
'technosolutionism' 275
TESSEA 100
The Theory of Economic Development
    (Schumpeter) 268
Thornton, P. 102
Tidmarsh, Chris 66–8, 70, 71
Tokayev, Kassym-Jomart 226
Tov, Moish 71
traditional employer–employee relationship
    62
traditional entrepreneurial activities 61
traditional Western culture 3
tuition-free business planning training 148

UNCRPD *see* United Nations Convention
    on the Rights of Persons with
    Disabilities (UNCRPD)
'underdog' entrepreneurs 20
    framing visually impaired research
        21–4
    literature on opportunity creation 24–5
    potential contributions 29–30
    reflections on further research 30–31
    research on visually impaired
        entrepreneurs 26–9
unemployment rate for disabled people 118
United Kingdom DDA 120
United Kingdom social model of disability
    37
United Nations Convention on the Rights of
    Persons with Disabilities (UNCRPD)
    4, 37, 133, 135, 222, 225, 230, 242,
    281
United Nations (UN) Decade of Action 184

United Socialist Soviet Republic (USSR) 224
United States Census Department (2011) 132
'universally accessible' event 154
university
    Spanish university research (*see* Spanish university research)
    students as future social entrepreneurs 103
US 1974 Rehabilitation Act 121
US Department of Labor Office of Disability Employment Policy (ODEP) 146
utilization rate of free offices 173

value creation
    perspective in disabled entrepreneurs 293
    through disabled entrepreneurship 290–92
venture creation 5, 21, 22, 26, 27, 29, 30, 77, 78, 80–83, 143, 144, 146, 147, 151, 156, 157, 183, 184, 214, 215, 217, 247
visible and invisible impairment 77–83
visionary leadership 156
visual impairment (VI) 29, 80
    entrepreneurs 21, 23, 26–9
    entrepreneurship 28, 30, 31
    research, framing 21–4
vocational rehabilitation 2, 4
    agencies 12
    organisations 36
    programme 126
    programs 272
von Schrader, S. 69

wage-based employment 146
Watson, T.J. 251
wealth creation and financial security 7
Weber, K. 145

Weber, M. 269
    The Protestant Ethic and the Spirit of Capitalism 268
Wei, X. 64
'welfare benefit trap' 137
well-designed accessibility facilities, low-rent housing with 169–70
wheelchair-bound entrepreneur 256
WHO *see* World Health Organization (WHO)
'wholesale strategy' 145
Wiklund, J. 69, 82, 83
Wilton, R. 102
Winschiers-Theophilus, H. 25
WISE *see* work integration social enterprises (WISE)
Women's Empowerment Principles 185
women's entrepreneurship, microfinance and 197–8
women with disability (WWD) 52, 183–92, 196, 198, 199, 202, 204, 240, 243
Wonder, Stevie 23
work integration social enterprises (WISE) 99–103, 107, 109, 110
World Economic Forum (WEF) 226
World Health Organization (WHO) 88, 183, 223, 238, 301
Wright, A.D. 68
WWD *see* women with disability (WWD)

Xiaotong, Fei 162

Yam, K. 71
Yamamoto, S. 2, 7, 8
Yerdildinova, Dina 221
Yin, R. 298
Yunis, Muhammad 144, 146

Zhan Shuak award 230
Zimiles, Jonah 71